CONGRESSIONAL PRIMARY ELECTIONS

Congressional primaries are increasingly being blamed for polarization and gridlock in Congress. Most American states adopted congressional primaries during the first decades of the twentieth century as a means of breaking the hold of political "bosses" on the nomination of candidates. Yet now, many contend that primaries have become a means by which the most dedicated party activists choose candidates unrepresentative of the electorate, and so general election voters are forced to choose between two ideologically extreme candidates. Consequently, there have been recent instances in both parties where nominees were chosen who were clearly not preferred by party leaders, and who arguably lost elections that their parties should have won.

This book is the first to focus solely upon congressional primary elections, and to do so for a student readership. Boatright organizes his text around the contention that there are important differences between types of primaries, and these differences prevent us from making blanket statements about primary competition. He focuses on explanations of two sources of difference: differences in electoral structure and differences brought about by the presence or absence of an incumbent seeking reelection. The first three chapters introduce these differences, explore how they came to exist, and outline some of the strategic considerations for candidates, parties, interest groups, and voters in primary elections. The subsequent four chapters explore different types of primary elections, and the final chapter evaluates actual and proposed primary reforms.

Congressional Primary Elections is the first book to provide a history and analysis of congressional primary elections and will serve as a crucial part of courses on political parties and campaigns and elections. The book gives students the tools for understanding arguments for and against the reform of primary elections and for understanding the differences between types of primaries.

Robert G. Boatright is an Associate Professor of Political Science at Clark University. He is the author of three other books, including *Getting Primaried: The Changing Politics of Congressional Primary Challenges* and *Interest Groups and Campaign Finance Reform in the United States and Canada*. His research interests include campaign finance, congressional elections, and interest groups.

CONGRESSIONAL PRIMARY ELECTIONS

Robert G. Boatright

NEW YORK AND LONDON

First published 2014
by Routledge
711 Third Avenue, New York, NY 10017

and by Routledge
2 Park Square, Milton Park, Abingdon, Oxon OX14 4RN

Routledge is an imprint of the Taylor & Francis Group, an informa business

© 2014 Taylor & Francis

The right of Robert G. Boatright to be identified as author of this work has been asserted by him in accordance with sections 77 and 78 of the Copyright, Designs and Patents Act 1988.

All rights reserved. No part of this book may be reprinted or reproduced or utilized in any form or by any electronic, mechanical, or other means, now known or hereafter invented, including photocopying and recording, or in any information storage or retrieval system, without permission in writing from the publishers.

Trademark notice: Product or corporate names may be trademarks or registered trademarks, and are used only for identification and explanation without intent to infringe.

Library of Congress Cataloging-in-Publication Data

Boatright, Robert G.
 Congressional primary elections / by Robert G. Boatright.
     pages cm
 1. Primaries—United States. 2. United States. Congress—Elections. 3. Representative government and representation—United States. I. Title.
 JK2071.B63 2014
 324.273'154—dc23
 2013049213

ISBN: 978-0-415-74199-6 (hbk)
ISBN: 978-0-415-74200-9 (pbk)
ISBN: 978-1-315-81494-0 (ebk)

Typeset in Bembo
by Apex CoVantage, LLC

Printed and bound in the United States of America by Publishers Graphics, LLC on sustainably sourced paper.

CONTENTS

List of Figures and Tables vii
Acknowledgments xi

1. Why Study Congressional Primaries? 1
2. Primary Elections and the "Democratic Experiment" 24
3. The Strategic Context of Congressional Primaries 75
4. Open Seat Primaries 111
5. Challenger Primaries 143
6. Incumbent Primaries 169
7. Race, Redistricting, and Primary Elections 204
8. Primary Reform 233

References 259
Index 279

FIGURES AND TABLES

Figures

3.1	Primary Turnout as a Percent of Eligible Voters, Midterm Election Years	79
3.2	Primary Turnout as a Percent of Eligible Voters, Presidential Election Years	80
3.3	Democratic and Republican Primary Turnout as a Percent of Eligible Voters, Presidential Election Years	81
3.4	State-Level Primary Turnout in Presidential and Midterm Election Years Compared	82
3.5	General Election Turnout, Midterm and Presidential Election Years	83
3.6	Presidential and Nonpresidential Primary Turnout Compared, 1972–2008	106
4.1	Number of Contested and Uncontested Open Seat House Primaries by Year and Party, 1970–2012	118
4.2	Average Receipts for Winning and Losing House Primary Candidates by Source, 2012	130
4.3	Receipts for Victorious Democratic and Republican House Open Seat Primary Candidates, 2000–2012	133
4.4	Number of Contested and Uncontested Open Seat Senate Primaries by Year, 1970–2012	135
5.1	Number of Uncontested Incumbents by Year and Party, 1970–2012	147
5.2	Challenger Party Primary Competition and General Election Results, 1970–2012	150

5.3	Challenger Party Primary Competition by the Incumbent's Ideological Fit to the District, 1970–2012	154
5.4	Challenger Primary Competition by Party, 1970–2012	155
5.5	Sources of Funds for Challenger Primary Winners and Losers, 2012	158
5.6	Average Total Receipts for Challenger Primary Winners, by Party, 2000–2012	159
5.7	Average Total Receipts for Primary Winners, by Party and Competitiveness, 2000–2012	161
5.8	Number of Contested and Uncontested Senate Challenger Primaries by Year, 1970–2012	163
6.1	Number of Primary Challenges to Incumbent House Members, 1970–2012	173
6.2	Number of Primary Challenges to Incumbent House Members, 1970–2012, by Level of Competitiveness	174
6.3	Primary Challenges to House Incumbents by Region of the Country, 1970–2012	175
6.4	Competitive Primary Challenges to House and Senate Incumbents Compared	177
6.5	Average Receipts for Competitive Primary Challengers to Incumbents, by Party and by Level of Competitiveness	179
6.6	Sources of Receipts for Primary Challengers	180
6.7	Average Percentage of Small and Large Contributions to Primary Challengers	181
6.8	Number of Ideological Primary Challenges to Incumbents, 1970—2012	190
6.9	Incumbents Defeated in House and Senate Primaries, 1946–2012	196
7.1	Ohio Congressional Districts	207
7.2	Number of Minority Representatives by Year	213
7.3	Majority-Minority Districts and Minority Representatives Compared	214
7.4	Primary Challenges to Majority-Minority Incumbents and Democratic Incumbents, 1970–2012	220
7.5	Number of Open Seat Races by District Racial Composition	223

Tables

2.1	Adoption of the Direct Primary by Year	37
2.2	Congressional and Presidential Primary Dates, 2012	63

2.3	Primary Type by State, as of 2012	65
3.1	Comparing Primary Voters and Other Types of Voters, 2010	88
3.2	Ideology and Partisanship of Primary Voters, 2010	89
4.1	Determinants of the Number of House Open Seat Primary Candidates, 1970–2012 (Poisson)	121
4.2	Predictors of the Second-Place and Third-Place House Primary Candidates' Vote Percentages, 1970–2012 (OLS)	123
4.3	Determinants of Fractionalization in House Primaries, 1970–2012 (OLS)	125
4.4	Determinants of Vote Share, Democratic and Republican House Open Seat Primary Candidates, 2000–2012 (OLS)	132
4.5	Average Receipts for Victorious Senate Open Seat Primary Candidates, by Partisanship of State, 2000–2012	137
5.1	Determinants of the Number of House Challenger Party Primary Candidates, 1970–2012 (Poisson)	151
5.2	Determinants of Fractionalization in House Challenger Primaries, 1970–2012 (OLS)	152
5.3	Determinants of Vote Share, Democratic and Republican House Challenger Primary Candidates, 2000–2012 (OLS)	162
5.4	Average Receipts for Victorious Senate Challenger Primary Candidates, by Partisanship of State, 2000–2012	165
6.1	The Relationship between State Primary Laws and Challenges to Incumbents	176
6.2	Campaign Finance for Senate Primary Challenges, 1980–2012	181
6.3	Types of Primary Challenges to Incumbents, 1970–2012	189
6.4	Top Interest Groups Spending in Congressional Primary Challenges, 2000–2012	200
7.1	Competition in Majority-Minority District Incumbent Primaries, 1970–2012	219
7.2	Common Reasons for Primary Challenges in Majority-Minority Districts, 1970–2012	222
7.3	Incumbent vs. Incumbent Primaries, 1992–2012	229

ACKNOWLEDGMENTS

Almost a decade ago, I was invited to a conference on the subject of political polarization—a common theme, I'm sure, for exclusive gatherings of academics. In preparing my remarks for this conference, I was struck by the fact that primary elections are often blamed for the ideological divisions we see in Congress today. Where, I wondered, is the evidence that primaries do in fact lead to the election of ideologically extreme candidates? And if there is such evidence, why is it that primaries were with us for nearly a century before our parties became so polarized?

As I was beginning to explore the subject, I was surprised to see that there had not been a comprehensive text on primary elections written since 1928. This may be—as some of my friends have been quick (perhaps too quick) to point out—because they aren't an interesting enough subject to merit a full book. Yet it is no exaggeration to say that the nation's best political scientists were extremely preoccupied with primaries for much of the 1900s, 1910s, and 1920s. The idea of primaries, it seems, used to matter a lot. This book is based on the contention that congressional primaries still do matter. Claims are frequently made about primaries, but in fact we know little about them. I will let readers determine whether they are interesting enough to deserve a book. I can say at a minimum that enough of my colleagues were interested when I described the project to them to provide assistance and encouragement.

As this project developed, I received input and guidance from several colleagues. In particular, Jeff Berry, Michael Crespin, Vin Moscardelli, and Seth Masket provided feedback or helped with difficult points in the project. Mark Miller provided valuable advice on the task of writing the book, as well as cheerfully loaning me his books on Congress. Hans Hassell, Thad Kousser, Eric McGhee, and Andrew Sinclair graciously provided me copies of their unpublished work on primaries. Gary Jacobson provided his challenger quality data, which served as a starting point for putting together the datasets used here. The campaign finance datasets here also built upon data collected at the Campaign Finance Institute; I thank Michael Malbin and Brendan Glavin for their help in understanding and using these data. At Clark University, Marc Kadushin and Amanda Gregoire provided dependable research assistance in constructing the open seat and challenger datasets. Thank you as well to Nick Giner for help with the Ohio map in Chapter 7.

I thank Michael Kerns, Darcy Bullock, and the rest of the editorial staff at Routledge for their support of this project. The anonymous reviews provided by Routledge also were extremely valuable in helping me shape and present my ideas here. I would be remiss, as well, not to note the debt this book owes to my earlier book on primaries, *Getting Primaried: The Changing Politics of Congressional Primary Challenges*. The University of Michigan Press, and political science editor Melody Herr in particular, provided valuable support in my first foray into writing about primaries. That book is written for a somewhat different audience and is focused more on a particular type of primary challenge, but my experience in writing it certainly shaped my views on the content here.

Some of the research for Chapter 2 was supported by a Congressional Research Award from the Dirksen Congressional Center. I greatly appreciate the center's financial assistance for this project. I also gratefully acknowledge the travel and research support for this project provided by the Francis Harrington Fund at Clark University, and the Faculty Development Grant I received from Clark University in 2011.

My family has also tolerated several years now of frantic book writing. I thank my children, Jacob and Dara, for being patient about the distractions that come with writing, and my wife, Audrey, for her support, love, and encouragement.

1
WHY STUDY CONGRESSIONAL PRIMARIES?

The state of Massachusetts endured four different Senate elections between 2006 and 2012. The first of these, in 2006, was not much of a contest. Democrat Edward Kennedy was seeking his eighth full term in office, and 2006 was widely expected to be a good year for Democrats. The seventy-four-year-old senator had no primary opponent and had little need to campaign aggressively in the general election. Kennedy had occasionally had serious Republican challengers in the past, but there were few indications that a well-known Republican in the state would step up to challenge him this time. Andrew Card, the former chief of staff for President Bush, considered running but ultimately decided against it. A competitive primary did, however, break out in the Republican Party. Businessman Ken Chase and a former selectman from the small town of Wakefield, Kevin Scott, fought nearly to a draw in the Republican primary, with Chase ultimately winning by 1,300 votes, a 51 to 49 percent victory. The Republican primary was a draw financially, as well; both Chase and Scott raised approximately $500,000. The Massachusetts voters, however, appear not to have been paying very much attention; the only poll conducted in February of 2006 of voter preferences in the Republican primary gave Chase 8 percent of the vote, Scott 3 percent, and "don't know" 76 percent.[1] Things surely got better for both candidates as the September primary neared, but there were never very many indications that the nomination was a likely stepping stone to a seat in the Senate. Kennedy won the general election by a 69 to 31 percent margin.

In 2008, another veteran senator, John Kerry, was up for reelection. Republicans again saw little hope of winning the seat, in part because of Kerry's popularity and in part because he had over $20 million dollars at his disposal, money left over from his 2004 presidential run. There was no Republican primary in 2008,

2 Why Study Congressional Primaries?

and the party nominee, businessman and conservative activist Jeff Beatty, received the same vote percentage as the party's 2006 nominee, 31 percent. Kerry did, however, face a spirited but underfunded challenge for the Democratic nomination from Gloucester City Councilman Ed O'Reilly. Kerry had not spent very much time in Massachusetts during his unsuccessful presidential bid, and he had taken some votes during his past term that angered Massachusetts progressives. O'Reilly was particularly incensed that Kerry, whose career had begun with his denunciation of the Vietnam War, had not spoken out more forcefully against the wars currently being waged in Iraq and Afghanistan. O'Reilly sought to cultivate a following among progressive activists, particularly those who frequently read popular left-wing blogs. O'Reilly was seeking to catch the anti-incumbent wave that was to nearly topple Senator Joseph Lieberman in nearby Connecticut's primary. O'Reilly was unsuccessful, but he arguably posed a more serious challenge to Kerry than did the senator's general election foe.

Senator Kennedy became ill in 2008 and passed away in August of 2009. A Massachusetts law passed in 2004 allows the governor to appoint an interim senator when there is a vacancy, but requires that an election be held within six months to complete the term. Massachusetts Governor Deval Patrick's appointee, Paul Kirk, made it clear that he had no interest in running to complete Senator Kennedy's term. Massachusetts would have an open senate seat for the first time since 1984. The state's all-Democratic House delegation clearly featured many representatives who had been waiting to run for the Senate, and the state government, also full of Democrats, featured many Democrats with experience running statewide races. The primary could well have become a free-for-all. Ultimately, all but one member of the state's House delegation decided not to run, and the December 2009 primary wound up being a four-way affair. State Attorney General Martha Coakley secured the endorsements of many of the state's Democratic leaders and of women's groups. Representative Michael Capuano, among the more liberal members of the state's House delegation and a candidate adept at courting minority voters, ran to Coakley's left. Alan Khazei, the former director of City Year, a nonprofit organization encouraging students to do volunteer work in underprivileged neighborhoods, ran as an outsider candidate, with substantial support from some liberals and on college campuses. Finally, Steve Pagliuca, one of the owners of the Boston Celtics, mounted a campaign touting his business expertise, largely funded out of his own pockets. Coakley had to work hard to win the primary, but she did ultimately triumph by a comfortable margin. Coakley was clearly a formidable candidate, but much of the story of 2010 will likely never be told—there were many other Democrats who might have given Coakley a more spirited challenge, but these potential candidates never ran.

The story of the 2010 special election has been recounted in many books and articles documenting the travails of the Democratic Party during Barack Obama's first term. Coakley, widely expected to cruise to victory in the 2010 general election, took the holidays off from campaigning and never gained her footing in the general election. Money surged in from out of state to support the Republican nominee, Scott Brown, and the 2010 special election became the first big victory for the Tea Party in its quest to fight back against the Obama administration. There was, however, little indication during the Republican primary that Scott Brown would be the candidate he turned out to be. Brown was a relatively obscure state senator, and his primary campaign was barely visible. Brown had a primary opponent, perennial candidate Jack Robinson, but the Republican primary attracted virtually no attention from a media focused on the Democratic race. The Republican primary attracted barely one-fourth as many voters as did the Democratic primary. Despite the fact that there would be no incumbent for the victor to face, the Republican primary looked little different from the primaries to select the opponents of Kennedy and Kerry in past years.

Finally, in 2012 Brown was up for reelection again, for a full six-year term. Brown had shown during his time in office that he was a likeable politician, and he stressed throughout his short time in office that he understood that Massachusetts was more liberal than the home states of his Republican colleagues. Brown frequently broke ranks with the Republican Party, often voting as a bloc with Maine's two centrist Republican senators, Olympia Snowe and Susan Collins. This earned Brown some enmity on the right—Tea Party activists, who took credit for Brown's victory, grumbled about fielding a primary challenger to run against him in 2012. No such challenger ever did emerge.

Meanwhile, however, many Democrats realized Brown would be tough to beat yet still contended that his election was a fluke and that in a presidential year he could be beaten by the appropriate candidate. Once again, the names of many House members and state elected officials were floated as potential nominees. Members of the Obama administration, in the meantime, had found a candidate to their liking, Harvard Professor Elizabeth Warren. Warren had been one of the main proponents of the creation of the Consumer Financial Protection Bureau, a government agency created following the 2008 market crash to police the financial services industry. When it became clear that Senate Republicans would block Warren's nomination to head the bureau, she became somewhat of a star on the left. Warren would, in the eyes of many Democrats, be the perfect Senate nominee for Massachusetts—she would come into office with star power and political expertise, yet she was not a politician. Massachusetts politicians grumbled about the Obama administration's meddling in their politics, but the governor was an early supporter of Warren and no one else of stature emerged to run for the seat. On her way to a November victory, however, Warren did receive an important assist from the state's peculiar primary process. The two major parties in Massachusetts hold conventions before the primary, and state law allows the parties to limit ballot access. Democratic Party rules require that candidates for statewide office receive the votes of at least 15 percent of convention delegates.

4 Why Study Congressional Primaries?

During 2011 a number of Democrats—mayors of small cities, party activists, and so forth—announced their candidacy, and in the fall of 2011 there was a six-candidate debate among the primary candidates. Ultimately, however, most of these candidates stepped aside for Warren. One candidate, however, did not. Immigration lawyer Marisa DeFranco took her candidacy to the convention, arguing simply that the primary voters should have a choice. De Franco appeared up until the convention to have the backing of enough delegates to make it into the primary ballot. News reports, however, indicate that Governor Patrick and his allies worked hard at the convention to deny DeFranco a place on the ballot, arguing that Warren would inevitably win the nomination, and that the distraction of a primary opponent would impede the party's attempts to unseat Brown.[2] Patrick was apparently successful; Warren received over 95 percent of the delegates' votes, and there was no Senate primary.

Four elections, four very different sets of primaries. What can one conclude from these races? To start with, let us consider how exhausting these primaries were—for candidates, for political elites, and for the media. Yet it is not at all clear that the voters of Massachusetts were particularly swept up in any of these.[3] Turnout, as we saw, was very low in each year's Republican primaries. Massachusetts holds its primaries in September, so even in years like 2008 when the state's presidential primary is consequential, congressional candidates do not appear on the presidential ballot. Turnout was low in John Kerry's 2008 primary, and given the fact that no one really thought Kerry was likely to lose, it is quite plausible that many of the people who showed up to vote in that primary were enticed by more competitive races further down the ballot. The 2009 special primary election included a total of approximately 800,000 votes cast—slightly over one-third as many as were cast in the special general election, less than one-fifth of the votes cast in the 2012 general election, and approximately 13 percent of the state's registered voters. In 2012 Massachusetts Secretary of State William F. Galvin told reporters that turnout in state primaries fluctuates between 15 and 50 percent (Valencia 2012), depending on how exciting the primary matchups are, but the Senate primary results above make this estimate appear somewhat optimistic. So yes, these are a lot of races, but the stories to many of them are known to few of the people represented by the victors of these races.

Let us, however, put these Senate races in a broader context. Are these races representative? Can we speak meaningfully of patterns in congressional primary elections based on these cases? These Massachusetts races are all Senate primaries. Are Senate primaries different from House primaries? Obviously, they involve a larger number of voters, and Senate seats are arguably more desirable than House seats. There are, however, many equivalent stories one can tell about House primaries. During this same time period, Massachusetts saw a large number of uncontested primaries, races for the Republican nomination in safe Democratic seats—a nomination whose value was questionable. There were also some spirited primaries like the Chase-Scott affair, even if in doomed causes. In 2010, a three-way Republican primary broke out in the state's third district, a relatively safe Democratic seat. The three Republicans—a state legislator, a Tea Party activist, and a businessman—clearly saw themselves as representatives of different factions in their party and their primary was quite exciting, even though it yielded a nominee who lost by quite a few votes. There were competitive primaries for open seats, as took place in one of the state's more conservative districts, the district where Cape Cod is located, in 2010. And there were challenges to incumbents, as well; in 2012, for instance, longtime Democrat Richard Neal faced a spirited challenge from a state legislator who felt that Neal's political interests, buttressed by support for organized labor and the politics of one of the state's poorer industrial cities did not match the views of progressive, wealthier liberals in the Berkshires. In short, the Senate races discussed above seem all to have clear analogues among House races.

But, one might add, the races summarized here all took place in the liberal bastion of Massachusetts, during a period of time where Massachusetts Democrats were (mostly) in control of things. These case studies were listed in part because of the fluke that they all took place one after the other. A senate race every election year—how exhausting! And yes, these Massachusetts races also start the book because your author teaches there. There is, however, little in this summary to indicate that Massachusetts primaries ought to be that different from primaries elsewhere. The jockeying for position among Democrats in 2010 and the lack of interest among Republicans in seeking the 2006 and 2008 nominations is arguably paralleled by, for instances, the competition among Republicans for the 2012 Senate nomination in Texas, and the lack of interest in the seat among Democrats. The concern among Democrats about securing the strongest candidate in 2012 is similar to the concerns of party activists in purple states as well. And the challenge to Kerry and the threats of a challenge to Scott Brown look much like challenges to incumbents in both parties in recent years—and, as we shall see, they are not that different from challenges to incumbents decades ago. In short, there is nothing about the partisanship of a state that indicates that its primaries should be that unique. What arguably matters, instead, are the peculiar rules that Massachusetts has to limit primary competition. Many states, as we shall see, have unusual primary election procedures, and these are a legitimate subject for study precisely because variations among states have consequential effects on primary competition.

If we are to take this collection of Senate primaries as being somewhat representative of congressional primaries overall, then, what do they tell us? First, they suggest that congressional primary elections are undeniably messier than congressional general elections.[4] Primaries tend to feature multiple candidates, and they often can be completely upended by the entry of new candidates. They are thus shaped in unpredictable ways by the number of candidates who run and by the decisions of potential candidates about whether or not to run. Second, primaries take place before a small, and, again, unpredictable audience. Turnout tends to fluctuate wildly, and it is difficult for candidates to gain a clear understanding of what is going on simply because the measurement tools available in general elections—polling data, previous voting patterns, and so forth—do not necessarily apply. And third, just as in congressional general elections, the presence or absence of an incumbent largely shapes primary elections. Open seat primaries tend to follow a very different logic than do primaries featuring an incumbent or primaries for the nomination to run against the incumbent in a general election. In the case of these Massachusetts races, we saw a mix of political superstars and relative unknowns, we saw campaigns that energized large numbers of voters, and campaigns that voters largely ignored, and we saw, in 2012, the consequences of the state's political culture and its own history in developing its primary system shape the election.

We can simplify our discussion here and say, in the end, that these primaries were fundamentally about Edward Kennedy, John Kerry, and Scott Brown. This serves, perhaps, as a good starting point, but only that. Ultimately, congressional primaries give us a unique, and uniquely American, view of representative democracy. Congressional primaries are messy and they often have serious flaws. However, in a political system where there is often little change from one election to the next in the party holding power, in the outcomes of general elections, or in the policies produced by government, primaries have since their inception represented, at least in theory, an opportunity for citizens, rather than politicians or party leaders, to have their say in the machinations of government.

Why Congressional Primaries Matter, and What Matters in Congressional Primaries

The twin aims of this book are to make sense of congressional primaries and to provide a comprehensive overview of patterns in congressional primaries over the past several decades. There is a vast literature on congressional elections, and there are several well-established textbooks on congressional elections. While some attention has been paid by scholars to the questions that touch upon primary elections, questions such as who runs for Congress or what role political parties play in shaping congressional elections, studies of congressional primaries are few and far between. In fact, by my count there have been only two books published over the past eighty years—excluding my own book on the subject, *Getting Primaried* (Boatright 2013)—to have nonpresidential primary elections as their main subject; one of these books was a historical inquiry into the development of primary elections (Ware 2002) and the other was an edited volume covering various aspects of congressional primaries (Galderisi, Ezra, and Lyons 2001). Congressional primaries have clearly not been at the top of scholars' minds for a long time.

This is, however, a problem that needs correcting. Primary elections have come to play a large part in the way we talk about national politics. Let us consider three illustrations of this:

First, consider the plight of the Republican Party following the 2012 election. Despite uncertainty within the party about whether President Obama would prevail in the presidential election, there was near-universal agreement that the Republicans would pick up the four (or three, depending on who held the presidency) seats necessary to become the majority party in the Senate. Democrats had more Senate seats to defend in the election, and many of the seats they did have to defend were in states that were not particularly friendly to the party. Yet when all of the votes had been counted, all of the Democratic incumbents up for reelection had won, and the Democratic Party had actually gained two seats. Part of the reason that Republicans did so poorly in this election, according to many political pundits, was that Republican primaries produced candidates who could not win general elections. In Missouri, for instance, the victor in the three-way Republican primary, Todd Akin, was not particularly well-liked by party leaders and had a history of intemperate comments. Akin effectively ended his hopes for winning the general election shortly after the primary when he told a television interviewer that "legitimate rape" could not result in pregnancy. Akin's gaffe may have cost him the election, but many Democrats and Republicans saw it coming. The Missouri race was, according to some Republicans, one of as many as five races that the party lost in 2010 and 2012 because it was unable to nominate the strongest candidates (see LaTourette 2012). Republicans, however, are not unique in this regard, although they do appear to have had a run of bad luck; Democrats also have lost House and Senate races they should have won in states such as California and Illinois because their primaries have not produced strong candidates. All of these elections bring into question the role of political parties in the nominating process. Should parties be able to control nominations? Have they lost control of nominations, or did they ever even have control? What are the consequences of party control for American democracy?

Second, there is a growing perception among the political class that incumbent members of the House and Senate have reason to fear primary challenges if they stray from the party line. There are many recent examples of politicians who appeared to have great appeal to the general electorate of their state who failed to make it through the primary. Among the misfortunes that befell the Republican Party in 2012 was the loss of Senate seats in Indiana and Maine. In Indiana, veteran Senator Richard Lugar, first elected to the Senate in 1976, had rarely had difficulty winning reelection and had never, until 2012, been seen as a particularly liberal Republican. Nonetheless, Lugar lost his 2012 primary to a challenger who claimed he would never seek to compromise with Democrats. Lugar's opponent went on to lose in the general election. Lugar was, however, not alone. Many Democrats, including senators Joseph Lieberman and Blanche Lambert Lincoln and representatives Albert Wynn and Silvestre Reyes, either lost or nearly lost primaries to challengers who claimed they were too moderate. These instances of "primarying," according to many, make Congress more partisan and extreme. Furthermore, it has been claimed, the *threat* of a primary causes many incumbents either to flee the political center or to decide to get out of the business altogether. Maine Senator Olympia Snowe, for instance, abruptly retired from Congress in 2012, in part because she was about to face a primary opponent. Snowe's retirement handed yet another Republican seat that was not expected to be competitive to the Democratic Party. Events such as these are not as much a reflection on the parties as on the primary electorate; they prompt us to ask whether incumbent members of Congress are, indeed, more at risk of losing primaries today than in years past. They also lead to a variety of normative questions. The most obvious such question has to do with the effect of primaries on how Congress functions. Do primary challenges to incumbents prevent incumbents from compromising with each other, or are they a means of ensuring that politicians remain true to the views of the voters who got them there in the first place?

Third, primary elections present us with many examples of the messiness of democracy. Absent the cues provided in a race between a Democratic and a Republican nominee, voters may well lack the ability to make intelligent decisions about who is the better candidate. Without the tendency toward two-candidate competition that our first-past-the-post electoral system provides, primary elections often feature a bewildering array of choices. Primaries featuring ten or more candidates are not uncommon; in such races, the victor may well have received a quarter of the vote or less. When one combines this with the fact that congressional primaries are often low-turnout affairs, it is possible to win with a relatively small number of votes. Consider, for instance a recent election in Arizona's Third District, a safe Republican district comprised of the wealthier parts of Phoenix and Phoenix's northern suburbs. Here, over 200,000 people routinely vote in general elections. When incumbent John Shadegg retired in 2010, the battle for the Republican nomination to replace him featured ten candidates. The victor, Ben Quayle (son of the former vice president), received 14,266 votes, or 23 percent of the vote. On the one hand, then, primary elections provide an exercise in unfettered democracy—the winner may well not be the candidate with the most money, and in the right circumstances a candidate with a small but dedicated following can parlay that support into a seat in Congress. It may not even be a problem that voter turnout is often so low—perhaps the voters who turn out are simply more knowledgeable about politics than those who stay home. Yet on the other hand, the complexity of multi-candidate competition is sufficiently problematic that some states have developed means of restraining this competition; some hold preprimary conventions to limit the number of candidates who appear on the ballot while others hold runoff elections if no candidate receives 50 percent of the vote. Do rules such as these improve the nomination process?

Even if one puts aside concerns about party extremists in Congress or the electorate, it is still worth asking whether the primary election process can be improved without stifling popular involvement in the choosing of candidates. Asking questions such as these inevitably leads one to the question of what voters know about primary candidates and how elections differ when they lose the structuring effect of two-party competition.

These three examples show us not just that congressional primaries matter, but that there are particular features of congressional primaries that we should consider. We shall explore many of these in greater detail in subsequent chapters. Briefly, however, these examples show us that congressional primary results are shaped by the following variables:

- *The presence or absence of an incumbent*: Just as is the case in treatments of general elections, the presence of an incumbent transforms a race from a competition of ideas between candidates to a referendum on the incumbent and the incumbent's actions in office. Even in primaries where an incumbent is not running, however, the incumbent still plays a role. In races to take on an incumbent, prospective general election challengers will choose to run or stay home based on whether they believe the incumbent will be beatable. In open seat races, the incumbent may have endorsed a candidate to succeed him or her, or the incumbent may be sufficiently unpopular by the time he or she leaves that candidates of both parties will take no notice of him or her. In any type of primary, however, the current or prior officeholder can determine the dynamics of the race.
- *The structure of competition*: How many candidates are running? Competition between two candidates will, by definition, yield a majority winner. Competition between multiple candidates may not. Primary elections are also shaped by the threat of competition—candidate filing deadlines are often very close to the primary election date, so in many instances primary candidates do not know exactly who their competition is. While we can address patterns in the number of candidates who run and the number of competitive candidates who run, we cannot necessarily study other factors of this competition. All political parties have factions, and all state and congressional districts have distinct geographic interests within them. Primaries often are structured in that a candidate from one population center runs against a candidate from a different area, in that candidates of two different ethnic groups compete with each other, or in that a liberal runs against a conservative. With the exception of races against incumbents—which are few enough in number and usually deemed remarkable enough that we can categorize the reasons for the challenge—we do not have the tools to measure factional support, but we must be aware that primaries are often highly structured affairs in which groups within the electorate, not just candidates, compete with each other.

- *Partisanship and partisan swings*: The partisanship of a district—that is, the relative strength of the two major parties in presidential voting, general election voting, or party registration—can determine how realistic one party's chance is of winning a general election. This, in turn, affects who runs for the nomination, how many voters turn out in the primary, and how voters evaluate the primary candidates. There are also, however, important changes in the value of one party's nomination across time. In a presidential election year, for instance, the nomination may be more valuable to candidates of one party if they expect their presidential candidate to be popular. In states where congressional and presidential primaries occur on the same day, competition for the presidency can also shape candidate strategy in the congressional primary. The partisanship of the district matters, but so do larger trends in partisanship as well as short-term effects. There are good years and bad years to run for Congress.
- *Rules and state variations in rules*: There are two sets of rules that influence congressional primaries. First, there are rules that govern the involvement of parties in the primary process. Are political parties able to winnow the field by endorsing a candidate or determining which candidates will appear on the ballot? Although primaries developed largely as internal affairs for political parties, today there are many different levels of engagement for parties across states. Second, states differ in their determinations of who can vote in a primary election. Some states allow anyone to vote in any primary (as long as he or she does not vote in more than one primary at a time) while others allow parties to restrict voting to individuals who have registered as members of the party well in advance of election day. A small number of states do not even hold separate Democratic and Republican primaries, instead placing all candidates on one ballot and using the primary to winnow the field to the top two candidates, whether are not these two are comprised of a Democrat and a Republican. Many past studies of primaries have dwelt upon the differences in outcomes according to primary rules. This literature can often seem somewhat arcane, but beneath it all is an important point: in most states, the rules that determine who can appear on a primary ballot and who can vote in a primary were determined through conflicts between reform factions and parties, or between the two major parties, and the differences reflect who won and lost these battles. These battles were fought because the competitors anticipated different results from different types of rules, so it is worth asking, even if these battles took place nearly a century ago, whether these different expectations have truly yielded different types of results across the states.
- *Money and the sources of it*: There is, as I have noted above, a lot we cannot measure about primary candidates, let alone about potential candidates who do not emerge. The one piece of information we can acquire about candidates, apart from how many people voted for them, is how much money they raised and where it came from. In a few cases, we can use this information to make claims about the role of parties; parties rarely give money to primary

candidates but when they do it is worth noting. In some cases we can infer traits of a candidate according either to her level of interest group support or to the characteristics of the groups supporting her. That is, we do not have to research a candidate's views on guns if we can simply note that the National Rifle Association has given her money. Measuring the relationship between money and competitiveness, however, is complicated. As we shall see, many congressional primaries feature winners who spent negligible amounts of money while other primaries are multi-million dollar affairs. We cannot even attribute this to the value of the nomination—some candidates may raise money during the primary in order to spend it attacking prospective general election opponents, and other candidates may enter the primary late, raise little money, but win based on name recognition. Money, then, is harder to study than it is in general elections, but it is an important part of the puzzle.

The examples of primary results provided above are not exhaustive of all the questions one might ask about primaries, but they serve as evidence that primaries matter. The list of variables provided above is also not exhaustive, but it gives one a sense of what we can and cannot measure in congressional primaries. In a political system where 90 percent of incumbent members of Congress are reelected, where a shift of three or four Senate seats represents a sea change in American politics, it is worth asking what happens before the general election begins—but we must also do so with an awareness that much of what we know about general elections either does not apply or cannot be measured in primary elections. As we shall see in Chapter 2 of this book, congressional primaries were once a topic of heated discussion among politicians and academics. In the early years of the twentieth century, Progressive reformers railed against party bosses and their undemocratic means of choosing candidates. Primary elections were presented by reformers as a surefire way for the people to take back political power from corrupt, unelected political bosses. Uniquely among Progressive reforms, primaries took root absolutely everywhere in the country, to the point that we do not even seriously think about giving them up. Yet it is not at all clear that primaries cured the problems that motivated the Progressives, and primary elections also present many of their own problems. Understanding the problems introduced in primaries and the dynamics of primary competition can help us to understand the dynamics of congressional general elections, the behavior of legislators, the policies produced by the government, and, perhaps, the tools citizens have to change aspects of primary elections that they do not like.

Primary Elections in Comparative Perspective

Before we consider differences among American congressional primaries, it is worth considering the uniqueness of American primary elections. To put matters simply, the creation of primary elections was hardly inevitable, and there is little evidence that primaries are a particularly good means of choosing candidates. Plenty of other democratic nations are able to choose political leaders who are clearly qualified for elected office and are representative of the views of the public without the complications of primary elections. In the premier cross-national study of candidate selection methods, Israeli political scientists Reuven Y. Hazan and Gideon Rahat (2010, 4) assert that the United States is the only democratic nation in which candidate selection is heavily regulated by the government. Hazan and Rahat distinguish candidate selection methods along two dimensions— inclusiveness for candidacy (that is, how easy it is for anyone to run for office) and inclusiveness of the selectorate (how easy it is to vote in candidate nomination candidates). The United States is the only nation with high inclusiveness on both dimensions—where almost anyone can run for a party's nomination and almost anyone can vote in those contests.

The United States is not the only nation that holds primaries, and political parties in several other countries have in recent years been moving to democratize their candidate selection processes. Iceland, Taiwan, Mexico, and Spain are the most noteworthy examples of countries that have recently established primary elections for legislative office (Hazan and Rahat 2010, 40). In some countries, political parties can choose whether or not to hold primaries, while in others (such as Germany, Finland, and New Zealand) there are legal strictures that govern how parties may select candidates. Party leadership elections, in particular, have increasingly been scrutinized by many governments to ensure that candidate selection and the financing of candidates' campaigns are transparent (Hofnung 2008; Sandri and Seddone 2012). Few nations provide public funds for the administration of elections, so in most other countries where there is even the option to hold primaries, parties (or in some instances, candidates) must pay for these elections themselves. In no other nation have primary elections become as formal a part of the electoral process as in the United States. There are many reasons why this may be so; before considering those reasons, however, let us briefly consider other ways of choosing party nominees.

Candidate Selection in Other Democratic Nations

The United States is one of the few Western democracies to use a first-past-the-post, or plurality rule, system of elections. There is, furthermore, little movement to change this system. While other countries that use plurality rule have lively discussions about abandoning it (as is the case in Canada) or have abandoned it (as in France and New Zealand; see Farrell 2011, 179), the United States has had few serious discussions about such dramatic changes. The United States is also among the few nations to employ a system of checks and balances where different branches of government may be controlled by different political parties. Most European democracies use either a proportional representation system or the so-called Westminster Model, in which candidates win plurality elections in individual districts but where the party with the most seats in parliament governs. Proportional systems tend to produce multiple political parties and to feature little ideological diversity within the parties. Westminster systems may contain distinct ideological factions, but these factions work to resolve their disagreements privately—parties in both types of systems vote as a bloc in parliament. A common means of selecting candidates in proportional systems is to create ranked lists of candidates; if a party wins, for instance, fifty seats in the legislature, the top fifty candidates on the party's list will be seated. Candidates may compete with each other to receive a higher position on the list (see Hazan and Rahat 2010, 11), but it is hard to imagine procedures by which such competition could be resolved by voters. Westminster systems, such as those in the United Kingdom and Canada, have candidates running in particular geographic districts, but it is not uncommon for parties to place their preferred candidates in districts that the party expects to win—even if those candidates have no connection to that district.

In both types of systems, candidates have little opportunity to distinguish themselves. They cannot promise to vote any differently than any other candidate in the party would, thus removing one source of appeals to the public. Candidates may tout their skills or expertise, but it is not at all clear that the voters are the best judges of this. As a result, even when candidate selection moves in a more democratic direction in parliamentary systems, it stops well short of resembling the American system. Canada, for instance, has experienced some of the same political movements as the United States, but these movements have affected its party system in different ways. The Nonpartisan League (which we shall discuss further in Chapter 2) fielded candidates in Republican (and occasionally Democratic) primary elections in North Dakota, Minnesota, and other prairie states in the early twentieth century, yet in the neighboring Canadian provinces of Saskatchewan and Alberta it chose to constitute itself as its own political party (Schwartz 2006).

Canada has traditionally had what is often referred to as a "two and a half" party system—two strong parties that compete to win elections, along with at least one party (and in some elections as many as three or four parties) that advocates for a particular part of the country. Canadian parties have at times had strong ideological factions, but for the most part Canadian parties have been less ideologically distinct than American parties, and Canadian voters have been less attached to parties than have American voters. Candidates are chosen by party constituency associations at the district (or, in Canadian terms, riding) level, but it is rare for these associations to contravene the instructions of the national party, and the party leadership, when such instructions are given. The procedures for making these choices more closely resemble a caucus than a primary—only a fraction of party members attend, and the decisions are made on one particular day and in one particular place, not at scattered voting booths (Hazan and Rahat

2010, 40). Proposals have been made by some Canadian parties to decentralize this process, but the ultimate decision about this is a matter for the parties, not for the government. Most funding for local parties is provided from the national party organization, and fewer than 2 percent of Canadian citizens are formal members of the political parties. Even if multiple candidates compete for the support of the party in a particular riding, then, their competition is predicated upon a decision by the national party to allow this competition to take place, and it takes place before a tiny sliver of the population of the riding. There are many good reasons why Canadian parties would allow competition for the party's nomination; as Cross and Blais (2012, 15) argue, parties can try to generate broader public support by making competition for the nomination more visible; this often occurs following a defeat or in regions of the country where the party is weak. In Canada, as in other parliamentary democracies, there has been broad public support for making competition for the nomination more visible, more highly regulated (in terms of the financing of these races), and more democratic, but the easiest way for political parties to satisfy this public demand has been to do so in races for the party leadership (which are easily more visible than legislative races).[5]

In Latin America, where parliamentary systems are less common and American-style presidential democracies are more frequent, candidate selection can at times more closely resemble American primaries. Few of these nations have laws that require primaries to be held, however. As a result, parties can hold (and pay for) primaries when it is to their advantage to do so. Two recent articles on Latin American primaries (Carey and Polga-Hecimovich 2006; Kemahlioglu, Weitz-Shapiro, and Hirano 2009) have found that when Latin American parties hold primaries, they tend to benefit in the general election from doing so. Put in other words, Latin American parties may hold primaries only when it will benefit them in the general election to do so. Kemahlioglu, Weitz-Shapiro, and Hirano find that primaries are more commonly held by coalition parties, larger parties, and centrist parties; in each case, these parties may have a diverse enough set of factions that primaries are an effective means of resolving tensions within the party. Both articles find that GDP growth is positively related to the occurrence of primaries, indicating that primaries are more common in nations where the parties can afford them. And neither article found any evidence that having held a primary in the past makes a party any more likely to hold primaries again. That is, parties do not simply get in the habit of holding primary elections, but instead use them to resolve tensions related to the election at hand.

Studies of Latin American elections can, as Carey and Polga-Hecimovich point out, shed light on many arguments made about primaries in the United States. We cannot truly see whether primaries are beneficial in the United States because parties do not get to decide whether or not to hold them. These studies also, however, show that any nation's primaries are shaped by cultural factors unique to that country. Two other studies of primaries provide even stronger evidence of this. First, in 2011, Kathleen Bruhn conducted almost two hundred interviews with candidates in primary elections for the lower House of the Mexican legislature. Although the selectorate in Mexican elections can be quite small (ranging from 8 to 50 percent of eligible voters), Mexican primaries operate similarly to American primaries, although legislators are prohibited from serving consecutive terms. Parties are not required to hold primaries, but legislative primaries are relatively frequent. Bruhn found, however, that the logic of primary election results is almost the opposite of the American conventional wisdom. She found that candidates chosen in primaries are more moderate than candidates chosen by party leaders, and she found that candidates chosen in primaries are more likely to be party insiders than are those chosen by party leaders. Bruhn attributes this to the interaction of money and the parties' strategic considerations. In districts where a party expects to win or at least to be competitive, multiple candidates may express interest, and parties are likely to let these candidates sort out their differences in a primary. Candidates will be willing to spend money in the primary because they foresee the chance of winning the general election should they make it through the primary. In uncompetitive districts, few aspiring candidates will want to spend money in a primary because victory in the primary will not yield general election victory; as a result, parties will simply choose candidates without having a primary. One result of this is that, particularly when a party has multiple factions, primary candidates will have a track record within the party and will need to appeal to multiple factions to win the nomination. In districts where parties are less competitive, parties may choose candidates who will have appeal beyond the party's core supporters; such candidates may have experience doing something other than working in the party, and such candidates may have substantial appeal to a particular faction. Overall, Bruhn argues, when party elites choose candidates they may seek to balance the demands of different factions by choosing the candidates preferred by these factions. The candidates themselves, however, will have little need or opportunity to make appeal to multiple factions—that is, to be moderate in their appeals.

Second, research by Ichino and Nathan (2013) on legislative primaries in Ghana shows that many primaries may have little or nothing to do with factions or with ideological conflict. The selectorate in Ghana can be quite small—consisting of as few as one hundred to three hundred voters. Primary candidates in Ghana can easily provide material favors to enough primary voters to win, and many of them do just this. It is in the interest of voters, then, to have primaries because they can profit from them. According to Ichino and Nathan, some primary voters can bargain with the candidates—in a multi-candidate primary, voters can and do accept gifts from more than one candidate, and they frequently let candidates know what their opponents have given them. Actions by a party to cancel a primary or reduce primary competition can thus alienate voters. Because Ghanaian legislators have little independence from their parties, appeals based on ideology would be worthless. However, the cost of switching parties or going outside of the party system can be high; parties are often based on ethnicity, so candidates and voters may have little choice about which party to join. The primary is, then, a more important venue than the general election for making personal appeals to voters.

All of these examples give us some sense of why the United States has primary elections for virtually every level of office while other nations do not, but they also show that even comparing American primaries to other nations' primaries can be difficult. Cross and Blais (2012, 158–160) emphasize reasons for this that have to do with American culture—the United States has long had a stronger preference for direct democracy than have other countries, and the Progressive Movement (about which we will hear more in the next chapter) set the United States on a historical course that is largely irreversible. There are, however, noteworthy institutional reasons why primaries make sense in the United States. The two-party system (a byproduct of the plurality rule system enshrined in the constitution) results in political parties that are unable to control their members, that feature multiple ideological points of view, and that are unable to effectively resolve disputes among members. There is, in addition, no formal definition of party membership in the United States, so parties do not have the latitude to limit participation in candidate selection in the same way as do parliamentary parties. The United States does, however, have strong enough legal institutions to restrain the sort of favor-seeking that characterizes nomination contests in developing democracies. While there may be some downsides to ideological competition within parties, ideological battles may be preferable to primary competition devoid of issues.

As Kemahlioglu, Weitz-Shapiro, and Hirano (2009) note, the trade-off in the decision about whether to have primaries echoes the distinction between "voice" and "exit" made by economist Alfred O. Hirschman (1970). Hirschman contended that dissent within organizations can either be resolved by deciding to remain within the organization and work for change (that is, to exercise voice) or to exit the organization. Hirschman's distinction applies to both candidates and voters. In a two-party system, an aspiring office-holder must work within one party or the other, and there are steep barriers to party switching. As in the Ghana case, moving from one party to another entails a loss of status, and party-switchers are rarely greeted warmly by their new party. Although voters can easily switch parties in the United States, they only have one other choice, so it takes a great deal of dissatisfaction to switch. In a system with multiple parties, or in which new parties can easily be formed, on the other hand, competition within parties makes less sense than does leaving the party entirely. Parties, especially strong parties of the European variety, may be resistant to change from within, and candidates and voters alike are more likely to find ideological or political satisfaction by leaving.

The fact that primaries are an established part of American elections, that they are taken for granted by politicians and voters alike, is testament to the fact that they fit the American political system of the twentieth and twenty-first century quite well. This does not, as I have noted, make them a good means of choosing candidates. In their evaluation of candidate selection mechanisms, Hazan and Rahat (2010) explore the role of public participation in bringing about responsiveness to public sentiment on the part of candidates and political parties. The United States scores high in terms of public participation and high in terms of responsiveness to the public, but low in terms of the responsiveness of the political parties to the public. Although more Americans participate in candidate selection than is the case (arguably) in any other democratic nation, they frequently choose candidates in races with little competition. They may give candidates a mandate to pay attention to their views, but primaries clearly do not give the political parties a mandate to do anything. There is much to celebrate in the openness and democracy that characterize American primaries. Primaries are appealing in that there are examples of dramatic victories, unexpected reversals for veteran politicians, and charismatic new faces—this is an appeal that has been noticed by politicians in many other countries, and it is an appeal that has led many nations to move toward greater public participation in primaries. But whether it is an appeal that has served Americans well is a story worthy of careful exploration, and which we shall explore in this book.

Congressional Primaries and the Study of Congressional Elections

As I have noted above, this is, to my knowledge, the only recent effort to write a comprehensive study of congressional primary elections. There are many fine texts that cover the congressional election cycle in its entirety. Before setting forth on this study, it is important to consider how these books have treated primary elections—what lessons we can draw from studies of the full election cycle, why congressional primaries have traditionally received little attention in these books, and what relationship there is between conventional wisdom about general elections and the dynamics of primary elections.

The two standard congressional elections textbooks today are Gary C. Jacobson's *The Politics of Congressional Elections*, now in its eight edition (2013), and Paul S. Herrnson's *Congressional Elections*, currently in its sixth edition (2012). Both of these books developed from their authors' earlier research on particular aspects of the congressional election process. Jacobson, for instance, published several articles and books during the 1980s on the effect of national political trends in congressional elections and on reasons for the emergence of so-called "quality challengers" in congressional elections (Jacobson and Kernell 1981; Jacobson 1987, 1989). Jacobson sought to distinguish between congressional candidates with political experience and those without, arguing that experienced candidates (those who had been elected to political office before) tend to be more strategic than other candidates, and to run against incumbent members of Congress at moments when those incumbents were particularly vulnerable. Jacobson's effort to document the declining number of quality challengers in incumbent-challenger races was an indication of the growing security of incumbents and the declining turnover in Congress. As Jacobson continued to publish revisions to his textbook, he noticed the increased nationalization of congressional elections, as shown in the "wave" elections of 1994 and the late 2000s. Jacobson's focus in his textbooks has been on viewing congressional campaigns in the aggregate, looking at voter turnout patterns in congressional races, the role of partisanship, the role of national political forces, and public sentiment about Congress.

Paul Herrnson began his career slightly later than Jacobson. Herrnson's first book, entitled *Party Campaigning in the 1980s* (1988), documented the growing role of the party campaign committees in directing resources to candidates and in recruiting promising candidates to run in districts that they believed looked winnable for their party. Whereas Jacobson's efforts relied primarily on aggregate data, Herrnson (who had the good fortune to be based in the Washington, D.C., area) developed an approach based on interviews with candidates, prospective candidates, and party leaders. Herrnson thus takes a more "micro" view than Jacobson, walking the reader through the different stages of campaigns and outlining the different players in campaigns. His textbook contains, for instance, chapters on the role of money, on the role of the party committees, and on the role of interest groups. In each revision of his textbook, Herrnson has highlighted the stories of recent candidates of particular types—that is, he always presents a competitive open seat candidate, a competitive challenge to an incumbent, and a less competitive challenge to an incumbent, and he follows the candidates in these races through the book.

Primaries thus play a role in these books, but the research designs of these books take much of what happens in primaries as a given. Jacobson makes reference to declining party control over nominations and gives his reader a brief (three page) summary of how primaries came into existence. He also briefly compares competition in Senate and House primaries. Overall, however, Jacobson's argument assumes that strong candidates will emerge from primaries when there is a good chance that the primary winner will ultimately win the general election. It may be that sometimes mistakes happen, but this is not relevant to the overall patterns in congressional elections that Jacobson discusses. Herrnson spends slightly longer talking about primaries; in the most recent edition of his textbook, fourteen pages are devoted to summarizing why and how candidates decide to run for office, and seven more cover campaigning in primaries. Herrnson does discuss patterns in the types of candidates who run in primaries (and who win primaries) and he discusses some particularly unusual recent primary elections. There is also some discussion of the role of political parties in recruiting candidates and providing assistance to candidates during the primaries. Herrnson makes it clear that political parties have favorites in many primary elections and that they occasionally work behind the scenes to ensure that their preferred candidates win the primaries. Herrnson appends a brief commentary on the Tea Party and its role in upending many of the 2010 Republican primaries.

It is not only, then, that the scope of these books precludes lengthy discussion of primary elections. It is also that they originated from efforts to document particular problems that assume some role for primaries but are not directly about primaries. For Jacobson, primaries tend to produce general election candidates who befit the already established characteristics of the general election race. For Herrnson, political parties want to use primaries to their advantage; sometimes they do not do this, but usually they do. The real story in both of these books is what follows.

These are the two dominant textbooks on congressional elections today. They build on many developments in scholarship on congressional elections that began in earnest in the 1970s. David Mayhew's *Congress: The Electoral Connection* (1974) called for seeing all of the actions of members of Congress as natural outgrowths of the desire for reelection. The work of Joseph Schlesinger (1966, 1994) focused upon delineating the desires of the ambitious politician; for Schlesinger, politicians, including members of Congress, sought to be reelected but also sought to advance their own careers, either within Congress or beyond Congress. Richard Fenno's two masterpieces of participant observation, *Home Style* (1978) and *Congressmen in Committees* (1973) showed that members of Congress have very sophisticated understandings of the relationship between what they do in Congress and how the electorate perceives their actions. Morris Fiorina, in his book *Congress: Keystone of the Washington Establishment* (1989), built upon Mayhew's argument to explore ways in which the drive for reelection affected not only the actions of individual members of Congress, but shaped the committee system within Congress and the ways in which Congress legislates. Finally, John Aldrich's *Why Parties?* (1995), as well as subsequent work by Aldrich and his colleagues, outlined the goals political parties have in pursuing their ends through Congress. All of these books have shaped a modern view of congressional elections that sees them as tools used by parties, or as inconveniences endured by elected officials as they pursue their own ends. The uniting feature of all of these approaches to elections is that elections tend to be shaped by incumbent politicians and by political parties in order to meet their own ends.

All of these accounts have undoubtedly provided political scientists with an excellent way to make sense of the relationship between elections and congressional politics. Much of the conventional wisdom derived from these works is undoubtedly true. In this book I adopt the same framing device, for instance, that Herrnson uses—I separately consider open seat primaries, primaries for the nomination to challenge an incumbent, and primaries featuring an incumbent. The dynamics of these races are so different from each other that it is hard to imagine studying primaries any other way. It is clearly true that incumbency is the most important defining feature of primaries. Similarly, political parties clearly have a stake in controlling primary elections—even when, as I shall explain later, there is no compelling evidence that they consistently do so or need to do so. The literature on congressional elections is surely right on both of these counts.

In what follows, though, I go to great lengths to discuss the unpredictability of congressional primaries and to try to get a handle on all of the things we do not know but should, or do not know and cannot systematically measure. What makes congressional primaries fit so uneasily into the accounts of Mayhew, Fiorina, Schlesinger, Fenno, and Aldrich—and what makes them deserving of more attention than what Jacobson and Herrnson are able to provide—is the role of the public in them. Congressional primaries developed, as I shall show in Chapter 2, as perhaps the single most successful outgrowth of the Progressive Movement of the early twentieth century. Primary elections, argued the Progressives, were a means of taking power away from political bosses. Primaries, as we saw in our comparison above of American candidate selection methods to those of other countries, are unique in their insertion of voters into a task traditionally reserved for parties. Although, as Alan Ware (2002) has shown, parties have consistently worked to harness the primary process for their own ends, they have never been completely successful in this. Primaries thus insert far more unpredictability into the political system than do other types of elections or other types of interactions between the public and the government. They do not always do this, but they do this enough that they are worthy of study in this regard.

Furthermore, it is not just that primaries represent a moment in which the public can play a role in parties' decision-making. It is that we have never known exactly who that public is. Not very many people vote in primaries. This means that parties and candidates must do a fair amount of guessing in order to determine whose views are being represented in primaries. It is one thing to summarize the views of voters in presidential elections or in congressional general elections—the percentage of people who vote in these races is similar from one election to the next, and much has been learned about the role of socioeconomic factors, partisanship, and so forth in voter decision-making. Clearly some of this matters in primary elections as well, but in races where turnout can hover around 15 percent of the electorate—less than half of the turnout in congressional general elections and less than a third or even a quarter of turnout in presidential elections—it is hard to make predictions about voters. When this is coupled with lack of partisan labels in primaries, the unpredictable number of candidates, and the fact that the number of candidates running in any given primary can change over the course of the race, it becomes apparent that primaries can be unpredictable even when using the measurement tools perfected in the study of other kinds of races. Sometimes, some factions within the electorate have their say in primaries, but it is hard to know when this has happened.

A final piece of conventional wisdom that emerges from many of the studies of Congress that matters in this study of primaries is the consensus among scholars that Congress as an institution has changed substantially over the past three decades. Voting on congressional legislation is far more polarized along party lines than it has been at any time in the past century (McCarty, Poole, and Rosenthal 2006). The career advancement of members of Congress is now predicated on party loyalty, both in terms of voting and in terms of providing financial support to the party committees and to one's fellow party members (Heberlig and Larson 2012). The narrow margins of majority control that have been the norm since the early 1990s have required substantial ingenuity on the part of congressional leaders in order to advance legislation, and they have required more aggressive "whipping" by the parties than was the case in less polarized times or in times where one party enjoyed a larger majority, and hence could afford to lose more members on any vote (Sinclair 2011). These developments have brought about more competitive general elections, but they also pose three possibilities about primaries: parties may be more concerned about getting the right candidate from the primary, incumbents who stray from the party line may wind up with a primary challenge, and incumbents who stick to the party line may take enough unpopular positions that they make themselves vulnerable to a general election challenger—thus making the challenging party's primary more competitive. The time trends identified in the Herrnson and Jacobson books, in other words, should lead us to think about whether primaries today are more consequential than they once were. In taking this look, however, one must go back and look at previous years' primaries, to see whether anything really has changed or whether primaries were always as they are today but less studied.

This book, then, is meant as a complement to standard books on congressional elections. There are many reasons why primaries have not been a major component of previous works on congressional elections. Primary results were not integral to the larger issues in congressional politics that interested researchers of the 1970s, 1980s, and 1990s. Primaries did not seem all that interesting during these eras, perhaps, and there was nothing anyone thought to be "wrong" with them. And perhaps primaries are a daunting thing to study because the data that we take for granted in studies of Congress—survey results, legislators' voting records, and the like—are not there. In this third regard, this book may strike some as being foolhardy in its effort to make sense of primaries using the piecemeal data that we have. In regards to the first two reasons, however, the aim here is to help the reader think about the role of primary elections in shaping general elections, party politics, and legislative politics, and to help sort out whether and how primaries have changed in recent years, and how we might judge any such changes.

Organization of the Book

The next two chapters of this book provide a context and a structure for looking at different types of primary elections. Chapter 2 provides a historical overview of primary elections. Congressional primaries have existed for barely a century, and they have taken on numerous forms over that time. In this chapter I summarize the reasons for the development of primaries, the goals that advocates of primaries had, and the ways in which these goals were or were not realized over the course of the twentieth century. I also consider the development of presidential primaries in the 1960s and 1970s and the ways in which the establishment of presidential primaries shaped the rules for congressional primaries and the expectations that researchers have had about primary election voting and results.

Chapter 3 discusses primary election strategy and voting. It has been well established for decades that multi-candidate competition differs from two-candidate competition in that candidates cannot reliably identify winning positions, and in that there is no guarantee that the winning candidate will be "best" candidate in terms of voter support or candidate positions. This chapter summarizes what is known about efforts by parties and outside groups to shape primaries, and it provides a look at data on who votes in primaries and how primary voters differ from voters in other elections. In this last regard, it is worth noting that the chapter shows that there is very little support for the widely held claim that primary voters are more politically extreme than general election voters or the electorate as a whole.

The book then turns to distinguishing between different types of primaries. Chapters 4, 5, and 6 consider open seat primaries, primaries for the nomination to challenge an incumbent, and primaries featuring an incumbent. In these chapters, we shall consider what causes candidates to run in primaries, how parties seek to restrict competition, and how district partisanship affects the competitiveness of primaries. The chapters make use of different types of data. In the case of open seat primaries, presidential voting in the district gives one a reliable measure of district partisanship—in many instances presidential voting tells us more about a party's prospects in a district than does the party of the departing incumbent. In the case of challenger primaries, the popularity of the incumbent and the incumbent's ideological "fit" to the district play a greater role in determining the level of competition to oppose the incumbent in the general election. Finally, primaries featuring an incumbent are sufficiently rare that the reasons for the challenge can usually be known. In such cases, we can gather information about the strategy of the primary candidates, something that is either entirely absent or can only be inferred for other primary types.

Chapter 7 considers the effects of race and redistricting on primary elections. The redrawing of districts can create particularly competitive primaries, and in recent decades some states have been forced to do this because of the need to create or maintain majority-minority districts. Most majority-minority districts are not competitive in general elections, and hence winning the primary is tantamount to winning the election. This has led some primary elections in these districts to be more competitive than are other types of primaries, and it has also created unusual patterns of competition in neighboring areas. These are primaries that do not quite fit the typology presented in other chapters, and the changing role of primaries from discouraging to encouraging the participation of minorities in the political process merits consideration separately from other primary elections.

Finally, Chapter 8 discusses efforts to reform primaries. This chapter begins by outlining the legal status of primary elections and the legal protections in place for primary elections. It then summarizes normative concerns that have been raised about the conduct of primaries and discusses parallels between these concerns and those concerns raised in the early twentieth century. The chapter concludes by describing some calls for reform that have been raised by academics and advocacy groups and by summarizing three major changes in primaries: the move to establish closed primaries in South Carolina and Idaho, the "top two" primary implemented in California in 2012, and the efforts by Tea Party activists in 2010 and 2012 to use Republican primaries to elect candidates of their choosing.

Congressional primaries are clearly here to stay. Despite the unusual nature of American candidate selection laws, there is little chance that there will be radical changes to them in the years to come. This is as it should be. Despite their imperfections, primaries represent a triumph of democracy, a tool that ensures that political parties and their leaders cannot monopolize campaign discourse (Geer and Shere 1992). Accordingly, I argue here, they are deserving of more than a footnote in books on presidential primaries, on congressional elections, or on political parties. We discuss congressional primaries often enough, and we bring them into debates about what ails American politics enough, that they are deserving of study in their own right.

Notes

1 These results are from a Suffolk University Poll, available from *National Journal*'s 2006 Poll Track, http://uselectionatlas.org/POLLS/SENATE/2006/polls.php?action=indpoll&id=25200610230 (accessed February 8, 2014).
2 For discussion of these developments, see Goodnough 2011, 2012; Seelye 2012.
3 This chapter has not even discussed the special election primary held in April 2013, following John Kerry's appointment as secretary of state. Primaries in both parties to fill that seat were plagued by apathy, a consequence, according to many in the Massachusetts media, of voters' exhaustion following the 2012 election.
4 By "congressional" here I am referring to the House and the Senate.
5 On these points see Eagles, Jansen, Sayers, and Young 2005; Erickson and Carty 1991; and the essays in Bakvis 1991.

2
PRIMARY ELECTIONS AND THE "DEMOCRATIC EXPERIMENT"

> This was the makeup of the ticket that on the last day of March, 1916, agitated the office-holders, perplexed the politicians and set the whole state to wondering whether they were witnessing a huge joke or a revolutionary political movement.
> —Herbert E. Gaston (1920, 109)

The proponents of democratizing American political nominations have always sought to frame primary elections as a means of wresting control away from political parties and giving greater power to the American people—not as a joke or a revolution, as Herbert Gaston's description above of the 1916 North Dakota Republican primary results suggests, but as a means of enhancing democracy. The call for democracy, for wresting control of government away from unelected party bosses, resonated for several decades before and after the turn of the twentieth century, and took a variety of forms. In the late 1800s, it tended to take the form of third-party movements. Populist leader Milton George rallied American farmers in the 1880s with the cry that "the government is the people, and we are the people" (quoted in Wiebe 1967, 61). Historian Robert H. Wiebe (1967, 61) summarizes George's appeal, saying that "The only proper party was the people themselves; the only valid laws [according to George] were the people's truths phrased in the people's language." By the 1910s, however, the drive for greater voter choice had been taken up by the Progressive Movement, and it featured a call for an increased role for voters within the two major parties. Richard Hofstadter (1955, 257–61), describing the Progressive Movement that would build upon the Populists' anger, argues that the Progressives sought to restore American government to the way it had been in an earlier age, before political parties had successfully seized control of American elections and limited the choices of American voters. For Hofstadter, the Progressives sought to appeal to citizens as individuals, not as partisans, not as representatives of class or ethnic interests. The Progressive Movement, in his telling, sought to draw links between societal problems and government institutions, and to use the power of enlightened individuals—"men of good will"—to free government from parties and pressure groups. Both reform movements had many goals, but none of these goals was so widely accepted as the establishment of direct primary elections of local officials, including governors, state legislators, and members of Congress.[1]

There are two noteworthy features of these historians' accounts of the origins of primary elections. First, the rhetoric presented in these accounts seems timeless; it is easy to see Tea Party activists today using the same sorts of rallying cries that Populists and Progressives used, seeking to appeal to citizens as individuals to rise up in opposition to the agendas presented to them by political party leaders. Second, there is also something uniquely American about the emphasis here on the power of the individual voter and the skepticism about parties. Arguments in favor of primary elections have been with us for some time, and were once a major subject of political science research. While Americans today take primary elections somewhat for granted, and the literature on primary elections (at least at the subpresidential level) has largely been left behind, it is worth noting that no other Western democracy provides voters with so much leverage in determining the nominees of the two major parties.

It is also worth noting before we describe the history of primary elections that there is no reason to assume that primaries are always the "best" way to choose party nominees. During much of the nineteenth century, American parties chose their nominees through party conventions or caucuses. Such meetings were held at the state level and also at the level of individual towns. In 1897, Massachusetts state senator Frederick Dallinger published a book entitled *Nominations for Elective Office*, in which he summarized nominating procedures in the United States up until that time, with particular emphasis on his home state. In much of New England, Dallinger argued, party caucuses functioned like town meetings—there were opportunities for all citizens in attendance to deliberate over whom the party should nominate, and the offices for which they sought to nominate candidates often had such small constituencies that those in attendance could be expected to be reasonably familiar with the potential nominees and the tasks that would lie before them should they be elected. As far as Dallinger was concerned, this procedure worked quite well. However, he noted that in some larger cities such as Boston, constituencies were simply too large for the town meeting format to work. Dallinger feared that primaries would become popular in such instances, and that uninformed voters would make poor choices about whom to nominate. Five years later, Ernst Christopher Meyer, an American diplomat, self-published for European and American audiences another voluminous history of nominating procedures (1902); Meyer, as well, felt that caucuses had worked well and had been an admirable forum for democratic deliberation and self-government. Meyer, however, showed that even in Dallinger's home state, town meetings had become impractical as early as the 1820s. By that time, party machines in Massachusetts and New York had begun to offer slates of candidates, and caucuses merely ratified these slates. The caucus, argued Meyer, was ill-suited to evaluate candidates because there were so many offices and because the constituencies for these offices were sufficiently large (both in terms of population and the distances participants needed to travel) that delegates needed to be selected for the purpose of deliberating. Given the low level of information participants had about the candidates (especially for lower-profile offices), party slates tended to place well-known candidates at the top and lesser-known candidates further down the list. The larger scale of these elections also made corruption, or mere carelessness in vote counting, more of a problem; in a small meeting one might assume that consensus could be reached more easily or that nominating procedures that satisfied the participants could be developed in an ad hoc manner, but the counting of the votes or the nominating procedures needed to be done in a more oligarchical fashion in larger gatherings.

One might ask, of course, how democratic the small-town meetings favored by Dallinger actually were. Dallinger (1897, 23–25) provides examples of letters offered to caucus attendees from local businessmen touting the probity of their preferred candidates; whatever appeal such letters might have had, they do suggest that a select number of local luminaries exercised a great deal of control over nominations. Be this as it may, however, the small-town environment of early nineteenth century New England towns seems a more idyllic forum for choosing nominees than was the case in the sprawling, heavily agricultural states admitted to the union later in the century. It seems impractical to assume that more than a small fraction of the residents of South Dakota or Wisconsin had the time, knowledge, financial means, or motivation to take part in similar meetings. Thus, both in rapidly growing industrial cities and in less populated agricultural areas, political parties took the lead in selecting nominees. Primary elections were introduced in a few places in the United States in the 1860s—California Republicans held primaries in 1866, and Crawford County, Pennsylvania, implemented primary elections in 1868 (Meyer 1902, 84)—but where primaries were held they tended to be optional.[2] Parties could choose to hold primaries when they felt it beneficial to stimulate interest in their nominations among the broader electorate, but when they did so they were responsible for publicizing the primaries, paying the costs of establishing voting places and procedures, and for tallying the votes.

In many parts of the United States, in the late nineteenth century as today, winning a party's nomination could be tantamount to winning an election. As we shall see in this chapter, then, the introduction of primary elections thus represented a step toward democratizing elections. It is clear that many Americans were effectively shut out of the political process in the late nineteenth century because they were presented with a fait accompli when they showed up at the polls on Election Day. As Progressive reformers began to focus their attention on the corruption of party machines in the first decades of the twentieth century, it was abundantly clear that the undemocratic nature of nominating procedures was a problem for many voters. Some historians of this period have argued, however, that nominating procedures had also become a problem for the parties themselves, and that American political parties also stood to gain from acquiescing to state-sponsored primary elections.

Between 1899, when the Minnesota legislature passed a direct primary law for Minneapolis elections, and 1916, over half of the American states introduced some form of primary elections, and by 1958 every state had primary elections for most elective offices. This spread took place with surprising speed, and, perhaps most remarkably, occurred almost unnoticed by political scientists. There was an outpouring of research on primary elections between the publication of Dallinger's 1897 book and the publication of the final edition of Charles Merriam and Louise Overacker's *Primary Elections* in 1928, but it was not until 2001 that another book would be written about primary elections at the subpresidential level. Several books written on the problems of particular parts of the country (most notably the South) would make reference to primary elections, and many books written about presidential primary elections in the 1970s and 1980s made note of the Progressive Era reforms, but no researchers thought to connect the ferment of the early twentieth century to the sometimes unusual procedures many American states have developed to choose nominees for Congress and for state offices.

This chapter, then, seeks to explain the enduring legacy of the debates over primary elections in the early twentieth century and to draw a line from those debates to current primary elections. We shall pay particular attention here to regional differences—primary elections today are not the same everywhere and they were implemented in different parts of the country for different reasons. As this is a book about congressional primaries, we shall pay particular attention to noteworthy developments in such primary elections over the course of the century, but it is important to note at the outset that congressional candidates have largely been bystanders as primaries have developed. In the early twentieth century, primaries were advocated as a means of reining in big city party bosses, but the concerns of reformers had as much or more to do with the nominations of mayors, governors, and even judges than they did with the nomination of candidates for the House of Representatives; senators were not even elected at the time the movement for primary elections took off, although the direct election of senators was another major (and successful) Progressive goal. Similarly, when Americans again became interested in the conduct of primary elections following the debacle of the 1968 Democratic Convention, the focus was largely on presidential candidates, and to the extent that congressional nominations were influenced by changing primary laws in the 1970s, these candidates were again innocent bystanders. We thus have a system (or, to put it more accurately, fifty different state systems) for conducting congressional primaries that has never been specifically about producing better, or more democratically chosen, congressional candidates.

Periods of Primary Reform

It is useful in looking at congressional primaries to consider the periodization schemes that scholars have proposed in talking about presidential primary elections. Among the more authoritative books written on presidential nominations in the late 1960s was James W. Davis's *Presidential Primaries: Road to the White House*, first published in 1967. In the 1980 edition of the book, Davis identifies four different eras of presidential primary reform. Davis identifies the Progressive Era, from 1905 to 1916, as the initial period of primary reform, in which at least half of the states experimented with mandatory primary elections.[3] Davis contends that the period from 1917 to 1945—in which eight states repealed their primary laws, other states saw efforts at repeal of or restrictions on primaries, and in which most presidential candidates largely ignored primaries—comprises a second period. Third, Davis argues that between 1948 and 1968 there was a renewed interest in primaries among states and among candidates, as some presidential aspirants saw primaries as a path toward nomination even though success in the primaries did not automatically translate into support at the party's convention. Finally, Davis discusses the period from 1968 to 1976, in which the major parties enacted formal delegate apportionment rules for the states and encouraged the use of primaries as a means of selecting convention delegates. Given that Davis was writing in 1980, it makes sense to consider subsequent developments as a further part of the post-1968 period.

In thinking about Congress, Davis's scheme still has much to recommend it, although one might quibble with the exact dates. It is clear that the direct primary laws passed during the Progressive Era changed congressional nominating procedures, and it is equally clear that there was a retrenchment in subsequent years. It is difficult to adequately gauge when this retrenchment began, however. Davis (1980, 42–49) lists the twenty-five states that introduced presidential primary laws, and then provides a list of eight states that repealed their presidential primary laws between 1917 and 1935. Ware (2002, 227–29) shows that by 1919 all but three states—Connecticut, Rhode Island, and New Mexico (which became a state in 1912)—had some sort of primary law on the books, but that over 70 percent of the states that had primary laws endured repeal efforts between 1919 and 1926. Most repeal efforts were, however, unsuccessful, and as we shall see below, many early primary laws had problems and it is difficult in many instances to distinguish between efforts to fix problems with primary laws and efforts to roll them back. Many academics writing about primaries during the 1920s (see, e.g., Ray 1919; Boots 1922; Kettleborough 1923a, 1923b; Overacker 1928, 1930, 1932a) seem reluctant to categorize developments during that decade as part of a larger effort to do away with primaries. The three remaining states implemented primary laws by 1957 and newly admitted states also introduced primary laws shortly after admission to the union. Literature from the 1950s shows that for the most part the states tinkered with their primary laws and voters became accustomed to primaries, but there is no real sign of any sea change in congressional primaries at any point between the late 1920s and the late 1960s outside of the South. With the abolition of the South's white primary in 1944, most Southern states developed a system of primary elections (at least within the dominant Democratic Party) with runoff elections in instances where no candidate won a majority.

It makes sense in talking about subpresidential nominations, then, to focus our attention on three periods—the Progressive Era, the subsequent decades, and the contemporary period from 1968 onwards. In doing so, it is important to distinguish the changing rationales for primary elections. Progressive reformers saw primaries as a means of making government more accountable to the people; for them, there was a clear relationship between the way in which politicians reached office and the attention (or lack thereof) of politicians to contemporary social and economic problems. Primary elections were thus one of many Progressive reforms aimed at making government more accountable, but much of the literature on primary elections in that era focused upon problems primaries might introduce—either actual problems that had been observed or theoretical problems with giving voters (the so-called party in the electorate) a say in nominations. Throughout this literature, however, the animus against political bosses is tempered by a concern that parties still be able to produce candidates who could advocate for the policy views of their parties. In the subsequent decades, the rather scant body of work on primaries continues to focus on technical problems in the administration of primary elections, but with a growing acknowledgment that in states where one party was not competitive, primary competition provided clues about intra-party factionalism that one could not identify by looking only at general election results. That is, there was less advocacy for primary elections of any type but more attention to the nature of primary competition. Finally, in the 1970s and beyond, in an era of dealignment of voters from the parties, the attention of reform advocates shifted to a more full-throated argument about including not only loyal partisans but all voters in primary elections. These changes tell us much about changes in what American parties represent—changes that were wrought in part by the introduction of the direct primary but that also have influenced debates about what the consequences of primaries should be.

The Progressive Era and the Direct Primary

It is striking how much attention political scientists and journalists devoted to primary elections during the first two decades of the twentieth century. In addition to the early compendia by Dallinger and Meyer (discussed above), there were, by my count, thirty-three articles on the subject written in the *American Political Science Review* and the *Annals of the American Academy of Political and Social Sciences* between 1902 and 1931. Many of these took the form either of state-specific case studies of how direct primaries were faring or of annual or biennial updates on the passage of laws in the different states. In addition, renowned University of Chicago political scientist Charles Merriam—one of the founders of the field—published a comprehensive text on primary elections in 1908, and updated the book in 1928 with co-author Louise Overacker. Overacker, along with another political scientist, Charles Kettleborough, took on the role of monitoring the spread of primaries and the repeal or adjustment of existing laws. An edited volume focused upon direct primary laws in Minnesota and Wisconsin was even published in 1905 for the use of high school debating leagues (Fanning 1905). The major political opinion magazines of the era, such as *The Nation, Harper's Weekly, Outlook,* and *The Atlantic Monthly* published frequent articles pushing for the adoption of direct primary laws and championing the results of these laws. There was substantial diversity in the laws passed, in terms of voter registration requirements for primary voters, the offices covered by primaries, and the role of state governments in administering (and paying for) primaries. Literature on state policymaking often touts state governments as "laboratories of innovation." This was certainly the case for primaries; while primary laws were clearly contagious, this is one era in which the multiplicity of state primary laws drew substantial public interest and drew many into the process. Despite this, however, the literature on primaries is decidedly one-sided. Merriam, as we shall discuss later, was a strong advocate for direct primaries, and almost all of the literature on primaries (with the exception of the Fanning reader) was written by those who supported them.

An 1898 editorial in *Outlook*, a New York-based Progressive weekly, opined that "the reform of the primary is the foremost question to-day in American politics."[4] The editorial went on to argue that "the people elect officers, but do not nominate them, and consequently the election is often a choice between candidates neither of whom are acceptable ... How to translate the power of the nomination from the few to the many, from the machine, which can be and often is purchased, to the people, who may be deceived but are not corrupt, is the most important present problem which democracy has to solve." Whether it was the foremost question for all Progressive reformers is debatable, however. For many contemporary historians, of course, the enduring legacy of the Progressive Era lies not as much in governmental reform as in reform of working conditions in America's factories, acculturation of immigrants, and the restraint of industrial power. Even within the sphere of governmental reform, the primary was one of many goals. At the municipal level, Progressives had much success in pushing for nonpartisan elections, in reducing the role of patronage in government, in reducing the number of elective offices, in establishing off-year elections, and in shifting power away from elected officials to trained bureaucrats and appointed public servants. At the state level, Progressives championed establishing laws allowing for referenda and voter initiatives to enact or overturn legislation, lengthening the terms for some elected officials, and allowing for the recall of elected officials. At the federal level, Progressives were responsible for the constitutional amendments requiring the direct election of senators and for the enfranchisement of women. Many Progressives also pushed for reforms that never did come to pass, including cumulative voting, preference voting, and even proportional representation.[5] In Meyer's account (1902, 435–64), all of these goals are related to the direct primary—for instance, reducing the number of elected offices will allow for more informed voting in the primary and lengthening legislators' terms in office will give voters more of a record to judge—but the primary was clearly only part of a long list of ideas.

The push for the direct primary was also clearly related to one innovation in elections of the late nineteenth century, the introduction of the secret ballot (also known as the Australian ballot). For much of the nineteenth century, voting was hardly the secret affair it is today. Parties distributed colored ballots to voters, and many accounts of the era describe voters entering the polling place prominently displaying their ballots for any interested observers (such as party workers) to inspect. The Australian ballot was first introduced in Massachusetts in 1884, and it spread to all states by 1891. The Australian ballot was initially opposed by the parties, but the appeal to the public was irrefutable. Although the Australian ballot allowed for split-ticket voting, by most accounts the parties adapted to it quickly (and found that they could appear on the side of reform without sacrificing very much control over the election process).[6] In some states (such as the machine bastion of Illinois), voters were still given the option of pulling one lever to vote a straight party ticket or of having candidates of the same party grouped together to facilitate voting a straight party ticket; in others (such as Massachusetts) voters were given an "office block" ballot, where candidates were grouped by office sought, not by party. With the introduction of the Australian ballot, however, states had, for the first time, given themselves a clear role in the administration of elections. If states were to require secret balloting in elections, they also would assume the financial responsibility of operating polling places, counting votes, and so forth (Ware 2002, 38).

As noted above, political parties in some states experimented with holding primaries as early as the 1860s—in some cases because they were required to, in others because they felt it would be advantageous to involve voters in the selection of nominees. We saw in Chapter 1 that optional primaries were at the time occasionally used in other democracies as well (and still are), although they rarely go by that name. A primary election can generate excitement about the party's candidates and can compel candidates to campaign for the nomination—something that may aid candidates in the general election or can ensure that the party nominates someone with sufficient popularity to win the general election. In short, if primaries are optional they will be held when they benefit the party. Mandatory primaries, on the other hand, deprive the parties of substantial autonomy in determining how their nominees will be chosen, but this deprivation is not necessarily something harmful to parties. In Alan Ware's (2002, 64) account, immigration and urbanization during the late nineteenth and early twentieth centuries changed American parties in four noteworthy ways, ways that shaped the tactics that proponents of primaries used. First, questions were raised about the sorts of people who should be participating in elections and whether the enactment of closed primary laws (that is, primaries in which only previously registered party members are permitted to vote) would reduce the possibility that uninformed voters would play too large of a role. Second, because states had taken over some aspects of election administration with the Australian ballot, the introduction of mandatory primaries would absolve parties of the need to develop rules for choosing nominees. Third, the transparency of primaries would arguably reduce fraud and corruption; at a minimum, arguments about the prevalence of fraud in less visible nominating procedures were a rhetorical tool to use against party bosses. And fourth, just as parties lost the ability to determine the rules of selecting nominees, they also lost the ability (or need) to balance the demands of competing geographic or ethnic constituencies within the party.

The other major account of the development of the direct primary, John Reynolds' (2006) *The Demise of the American Convention System, 1880–1911*, also claims that the Progressives latched onto the idea of the direct primary some years after parties had begun to explore using it. In Reynolds' telling, political parties began using primaries at the county level as early as the 1860s, largely as a cost-cutting measure—it was less expensive to have party members in some areas cast votes on a particular day than to bring them all together. These primaries had become problematic, however, in part because they were primaries to select delegates to the state convention, and voters often had no idea what the delegates would do when they arrived at the convention. At this time, a new breed of candidate also emerged, the so-called "hustling candidate." Such candidates actually put themselves forward for the nomination and sought to organize slates, rather than allowing others to do this work for them. Although voters in a direct primary could hardly be expected to know about all of the candidates seeking office, when they were familiar with a candidate they could at least have a chance to help him get the nomination. By the time Progressive academics and political leaders gathered for the 1898 conference on the "Practical Reform of Primary Elections"—the one and only formal gathering of primary advocates of the time—political parties in many states had made it clear that they would use primaries; the question was not whether to have primaries but how to reform them so as to ensure that they took place in an orderly, transparent way. Doing this required the involvement of state governments.

The Enactment of Direct Primary Laws in the States

Drawing inspiration from the Crawford primary and the California experiment of the 1860s, parties in several American cities (most notably, Cleveland) experimented with primaries in the 1890s. The first mandatory primary election enacted by a state legislature, however, was the Minneapolis primary of 1900. In Alan Ware's (2002, 110–13) telling, the Minnesota legislature passed a primary law largely because legislators from Minneapolis had championed it and few city politicians objected to it. As discussed above, there was an outpouring of journalistic interest in this experiment, but the advocates of the primary appeared to have few expectations of what might happen and they did not appear to be motivated by an animus against the city's political leaders. Although the primary was nominally closed, there were by most accounts few efforts to ensure that crossover voters (for instance, registered Democrats who reregistered as Republicans in order to vote in the primary) were excluded. A 1902 evaluation of the primary (Anderson 1902) concluded that turnout exceeded expectations, that there was no evidence of malicious intent on the part of crossover votes, and that the quality of most candidates nominated was not demonstrably worse than the quality of previously nominated candidates. There was, however, one glaring exception to this pattern—the mayor nominated by the Republican Party, and subsequently elected, was, according to virtually everyone offering an opinion on the election, a bad candidate. A.A. "Doc" Ames had served as mayor for three terms in the 1870s, as a Democrat, and was a well known quantity. After winning election, Ames chose his brother to lead the Minneapolis police, and he and his brother quickly became embroiled in allegations of corruption and dealings with organized crime. According to many political insiders, Ames's behavior could clearly have been predicted in advance of the election, but, although everyone writing about the primary expressed dissatisfaction with Ames's nomination, few saw it as a sign that the direct primary should be abandoned.[7] Perhaps equally troubling, but again rarely used as an argument against the direct primary, was the admission of a man named Johnson that he was completely unqualified for his job as parks commissioner but had nonetheless won the nomination because of the popularity of his surname among the predominantly Swedish voters in his district.[8]

Even in accounts that made hey of the Ames nomination, most journalists judged the Minnesota primary a success because voters liked it—they agreed with the idea of the direct primary, and no respectable politician would be able to garner support for repealing it. The most critical articles about Minnesota's experiment tended to come from the Wisconsin media; this was so because Wisconsin's

Progressive governor, Robert La Follette, had made the direct primary the centerpiece of his reform agenda. La Follette's opponents concluded that Minnesota showed that once primaries were established there was no going back. La Follette was unusual in that he was one of the few Progressive leaders to make the case for the full range of Progressive reforms while in office. As the leader of an insurgent movement within the state's Republican Party, La Follette framed the primary as an attack on the status quo, and the agents of the status quo—within his party and within the opposition party—responded by waging a protracted war in the legislature against the direct primary. One contemporary account of the floor proceedings regarding the direct primary alleges that anti-primary legislators and their allies used whatever means they could to keep their opponents from voting, including getting them sufficiently drunk that they either would change their minds about voting for the primary law or would become unable to vote altogether (Meyer 1902, 252–55).[9] After failing to push primary legislation through the legislature, La Follette (who had been more successful in pushing for referendum laws) went over legislators' heads and was able to get a direct primary law, applicable to all state offices, on the general election ballot in 1904. It passed with 62 percent of the vote, although it allowed for crossover voting, something La Follette had opposed. As governor, La Follette also encouraged other states to adopt the direct primary, winning over, among others, California Governor Hiram Johnson and New Jersey Governor Woodrow Wilson (Unger 2000, 194, 223). Despite the claims of La Follette and his opponents, studies many decades later concluded that the Wisconsin primary had in fact done little to upset the political status quo (Ranney and Epstein 1966; Ranney 1968, 1972). To the extent that primaries had resulted in different types of elected officials, some accounts have merely noted that candidates of significant personal wealth or with the right ethnic origins for their constituency had an advantage (Margulies 1968, 99).

Minnesota and Wisconsin were, at the time, highly unusual states. They had weak party systems, and they had vigorous reform movements that operated both within and without the major parties and that brought together industrial workers and farmers. It is unsurprising, then, that other weak party states, such as South Dakota and California, also quickly introduced primary laws. What is more surprising, however, is that states where parties had traditionally been much stronger also adopted the primary with little conflict. Between 1896 and 1911, Massachusetts slowly developed a primary system, beginning with council offices in Boston and gradually expanding the law to cover all state offices (Ware 2002, 110–17). There was clearly some conflict going on between urban machines and small town reformers here—Massachusetts had previously enacted laws mandating odd-year elections for municipal offices (so as to insulate city elections from higher turnout state and federal elections) and making elections in the state's larger cities nonpartisan affairs. To introduce some order into these nonpartisan elections, Massachusetts also introduced preliminary elections, in which the field was winnowed to two competitors for each office.

Several other northeastern states also introduced primaries in similar exhibits of conflict between urban and rural (or small town) interests. It was not clear that the cities lost in these efforts. In Maine, for instance, the parties had traditionally sought to balance their tickets by slating candidates from numerous regions of the state; absent the ability to slate candidates, the city of Portland now dominated party nominations (Hormell 1923). The same concerns raised in Minnesota were also brought up in evaluations of the Maine reforms; Hormell's conclusion about the consequences the Maine direct primary was that there were few changes that could conclusively be linked to the introduction of primaries, but that "there are fewer dominating leaders in the legislature than in former years"—perhaps a reflection of the quality of candidates chosen by uninformed voters. The two main holdouts in the trend towards primaries were Rhode Island (which would not enact a primary law until 1948) and Connecticut. In the Connecticut case, the state's egregiously malapportioned legislature, in which many small towns enjoyed far more representation than their population merited and the lack of a single dominant urban area to draw reformers' ire made it the last state to pass primary legislation (Lockard 1959b).

Another state with a protracted (and amusing) battle over the primary was New York. New York resembled Massachusetts in that Progressive ideas had substantial appeal at the state level while party leaders in the state's dominant metropolis dragged their feet. New York City politicians, however, put up more of a fight than did Boston politicians. New York passed a primary law in 1912, at the behest of Governor (and future presidential candidate) Charles Evans Hughes. Hughes was aided in his push for a direct primary law by fellow New Yorker and former President Theodore Roosevelt (Beard 1910, 197). Whether because of poor planning or in a deliberate attempt to mock the new primary law, New York City politicians produced a primary election ballot that was fourteen feet long, and an inadequate number of ballots and tally sheets were made available at the city's polling places (Feldman 1917). This sort of opposition makes it difficult to distinguish between efforts to tweak the primary law from efforts to water it down in the years that followed. There truly were problems in New York. New York has traditionally had far more parties on the ballot than most other states; in part because the state permits fusion balloting there are many parties other than the Democrats and Republicans,[10] and these minor parties, too, were covered by the primary law.[11] In the American Party's 1912 primary, the winner received thirty-eight votes statewide, and the Socialist Party nominee in one district won with a total of two votes (Feldman 1917). This all wound up being very costly for the state. Yet these correctable flaws were not easily corrected without inducing legislative debate over the broader purpose of the primary, and as a result New York replaced its primary with a convention in 1921 and did not fully reimplement a comprehensive primary law until 1967 (Zimmerman 2008).

New York's woes, and its difficulties in fixing primary laws in the face of a legislature hostile to the idea of the primary, are similar to those of Illinois and

Michigan. In Illinois, conflict over the enactment of primary laws was again a battle between an urban political machine and the rest of the state. Even with provisions maintaining the ability of parties to publicize their candidate slates in advance of the primary, passage of the law was complicated by the fact that Illinois required preference voting in state legislative districts in the general election, and the state court rejected several versions of the primary law because it argued that primaries, too, should require preference voting (Aylsworth 1910; Jones 1910). In Michigan, candidates and parties appear to have devised ways to subvert the reformers' intent almost from the start (Reynolds 2006, 227). For example, the primary law did not prohibit candidates from running for multiple offices and no one was responsible for checking the credentials of candidates to ensure that they were, in fact, real people. The result of this was that politicians exploited these loopholes. Some candidates filed for several offices, waited to see who the competitors for each office would be, and then dropped out of all of the races save the one they felt they had the best chance of winning. In one instance, a political aspirant filed his own name along with the names of a number of fictitious candidates with politically popular last names in order to scare away opponents, and then withdrew the names of the fictitious candidates and won the nomination without opposition (Dorr 1937; see also Millspaugh 1916). It was not until 1935 that Michigan was able to begin cracking down on this process. Nebraska faced a similar problem; in 1931 the state addressed it by requiring candidates to list their home addresses on the ballot (Overacker 1932a). Missouri had a problem with well-known candidates filing to run, scaring away other potential candidates, and then dropping out at the last minute, after tipping off other potential (but weaker) candidates (Loeb 1910). And in Oklahoma, "spot" candidates were reportedly a regular feature of primary elections (Ewing 1953, 11); these were candidates who were not seriously aiming to win the primary but who were running in order to weaken one candidate in order to help another—for instance, a spot candidate might hail from the same town as the incumbent and could split the vote in that town with him, thereby aiding another candidate from a different region.

Primary elections, then, presented a smorgasbord of confusing options for political parties and for voters, and they offered a variety of new opportunities for political skullduggery. While many of the anecdotes above suggest clear problems with the administration of primaries, there were also many fascinating innovations. In an effort to ensure that voters would at least be minimally informed about candidates, Oregon required candidates for all offices to include on the ballot a brief statement explaining their candidacy, a provision the state still has.[12] Under South Dakota's Richards Primary law, enacted in 1912, parties were required to hold representative conventions before the primary in which they would choose a "majority" candidate and a "protesting" candidate.[13] Parties were also required to vote on what the themes of the campaign would be. In the case of presidential nominees, they chose these themes without the approval of the candidates themselves. While on its face an admirable effort to encourage deliberation on issues within the parties, the results were rather comical, as parties announced themes such as "true democracy" and "equitable adjustment, economy, progress, and prosperity," themes which hardly provided voters with a clear choice (Berdahl 1923). R.O. Richards, the law's namesake, was reportedly unhappy with the parties' cavalier treatment of his law and wondered whether the courts might require parties to adopt themes that actually said something concrete about their objectives. Despite efforts by legislators to repeal the law, it was overwhelmingly popular among South Dakota voters and remained in place until 1929 (see Merriam and Overacker 1928, 91; South Dakota Legislative Research Council 2005).

Table 2.1 shows a timeline of the adoption of direct primary laws in the states. In this table I show the date at which the state first implemented primary elections for the majority of statewide offices. In a few instances states established primaries for all offices all at once. More often, however, states gradually implemented primaries, moving from the municipal level up to the state level, often in fits and starts

TABLE 2.1 Adoption of the Direct Primary by Year

Year	States
1903	Wisconsin
1904	Alabama, Oregon
1905	Montana, Texas
1906	Louisiana, Mississippi, Pennsylvania
1907	Iowa, Missouri, Nebraska, North Dakota, South Dakota, Washington
1908	Illinois, Kansas, Ohio, Oklahoma
1909	Arizona, Arkansas, California, Idaho, Michigan, Nevada, New Hampshire, Tennessee
1910	Colorado, Maryland
1911	Maine, Massachusetts, New Jersey, Wyoming
1912	Kentucky, Minnesota, Virginia
1913	Delaware, Florida, New York
1915	Indiana, North Carolina, South Carolina, Vermont, West Virginia
1933	Georgia
1937	Utah
1947	Rhode Island
1953	New Mexico
1955	Connecticut
1960	Alaska
1970	Hawaii

Source: Merriam and Overacker 1928, 61–64; Galderisi and Ezra 2001, 17. Dates listed are for adoption of primary for most state offices; many states introduced laws covering some offices at an earlier date, others subsequently repealed parts of their laws. For different argument about sequence, see Ware 2002, 123–24; Lawrence, Donovan, and Bowler 2013.

over a period of many years. In the early states, this process effectively created a constituency for primaries—candidates who could win primaries became enthusiastic proponents of expanding the use of the primary (Reynolds 2006, 225).

Among many of the later states, particularly among Southern states, the direct primary was adopted with substantially less intrigue. In some of the early states, primaries were implemented at the behest of a single crusading politician—as was the case for Robert La Follette in Wisconsin and Hiram Johnson in California. One common theme among the later states, however, was that most individual candidates—and particularly congressional candidates—are relatively absent from the debates. It had become apparent that these laws had substantial appeal to voters. Writing long after the dust had settled, V.O. Key (1956, 92) argued that advocacy for the direct primary took on "an evangelical tone" in which any opponent "was made to appear to be, ipso facto, an enemy of democracy." This explains why many incumbent candidates merely bowed to the inevitable and accepted the new laws, while aspirants for office either sought to use the laws as they stood or reconsidered their decision to seek office. In the much later case of reforms to the presidential nominating process, it is easy to find instances of candidates who used newly enacted primary laws to their advantage.[14] This was likely the case for congressional candidates in the early years of the twentieth century, but the stories of these candidates are largely lost to history.

Evaluating the Progressive Era Reforms

What lessons can we draw from the early primary laws that can help us to understand the development of congressional primaries? First, it is important to note that the problems reformers focused upon, and the metrics they used for evaluating how well primaries worked, are still highly relevant. Charles Merriam's 1908 book on congressional primaries and Ernst Meyer's 1902 tome identified thirteen broad questions contemporary observers might ask about primaries. These were questions that were all taken up in the scholarly literature on individual states during the first three decades of the century.

1. *Should primaries be optional or mandatory?* As we have seen, primaries during the late nineteenth century were often optional. Reform advocates almost universally argued that primaries should be mandatory; this shifted control of election procedures from the parties to the states. Given that the problem, in the eyes of reformers, was that party leaders used nominating procedures in a manner that gave voters inadequate choices, optional primaries would still limit the involvement of voters in the elections of most concern to party leaders.
2. *Should primaries be open to all voters or closed to all but registered party members?* Reform advocates wrestled with the question of how to ensure that the

voters had the best interests of the parties in mind. Many analysts of early primaries asked whether voting by unaffiliated voters or registered members of opposition parties would produce candidates who did not agree with the party's goals. Some worried that crossover voters would deliberately sabotage primaries by voting for weak candidates, while others worried that registered party members' votes would be swamped by new voters who turned out to support a well-known candidate with substantial appeal outside of the party or an insurgent candidate who sought to take positions at odds with others in the party. While studies of open primaries found little evidence that this was in fact the case (see, e.g., Merriam and Overacker 1928, 69), this is a concern that has lingered to this day.

3. *How close to the general election should primaries be held?* Kettleborough (1923a), to take one example, argued that if primaries were held too close to the general election, nominees would have few opportunities to make themselves known to the general electorate or would be unable to heal rifts within the party caused by the primary. On the other hand, a primary held too far in advance of the general election would in effect require that candidates would have to run one campaign in the spring of the election year, and would then have to run a new campaign several months later. Separating primaries from the general election by too long a time period thus would be more costly for candidates—potentially providing an advantage to wealthier candidates—and would mean that any enthusiasm generated by the nominees during the primary would dissipate well in advance of the general election. Some observers asserted that primaries held too far in advance of the general election harmed government because incumbents would spend their time campaigning instead of governing (Geiser 1923). Complicating matters further, turnout varies according to the time of year; primaries held during the summer might yield lower turnout because many voters would be less attentive to the primary because of vacations or seasonal employment (Horack 1923). Some reformers thus argued that primaries should be held during September, but there was (and is) no consensus on the optimal timing of primaries.

4. *Should the two parties' primaries be held concurrently?* The answer to this, according to reformers, was yes. Because states and municipalities bore the costs of conducting elections, concurrent primaries would be less costly than holding two or more separate primary elections. In addition, sequential primaries provide an advantage to the party voting second. This party can observe the results of the first party's primary and choose candidates best able to compete with the first party's nominees. In instances where a party has unexpectedly chosen a lackluster candidate, the second party's potential candidates might take advantage of this. While this might be better for democracy, in that better candidates would emerge in the second party, the consensus among primary advocates was that this provided an unfair advantage to the second party.

5. *Should candidates be required to pay filing fees?* The principal argument against filing fees was simply that they would require candidates to raise more money and would deter some potential candidates who could not afford the filing fee (Merriam 1908, 142; Dorr 1937). As we saw in the Michigan case above, however, there are compelling arguments in favor of filing fees. They help defray the costs of holding primaries and they ensure that all of the candidates who file are reasonably serious about running. Michigan's filing fees were refundable, which meant that candidates could reevaluate their prospects once they saw who else was running, but candidates were able to use the fees to their advantage in filing for multiple offices.
6. *How should parties address the problem of plurality winners? Are they a problem?* Many analyses of early primaries raised the question of whether plurality winners—nominees who emerged from a multi-candidate field with less than 50 percent of the vote—would either be at a disadvantage going into the general election because a majority of their party had voted against them, or would have failed to win the nomination were they in a head-to-head battle with one of the other candidates (Meyer 1902, 277; Hormell 1923; West 1923). Merriam and Overacker (1928, 211) contend that, despite the fears of some primary opponents, instances of plurality winners were rare in the direct primary's early years. This hardly seems, however, like a sufficient reason to entirely abandon the concern about what should be done when this does happen. While, again, there was not compelling evidence that plurality winners tended to be at a disadvantage in either sense, states took this possibility very seriously and responded in a number of different ways. Several states experimented with preference or "second choice" voting, but were disappointed with the results (see Verplanck 1906; Lush 1907; Holcomb 1911; Lowrie 1911; Williams 1923). Six Southern states instituted runoff elections, in which the top two candidates ran in a separate election following primaries where no one garnered a majority of the vote; this system, while still in place today in many of these states, hardly satisfied those who argued that primaries increased the cost of campaigning. In the decades following the height of the Progressive Era, some states adopted the practice of holding endorsing conventions, in which parties would seek to confer the advantage of a party endorsement upon one candidate in an effort to increase his or her primary vote totals. Illinois allowed parties and other organizations to publish slates of endorsed candidates, again in an effort to help their preferred candidates and limit primary competition to a smaller number of candidates. Several other states, including Massachusetts, New York, and (in the 1950s) Connecticut introduced challenge primaries, in which candidates were required to get a threshold percentage of the vote (25 percent in New York and Connecticut, 15 percent in Massachusetts) at the party convention in order to appear on the primary ballot. In Utah, only the top vote-getters at the convention are given a line on the primary ballot; the convention procedures allow, in place of preferential voting, multiple rounds of voting with the

lowest-finishing candidates removed in order to settle upon candidates.[15] The runoff and preprimary convention are still in place and still draw attention for the maneuverings that take place in securing ballot access—in Utah, a sitting senator failed to win enough of the vote at the convention to appear on the ballot in 2010, while in 2012 another unsuccessfully maneuvered to limit the vote totals for an opponent at the convention in order to spare himself a primary challenger. And as we saw in the Massachusetts example in Chapter 1, preprimary conventions often feature maneuvering behind the scenes to discourage convention attendees from voting for a challenger or even to encourage strategic votes for a third "spoiler" candidate. While winnowing the field thus has much appeal, the behind-the-scenes politics involved in using unrepresentative conventions to limit primary competition have drawn harsh criticism.

7. *Should primaries be paired with "sore loser" laws?* In states with strong third-party movements, or with ballot access laws that did not prevent independent candidacies, a primary loser could easily turn around and run in the general election, potentially either splitting the vote of the loser's (former) party and enabling the other party to win, or allowing the primary loser to appeal across party lines and win the election. Recent general elections have included some winners who were "sore losers"—most notably, Connecticut Senator Joseph Lieberman in 2006 and Alaska Senator Lisa Murkowski in 2012.[16] Early primary advocates sometimes spoke in behalf of sore loser laws, but some Progressives argued against them on purely self-interested grounds—in California, for instance, Progressives apparently felt that they stood the best chance of winning office as Republican nominees, but that they stood enough of a chance running on their own that they could run in the general election as Progressives if they lost the primary. The absence of sore loser laws effectively gave them two chances to win (Delmatier, McIntosh, and Waters 1970, 171).[17] By the 1990s, however, all but three states had enacted some form of sore loser laws (Kang 2011).

8. *Do primaries help or hurt parties' general election prospects?* This was another major line of inquiry; contested primaries at the time (and again, this remains true today, as we have seen in both major parties' presidential primaries in 2008 and 2012) were viewed by some as a detriment to party unity (see Millspaugh 1916). There are few conclusive ways to measure the effect of party conflict on the morale of the supporters of the losing candidate, just as there are few ways to measure whether attacks on a winning nominee are picked up by general election opponents. There was at the time much anecdotal support for arguments for and against this notion, but for most supporters of primaries this was not a sufficient reason not to hold primaries. There is much contemporary literature on the relationship between primaries and general elections; we shall explore some of this literature in subsequent chapters.

9. *Do primaries increase the cost of elections for candidates, and do they provide an advantage for wealthy candidates?* Many reformers worried that primaries would

increase the cost of campaigning, both because they required candidates to appeal to a larger number of people to win the nomination and because they forced candidates to run two—and in some instances three—separate campaigns. Some contemporary students of the Progressive Era fault reformers for bringing about changes that led to the prominence of self-funded candidates today. Historian Philip Ethington (1999, 193), for instance, claims that "weak party institutions and strong direct democracy institutions have also supported waves of independent millionaire candidates." While such direct linkages seem a bit unfair to Progressive reformers, the concern about the role of money was present in debates at the time. The solution, for some, was simple—states should introduce regulations on spending or public financing of elections in order to aid less wealthy candidates (Hormell 1923; West 1923). Such ideas did not go far during the Progressive Era, but they are evidence that Progressives were sensitive to these concerns yet unwilling to abandon their advocacy for primaries because of them.

10. *Do primaries produce higher or lower quality candidates than indirect nominations?* There is obviously no metric to gauge whether primary election winners were better or worse than nominees chosen through other means. The Minneapolis and Maine cases showed, however, that this was a concern. Progressives struggled with the fact that primaries would take nominating power away from party bosses, but would then give that power to potentially uninformed voters. While Progressives praised the power of the common man to make savvy political choices and pushed for referenda and initiatives in order to take power from politicians and transfer it to citizens, they were also quick to bemoan the failures of citizens to rise to the occasion. In his analysis of the Illinois primary, State Legislator Walter Clyde Jones (1910) cautioned that before the direct primary could be effective, voters would need to show a willingness to vote intelligently. "This," he added, "is a matter which cannot be corrected by statute but only by personal reformation." Although many contemporary observers professed to see no difference in the candidates produced by primaries, in retrospect, historians have claimed to see many differences in the types of candidates, if not necessarily their quality. V.O. Key (1949) and other students of Southern politics (discussed below) noted that primaries there tended to confer advantage on demagogues or other candidates who could create distinctive, memorable candidacies. Modern historian Alonzo Hamby (1999), on the other hand, argued that the machine-produced candidates were, in fact, often quite colorful characters, and that early primary elections tended to feature less interesting candidates engaging in serious, but dry, discussions of the issues of the day—discussions that held little appeal for the average citizen. More recently, Branton (2009) has argued that if there is one minority candidate running in a field of white candidates, he or she can benefit by standing out from the field, and some students of gender and politics have argued that women can succeed in the same circumstances. These modern observations, then, lend credence to the early claim that candidates

with an easily observed means of differentiating themselves from the others, whether through ideological views, campaign style, or easily observed personal attributes, may have an advantage.

11. *Do primaries provide an advantage to particular regions of the state or groups of voters?* A core function of political parties, as we saw in the Maine example, was balancing representation of all regions of states. Parties could thus reduce geographic rivalries and foster alliances between disparate constituencies. This ability was clearly lost with the institution of the direct primary. Is it a problem that it was lost? For small town politicians in the New England states, the answer was arguably yes. Ticket balancing was an established feature of American elections in the 1800s, as the North/South combinations of presidential and vice-presidential candidates shows, but parties still retained the ability to balance tickets in less formal ways—by, for instance, choosing lieutenant governors from different parts of the state from their gubernatorial nominees or providing party leadership roles or cabinet positions to people from diverse constituencies. There is, after all, nothing inherently democratic about ticket balancing, and, as Alan Ware (2002, 127) suggests, this may have been an activity that brought enough grief to party leaders that they welcomed the intervention of state governments in forcing them to give up this power. In the opinion of some Progressives, balancing was suspect because it was a means of satisfying ethnic blocs at the expense of quality candidates. While in today's politics (in the United States and elsewhere) balancing a ticket to ensure representation by women or by minority racial groups is often a goal for liberals, in the context of the 1910s Progressives saw inclusion of European immigrant groups as a way to avoid addressing the issues voters wanted discussed (Reynolds 2006, 187).

12. *Will the news media play too large of a role?* Just as they worried about the types of candidates who would win primaries, so reformers worried that, given a potentially uninformed electorate, newspapers would play a dominant role in determining the winners of primary elections (Norris 1923). On one hand, this would be no better than having parties choose candidates—a local newspaper owner would merely gain the power that party bosses had previously had. On the other hand, as Victor West (1923) argued in his discussion of the California primary, it had not been demonstrated that newspapers would do a worse job than party leaders.[18] Of equal concern for some was the possibility that local newspapers would not devote *enough* attention to primaries, and they would thus be derelict in their duty to inform voters about the candidates (Fanning 1905, 53; Boots 1922).

13. *Will primaries increase citizens' engagement in the political process?* Finally, there was near universal agreement when primaries were introduced that they would prove to be popular among voters. It is not really accurate to argue that they would increase turnout, since one cannot really compare the number of people involved with the numbers who participated in nominating conventions. Yet most early works on primaries noted the impressive percentage of

citizens voting (Feldman 1917, Boots 1922, Guild 1923). This increase, however, would prove to be short-lived. As the novelty of primaries wore off, and as it became clear to some that the outcomes were not demonstrably different because of the increased participation, voter turnout declined precipitously.

There are several messages one can take away from this set of concerns. Many of these concerns are still relevant today; it is certainly not the case that primaries have evolved in ways completely alien to the path that Progressive reformers (and their foes) saw for primary elections. Many of these concerns also have eluded our measurement abilities. Things that seem evident to us today about primaries—the possibility that unorthodox candidates may have an advantage or that candidates may use primaries to attract large numbers of previously unaligned voters—are difficult to prove. No matter how many anecdotes we can summon about the consequences of, for instance, the battle between Barack Obama and Hillary Clinton in 2008 or the staying power of Ron Paul in the 2008 and 2012 presidential primaries, we cannot really prove that these candidacies and their consequences are determined by the existence of primaries or the rules of particular states' primary systems.

Most notably, however, these concerns show the ambivalence of Progressives about the abilities of the average citizen. Progressive reforms were a mix of the democratic (e.g., the referendum and the initiative, the direct election of senators) and the undemocratic (shortening the ballot, shifting power in cities away from elected officials toward an appointed city manager). The more ostensibly democratic reforms, such as the initiative, referendum, and recall, have proven to have effects that cripple the abilities of democratically elected officials to govern and, in the eyes of some, give wealthy citizens means of overly influencing politics. In the case of primaries, many Progressives argued that the direct primary would limit the power of the parties, but at the same time they clearly saw a role for parties and worried that politics without parties would not be preferable. The primary election laws enacted in the 1900s and 1910s were clearly part of a grand experiment, but they were part of an experiment that may well have ended prematurely.

Why Did Primaries Spread so Rapidly?

It seems clear that the enactment of primary laws in many states was framed as an exertion of power on the part of Progressives, as a strike against the power of political machines. Yet it is striking—and perhaps a little bit suspicious—how complete the reformers' victory was, especially given that parties would reassert their dominance in the years that followed. Why did so many states adopt direct primaries in some form or other? There is little evidence that Progressives had either a coherent nationwide strategy in regards to election reform or any sort of centralized resources to use for that purpose; instead, it seems in many states that reformers operated with complete independence from Progressives in other states (Ware 2000, 16). For many years, the dominant account of the movement for the direct primaries was that of Charles Merriam (Merriam 1908; Merriam and Overacker 1928). Merriam clearly establishes that there was a contagion effect. Merriam's books, as well as the various state studies of the era, show that voters were highly receptive to the idea of the direct primary. In some instances, politicians made vague promises to enact primary laws, then found themselves trapped by their own rhetoric and were unable to backtrack, as the Wisconsin stories suggest. Progressive journalists were eager to argue that primaries had been successful, even where the evidence was mixed. In states such as Wisconsin and Minnesota, legislators found that it was easier to enact primary laws than to scale them back once they had been shown to have problematic results. In 1912 Minnesota's newly elected governor, Winfield Hammond, parried any efforts to do away with the primary by simply remarking that, whatever the results are, people like it (Chrislock 1971, 84); similarly, in 1914 the Wisconsin Republican Party's platform committee entertained calling for doing away with the primary but concluded that there was no way to generate public support for the plan (Margulies 1968, 157). Given the inconclusive nature of so many studies, however, perhaps opponents of the direct primary took some consolation in the apparent fact that primaries had not really had the sorts of effects advocates such as La Follette predicted. If they were not that bad but voters liked them, there was no reason to stand against them, and if poorly designed laws cost the state money or sowed confusion among voters, this was not in the end a substantial threat to legislators' reelection.

Merriam's account, as unquestioned as it was for decades after the Progressive Era ended, is suspiciously light on political detail. Merriam does not frequently provide the sorts of blow-by-blow accounts of state politics that one can glean from the various journal articles of the time, and where he does, he dwells on the exciting conflicts between Progressives and urban machines. In case after case, the power of ideas triumphs. In Alan Ware's 2002 reassessment of the enactment of primary laws, the problem is that Merriam was not a disinterested observer but an active participant in the Progressive Movement. Ware, a British political scientist who has made something of a career of challenging the conventional wisdom in American political history, accuses Merriam of dwelling too much on the most exciting battles of the era and failing to study the states where primary laws passed with little opposition. Did the parties really do all that they could to fight the movement toward the direct primary? According to Ware, some urban machines did what they could to sabotage the law, but for the most part the machines decided quickly that not only could they continue to nominate their preferred candidates through primary elections, but they could in fact benefit from having states assume the responsibility for regulating their nominations. Primaries alleviated the problem of ticket balancing, they enabled parties to avoid conflict over how to choose candidates, and, perhaps most importantly, they transferred to the states and candidates the costs of funding the nomination procedure. At the same time, parties could use their organizational strength to help preferred candidates win their primaries and could abstain from elections in which they truly did not care which candidate won. Particularly in the case of low-profile offices, it cost the parties little to ensure that good candidates were nominated.

John Reynolds' study (2006) of the demise of the convention system concentrates less on the decisions of urban party bosses, but Reynolds also suggests that parties had been moving toward using primaries to choose their nominees, had found their own internal efforts to democratize candidate selection to be chaotic, and subsequently welcomed state regulation of the process. For Reynolds, the emergence of the "hustling candidate"—the candidate who actively seeks the nomination rather than waiting for it to be conferred upon him—preceded the establishment of primaries but could only be addressed by the parties by working with the states to establish primary rules.

For Ware (2002), Merriam is not only a bit too celebratory about primaries; Merriam, says Ware, is wrong about what happened. First, Ware claims, Merriam contended that primaries were an innovation that began in the West and the less industrialized Midwestern states—places where parties were weak enough that they could not resist. While states like Minnesota, Wisconsin, South Dakota, and California all fit this description, they were not, according to Ware, the first adopters of direct primary laws. Primaries were adopted as quickly in the Northeast and the industrial Midwest, showing that party strength (or lack thereof) had nothing to do with the timing of reform. Second, Merriam (and subsequent students of party politics such as V.O. Key, E.E. Schattschneider, and Walter Dean Burnham) saw primaries as most advantageous in one-party states. It is true that Southern states had vigorous primary competition for much of the twentieth century, but there is again no relationship between interparty competitiveness and the timing of primary laws outside of the South, indicating that parties did not see primaries as a threat to their ability to win elections. And third, Ware faults Merriam for overselling the relationship between public opinion and governmental action. Yes, primary laws were popular, but so, he says, are many other policy ideas that never become law. It is one thing to say that there were no popular arguments against primaries, but it was another to assert that anyone other than Progressives had the interest or the political skills to compel legislators to establish primaries. Ware finds the arguments for the direct primary problematic because the connection between primaries and the social agenda of Progressives was never explained convincingly at the time. Progressives clearly argued that primaries were the answer to a problem, but (in part because they remained sympathetic to the idea of giving parties a role as an intermediary institution in politics) they failed to clearly explain what the problem was.

Ware's explanation clearly fits some contemporary political scientists' rational choice approach to understanding political party strategy more than does the somewhat idealistic account presented by Merrian. It is ironic, then, that a recent statistical test of the Merriam and Ware arguments, done by Lawrence, Donovan, and Bowler (2013) shows more support for the Merriam account than the Ware account.

Ware is less sanguine, however, about the consequences of primaries. While they posed little threat to parties at the time, they would, he argues, play a role in creating the candidate-centered elections that would become the norm by the 1960s. When changes in communications technology enabled candidates to run for election (or, more commonly, re-election) without the blessing of their parties, the Progressive Era laws coupled with these changes to substantially weaken parties. This would lead, according to Mileur (1999, 268) to the creation of a new type of party, the party-in-service, which is now the major function of the party congressional campaign committees. This is, however, a story that we must explore only after we discuss the politics of congressional primaries between 1930 and 1968.

Before we do that, however, it is important to note one other possible explanation for the passage of direct primary laws. In an unpublished 2004 piece, Michael Crespin contends that one reason why primaries were appealing to parties is that they encouraged candidates to seek the nomination of one or the other major parties, as opposed to running as third-party candidates. One key difference between the Populist Movement and the Progressive Movement was that Populists seeking office tended to run as the nominees of minor parties such as the Greenback Party or the Populist Party (see Ritter 1997; Ware 2006, 53). The Progressives attending the 1898 primary reform conference explicitly stated that they were not interested in subverting third parties (Reynolds 2006, 158), but the practical effects of primaries show that they could not but have harmed minor parties. If we assume that candidates will evaluate their options for getting on the ballot and choose the one most likely to yield victory, running within a major party provides organizational advantages that a minor party cannot provide. In addition, if we assume that parties are more concerned with winning elections than with purity on policy matters, parties should also be receptive to allowing candidates with reasonably diverse views to seek the nomination through primary elections. Although there are instances where Populists worked within the major parties (the most obvious example being the campaign of Democratic presidential nominee William Jennings Bryan) and instances where Progressive went the third-party route, Crespin provides compelling evidence that the number of third-party candidates on the general election ballot declined in the years after primaries were introduced. This was one reason why, perhaps, parties supported the direct primary—as Peter Argersinger (1995, 170–75) argues, it forced populists to choose to be Democrats or Republicans, and in some states the direct primary effectively secured one-party dominance for decades to come.

Retrenchment and Maturation: Primary Elections from the Progressive Era to the 1960s

It is clear that primary elections had their problems. In many cases, these were technical problems that could be resolved without abandoning primaries entirely. One of the most compelling arguments about the primary, however, was that it would increase citizens' involvement in the political process; this claim quickly proved to be untrue. Turnout in primary elections was impressive in the 1910s, but it declined rapidly in many states during the 1920s. In some instances, this may have been because the novelty of the direct primary had worn off. It is also, however, difficult to draw firm conclusions because the electorate had expanded substantially with the passage of the Nineteenth Amendment, guaranteeing women's suffrage throughout the United States, in 1920. Women, as elections during that decade would show, were slow to take advantage of their new right, voting in lesser numbers than men in general elections and primary elections alike.[19]

The overall data, however, do not mean that primaries had lost their ability to frighten party regulars and to invigorate political outsiders. Then, as now, a few isolated dramatic events may well have shaped national perceptions of what was going on in politics far more than did overall national trends. There were, in other words, some dramatic upsets in primary elections once these elections had become widespread. Whether despite this or because of this, however, it is clear that the Progressive Movement lost clout during the 1920s and 1930s, and that with its decline vigilance over protecting existing primaries also waned. Most states retained some form of primary elections but many limited ballot access or limited the offices for which primaries were held. In the mean time, however, all three of the holdouts enacted primary laws.

The study of primary laws also lost its appeal to political scientists. Above, I noted that thirty-three articles were written on primaries through 1931; by my count, there were only five articles on primary elections written between 1932 and 1960.[20] Why did primary laws become weaker, less consequential, and less interesting to academics and the public after the high-water point of the Progressive Movement? James W. Davis (1980, 42–49), the author of the presidential primaries text, provides a three-piece argument about the American political psyche. In the 1920s, general prosperity reduced the power of arguments that something was wrong with the conduct of American elections. In the 1930s, the Great Depression shifted Americans' focus from matters of political process to broader economic worries. And in the 1940s, of course, matters of foreign and military policy dominated the national political discourse. Merriam and Overacker (1928, 94–95), in fact, go further than this, claiming that the public lost interest in primary reform during World War I and never really became interested again. Hiram Johnson's biographer Richard Coke Lower (1993, 101) contends that the leading Progressives did not agree about World War I and that it was this dissension that ended the Progressive Movement. And Herbert Gaston (1920, 266), in his history of primary reform in North Dakota, even argues that the influenza epidemic that raged from 1918 to 1920 prevented reformers from traveling enough to start an anti-party movement in parts of the country. There is no way to prove or disprove these sorts of arguments, but one can certainly draw links between the country's economic and military well-being and other periods of concern with process issues, such as the campaign finance reform movement of the 1990s.

The Direct Primary Outside the South

It makes sense in looking at the first decades of the direct primary to consider the South separately from the rest of the country. In Northern and Western states, primaries had already become nearly universal by the 1930s, but their impact in many states was limited, both by the nature of primary competition and by the growing opposition to primaries.

During the first decades of primary elections, however, it did occasionally appear that primary conflict would become as important, if not more important, than general election races. Because the development of primaries coincided with the Progressive Movement, and because Progressives tended to run as Republicans, there were a number of heated Republican Senate primaries during the late 1910s and 1920s. These primaries also, as many opponents of primaries feared, often featured candidates who were able to finance their campaigns out of their own pockets. A 1918 Michigan election, for instance, featured a Republican primary won by wealthy financier Truman Newberry, while the Democratic primary was won by automaker Henry Ford. This race became somewhat of a cause célèbre for those who sought to control the costs of primary elections (see Baker 2012); the recently enacted Federal Corrupt Practices Act placed strict limits on campaign spending, but the language of the statute made it unclear whether it applied to primaries or not. In its 1921 *Newberry v. U.S.* decision, the court made it clear that Congress had no authority to regulate spending in primaries. Subsequent primary elections in Pennsylvania and Illinois provided evidence that the development of primaries would substantially increase the costs of running for office.

With the decline of the Progressive Movement, however, came a decline in Republican factionalism and a decline in the competitiveness of primaries. Several studies have demonstrated that, as Alan Ware (2002) claimed, parties still seemed to ensure that their preferred candidates received the primary nomination. One study of Senate elections during the 1940s and 1950s concluded that there were no noticeable differences in the party unity scores of senators that related to the way in which they were nominated (Telford 1965). A 1980 study of gubernatorial and senatorial nominations concluded that in states that held endorsing conventions or other sorts of preprimary conventions there was less primary competition than in primary states (McNitt 1980). Where there was competition, it tended not to be about ideology, and it tended to happen within the state's dominant party; the occasional strong candidate to emerge within the minority party was often able to coast through the primary with little opposition in states such as Massachusetts and Rhode Island (see Moakley and Cornwell 2001). Anecdotal reports often identified newly elected politicians who appeared unlikely to have been able to win the nomination had it been decided by a party convention. For instance, Ware (2002, 234) discusses the career of Idaho's William Borah, a Republican first elected by the state's legislature in 1907. Although Borah first reached office as a conventional Republican, once Idaho implemented a direct primary for Senate nominations Borah (who served until 1940) developed a personal coalition and established himself as a figure who kept his distance from the state's Republican Party. In an ironic development, Robert La Follette, Jr., appointed to the Senate upon his father's death in 1925, was defeated in the 1946 Republican primary by Joseph McCarthy. La Follette, Jr. was by most accounts a less charismatic and more serious senator than his father; he also was not beloved within the Republican Party, but McCarthy was clearly not supported by party insiders either (Fowler 2008, 133, 171). McCarthy won the 1946 primary and general election, and in 1952 he beat back a primary challenger who did have the support of party regulars with 72 percent of the vote. McCarthy and Borah certainly were not similar in ideological terms, but both were able to use primaries to go over the heads of party regulars and create a personal campaigning style that appealed to the party in the electorate. Ware cautions, however, that such anecdotes may say more about state culture than they do about the nature of the direct primary.

Nowhere did the direct primary and state culture collide in a more dramatic way, however, than in North Dakota. North Dakota's experience merits retelling in part because it symbolized the threat primaries could pose to the parties and in part because, despite North Dakota's relative isolation from the major urban areas of the country, it does appear that the insurgents in the state's primary made credible claims about beginning a national, or at least regional, movement.

Observing that late nineteenth century agrarian movements such as Populism and Grangerism had had little impact in North Dakota, A.C. Townley in 1914 sought to organize a movement of farmers that would take advantage of the state's new direct primary law to elect a slate of candidates who had pledged to advocate for, among other things, state ownership of grain elevators and mills, state hail insurance, the establishment of rural credit unions, and favorable tax treatment for farm improvements.[21] Townley's group, the Nonpartisan League (NPL) would be different from Progressive groups in neighboring states because of its emphasis on using the primaries, on electing farmers, and on ensuring that movement leaders such as Townley were not among those seeking political office. In *Political Prairie Fire*, the definitive book on the NPL, Robert L. Morlan (1955) describes the extensive effort by the NPL to engage farmers at the precinct level, to construct a financial base through postdated checks from farmers, and to coordinate precinct-level endorsing caucuses that would recruit local farmers who would run, pledged to the NPL's principles but without direction on other political issues. NPL candidates would run in the primary of whichever party appeared to have the strongest support in the area. According to Morlan, Townley decided to focus upon this unorthodox strategy—using a disciplined organizing method that resembled what a party might employ, but in the service of a group that would studiously avoid becoming a party itself—because of his experience as an organizer for the Socialist Party. Socialist policy ideas, Townley found, were far more popular than was the party itself. Many farmers were receptive to the idea of state ownership of mills, elevators, and so forth but refused to abandon their party—especially when the party soliciting them carried as much baggage as did the Socialists. The NPL endorsed a large enough slate of state legislative candidates in 1916 that it won the governorship, control of the state House, and (with the help of senators who were not NPL members but supported many of their plans) enough of a working majority in the state Senate to pass much of its agenda. The NPL held power for four years, but those four years featured vicious infighting between the NPL and its opponents, as well as between developing factions in the NPL.

Although the NPL was originally formed in order to play a role in state politics, the group had an opportunity to win a House seat when incumbent Republican Henry Helgeson died in the spring of 1917. There was not actually a primary in the special election to fill Helgeson's seat, but the candidate recruited by the NPL, John Miller Baer, ran as a Republican, defeating a Republican regular and a Democrat in the election.[22] Baer withstood a primary challenge in 1918 but fell to another challenger in the 1920 Republican primary. Baer's brief congressional career shows the limitations of the NPL's approach at the congressional level. To start with, Baer was no politician, but he was somewhat of a celebrity. Baer was somewhat of a household name in North Dakota as the cartoonist for the NPL's paper, the *Leader*. This clearly enabled him to stand out in the special election race, and it also at least theoretically gave him the ability to be his own man in Congress. Although Baer caucused with House Republicans, there is no evidence that he had reason to expect to advance within the party. Baer also had the misfortune of having a German surname, which doomed him when World War I got underway and many American Germans were accused of sympathizing with the enemy. Baer was the only House or Senate member who clearly ran and won because of his NPL ties; although the NPL did support North Dakota's two other House incumbents, both initially reached office before the appearance of the NPL.

Baer's fortunes echoed those of the NPL. What is most striking about the Morlan book is the sheer hostility that the NPL faced, in North Dakota and the nation. Morlan describes the period between 1916 and 1920 as "one of almost unparalleled ill-feeling in those states where [the NPL] was a significant political force" (Morlan 1955, preface). NPL candidates were relentlessly accused of being socialists (which some, in fact, were), of being unpatriotic, and of being the puppets of group leader A.C. Townley. Party leaders in neighboring states played up these alleged threats, and the national press treated the NPL—and in particular, the candidates sent to Washington by the NPL—as curious specimens from a remote and backwards state. There was no party infrastructure to defend the NPL; while in North Dakota the NPL had its newspapers to present its point of view, it had no means of doing so outside of its home state. Townley may well have been calling the shots for the NPL, but it seems reasonable to expect an upstart group to be reliant on the charisma of one individual.

Outside of the Midwest, Townley was treated as somewhat of a curiosity by leftists. He embarked on an Eastern speaking tour in 1917, giving a well-received talk at Cooper Union in New York, and meeting with labor leaders and the national news media (Morlan 1955, 147). At home, however, Townley was repeatedly arrested and jailed. The NPL faced obstacles in expanding into other states, but it also faced obstacles at home, as conflicts within the organization led to factionalism. A variety of other "leagues" were formed in order to confuse voters. Some Republican and Democratic politicians were happy to court NPL followers; the Republican Party even purchased advertising in NPL papers for races the NPL was not contesting (Gaston 1920, 173). Meanwhile, Republicans and Democrats outside of the NPL were also happy to support NPL dissidents and to adopt their own versions of the group's ideas. As a consequence, the parties could implement parts of the NPL agenda while alternately attacking the group itself and making appeals to NPL supporters. As Republican regulars reasserted control over North Dakota primaries, the NPL lost its role as an organized group. The newspaper folded, Townley began to speak of reconstituting the group as more of a conventional interest group, and NPL politicians began seeking to establish careers as individuals rather than as agents of the NPL. Individual politicians would be elected with the help of the NPL at the state level, but the NPL lost its role as an insurgent threat in primaries. In 1956, North Dakota Democrats established a formal alliance with the NPL that endures to this day but rarely spills over into primary factionalism (Omdahl 1961). Some studies have alleged that the NPL exerted its own influence in elections as late as the 1970s, but this influence was felt in general elections rather than primaries (Pierce 1973).

Why were NPL candidates successful in North Dakota, but not in other states? Morlan begins his book by showing just how unique the circumstances of North Dakota were. It was not just that North Dakota was (and is) a low-population, predominantly agricultural state where farmers' grievances play a large role in politics. At the time 27 percent of the population was foreign-born and a majority of residents were born outside of North Dakota.[23] North Dakota had no cities of significant size, and was thus entirely dependent on Minnesota cities and Minnesota grain buyers for its well-being. Morlan provides a catalog of abuses of North Dakota farmers by Minnesotans to show that the state was, perhaps more than any other American state, entirely dependent on outside political and economic actors. As a consequence of this, "a strong persecution complex had developed over the years" (Morlan 1955, 348), and although citizens tended to vote Republican there was neither a strong party organization nor an allegiance to incumbent Republican leaders. The sort of retail politics practiced by the NPL, coupled with the establishment of a party newspaper, enabled the NPL to reach farmers far more effectively than did communications from party regulars. Finally, the political issues at stake in North Dakota had virtually nothing to do with conflicts between the parties at the national level, so North Dakotans were receptive to what was effectively a reorientation of political conflict from the general election conflict between the parties to a conflict during primary elections between NPL and anti-NPL forces. As theories of issue cleavages predict (see Sundquist 1983), by the 1950s the Democrats and Republicans in North Dakota had reconstituted themselves such that the Democrats allied with what remained of the NPL and the Republicans constituted the opposition to it.

Although the NPL sought to play a role in other states' primaries, its success in doing so was limited by the economic geography of these states and the fact that the parties, seeing what had happened in North Dakota, had plenty of time to prepare. In some instances, preparation involved doing away with or substantially weakening the primary itself; Montana, Idaho, Nebraska, and Kansas all abolished their primary laws, although all of these states would reinstitute primaries once the NPL threat had waned (Morlan 1955, 239). Voter referenda brought the direct primary back quickly in Nebraska and Montana. In other instances, preparation involved the seeding of reform groups that were less openly hostile toward business; this was particularly the case in Iowa. Urban interests played a greater role in Minnesota, Wisconsin, and Nebraska. Recognizing that it had no chance to compete in as many races as it had in North Dakota, the league selected vulnerable incumbents to challenge, hoping to draw attention in a small number of races in order to build its fortunes (Gieske 1979, 37).

Many of these states also had indigenous Progressive movements that had been instrumental in establishing primaries; whereas in North Dakota the NPL saw the primary as a tool to be used, in Wisconsin, Progressives had already established their own power within the Republican Party, and the primary was a result of their power, not a tool to be used to establish it. In Minnesota, the Republican Party was able to keep NPL candidates from gaining power during the late 1910s; as it began to appear that the group's power had ebbed without yielding control of the Republican Party, agrarian reformers instead established a third party, the Farmer-Labor Party, which would hold primaries and elect candidates on its own before eventually merging with the Democrats (Gieske 1979, 41–44). Most crucially, however, there were already enough politicians sympathetic to the NPL's goals that the NPL endorsed many candidates, such as Idaho's Senator Borah and Montana Congresswoman Jeanette Rankin, who had initially come into office without the NPL's help. Given the alleged ties between the NPL in North Dakota and socialism, pacifism, and pro-German sentiment, politicians had good reason to keep their distance from the NPL even if they championed its agenda. Outside of North Dakota the NPL behaved more like a contemporary interest group and less like the disciplined anti-party force it was in North Dakota. One result of the NPL's lesser role in these states, however, was that it could not prove it had made a difference in elections; individual politicians could control their own fate in these states more than they could in North Dakota. States and politicians, then, saw the primary threat coming and took steps to shore up their parties and their primaries. At the height of its strength, the NPL could count a dozen or more House and Senate members, but these members were generally elected as Republicans, and it was not clear how many of them would have been elected without NPL backing; Baer remains the only House member who clearly reached office because of the NPL.

The case of the NPL may show that organizations that seek to gain power through primary elections are inherently unstable or ephemeral. It does, however, also show that primaries had the potential to be every bit as disruptive as anti-reform forces feared. It would be easy to write off North Dakota as an unusual state, an aberration. California's odd experience with the direct primary (discussed in Chapter 8) may well have been disregarded by many as well. Yet perhaps the fact that the NPL was able to establish a foothold outside of North Dakota led politicians to take the NPL and its primary strategy seriously. Even outside of the agricultural regions where the NPL was a threat, therefore, many states' primary laws were weakened. Few states repealed their primary laws entirely, but the parties did reassert themselves. In addition, presidential candidates tended to ignore primaries, leading to declining voter turnout. As noted above, states such as Minnesota, New York, and Massachusetts reduced the number of offices subject to primaries, and one contemporary study documented an increase in the restrictions on voting in closed primaries (McClintock 1922).

Opposition to the primary in the 1920s was led by Charles Dawes, Calvin Coolidge's vice president. Former President William Howard Taft did not explicitly call for doing away with the primary but he did call for placing limits on primaries. Taft, who had had an uneasy relationship with Progressives during his presidency, lamented the abandonment of deliberation within the party and the difficulty of arguing for conventions: "The initiative, the referendum, and the recall, together with a complete adoption of the direct primary as a means of selecting nominees and an entire destruction of the convention system are now the sine qua non of the real reformer. Everyone who hesitates to follow all of these or any of them is regarded with suspicion and is denounced as an enemy of popular government and of the people" (quoted in Milkis 1999, 13; see also White and Mileur 2002). Few elected officials were willing to publicly side with Dawes and Taft, however, in part because most of them had either gained office through primary elections or had learned to live with primaries and won renomination by running in primaries (see Hannan 1923). There were few advantages to explaining to the public why primaries did not work, but many governors and legislators worked behind the scenes to reduce the uncertainty primaries might introduce. Time after time, when repeal was put on the ballot, the voters chose (by substantial margins) to keep the primary (Merriam and Overacker 1928, 271).

The principal means of limiting the effects of primary elections was the preprimary convention. As noted above, the preprimary convention had some salutary aspects—it had the potential to limit the number of candidates in the primary and to reduce the likelihood of plurality winners. In addition, as one Illinois party chairman noted, a preprimary convention could ensure that qualified candidates ran for lesser offices and that party leaders had some limited means of ticket balancing for offices that attracted little interest from candidates (Wallace 1923, 103). As many as twenty states held preprimary conventions during the 1920s and 1930s, and twelve still do so today (Green and Herrnson 2002). Some preprimary conventions developed almost by accident; in Minnesota, anti-NPL forces understood that their best chance at defeating NPL candidates in the state's Republican primaries was to informally select one candidate to run head-to-head against the NPL endorsee. In races where multiple candidates sought to run as "regulars" or "stalwarts," some sort of informal preprimary selection process was necessary, with the tacit agreement of all involved that the losers in this process would drop out.[24] In his history of the Progressive Era in Minnesota, Carl Chrislock (1971, 62, 187–88) points initially to editorials in partisan newspapers in 1912 urging a representative conference of state Republicans to prepare for primary conflicts with the NPL, and then shows that, ten years later, the state finally passed a law allowing parties to hold formal endorsing conventions. The state's 1922 law stated that the party's endorsed candidate would be designated as the party endorsee on the primary ballot; following victory in that year's gubernatorial election by an NPL-supported candidate, the legislature in 1923 rolled back the law somewhat, still allowing for endorsing conventions but removing the specification that the endorsee would be noted as such on the ballot.

The Minnesota battle shows that there are many different formats to these conventions. In some states, candidates are required to receive a threshold number of votes at the convention in order to appear on the ballot; in others the winning candidate receives the endorsement of the party at the convention. Still others, such as South Dakota, engaged in platform writing at the convention. It is unclear, then, whether preprimary conventions were an effort to sabotage the direct primary or a constructive effort to fix problems with it. In many states, preprimary conventions were optional, and there were concerns raised that the endorsement of the party might hurt candidates more than it helped (Wallace 1923). Research suggests, however, that while preprimary conventions and other forms of party endorsement can reduce the number of candidates running (Dominguez 2011), they have declined in effectiveness over the century—that is, winning a party's endorsement or placing first in the voting at the party's convention does not help candidates in the primary, even in states with relatively strong parties (Maisel and Bibby 2002).

Because it is difficult to estimate the effects of primaries during the Progressive Era—so many different types of states adopted so many different types of primaries, and events in the years after the Progressive Movement's decline may well have shaped elections and nominations more than did primaries—it is instructive to look at the experience of the states that adopted the direct primary after the wave of enthusiasm for it had crested. New Mexico did not enact a direct primary until 1938, for complicated reasons having to do with fears on the part of Latinos that they would lose influence without the balancing provided by convention nominations (Donnelly 1940, 238; cited in Ware 2002, 188n). In his history of New Mexico politics, Jack Holmes (1967, 221–27) concluded that interparty competition declined between 1940 and 1965 and that the primary became a scene of conflict between regions over nominations for statewide office. Meanwhile, incumbent legislators and members of Congress became more powerful, were rarely challenged in primaries, served for longer, and developed stronger personal connections to voters (this, of course, corresponds to a growing national trend for members of Congress to serve for longer and confront fewer strong challengers in their reelection bids; see Ansolabehere, Hansen, Hirano, and Snyder 2006, 2007, 2010; Carson and Roberts 2013). Similarly, after Connecticut, the last holdout, gave in in 1957 (Lockard 1959a, White 1983) and instituted a challenge primary, the occasional iconoclastic legislator was able to win office and win reelection without the help of his or her party—perhaps the best known case of this was Lowell Weicker, a Republican senator from 1970 to 1988, and later an Independent governor.

These developments in the North and West showed that certain types of individual politicians were able to use primaries to their advantage, but there simply were not enough of these politicians, especially in states where there was healthy two-party competition. As has arguably been the case in presidential nominations, some observers concluded that primary voters were just as capable of voting strategically—choosing the strongest general election candidate—at the congressional level as were convention delegates.

Southern Primaries

The anecdotal evidence of strong personal appeals occasionally overriding the judgment of party insiders is far more evident, however, in studies of Southern politics. In the one party South during these decades, the Democratic Party had no reason to be concerned about general election results. V.O. Key (perhaps Charles Merriam's most prominent graduate student at the University of

Chicago) published his magisterial account of Southern politics in 1949, at the height of Democratic dominance in the South. Key's interest in primaries was not so much related to how they arose—it seemed evident to him that the direct primary provided an excellent opportunity for Southern Whites to exclude African-American voters from politics—but in what primary competition said about the sorts of factions that did exist in the South. Between 45 and 70 percent of Southern Democratic primaries were uncontested during each election cycle between 1920 and 1946 (Key 1949, 381), but the types of competing candidates varied widely by state, and statewide primaries were much more likely to be contested.[25] Cortez Ewing (1953, 33) noted that over 90 percent of Southern Senate races were contested, and that it was not uncommon for more than ten candidates to enter a primary. Turnout in these primaries also varied widely during the 1930s, 1940s, and 1950s, from 10 percent in Virginia to a peak of almost 40 percent in Texas in 1940 (Davidson 1990, 24). In Texas, in fact, turnout in the Democratic primary routinely exceeded general election turnout until the late 1960s.

What did Southern primaries say about state culture? In Virginia, primary competition pitted two enduring factions against each other, a political machine dominated by Senator Harry Byrd and a much weaker coalition of urban interests. In Alabama, Mississippi, and South Carolina, sectional interests competed against each other, at times producing relatively liberal Democratic senators such as Alabama's John Sparkman but more often producing extremely conservative senators. Ideology was rarely an explicit factor in these races, however; race was always the primary concern. In a small number of Southern states, such as Tennessee and North Carolina, the Republican Party did have sufficient influence that Democratic machines sought to ensure that candidates with a broad appeal were nominated. In Arkansas, a series of prominent politicians with strong personal followings competed against each other in races devoid of ideological or sectional conflict. In Florida, a state with far more diverse economic and sectional interests, primaries were scenes of what Key termed "every man for himself" conflict, with no enduring factions. And in Texas, perhaps alone among Southern states, primaries produced a clear ideological split, as liberals such as Senator Ralph Yarborough fought against conservatives in the primaries.

Apart from race, the unifying feature of these primaries, and the reasons why they were so troubling to Key, was that few of the factions competing in the primaries had any permanence. They were too closely linked to individual politicians, and the transience of factions meant that elected officials often had no power to carry out a sustained course of action. This was a problem that had been observed in Northern states, as well (see Hall 1923), but where such factions existed in Northern states, they generally pitted Progressives against party regulars. In the South, in contrast, there were no clear distinctions between factions other than candidates' personalities. The lack of ideological appeals in these races meant that voters had no clear means of expressing preferences about policy.[26]

Candidates quickly learned that there need be no connection between ideological pronouncements made on the campaign trail and legislative pursuits in Washington. And, perhaps most troubling to Key, Southern primaries conferred an advantage upon demagogues such as Georgia senators "Pitchfork" Ben Tillman and Herman Talmadge. Racially charged rhetoric was a means of standing out from the crowd, and Southern politicians vied with each other to espouse the most incendiary rhetoric, both racial and otherwise. William Fulbright's challenger in the 1968 Arkansas Senate primary, for instance, took note of Fulbright's chairmanship of the Senate Foreign Relations Committee by referring to him as "Chairman Fulbright" in one breath, and discussing "Chairman Mao" in the next as a means of equating the two (Yates 1972, 285).

Key's observations set the research agenda for a generation of Southern political scientists. J. Morgan Kousser, writing in 1974, reached many of the same conclusions, contending that much of the rhetoric in Southern primaries consisted of candidates (including incumbents) proudly proclaiming themselves to be outsiders and to be voices for the disenfranchised—by which they meant Southern whites (Kousser 1974, 231). Moreover, Southern primaries required candidates to fabricate issues and to tear down their opponents precisely because there were no significant ideological disputes at stake. As David Lublin (2004, 13) would later note, there were also no repercussions for Southern legislators if they radically changed their ideological views during their tenure in office, as South Carolina's Strom Thurmond showed. The heated, demagogic conflict of Southern elections obscured genuine disagreements on policy.

Again, however, the Southern experience with primaries was different from the rest of the nation's experience because race, and the politics of racial exclusion, played such a large role. During the 1940s, Southern states created the "white primary," an explicit effort by whites to reach consensus on nominees without risking having African-American votes influence the result. As we shall discuss further in Chapters 7 and 8, Southern Democrats continually sought to devise a constitutional means of doing this. Following the Supreme Court's *Smith v. All-wright* (321 U.S. 649 [1944]) decision in 1944, however, Southern states stopped changing primary rules and instead adopted literacy tests, poll taxes, and other means of excluding black voters (Weeks 1948). As segregation began to crumble in the 1960s, African Americans occasionally attempted organized efforts (as had the Progressives in Wisconsin and the Nonpartisan League in North Dakota) to nominate candidates from within their state's dominant party instead of backing a rival party. This happened in Tennessee and Mississippi in 1966, but both efforts were unsuccessful (Fortenberry and Abney 1972, Greene and Holmes 1972). It would not be until the 1970s that African-American voters became a significant voting bloc within the Democratic Party, but even then the relationship between black votes and party nominees remained weak until the rise of the Republican Party in the South (and the corresponding exit from the party of conservative whites) provided African Americans with the clout within the Democratic Party to influence nominations. By this time, of course, Southern primary competition had begun to resemble primary competition elsewhere. Even then, strategic concerns among Democrats about producing viable general election candidates have had the effect of reducing overt racial conflict within the party, as some contentious Democratic primaries arguably reduced general election vote share and enabled Republicans to win in more diverse Southern states such as Florida (Craig and Austin 2008).

Just as some of the anecdotes about individual politicians who prospered after the adoption of the direct primary may say more about state culture than about the primary itself, so the history of Southern primaries may say more about the politics of the American South than about the consequences of primary elections. Nonetheless, there are common themes that run through the literature on primaries in different regions of the country during the middle decades of the century. Political parties adapted to primaries, and where they could not adapt, many state parties modified primary elections to fit their needs. However, in many parts of the nation primary elections distanced political candidates from their parties, increasing the power of individual politicians and benefitting many candidates who were at odds with their parties on matters of policy.

This distance was troubling for many academics. In a 1923 article, William Hannan surveyed governors, political scientists, party leaders, and newspaper editors about the direct primary. Unsurprisingly, governors (many of whom, by this time, had been elected in direct primaries) tended to favor it while party leaders tended to oppose the direct primary. Although Hannan only spoke with ten to fifteen people in any of these categories, the narrow majority of political scientists who supported the direct primary seems to accord with the balance in published work—most of the pieces written in the 1910s and 1920s were done by political scientists who at least cautiously supported primaries and had somewhat high hopes for them—though many also cautioned about overpromising. Apart from works specifically on the South, however, the most prominent statement of this time by political scientists about the direct primary was the report of the American Political Science Association's (APSA) Committee on Political Parties, entitled "Toward a More Responsible Two Party System." The report, published in 1950, is perhaps the most influential statement of mid-century political scientists' views on what the proper role of political parties is in the United States.[27] The report criticized American parties for their failure to take strong programmatic stances on the issues of the day and to differentiate themselves from each other. While the report clearly identified many problems with the parties that were unrelated to their nomination rules, it did contend that primaries had developed into a serious problem for the parties. The authors of the report reflected the consensus of the day that it would be impossible to repeal primary laws, and that there was no better alternative. They did, however, argue that the patchwork of state laws was problematic and that national legislation to create uniform primary procedures would be an improvement; that preprimary conventions were a salutary development; and that closed primaries were preferable to open or blanket primaries (Committee on Political Parties 1950, 10, 70–72). As Epstein (2002, 210–12) and Maisel and Bibby (2002, 74) have noted, the APSA Report did not have a discernible effect on parties' decisions about what types of primaries to hold, nor did it seem to offer ways of confronting the problem that voters have exhibited a strong preference for primaries, and for open primaries, at that. Yet the report clearly does demonstrate that if Progressive sentiments did dominate within the discipline of political science in the early years of the century, they no longer did so by 1950.

It would be oversimplifying matters far too much to argue that the direct primary, by itself, caused the increase in the incumbency advantage, the breakdown of party discipline, or the voter dealignment that were characteristics of American politics by the 1960s and 1970s, but the history suggests that primaries may have been a contributing factor.[28] Whether or not this is so, however, enthusiasm about primary elections was clearly gone. Perhaps they had not proven to be the answer to the problem of corrupt party machines, or perhaps the political world that emerged after the decline of party machines had its own more significant problems. When primaries again became a subject of concern in the late 1960s, they were discussed by reformers who had different goals in mind and different recommendations about the mechanics of primary nominations.

Creating the Modern Primary Election System, 1968–

Progressives did not single out any particular office in their push for primary elections; they advocated primaries for all elective offices, and congressional elections were simply part of the story. Reforms to the parties' nominating system following the 1968 election, however, were principally about altering the presidential nominating process. To the extent that congressional primaries were affected as well, it was because many states sought to save money by conducting all of their primaries at the same time, or because it was too complicated to have one set of rules about voting for presidential nominees and another set of rules about voting for nominees for other offices. Primaries in many states were unaffected by changes in the presidential nominating process, but enough were changed that the conduct of congressional primaries became far more uniform across the country than it ever had been.

As we have seen, all states had some form of primary law by 1968. Three changes in the early 1960s, however, also shaped the growing uniformity in congressional primary laws. First, a string of Supreme Court decisions, culminating in *Reynolds v. Sims* (377 U.S. 533 (1964)), established that states must redraw congressional districts after each census, and they must redraw them such that they are as close to equality in population as possible. As we saw in the Connecticut case, malapportionment was a device that states used to ensure voices for particular communities of interest. Southern states also used malapportionment—in some cases, allowing for at-large representatives—in order to dilute African-American voting strength. The consequence of these decisions was that by 1970 all members of Congress in each state represented districts of the same population size, and states became less able to direct political competition into the primary or away from the primary. Second, the Voting Rights Act of 1964, as well as other contemporaneous civil rights legislation, finally began the process of enfranchising African Americans in the South. Primaries were no longer a means of excluding African Americans. Even if states creatively drew districts, minority voters had to go somewhere, so their presence in the primary electorate would ensure that race, and ideological disputes about race, would ensure that the issueless primaries that characterized Southern politics during the 1940s and 1950s were endangered. And third, changes in communications technology increased the ability of politicians to appeal to voters independently of the parties. Not all congressional candidates had the resources to advertise or resided within districts with appropriate media markets, but the availability of television, radio, and later, direct mail to reach voters reduced the value of parties' organizational support and endorsing power in primary elections.

In a string of articles, Ansolabehere, Hansen, Hirano, and Snyder (2006, 2007, 2010) conclusively show that congressional primary competition declined steadily between 1910 and today. Even when one separates out the South, the decline is still evident. Ansolabehere and his coauthors conclude from this that primaries have fallen far short of the expectations Progressives had about intraparty competition. The 1970 election, however, serves as a turning point in our consideration of primaries. For the first time, representatives came from similarly drawn districts. We can, from this point on, argue that large scale data on elections are not complicated by differences in districting schemes. Vestiges of the old type of campaigning lingered, particularly in the South, well into the 1980s and even the 1990s. Yet two different trends were clearly afoot—first, candidates now had the means to seek the nomination without the need for party organizations, but second, as white conservatives began their movement toward the Republican Party, competition in the primaries was narrowed such that candidates waged their battles on one side or the other of the ideological spectrum. That is, liberals sought the Democratic nomination and conservatives sought the Republican nomination.

These changes did not precipitate the primary reforms initiated by the Democrats after their disastrous 1968 presidential convention, but these changes did play out amidst a debate about primaries that was quite unlike the Progressive Era debate over primaries. Yes, primaries were less frequent in the 1970s and 1980s than they had been in previous decades, but just as Key argued that the nature of primary competition said something about the political culture of different Southern states, now one could argue that primary competition said something about the American political culture, changes in American politics, and the cultures of the Democratic and Republican parties.

Most of the states that enacted direct primary laws in the early part of the twentieth century also established presidential primaries. While voting in presidential primaries followed the same rules as the primaries for other offices, these were not direct primaries—voters were choosing delegates to the party convention, and it was difficult to predict how these delegates would vote. In many states, governors or other prominent political leaders would run "favorite son" candidacies, in which they brought with them a slate of electors who would then vote for a candidate of the favorite son's choosing. Because presidential primaries were not binding, then, presidential candidates had little incentive to campaign in the primaries. From the 1920s through the 1940s, these primaries were generally ignored by candidates. During the 1950s and 1960s, candidates became more interested in campaigning, but they tended to campaign selectively, choosing primaries where success would send a signal to delegates and party leaders. In 1952 and 1956, Estes Kefauver ran vigorously in the Democratic primaries, outpolling all of his rivals, but was unable to win the nomination in either year. In 1960, John F. Kennedy ran in several early primaries; most notably, he campaigned extensively in West Virginia in order to show that he could win votes in states with small Catholic populations. And in 1968, Eugene McCarthy defeated sitting President Lyndon Johnson in the New Hampshire primary, arguably driving Johnson out of the race. At the 1968 convention, however, Democrats chose Hubert Humphrey as their nominee despite the fact that he had not run in any of the party's primaries.[29]

The 1968 convention was punctuated by demonstrations against the Vietnam War in the streets of Chicago and Chicago Mayor Richard Daley's decision to direct the Chicago police to use force against the protestors. After the convention, a party committee chaired by Senator George McGovern and Representative Donald Fraser issued a report calling upon the party to establish nominating procedures that were open and well publicized, and to select delegates who were broadly representative of each state's Democratic electorate (see Maisel and Bibby 2002). After the Democratic National Committee adopted the report's recommendations, many state parties concluded that the best way to ensure that they met these guidelines was to hold primaries in which delegates bound to the candidates were selected in proportion to the candidates' vote totals in the state primary. In many states, these new provisions were adopted by statute, thus binding the Republican Party to the new primary rules as well.

There is a well-established literature on the consequences of the new primary rules in subsequent elections, and there is also a substantial literature on the influence of these rules on candidate strategy. We shall review some of these discussions of candidate strategy in Chapter 3. For now, it is sufficient to note that conclusions about the effects of primaries on presidential candidates do not necessarily apply to candidates for other offices because presidential candidate strategy is dictated by the fact that there is a sequence of primaries as opposed to the one direct primary that applies to other types of candidates. As it became apparent in subsequent years how valuable early primary victories would be to presidential aspirants, states began to jockey amongst themselves to schedule primaries earlier and earlier. Not all states were required to hold all of their primaries on the same day, but many did—again, in part to reduce the costs of election administration. As of 2000, twenty-one states held their presidential and congressional primaries on the same day, and twenty states did so in 2012 (Galderisi and Ezra 2001, 21–22; author's calculations). The 2012 primary dates are shown in Table 2.2. Congressional primaries, again, are low visibility elections, so turnout

TABLE 2.2 Congressional and Presidential Primary Dates, 2012 (Listed by Date of Congressional Primary)

State	Congressional Primary	Presidential Primary	State	Congressional Primary	Presidential Primary
Ohio	March 6	March 6	Virginia	June 12	March 6
Alabama	March 13	March 13	Colorado	June 26	February 7
Mississippi	March 13	March 13	Oklahoma	June 26	March 6
Illinois	March 20	March 20	**Utah**	June 26	June 26
Maryland	April 3	April 3	Georgia	July 31	March 6
Texas	April 3	April 3	Tennessee	August 2	March 6
Pennsylvania	April 24	April 24	Kansas	August 7	March 10
Indiana	May 8	May 8	Michigan	August 7	February 28
North Carolina	May 8	May 8	Missouri	August 7	February 7
West Virginia	May 8	May 8	Washington	August 7	March 3
Idaho	May 15	March 6	Hawaii	August 11	March 13
Nebraska	May 15	May 15	Connecticut	August 14	April 24
Oregon	May 15	May 15	Florida	August 14	January 31
Arkansas	May 22	May 22	Minnesota	August 14	February 7
Kentucky	May 22	May 22	Wisconsin	August 14	April 3
California	June 5	June 5	Wyoming	August 21	March 6
Iowa	June 5	January 3	Alaska	August 28	March 6
Montana	June 5	June 5	Arizona	August 28	February 28
New Jersey	June 5	June 5	Vermont	August 28	March 6
New Mexico	June 5	June 5	Massachusetts	September 6	March 6
South Dakota	June 5	June 5	Delaware	September 11	April 24
Maine	June 12	May 5	New Hampshire	September 11	January 10
Nevada	June 12	February 4	New York	September 11	April 24
North Dakota	June 12	March 6	Rhode Island	September 11	April 24
South Carolina	June 12	January 21	Louisiana	November 6	March 24

Note: States with concurrent presidential and congressional primaries listed in **bold**.

Source: Author's calculations.

has tended to be far lower in congressional primaries than in general elections or in presidential primaries (or, at least, in presidential primaries where there is meaningful competition). In states where candidates for the congressional and presidential nomination are on the same ballot, the electorate is thus far larger, with uncertain results for congressional candidates. On the one hand, these voters may be ignorant of the characteristics of congressional candidates and simply vote based on name recognition; on the other, congressional candidates who can link themselves to a popular presidential candidate may benefit. For example, House challenger Donna Edwards faced off against incumbent Al Wynn in the Maryland Democratic primaries in 2006 and 2008. Edwards lost in 2006 but, with Barack Obama on the ballot, won handily in 2008. Many media observers attributed her victory in part to the fact that many of the voters Obama drew to the polls were sufficiently aware of and supportive of Edwards's campaign to make the difference (Helderman 2008).

The McGovern-Fraser Commission's rhetoric about openness, inclusiveness, and sensitivity to ensuring a role for women and minorities also had an effect on the nature of congressional primaries. The Progressives had been sympathetic to the idea that primary voters should have some sort of allegiance to the party in whose primary they voted. In practice, closed primaries required that a voter register as a member of the party in advance of the election, or at a minimum the voter profess his or her allegiance to the party and intention to support the party's eventual nominee in the general election. Open primaries, on the other hand, were those in which any registered voter, whatever his or her past affiliation, was permitted to vote in the primary of his or her choosing. In the 1928 edition of *Primary Elections*, Merriam and Overacker (1928, 69) counted four states that had open primaries. Many advocates of primary reform in the 1960s, however, argued against closed primaries. Austin Ranney (1975, 162), for instance, claimed that closed primaries tended to exclude some types of voters, were vulnerable to manipulation at the polls (that is, a party observer could challenge any voter suspected of trying to "raid" the opposition party's primary), and were at any rate not very effective in ensuring that voters did, in fact, have the party's best interests in mind. Furthermore, the Supreme Court, in its *Kusper v. Pontikes* (94 S. Ct. 303 (1973) at 308) decision stated that states needed to show a compelling interest in preventing anyone from voting in a primary; some registration requirements remained permissible, but most states instituted registration cutoffs that were only a month or so before the primary. By 2000, twenty-four states had open primaries (Kanthak and Morton 2001, 121). Table 2.3 shows the type of primary currently in place in each state. Primary laws vary substantially, so the labels placed on each primary type necessarily obscure many variations in registration procedures, challenge provisions, and so forth.

As Kaufmann, Gimpel, and Hoffman (2003) argue, it is not clear that openness is a good thing, but, like the arguments for the direct primary early in the century, there is substantial rhetorical appeal to the notion of allowing

TABLE 2.3 Primary Type by State, as of 2012

Type	States
Closed	Arizona, Connecticut, Delaware, Florida, Kentucky, Maryland, Nebraska, Nevada, New Mexico, New York, North Carolina, Oklahoma, Oregon, Pennsylvania, South Dakota, West Virginia
Semi-closed*	Colorado, Iowa, Kansas, Maine, Massachusetts, New Hampshire, New Jersey, Ohio, Rhode Island
Open	Hawaii, Idaho, Michigan, Minnesota, Montana, North Dakota, South Carolina, Utah, Vermont, Wisconsin
Semi-open**	Alabama, Alaska, Arkansas, Georgia, Illinois, Indiana, Mississippi, Missouri, Tennessee, Texas, Virginia, Wyoming
Nonpartisan/Top Two	California, Louisiana, Washington

*<i>Previously</i> unaffiliated voters or new voters may vote in a party's primaries, but not registered members of another party.
**Voter must publicly request a party ballot or declare membership in party.

Source: Kanthak and Morton 2001, 121; updated by author. Some details omitted; for further discussion of coding, see McGhee, Masket, Shor, and McCarty 2010.

everyone to vote. Open primaries have been said to have a variety of implications, which we shall discuss in more detail in Chapter 3. Briefly, they lend themselves to two very different types of interpretations. First, many researchers have contended that voters drawn into an open primary will be more centrist in their political views than previously registered party members; this might be expected to produce a candidate with more centrist views than would be the case in a closed primary. Second, open primaries might attract voters who prefer a candidate on nonpolitical grounds; for instance, voters might be attracted to a candidate with substantial personal or nonideological appeal but weak roots among party activists. For instance, both features may well have been at work in the 2000 Republican presidential primaries; some analysts speculated that John McCain, a candidate who had cultivated the image of a reformer and was somewhat more popular among Democrats than his rivals, might have benefitted in states with open primaries.[30] Open primaries can also attract opposition party voters who do not have an interesting primary to vote in; if, for instance, the Republican Party has a contested Senate primary and the Democratic party does not, some Democrats might take more of an interest in the Republican candidates. Studies of such instances of "crossover voting" have sought to distinguish between sincere crossover voters (those who enter the opposition party's primary because they generally think one candidate would be a better member of Congress than others in the primary) and strategic (or malicious) crossover voters, who seek to bolster the chances of an opposition party candidate who they think would be a weak opponent to their party's candidate. Most evidence to date suggests that the vast majority of crossover voters are sincere.[31]

Primary reforms also closely preceded another consequential change to the nature of campaigning, the reforms in campaign finance law enacted in the early 1970s. The 1974 Federal Elections and Campaigns Act (FECA) amendments established limits on the amount of money individuals can contribute to candidates, political organizations, and in sum. The original version of FECA (passed in 1971) also enhanced disclosure laws and established limits on candidate spending and on contributions by a candidate to his or her own campaign. These candidate spending limits were subsequently overruled by the Supreme Court in the *Buckley v. Valeo* decision (424 US 1 (1976)), but the court left the contribution limits in place. FECA had three consequential effects for congressional candidates. First, its contribution limits ensured that candidates would largely be responsible for raising their own money—support from party insiders would not be sufficient. Second, it conferred an advantage upon candidates with the personal resources to fund their own campaigns—so much so that parties now sought to encourage such people to run. And third, it gave a governmental stamp of approval to political action committees (PACs); as the years passed after FECA's passage, it became apparent that PACs tended to disproportionately support incumbents, and that congressional incumbents would be able to easily accumulate campaign war chests that would deter potential primary and general election opponents.

Although changes in primary rules and campaign finance laws clearly did much to make the American electoral system more transparent than ever before and to diversify the electorate in primary elections, it is easy to see why competition in primaries actually went down. In the South, realignment ensured that interparty competition would now be more important than primary competition. This meant that the battles which took place in Southern primaries now could transpire in the general election, and that political parties had reasons to try to limit primary conflict and to seek to work behind the scenes to discourage primary competition. In the nation as a whole, the evolving role of national party organizations in congressional elections (and the corresponding decline in the power of local and state political machines) meant that national parties sought primary competition only where it worked to their advantage. Although political parties generally tend to avoid taking an active role in endorsing or providing financial support for primary candidates, most accounts of party campaign committee activities suggest that national political leaders have actively sought to recruit potentially strong congressional candidates, to help them tap into national fundraising networks and to provide them with advice on strategy. Clearly the national parties will not recruit more than one strong candidate per district, so the role of national parties behind the scenes can also ensure that primaries are a foregone conclusion in many congressional districts.

If all of this points to a decline in primary competition even as primaries became more open than before, it does not necessarily address the growing polarization between the two parties. This polarization has been a long, gradual process that certainly cannot be covered in more than cursory detail here. Some political scientists have attributed the growing ideological divide between the parties to institutional changes within Congress (Theriault 2008), others have attributed it to changes in the news media (Sobieraj 2011) and the incentives of unelected political elites and nonparty political groups (Masket 2009), and still others have pointed to an ideological sorting of American voters (Levendusky 2009, Abramowitz 2010). At a minimum, some primary elections have clearly become forums for conflict between centrists and political extremists. With the exit of conservative whites from the Democratic Party in the South, the least one can say is that where there is ideological competition in primaries it must be between the center and the left (in the case of Democrats) or between the center and the right (in the case of Republicans). And, despite the increased role of national party organizations in seeking out candidates to run for office, the weakening of the parties that primary reforms, among other things, have provided ensures that parties cannot entirely mute this conflict.

As with many of the patterns here, it is hard to argue that primaries are the *cause* of broader changes in political competition and representation, as opposed to being a symptom of those changes. The political culture of different regions of the country, the idiosyncrasies of which candidates emerge where, and short-term political forces such as opposition to the Vietnam and Iraq wars or the Tea Party movement may influence primary elections, but there is no strong evidence that their influence is felt in any particular type of primary—or, for that matter, that matters would be substantially different if our nation had other means of nominating candidates. To take one example, much of our discussion above of primaries has speculated about whether candidates with extreme views or some sort of personal appeal benefit from running in primaries, and whether the nature of the primary influences the type of candidates that emerge. Yet quantitative evidence on this is mixed, as is anecdotal evidence. To wit, three of the more consequential races where a Tea Party candidate upended an establishment-backed opponent in the 2010 primaries took place in the closed primary states of Delaware, Colorado, and Nevada. And the insurgent candidate in the 2008 Democratic presidential primaries, Barack Obama, scored many of his greatest successes in caucus states. Anecdotes, then, can only get one so far.

The perception, however, that primary elections tend to produce ideologically extreme candidates has given rise to a renewed interest in a distinctly different types of primaries, such as the "jungle," "blanket," or "top two" primary. In a blanket primary, all voters receive the same ballot, and they may vote for one candidate of any party in each race. The candidate of each party with the most votes goes on to the general election. In a top two primary, the top two vote-getters, regardless of party, proceed to the general election. In Louisiana's jungle primary, used in every election since 1978 save one (2008), the top two vote-getters run against each other only if no candidate has received a majority of the primary vote. As we shall discuss in Chapter 8, the Supreme Court has ruled that the blanket primary is illegal, but prior to the Supreme Court's decision California, Washington, and Alaska had adopted it, and California and Washington have recently switched to a top two primary. The impetus behind these types of primaries is the belief that it will advantage centrist candidates and give greater power to voters not aligned with one party or the other. Louisiana is the only one of these states that has used any of these procedures long enough to have any basis for judgment, but any conclusions about the merits of this type of primary are colored by the fact that Louisiana has a rather distinctive political culture. At a minimum, the attention provided in the media to California's experience with the top two primary in 2012 suggests that the questions raised by the Progressives have not subsided, and that we may well be entering another era in which primary laws are scrutinized and debated.

Where We Stand Now

In a way much has changed in the study of primary elections over the past century, but it is striking how many of the concerns of Progressive Era reformers are still relevant. As we shall see in the remainder of this book, there is still a healthy debate about the consequences of open and closed primaries, about the effects of the timing of primary elections, about the effects of primary elections on general election outcomes, and about the types of candidates who are advantaged and disadvantaged by our system of primary elections. Of course, the debate today allows little room for the possibility of abandoning primaries. Primary elections had an intuitive popular appeal when they were introduced, which is one reason why there was no question of returning to the convention method even in the 1910s and 1920s. They certainly carry the risk of a full-scale disruption of party competition, yet when these disruptions happen, as was the case for the Nonpartisan League in the 1910s, these disruptions have, after a time, been contained by the parties. There is also, of course, no evidence that voters object to the possibility that parties will be threatened by primaries. Today there are no serious proposals to abandon primary elections, but there is still much concern about how the mechanics of primary elections might be tweaked to encourage voting by some types of citizens or discourage voting by other types. The California experiment with blanket primaries is one manifestation of this, as is the Idaho Republican Party's recent decision to shift from an open to a closed primary.[32]

In many regards, however, concerns about the nature of primary elections have been subsumed in larger debates about the financing of elections, the drawing of congressional districts, and the growing ideological gap between the parties. Although there were some early discussions about campaign finance when primary elections were introduced (see, e.g., Baker 2012), the contemporary candidate-centered election and the ideological sorting of the parties are concerns that are largely alien to most of this century's literature on primary elections. Accounts of nomination procedures in the 1890s discussed the deliberative nature of conventions—while reformers raised serious doubts that anything deliberative truly took place at party gatherings, the archetypal New England town meeting discussed by Dallinger, among others, was presented as a forum in which citizens could raise issues of governmental policy and weigh the relative merits of candidates in their ability to pursue these policies. Even among primary advocates, the preprimary convention, particularly in states such as South Dakota, was presented as an opportunity for parties to agree first on principles, then on candidates. The emphasis on deliberation among citizens during election campaigns, however, that has arisen since the 1960s presumes that deliberation is something that takes place outside the convention hall, with the aid of organized interests, the media, and, yes, advertising by candidates and their supporters.

One might well ask whether this sort of deliberation is any more meaningful than was deliberating at nominating conventions; whether one believes this to be the case rests largely on interpretation of century-old accounts of what went on in nominating conventions before primaries were implemented. There certainly is little evidence from contemporary party conventions that they are forums for meaningful deliberation. Yet in a way this is also a moot point, since there is no likelihood that the American experiment with primary elections will be abandoned any time soon. It is not only deliberation that has mattered for those who study primaries during the various eras of the past century, however; competition is also generally seen as something that goes along with deliberation. In the one-party South described by Key and Kousser, the rhetoric of primary candidates could frequently be ugly, but in some circumstances voters were presented with a meaningful contrast of ideas when they voted, something that would otherwise be lacking. Even though the level of primary competition has declined since the 1970s, where it does occur voters are, again, generally presented with meaningful contrasts. This is hardly a strong argument for encouraging primary competition, however. In contemporary America, despite gerrymandered districts and an uneven distribution of partisans, the general election also at least holds the possibility for such competition. If this is the case, then party polarization becomes a problem. If primary elections produce one candidate of each party who stands far from the political center of the districts, voters are denied the opportunity to choose a candidate whose views correspond to theirs. Primary competition in areas that are not overwhelmingly partisan can thus serve to deny the voters an opportunity to choose candidates who represent their views. The nature of primary competition can serve to discourage deliberation and democratic competition. One can debate the extent to which this has, in fact, happened, but it is clear that this is a possibility that has been discussed a great deal during the past decade.

This is, again, a possibility that indicates that our contemporary situation, whether it was caused by the rise of the direct primary or not, has left us far from where we were at the outset of the twentieth century. This possibility also indicates that understanding the nature of *congressional* primaries today is far more important than it was during prior waves of primary election reform. Throughout this chapter, I have sought to emphasize that changes in nominating procedures took place with little reference to their effects on members of Congress. And yet, as this is a book about congressional primaries, I have sought to emphasize the effects of different reform proposals on congressional elections. In closing, it is important to reorient our discussion of primary elections to place congressional candidates front and center.

It is easy to see why congressional candidates were orphans during the various eras of primary reform in the twentieth century. During the Progressive Era, members of Congress had far less autonomy than they do today—they served fewer terms than they do today, and they did not have a role in actually crafting the rules under which they were nominated. Although Congress has exercised some discretion in determining laws regulating voting and the financing of elections, no congressional legislation regarding primary elections emerged for much of the century. The Progressive reforms thus took aim at the party machines that controlled municipal governments, state legislatures, and gubernatorial politics. Although the House of Representatives has certainly been the subject of a substantial body of analysis for the past century, the views of members of Congress on primaries play a minor role in the literature of the Progressive Era. And senators, of course, were not even directly elected when the first wave of primary reform began. As the Progressive Era waned and primary elections became entrenched, members of Congress sought to control their own destinies just as did other elected officials, but they did so by seeking to use the system to their advantage, not by shaping nominating procedures. And finally, when the McGovern-Fraser reforms took effect, many members of Congress took a role in shaping the new party laws, but with the aim of shaping presidential elections, not congressional races.

Today, however, Congress is generally regarded as "the broken branch," to quote Thomas Mann and Norman Ornstein (2008)—as the component of the federal government most in need of repair—and many of those who have bemoaned Congress's ability to function properly have placed the blame in part on the nature of congressional primaries. Thomas Mann, for instance, singles out primaries, campaign financing patterns, and redistricting as three of the major sources of congressional partisan polarization (2006, 280). Scholars may debate the relative contribution of these three factors, but certainly there is much anecdotal evidence of primaries gone wrong—of instances where voters are denied responsible choices or where candidates are compelled to take their cues from a small percentage of ideologically extreme voters rather than from the general electorate. This is in many ways a problem unique to Congress and unique to the narrow majorities that have become the norm in Congress over the past two decades. The majority of state legislatures have arguably not had such a turbulent recent history, and statewide officials (to say nothing of presidents) have not had to face the sorts of ideological challenges that have bedeviled congressional candidates of late.

All of this points to the dilemma that we shall explore in the remainder of this book. There is no going back, nor are there compelling reasons to assume that even if we could we would create a system that works any better than primaries. By 1928, after having three decades to analyze the rise of primary elections, Merriam and Overacker (1928, 344) admitted that it was still conceivable that one day conventions could do a better job of producing outcomes that were preferable to those of primaries. They admitted then that the actual chance of this happening was low, and today it is surely even lower. It is clear that primaries have their problems today, and that they have always introduced normative problems for democracy, as well as basic problems of strategy. While there is not necessarily another wave of primary reform waiting for us in the near future, it is clear that there is a need for a comprehensive accounting of the strategic dilemmas that face primary candidates, primary voters, and the political parties whose nominees are produced by our primary system.

Merriam and Overacker (1928, 344–45) conclude their study of primary elections—a study, to reiterate, that would stand as the last word on primary elections for over seventy years—with the claim that "there is nothing sacred about our American nominating systems, direct or indirect, regulated or unregulated. They are all parts of a larger democratic experiment and should be subject to change and adaptation, as new experience of new conditions may indicate." Conditions clearly have changed substantially since 1928, but it is important to note Merriam and Overacker's reminder that the primary itself is an experiment. As such, its effects need, today as in the past, to be carefully measured if we are to understand how this decidedly odd, and decidedly American, experiment has shaped our polity.

Notes

1 In the remainder of this chapter, as well as in the literature on congressional primaries, this is referred to as the "direct primary" to distinguish it from primaries aimed at choosing convention delegates or writing a party platform.
2 Ware (2002, 62) claims that Crawford County's first primary election was actually held in 1842, but that Progressives did not know this until 1935. For discussion of California's primary, which was purportedly the first open primary, see Delmatier, McIntosh, and Waters 1970, 33.
3 This is Davis's time frame; historians disagree about the duration of the Progressive Era. Hofstadter (1955, 3) claims that the era lasted from 1900 to 1914.
4 *Outlook* 58: 261–62. Reprinted in Fanning 1905, 60–62.
5 See, e.g., Meyer 1902, 464; Merriam 1908, 76–83; Jones 1910; Dodds 1923; Kettleborough 1923a; Merriam and Overacker 1928, 83.

6 For discussion of this see, e.g., Burnham 1965; Converse 1972; McGerr 1986; Ware 2000, 2006.
7 Anderson 1902; Meyer 1902, 284–86; Fanning 1905, 25, 30, 119; Merriam and Overacker 1928, 61; Ware 2002, 115.
8 The Johnson anecdote is from an editorial in the *Milwaukee Sentinel*, reprinted in Fanning 1905, 119.
9 See also Lovejoy 1941.
10 Fusion balloting is the practice of endorsing a candidate of another party; for instance, if a candidate runs as the nominee of both the Democratic Party and the Liberal Party, that candidate's votes on both lines will be counted toward his total vote share. This enables minor parties to selectively aid major parties. Other states have used it in the past, although the Supreme Court, in *Timmons v. Twin Cities Area New Party* (520 U.S. 351 (1997)) ruled against the practice. We will discuss this ruling more in Chapter 8.
11 As Merriam and Overacker (1928, 120) discuss, most states set a threshold for what general election vote percentage a party must have received in the previous election in order to be compelled to hold a primary. This threshold generally ranged between 1 and 10 percent. New York also had no threshold, applying the direct primary requirement to all parties qualified to be on the ballot
12 See Merriam 1908, 82.
13 Three other states had platform-writing conventions in advance of the primary, but South Dakota's was by far the most elaborate (Merriam and Overacker 1928, 83–91).
14 Such claims have been made about the George McGovern and Jimmy Carter campaigns, among others.
15 As explained in the state's 2012 Republican convention guide: "In the case of multiple ballots, more than one candidate may be eliminated in each round, provided that the sum of the votes received by the candidates to be eliminated does not exceed the number of votes received by the next highest candidate, and that at least two candidates remain on the ballot. The two top candidates shall participate in the final ballot. A candidate for an office that receives 60% or more of the votes cast at any point in the balloting process at the state nominating conventions shall become the Party's candidate without the necessity of running in the primary election" (Utah Republican Party Constitution, online, http://utgop.org/pdf/Utah%20Republican%20Party%20Constitution.pdf, accessed February 8, 2014).
16 Lieberman was able to run because Connecticut does not have a sore loser law. Alaska, however, does; Murkowski therefore was unable to have her name listed on the ballot but was permitted to run as a write-in candidate.
17 Not only did California permit sore loser runs until the late 1950s, it also allowed cross-filing, in which candidates could run in the primaries of more than one party. According to the state's cross-filing law (discussed by Delmatier, McIntosh, and Waters 1970, 193; see also McWilliams 1949, 193; Masket 2007), candidates needed to affiliate with a party but did not need to disclose that affiliation to the public. If they won the primary of the party with which they affiliated, they could appear on the ballot as the nominee of that party *and* of any other party whose primary they won. If they lost the primary of the party with which they affiliated, however, they could not appear on the ballot even if they did win another party's primary. Affiliating with a party became, then, a strategic decision for politicians—their decision had to do with which primary they were most likely to win. This law, unique to California, was enacted in 1917, amended in 1952 to

require candidates to announce their affiliation publicly, and was repealed altogether in 1959.
18 Although West does not say so, he is likely thinking about *San Francisco Examiner* owner William Randolph Hearst, who had parlayed his successful media empire into a seat in Congress.
19 In the short run, women's suffrage also introduced problems in the administration of closed primaries, since women had rarely been registered as party members due to their inability to vote. While this problem would obviously wane over time, a more pressing problem for some reformers was that many states required registrars to verify the age of voters, and some states struggled to determine appropriate ways to ask women the sensitive question of how old they were. While this may seem amusing today, Colorado went so far as to pass a law allowing women not to provide their age, and New York passed a new law permitting all registrants (men and women) to decline to give their precise age if they were over thirty years old (Ray 1919).
20 This excludes biographical works on Progressive leaders, and (because I am listing articles here) I also exclude V.O. Key's work on the direct primary.
21 Argersinger (1995) discusses the 1907 direct primary law in North Dakota, arguing that it was a means for the Republican Party to split its opposition and ensure dominance in general elections.
22 Details here on Baer drawn from Morlan 1955 and from Reid 1977.
23 The high percentage of foreign-born residents apparently led some contemporary observers to claim that this was the reason why North Dakotans were receptive to socialist appeals and to anti-party rhetoric; Morlan (1955, 349), however, contends that the NPL's popularity across regions of the state with different types of populations shows that this claim was not true.
24 Agreements such as these are still common in nonpartisan municipal elections; the problem, of course, is that losers cannot be forced to drop out.
25 Ewing (1953, 34), using a slightly different sample (and therefore, a different definition of what "the South" is), states that 40 percent of Southern House races during the 1940s had only one candidates, and that the average number of primary candidates per race was 2.5.
26 One oft-discussed exception to this pattern took place in 1962, where many (Democratic) primary challengers explicitly linked themselves to the Barry Goldwater campaign; the most prominent example of this was the Alabama Senate primary between James Martin and incumbent Lister Hill, discussed in Lamis 1984b, 31, 77.
27 The APSA did not explicitly endorse the report, but it did note in the preface of the report itself that it "approved the publication" of it. The committee was chaired by E.E. Schattschneider, who is arguably, along with V.O. Key, among that era's most influential scholars of American parties. For discussion of the report, see Green and Herrnson 2002.
28 Carson and Roberts (2013, 92–94) conclude that the direct primary increased the incumbency advantage by approximately 2 to 4 percentage points.
29 The candidate who received the most primary votes in 1968 was Robert F. Kennedy, who was assassinated before the convention. It is thus debatable how deferential the party should have been to the surviving primary candidates in choosing its nominee.
30 Maisel and Bibby (2002, 67) argue that this happened in Michigan, which adopted an open primary because Governor John Engler mistakenly believed this would help

George W. Bush. Engler subsequently sought to discourage Democrats and Independents from entering the Republican primary to vote for McCain (Cain and Mullin 2002).

31 This was a major subject of discussion in the debate surrounding California's adoption of a blanket primary in 1998. See Alvarez and Nagler 1998, 2002; Gaines and Tam Cho 2002; Kousser 2002; Salvanto and Wattenberg 2002; Sides, Cohen, and Citrin 2002.

32 For discussion see the Idaho Secretary of State web page, online, www.sos.idaho.gov/elect/primary_election.htm, accessed June 12, 2012; for immediate postprimary analysis of the consequences of this decision, see political scientist Gary Moncrief's analysis (2012) of voting data, at, "BSU's Moncrief: Idaho GOP Closed Primary Failed to Stop Crossover Voting, If It Was Occurring at All," *Idaho Statesman Blogs*, online, http://voices.idahostatesman.com/2012/05/18/idahopolitics/bsus_moncrief_idaho_gop_closed_primary_failed_stop_crossover_vot, accessed June 12, 2012.

3
THE STRATEGIC CONTEXT OF CONGRESSIONAL PRIMARIES

> "Regardless of where one's sympathies happen to lie in this struggle, it seems clear to the author that the interests of the state of Wisconsin would be better served if there were a greater spirit of mutual toleration and understanding between the opposing factions. The spirit of irreconcilable factionalism is not conducive to the clearest-sighted statesmanship, or the most disinterested public service."

So wrote political scientist Arnold Bennett Hall in 1923, commenting on the divisiveness of his state's new direct primary system. Hall's comments seem, particularly in light of his home state's 2012 recall election, to embody everything that Americans fear about political conflict. While most Americans can correctly distinguish between the Republican Party and the Democratic Party on the most salient political issues, in survey after survey they profess to want politicians to work together to address the nation's problems. As we have seen, primary elections were touted by Progressive Era reformers as a means to take away the control that corrupt party bosses had over nominations and to give the power of selecting candidates to the people. Yet since that time, many observers of primary elections have made two major claims—that primaries encourage factionalism and drive the parties apart, and that in the absence of party labels most voters are ill equipped to make meaningful, policy-based choices in primaries. There is obviously some tension between these two claims, and the empirical support for them is also shaky. Yet, as we shall see in this chapter, beliefs about the consequences of primary competition have shaped the strategies employed by voters, by political parties, and by candidates in primaries.

Hall concluded his evaluation of the Wisconsin direct primary with a call for giving parties greater power in selecting candidates. Hall, like other writers of the time, saw that it would be difficult to return to the days in which candidates were chosen at party conventions, but he argued that "some method should be devised by which party responsibility can be preserved and the party's capacity to achieve effective compromises carefully safeguarded and secured." Political parties arguably have asserted a significant amount of control over primaries in recent decades, and even when primary laws were enacted it was not at all clear that these laws really were a blow against parties. The behavior of parties—again, as well as voters and candidates—is best seen as an adaptation to the institution of primaries rather than as an effort to combat them.

This chapter will explore the advantages and disadvantages of primary elections for each of these three actors, using theoretical literature and empirical literature. We will then briefly review what is known about congressional primaries and what can be learned about congressional primaries by studying presidential primary elections. Despite the voluminous literature summarized in Chapter 2 about the introduction of the direct primary, there has been little written about congressional primaries in recent years, and contradictions abound in what has been written. Presidential primaries are arguably better understood than are congressional primaries, although it is not always clear how well lessons learned in one type of primary can be translated to another type.

There is, however, a rich body of theoretical literature that is of use in understanding the dynamics of congressional primaries. Some of these theoretical issues were hinted at in early twentieth century articles on the direct primary but have been elaborated upon, often in rich mathematical detail, in considerations of very different types of elections. To mention just two examples, the dynamics of races between three or more candidates are very different than those between two candidates, and the likelihood that candidates will present claims aimed at winning over majorities of the voters declines with the number of candidates. This was a problem for those who feared "plurality winners" in congressional primaries, but it is also a phenomenon that has been analyzed by scholars looking at other countries. Similarly, the problems of sequential elections—of appealing to one set of voters in a primary elections and another in a general election—were discussed by many who feared that primaries would be too divisive or too costly. Yet, again, this is a problem that can be analyzed in an abstract fashion or with reference to other nations, and the results of these studies do not always accord with the assumptions that have often been made about primaries. In short, there are many ideas about primaries that shape political strategy. Some of these ideas appear to be true, others appear to be untrue, and many have never been proven one way or the other. We shall take these up in turn below.

Voters

As Chapter 2 shows, many Progressive reformers believed that citizens would be the main beneficiaries of the adoption of direct primaries. Citizens would be able to choose among more candidates, thus ensuring that parties could not collude to keep important issues from being addressed by candidates. Citizens would also be able to give greater scrutiny to candidates; those seeking office would have to campaign among the wider electorate rather than merely among party elites. Most studies of primary election competition (including this one) assume that the more candidates for office there are, the more of a role the public will have in primary elections. In this regard, then, the history of primary elections is one of disappointment. After a brief surge in the 1920s, the number of primary candidates declined in subsequent decades. Likewise, voter turnout in primary elections also declined in the 1930s and 1940s (Ansolabehere, Hansen, Hirano, and Snyder 2006, 2010). It is difficult to analyze voting behavior in congressional primaries in isolation from voting behavior in presidential primaries, or even gubernatorial primaries, but what we know about voting in general suggests several lessons about how voters approach congressional primaries. Despite a paucity of studies that are specifically about voting in nonpresidential primaries, all of the voting literature suggests that we should expect voter turnout to be low and the primary electorate to be unrepresentative of the public in many ways.

Measuring Primary Election Turnout

The most basic question to ask about congressional primaries is how many people vote. Yet this question is more complicated than it might seem. In a 1986 piece, Barbara Norrander discusses the differences we have in even measuring voter turnout. We can count how many people voted, but it is difficult to come up with percentages. What percentage of Democratic voters cast ballots in the party's primary? In order to answer this question, we need to first know how many Democratic voters there are. Party registration fluctuates from year to year, and differences in primary laws mean that in some states it is easier to register as a member of a party than in others. Furthermore, many reliably partisan general election voters (that is, people who always vote for one party but are not registered as a member of that party) could choose to vote in primary elections, but do not. Should we count these as eligible voters? Norrander concludes that there are many different measures we might use to assess primary voter turnout; at a minimum, we should be sensitive to differences across parties and across states.

For the most part, however, estimates of turnout in nonpresidential primaries have ranged between 25 and 35 percent nationwide. In their book on state political parties and election, Jewell and Olson (1988, 108–11) estimate that in gubernatorial primaries (which almost always are held concurrently with congressional primaries) held between 1960 and 1986, the total turnout as a percentage of the voting age population fluctuated between 25 and 35 percent; turnout was higher for Democrats than Republicans, and it was higher in Western and Southern states than in Northeastern and Midwestern states. Primary turnout as a percentage of general election votes varies more widely across this period, however, largely due to differences in party competitiveness across states. During this period Democratic primaries in the South were often more consequential than general elections, and it was not uncommon for Democratic primaries to have turnout levels 30 percent higher than general election turnout. Meanwhile, primary voter turnout tended to be less than half of general election turnout for both parties in other states, and less than 20 percent of general election turnout for Southern Republicans.

The most comprehensive account of primary election turnout across states and over time, however, is provided by the American University Center for the Study of the American Electorate (CSAE). CSAE compiles a report on primary and general election turnout every election year. As we shall see in Figures 3.1 and 3.2, the CSAE data generally support Jewell and Olson's claims about primary turnout during the 1960s and 1970s, but they also show that a precipitous drop in turnout was beginning at that time and has continued during the 1990s and 2000s.[1]

As noted above, one of the strongest determinants of voter turnout in congressional primaries is the presence or absence of a presidential primary battle on the same ballot. Figure 3.1 shows total primary turnout and Democratic and Republican primary turnout in midterm election years. The CSAE data divide the total vote cast in either the gubernatorial or senatorial primary (whichever has the highest number of voters) by the total number of eligible voters in the state.[2] Figure 3.1 shows the total percentage of eligible voters who cast ballots, as well as the percentages of Democratic and Republican voters. The Democratic and Republican percentages are also taken from the total number of eligible voters, hence the sum of these two adds up to approximately the total sum of votes cast. This figure shows that the percentage of votes cast in primaries has been declining since 1970, and that the decline has been more evident in Democratic primaries than in Republican primaries. The graph clearly shows the decline in Democratic support in the electorate, a decline that is mainly a function of the decline of the Democratic Party in the South. Although there is a slight movement upwards in Republican primary voting in 2010, which some might take to suggest that Republican voters were more enthusiastic than Democratic primary voters, there is little correlation either between primary and general election turnout or between primary turnout and partisan swings in elections other than 2010.[3] Total turnout may be the bigger story, however; over 30 percent of eligible voters cast primary ballots in 1958 and 1966, but fewer than 20 percent have voted in primaries since 1998.

The gradual decline shown in Figure 3.1 masks state-level variations in primary turnout. In many races, a hotly contested primary may inspire high turnout.

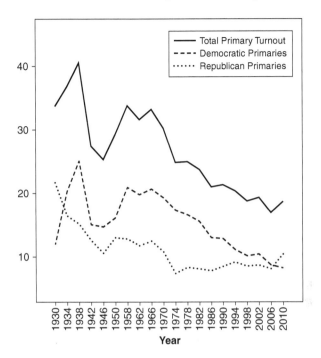

FIGURE 3.1 Primary Turnout as a Percent of Eligible Voters, Midterm Election Years

Source: Author's depiction of data provided by the American University Center for the Study of the American Electorate, www.american.edu/spa/cdem/csae.cfm.

Note: Data are for gubernatorial and senatorial primaries (using the higher of the two where states have both), taken as a percentage of all eligible voters. Data for 1954 are missing.

The states with the highest turnout in 2010 (in excess of 22 percent) had either bitterly contested senatorial or gubernatorial primaries (as was the case in Kentucky, Alaska, Arkansas, and Colorado), have for reasons of state culture traditionally had high turnout (as was the case in Washington, Oregon, and Maine), or exhibited both of these traits (as in Maine). Although the CSAE data neither break down turnout by congressional district nor show what turnout was in House races, given what we know about higher profile races driving turnout it seems very likely that voting in House primaries has fluctuated with state-level turnout.

Data on state-level primaries in presidential election years tell a different story. Were we to simply include data from state-level primaries in those years in our graph of midterm year primary voting, the pattern of decline would be much less evident. The reason for this is that presidential primaries clearly draw more voters to the polls than do primaries for other offices, and as we have seen, some states hold presidential primaries on the same day as congressional primaries

80 The Strategic Context of Congressional Primaries

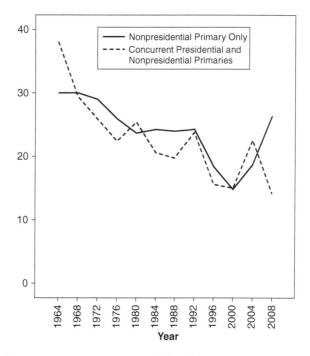

FIGURE 3.2 Primary Turnout as a Percent of Eligible Voters, Presidential Election Years

Source: Author's depiction of data provided by the American University Center for the Study of the American Electorate, www.american.edu/spa/cdem/csae.cfm.

Note: Data are for gubernatorial and senatorial primaries (using the higher of the two where states have both), taken as a percentage of all eligible voters.

while others do not. Figure 3.2 again uses the CSAE data to show turnout in state-level primaries held separately from presidential primaries (again, using the higher of the senatorial and gubernatorial primaries for each state) in comparison to turnout in states that hold their presidential and nonpresidential primaries concurrently.

The most notable feature of this graph is that the presence or absence of presidential primaries does not, in fact, seem to dramatically alter turnout, at least not as much as one might be led to believe. A story could be told about the duration of the primary election season—it is, for example, evident that the prolonged battle between Barack Obama and Hillary Clinton for the Democratic presidential nomination in 2008 increased turnout substantially on the Democratic side. When we further refine our distinction between separate and concurrent primaries by looking at turnout for each party, as shown in Figure 3.3, it also appears plausible that the protracted Democratic presidential nomination battles in 1968, 1972, and 1976 also increased turnout. There is, finally, the potential for

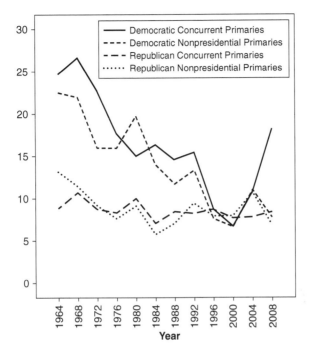

FIGURE 3.3 Democratic and Republican Primary Turnout as a Percent of Eligible Voters, Presidential Election Years

Source: Author's depiction of data provided by the American University Center for the Study of the American Electorate, www.american.edu/spa/cdem/csae.cfm.

Note: Data are for gubernatorial and senatorial primaries (using the higher of the two where states have both), taken as a percentage of all eligible voters.

selection bias—if we consider the 2004, 2000, and 1996 election years, years in which the presidential nominations of both parties were sewn up early, the concurrent states were clearly not states where the presidential nominees campaigned extensively or where the presidential primary outcome was in doubt. One way to think about the differences between presidential and nonpresidential election years is that the presence of a presidential race has made overall turnout in presidential election year primaries slightly more variable over the past two decades, as Figure 3.4 shows.

Who Votes in Congressional Primaries, and Why

Most studies of voting in congressional general elections have reached the same unsurprising conclusion about the difference between congressional and presidential elections—voters are simply less interested in congressional elections

82 The Strategic Context of Congressional Primaries

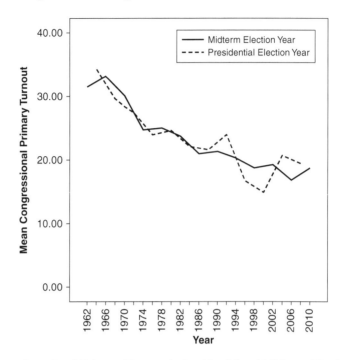

FIGURE 3.4 State-Level Primary Turnout in Presidential and Midterm Election Years Compared

Source: Author's depiction of data provided by the American University Center for the Study of the American Electorate, www.american.edu/spa/cdem/csae.cfm.

Note: Data are for gubernatorial and senatorial primaries (using the higher of the two where states have both), taken as a percentage of all eligible voters.

than they are in presidential elections. Figure 3.5 shows a well-known pattern: it is well-established in research on general elections that turnout in presidential election years is far higher than is turnout in midterm elections. In their textbook on political behavior, Flanigan and Zingale (2006, 45) summarize the existing literature on this difference, explaining that there are five major differences between presidential and congressional elections that drive turnout: there is more media coverage of presidential elections than of congressional elections, voters attach more significance to the presidency than to any individual congressional seat, more important issues tend to be raised in presidential elections, the presidential candidates tend to be "better" in the sense that they are more charismatic or attractive, and presidential elections tend to be more competitive than congressional elections. Although there is no literature proving that all of these factors apply to voters' views on congressional primaries, common sense tells us that these differences clearly relate to primaries, especially in states

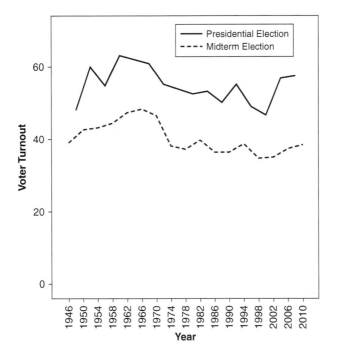

FIGURE 3.5 General Election Turnout, Midterm and Presidential Election Years

Source: International Institute for Democratic and Electoral Assistance (IDEA)'s *Voter Turnout Since 1945: A Global Report*, www.idea.int/publications/vt/index.cfm.

Note: Calculations made based on U.S. voting age population.

where congressional primaries are not held at the same time as presidential primaries.

Voters also have good reason to be less interested in primary elections than in general elections for several reasons. Although political scientists have told us for decades that the chance of any individual vote determining an election outcome is extremely low, voters' beliefs about competitiveness have been shown to affect turnout. That is, people are more likely to vote if they believe their vote will make a difference. Competition in primaries is, as we shall see in upcoming chapters, lower than in general elections, so even though we know that very few congressional *general* elections are competitive, there are even fewer competitive primary elections in any given year. The lack of competition in many primaries and the small sums of money spent make it difficult for candidates to communicate their views to voters, so even when citizens do choose to vote in congressional primaries, they may not know very much about the candidates. Furthermore, if citizens believe that there are differences between the parties, the policy or ideological consequences of one candidate defeating another in a primary are likely to be lower than the consequences of the general election. Research on voting behavior suggests that most voters know very little about the ideology of their member of Congress but that they use congressional elections to reward or punish the president's party. Such an option is, of course, not available in primary elections.

Voting in any election is a costly activity. Merely making the effort to show up at the polling place requires effort on the part of the voter; taking the time to review the differences between candidates and develop informed views about the candidates takes even more effort. In addition, many citizens who are eligible to vote are also not registered to vote, and registering to vote requires further effort. In states with closed primaries, furthermore, citizens must not just be registered to vote, they must be registered members of the party in whose primary they plan to vote. There are ways to reduce the costs of voting—organizations seeking to increase turnout may embark upon voter registration drives, may distribute campaign literature, or may even provide assistance to voters in getting to the polls. Political parties, labor unions, and other groups have traditionally sought to lower the costs of voting in general elections, but they generally have not done so in primaries. There are some exceptions to this rule, as the efforts by the Tea Party in 2010 and by organized labor in several recent elections show, but for these groups, as well, primary elections are simply less important than general elections. The burden of lowering voters' costs (or changing voters' perceptions of how important their votes are) is thus far more likely to fall upon candidates alone than it is in the general election.

Americans also are asked to vote far more often than are citizens of other democratic nations. Many American municipalities hold elections in odd-numbered years, with primaries immediately preceding these elections. In such parts of the country, citizens are asked to vote at least twice a year; in states where presidential primaries are separated from other primaries they are asked to vote three times. Many scholars of comparative politics have argued that voter turnout in the United States tends to be lower than that of other nations precisely because we are asked to vote so often and for so many different offices—many of which we have never thought very much about.[4]

Finally, even if citizens do show up to vote, they are not necessarily showing up to vote because of the congressional primary. For those states where presidential primaries are held at the same time as congressional primaries, voters may vote in the congressional race without knowing anything at all about the candidates, or they may simply leave that part of the ballot blank. The same applies, of course, for other offices—voters may show up because they care who wins the gubernatorial nomination, or, for that matter, they may actually care about a race lower down on the ballot such as a race for the state legislature.

What does all of this suggest about the primary electorate? An obvious conclusion is that this is an elusive electorate to study. There are many studies of turnout in presidential primaries, but there are only a few studies of turnout in House and

Senate primaries, and until 2010 there were none that employed a national survey sample. One study of turnout in Senate primaries (Kenney 1986) found that turnout is sensitive to characteristics of the primary itself—that is, whether the primary is open or closed, whether it is for the nomination to run in a competitive general election, whether the primary itself is competitive, and whether, of course, it is held at the same time as a presidential primary. Turnout in Senate primaries is also influenced by the state's level of education and turnout history—indicating that some states have a political culture that encourages voting in primaries while other states do not. These studies parallel studies of presidential primaries (Norrander 1991). Presumably House primaries exhibit similar patterns although they are harder to study. Drawing such conclusions about what inspires turnout, however, is different from drawing conclusions about *who* turns out.

There are three main areas of research about who tends to vote that are relevant to understanding turnout in congressional primaries. First, voters in all types of elections tend to be different from nonvoters. General election voters tend to be wealthier, better educated, and older than nonvoters (Wolfinger and Rosenstone 1980). This bias has been found in all types of elections, but it is more pronounced in less competitive presidential elections than in competitive ones, in midterm elections than in presidential elections, and in presidential primaries than in general elections (Norrander 1991). The lower turnout is, the less representative the electorate is. Hajnal (2010, 35–40) found that in local elections (where turnout is often lower than 20 percent of the eligible electorate) the bias toward the better off is even greater than in federal elections. All of these patterns lend support to Jewell and Olson's (1988, 107–11) claims that turnout in primaries is determined in part by the level of competition and in part by the existence of restrictions on voting. Some have argued that this is a function of barriers to voting (that is, younger or poorer people are less likely to have resided in the same home for the past two years than are older voters, and are thus less likely to be registered), while others have argued that older or wealthier citizens feel more connected to the political process and believe themselves to have more of a stake in the election outcome (see Rosenstone and Hansen 1993, 71–101; Wattenberg 2012). Still others have noted that people who have voted regularly in the past are likely to vote in the future, so candidates and parties are more likely to reach out to such citizens than they are to reach out to nonvoters (Arcenaux and Nickerson 2009).

Second, primary voters can be expected to have a different social or psychological orientation toward politics. Again, comparisons of voters and nonvoters give us some insight here. Voters in general elections tend to have more positive beliefs about politicians in general than do nonvoters, and they are more likely to believe that their views matter to politicians than are nonvoters. Meredith Rolfe (2012) argues that voting can be explained by the embeddedness of citizens in social networks where voting is encouraged—that is, some citizens have many friends and social contacts who regularly vote, volunteer for political causes, and so forth, and these citizens receive extra encouragement to vote just because it is socially sanctioned. Again, there are few studies of voting behavior that specifically focus upon congressional primaries, but the fact that citizens who vote in low salience elections tend to be more favorably disposed toward the political system than those who only vote in high salience elections (and who are, in turn, more favorably disposed toward the system than those who do not vote at all) suggests that the primary electorate should be more politically active than the general electorate. This does not suggest that primary voters will not turn out because of a dislike for individual politicians; it merely suggests that primary voters place a greater value on political activism than do other citizens.[5]

Third, one might expect primary voters to have different ideological views than the general electorate; it has even been suggested that the primary electorate for one party will be more extreme than the population of voters who choose that party's nominee in the general election. This is one of the claims that has most frequently been made regarding the role of primaries in encouraging polarization between the parties in recent years. Evidence for this claim is, however, mixed. Jewell and Olson (1988, 114–15) use the American National Election Studies seven-point scale of partisanship to show that voters in nonpresidential primaries in 1978 were more committed partisans than general election voters, but it would be wrong to equate partisanship with ideology, to argue that all strong Democrats are also liberals or all strong Republicans are necessarily very conservative. In her work on presidential primary voters, Barbara Norrander (1989) concludes that there is little evidence that voters in presidential primaries are more ideologically extreme than general election voters; they are, however, more ideologically sophisticated.[6] Norrander, Stephens, and Wendland (2013) refine this argument, arguing that there is also no substantial ideological difference between presidential primary voters in different primary types, once one has accounted for state partisanship. Finally, Norrander and Stephens (2012) consider congressional primary voting in California, concluding that there is again little strong evidence that there are systematic differences in ideology between primary voters and general election voters, although in some instances candidates may inspire higher primary turnout among their supporters.

The 2010 election was the first for which we have a national survey sample that enables us to compare primary voters to general election voters, all registered voters, and American adults in general. It is unsurprising that few surveys in past years asked about voting in nonpresidential primaries—apart from the limited amount of research on such elections, the percentage of the electorate that votes in these elections is small enough that the standard two thousand response survey would not yield a large enough fraction of primary voters to allow for meaningful analysis. The Cooperative Congressional Election Survey (CCES), conducted since 2006, combines survey modules from over thirty different teams with a limited amount of survey content used in common by all of these teams

(Ansolabehere 2012). The common content in 2010 included questions about voter registration, primary voting, general election voting, and a variety of political and demographic questions. The 2010 survey had over 55,000 responses, thus for the first time ensuring that we could obtain a full picture of the congressional primary electorate. Results from the 2010 CCES must be considered with a grain of salt, however, first because the percentage of respondents who reported voting far exceeded the percentage of the electorate who actually did turn out to vote (the CSAE data shown in Figure 3.1 have slightly over 20 percent of eligible voters turning out in 2010, yet 45.6 percent of CCES respondents claim to have voted in the primary)[7], and second because of the unusual nature of the 2010 midterm election. Considering 2010 is useful because we do not have to worry about the effects of presidential primaries, whether concurrent or not, but according to most media accounts turnout was unusually high among conservatives and among demographic groups that tend to favor Republicans. The results, nonetheless, provide support for some of the claims about the lack of representativeness of congressional primary voters, but the differences are not nearly as stark as some might expect. Table 3.1 compares primary voters with all general election voters, all registered voters, and all CCES respondents.

The data in Table 3.1 confirm most of the assumptions about primary voters that the above discussion suggests, but with a few surprises. Primary voters in 2010 were older, wealthier, better educated, and more likely to be male than registered voters and the general population. They were not, however, dramatically different from general election voters in any of these characteristics. Primary voters were slightly better educated and slightly more likely to be over sixty years of age than general election voters, but the percentages of white voters was actually higher in the general election than in the primaries, and lower-income voters were more common in the primaries than in the general election. The differences here are small but they are noteworthy in that we would expect primary voters to be wealthier and white.

Table 3.1 does not provide strong evidence that primary voters are more ideologically extreme than general election voters. There are larger percentages of registered Democrats and Republicans among primary voters than there are among other types of respondents, and there are also larger numbers of self-described Democrats and Republicans among primary voters than among any of the other three groups. There are fewer self-described independents among primary voters than among general election voters; there are, however, slightly more independents among general election voters than among all registered voters or among all respondents. To a certain extent, these differences are simply a consequence of the existence of closed primaries—in closed primary states one must register as a Democrat or a Republican in order to vote. It is possible that these numbers capture some polarization among voters but it is impossible to know for certain using such data.

TABLE 3.1 Comparing Primary Voters and Other Types of Voters, 2010

	Primary Voters	General Election Voters	Registered Voters	Full Sample
Male	52.3%	53.2%	49.1%	49.5%
White	78.5	80.1	77.3	77.9
60 Years Old or Older	36.0	34.2	27.1	24.8
30 Years Old or Younger	11.0	10.7	19.4	21.5
Family Income Below $40,000	33.1	32.5	39.0	42.2
Family Income Above $80,000	29.0	29.6	24.9	22.5
College Graduate	39.3	40.7	35.6	33.1
Voted for Obama in 2008	45.6	46.6	49.3	49.1
Voted for McCain in 2008	51.1	49.4	46.2	46.4
Liberal*	27.8	28.1	27.4	27.3
Middle of the Road*	19.3	20.5	24.2	24.4
Conservative*	50.5	48.7	42.7	42.4
Registered Democrat	42.5	38.0	36.3	37.5
Registered Republican	41.0	35.9	29.8	31.0
Describes self as Democrat**	38.0	34.3	35.1	34.7
Describes self as Republican**	34.3	30.6	27.2	27.1
Describes self as Independent**	23.6	30.4	30.0	30.0
Voted in Primary	—	65.5	51.9	45.6
Voted in General Election	91.6	—	73.1	71.8
Registered	—	—	—	88.4
Valid Percentage of Total Sample (N)	45.6 (24,303)	71.8 (32,707)	88.4 (48,249)	100.0 (55,400)

Source: Cooperative Congressional Election Survey (CCES), 2010 (Ansolabehere 2012)

* Ideology measurements created by conflating self-placements on seven-point scale; 1–3 = liberal, 4 = middle of the road, 5–7 = conservative.
** Partisan descriptions taken from pre-election survey.

Voters who describe themselves as "middle of the road" are less common in the primary and general elections than they are among registered voters and among the general public. Self-described liberals, however, are not substantially more common among primary voters than they are in the general electorate or in the population. The big story in terms or ideology is the much larger number of self-described conservatives among primary voters—over 50 percent of primary voters described themselves as conservatives, an 8 percentage point gap between primary voters and all registered voters. To some extent this is certainly a function of the enthusiasm of conservatives in the 2010 midterm; had Barack Obama and John McCain been facing off before either the 2010 primary electorate or the 2010 general electorate, McCain would have won. The overall conservative tilt among midterm election voters is clearly evident here, but the data also suggest that this tilt is present, and perhaps even more pronounced, among primary voters.

Claims about polarization between the two primary electorates, however, do not suggest merely that primary electorates are more conservative overall or that more partisans vote in the primaries than in the general elections. Such claims posit, instead, that Democrats who vote in the primaries are more liberal than Democrats who only vote in the general election, and that Republican primary voters are more conservative than Republican general election voters. These claims are such a common component not only of political punditry but of formal treatments of elections that they tend to be taken as a given. Table 3.2, however, shows that at least in 2010 there was little evidence that this is in fact true. The CCES followed the example of the National Election Studies and asked

TABLE 3.2 Ideology and Partisanship of Primary Voters, 2010

	Mean Party ID Score (7-Pt. Scale)	Mean Ideological Placement (7-Pt. Scale)	N*
Democratic Primary Voters	1.92	3.46	11,384
Registered Democrats	1.83	3.61	19,363
Self-Identified Democrats (Pre-Election)	1.71	3.54	17,881
Voted for Democratic Senate Candidate	2.01	3.28	11,560
Voted for Democratic Gubernatorial Candidate	2.18	3.34	12,473
Voted for Democratic House Candidate	2.08	3.31	13,573
Republican Primary Voters	5.96	5.70	11,970
Registered Republicans	6.17	5.68	15,407
Self-Identified Republicans (Pre-Election)	6.35	5.71	14,041
Voted for Republican Senate Candidate	5.67	5.66	13,832
Voted for Republican Gubernatorial Candidate	5.66	5.65	13,238
Voted for Republican House Candidate	5.60	5.63	16,649

Source: Cooperative Congressional Election Study (CCES), 2010 (Ansolabehere 2012).

* N is taken from the smaller of the two 7-point measurements, in most instances the ideology measurement. Ns are slightly different for the two questions because some respondents did not answer the questions.

voters to place themselves on a seven point scale for partisanship, ranging from "strong Democrat" (1) to "strong Republican" (7) with independents at a position of 4 on the scale. Similarly, the CCES asked respondents to place themselves ideologically, with 1 representing a "very liberal" respondent, 4 a "middle of the road" respondent, and 7 a "very conservative" respondent. Although these sorts of ideology questions have frequently been criticized by survey researchers,[8] they remain the purest way of seeing how voters think about their own views.

There is, of course, no such thing in congressional elections as the Democratic or Republican general electorate. Table 3.2, then, compares, within each party, primary voters to registered party members, self-identified partisans, and respondents who voted for the party's Senate, gubernatorial, and House candidates. To be certain, there is much overlap between Democratic Senate, House, and gubernatorial voters, but there is no compelling reason to simplify our measurement of general election voters. Within the Democratic Party, primary voters are stronger in their partisanship than are general election voters, but they are in fact slightly less liberal than Democratic general election voters. Republican primary voters in 2010 were actually less committed to the Republican Party than were all registered Republicans, but there is not very much ideological distance between Republican primary and general election voters. Republican primary voters are more conservative than Republican general election voters, but the distance is much smaller than it is for Democrats. One could explore numerous issue differences between primary and general election voters—for instance, one might look at different attitudes toward the Affordable Care Act, same sex marriage, and so forth; analyses by Jacobson (2012) and Sides and Vavreck (2013) that incorporate such measures show the same basic pattern as do the measures I use here.

Again, 2010 was an anomalous year, but it is the year for which we have the best data on congressional primary voters. The 2010 data suggest that much of what we have always assumed about characteristics of primary voters may well be true, but that the differences between primary voters and other types of actual or potential voters are not particularly large. We should, then, consider claims about the unrepresentativeness of primary electorates with caution.

Political Parties and Their Allies

Just as the story about whether voters are the main beneficiaries of primary elections has been far more complicated than Progressive reformers might have expected, so the story of whether political parties are the biggest losers in competitive primary elections is one that makes some theoretical sense but has in practice been quite complicated. The reasons why political parties might prefer to avoid primaries or to reduce competition in primaries are relatively straightforward: competitive primaries present the risk of producing ideologically extreme nominees, of creating divisions within the party that will hurt its nominees' chances in the general election, or at a minimum of wasting valuable campaign resources that might better be used to help the party's nominees in the general election. Political parties seek to win elections; the identity of the victorious candidates and the ideological views of those candidates are of secondary importance to the parties.

As Alan Ware's (2002) argument, detailed in Chapter 2, makes clear, however, political parties have always sought to maintain control over primary elections, and in some ways parties have even benefited from primaries. In Ware's telling, formal party interventions in primaries, such as endorsing conventions, and less formal interventions, such as the active support of party leaders, can discourage competition. And, one might add, competition is not always detrimental to the nominees. To take the most obvious recent case in presidential elections, an argument could be made that Barack Obama benefited from the protracted and often bitter Democratic presidential primary—his campaigning skills were sharpened, he received extensive media coverage, and the primary may well have had the effect of exciting Democratic partisans and swing voters. Was the 2008 presidential primary season an exception to the rule? Do stories about presidential primaries have any relevance to competition in congressional races? There is no consensus about the effects of primary competition in the literature on congressional primaries, but there is ample evidence that parties seek to control primary competition and to confer the nomination on their preferred candidates.

Parties' Hopes and Fears

The threats of primary competition barely require elaboration; every election provides instances where a weak general election candidate prevails over a potentially stronger candidate in the primary, thereby losing a seat for the party. Arguably, at least three such cases occurred in the 2010 Republican Senate primaries: in Delaware, perennial Senate candidate Christine O'Donnell defeated the state's lone member of the House of Representatives, Mike Castle; in Colorado, the former lieutenant governor was defeated by the district attorney for a rural Colorado county; and the former chair of the Nevada Republican Party was defeated by a much more conservative, and less experienced, state legislator. These were three Senate seats Republicans arguably could have won with better nominees. Similar stories can be told about other elections; perhaps the most notorious instances of this were former Ku Klux Klan leader David Duke's candidacies for the Senate and for governor of Louisiana in 1990 and 1991. The national Republican Party and the Louisiana Republican Party refused to endorse Duke and condemned his views, but neither could stop him from running as a Republican in the primary or as the de facto Republican nominee in the 1991 gubernatorial runoff (Kuzenski, Bullock, and Gaddie 2006).

Despite these high-profile instances, however, a case can be made that under some circumstances primaries can be helpful to parties. It is not always the case that party leaders can reach consensus on who the strongest nominee in a particular state or district would be; primaries enable party leaders to avoid having to make such decisions. Primaries also allow candidate to prove themselves to their parties and to voters—less well-known candidates can increase their visibility and demonstrate their capacities for running as the nominee, primary opponents can search for any disqualifying blemishes in each others' records, and candidates can acquaint themselves with important local leaders. From the party's point of view, primaries can serve as an audition, and it is better to find out during the primary that a potential nominee has damaging flaws than to find this out after the nomination has been made. If voters, party leaders, and campaign contributors are behaving strategically, they will use primaries to search for candidates who have broad appeal and can potentially win the general election. Even claims about wasted resources can be overblown—there are clearly some congressional primaries, such as the bitter incumbent-versus-incumbent battle between Democrats Brad Sherman and Howard Berman in California in 2012, in which the two candidates raised a combined total of over $4.5 million and spent over $5.5 million,[9] where money that, from the party's point of view, could better have been spent elsewhere was wasted. Yet one must remember that most congressional primaries are low-visibility affairs and such large expenditures are unusual. There are separate caps on individual contributions for primary election campaigns and general election campaigns, so a primary election victor can always return to his or her contributors and raise more money after receiving the nomination. It is far from clear that very much of the money spent by candidates in pursuit of the nomination would necessarily be available to them had they not been forced to raise and spend it for the purpose of winning the primary.

For the most part, national party organizations, such as the parties' congressional and senatorial campaign committees, have policies against becoming involved in primaries, except in instances where an incumbent is challenged. In the case of the two House campaign committees, there will be more nonincumbent candidates seeking the committees' support than there will be resources for the committees to dispense; party campaign committees can observe primaries in order to determine whether the nominee will be a viable general election candidate. While the leaders of the party campaign committees have at times recruited candidates to run, they usually withhold campaign assistance until it is certain who will be the nominee.

Assumptions about the parties' role in primary elections are, however, complicated by the fact that American political parties are not easily identified, monolithic organizations. In 2002, when George W. Bush's advisor Karl Rove reportedly encouraged St. Paul, Minnesota, Mayor Norm Coleman to run for the Senate (and pressured Coleman's strongest potential opponent, Minnesota House Majority Leader Tim Pawlenty, to run for the governorship instead), was Rove acting on behalf of the Republican Party (Edwards 2007, 111)? When Massachusetts Governor Deval Patrick worked to ensure that Elizabeth Warren would not face a primary challenge in her 2012 Senate campaign, was he acting on behalf of the Democratic Party (Seelye 2012)? Media accounts of primary races abound with discussions of party "insiders" and "outsiders," but there is no clear way to measure who is an insider and who is not, who is the candidate with party support and who is not, because most party interventions in primaries are informal and one cannot easily separate the actions of "the party" from the actions of individual politicians.

The foregoing discussion assumes, of course, that the nomination is worth having. In many congressional elections, this is a debatable assumption. The motives of parties in primary elections in districts where the party has no realistic assumption of winning the general election differ from those of parties in winnable seats. As I have noted in previous research (Boatright 2004, 142–81), the Republican nomination battle, where there is one, in a heavily Democratic district (or vice versa) is not completely worthless; there is symbolic value in winning the nomination even in hopeless districts. The right candidate can potentially increase general election voter turnout, thus helping other candidates up and down the ballot; he or she has the chance to convince the party—by exceeding expectations even in a losing cause—that a seat might be winnable in the future, or a candidate's nomination might inspire party extremists, who will have a candidate to rally around. The heated Republican primary battle in Massachusetts' Third District, discussed in Chapter 5, is an example of a race where the nominee was likely doomed to lose but where Republican Party leaders did take an interest in the three-way primary.

As we discussed in Chapter 1, the United States is one of the few nations in which political parties have such a limited role in selecting nominees. In most other democracies with geographic representation, parties either slate candidate to run in particular constituencies through the fiat of party leaders or at local party conventions. This does not mean that there is no competition for nominations in these countries; instead, it means that competition takes place before a limited electorate, an electorate with much narrower goals than those of American primary voters. In a list-based system, parties can choose established, faithful candidates for the seats the party is likely to win, and can make symbolic choices further down the list (see Hazan and Rahat 2010, 114). Ticket balancing is also possible in such systems, while this is one ability that American parties clearly lost with the establishment of the direct primary. The repertoire of what American parties can do is more limited, and this factor arguably accounts both for the independence from the parties that most incumbent legislators have and the role of unrepresentative groups in the primary electorate.

The Evidence: What Really Happens to Parties in Primaries?

Given the understandable downside of primary competition for parties, it may come as a surprise to the reader that there is little evidence either that parties can do very much to influence primary outcomes or that parties are disadvantaged by primary competition. Although there are clear problems with measuring party interventions or the consequences of primary elections, the existing literature on both subjects gives further evidence that, just as expectations about what would happen with the introduction of primaries were largely confounded, so the expectations of contemporary parties about primaries are often unsupported.

There have been occasional efforts to study the effects of party endorsements on primary elections. In 1980, Andrew McNitt conducted a study of the effect of party endorsements on the amount of competition; McNitt concluded that the existence of party nominating conventions limited the number of candidates running in primaries. This is to be expected. However, blanket primaries—which are theoretically the most "wide open" of primaries, in which the role of partisanship should be worth the least—were also particularly uncompetitive. Although state culture makes it difficult to assess the value of endorsements (different types of states have different types of party endorsement procedures), it appears that parties that play a formal role can limit competition.

This does not mean, however, that the endorsements themselves have a strong effect on the outcome; it merely means that formal endorsements can give the least competitive candidates a reality check. Casey Dominguez (2005, 2011, 2013) conducted a survey of congressional candidates running in the 2002 primaries, asking not only about formal party endorsements but about the endorsements of other partisan groups and prominent party members. Dominguez concludes that the low visibility of congressional primaries ensures that endorsements can have substantial value—in many instances voters know virtually nothing about the candidates, so the endorsement of a well-known politician may be the only piece of information they have when they go to the polls. This does not mean that parties play a unified role in selecting their nominees—witness the effect of Sarah Palin's candidate endorsements in the 2012 Republican congressional primaries, endorsements that often were given to candidates other than those favored by local leaders. It does, however, suggest that even when they cannot limit competition parties still have a role to play. If nothing else, parties can aid their preferred candidates in locking up the endorsements of key political elites, in providing access to donors and "party loyal" groups, or in ensuring that their preferred candidates have access to the best campaign consultants. Dominguez (2005) argues that party elites are more likely to converge around preferred nominees when they expect the general election to be competitive than they are in primaries for safe seats.[10]

A third approach, taken by Hans Hassell (2012), is to look at fundraising networks for congressional primary candidates. While national party organizations cannot formally endorse candidates, they can informally urge party benefactors to support candidates. Hassell finds evidence of indirect party support in primaries, in the form of contributions from individual donors well-established in the party's network. That is, individuals who have traditionally supported the party campaign committees as well as the party's most electable candidates nationwide tend to converge on particular candidates in primary elections—candidates who, one would suspect, are believed by party leaders to be the most electable general election candidates. This is an effect that is easy to see in the case of interest groups such as EMILY's List or the Club for Growth that promote primary candidates, but while interest groups tend to claim credit for doing this, party committees tend to avoid such credit claiming because of their need to remain officially neutral. Hassell also finds that over the past decade parties have become much more willing and able to engage in such unofficial candidate support than they were in previous elections.

All of these studies are complicated by the fact that the most crucial party intervention in primaries—recruitment to run, or "negative recruitment," encouragement *not* to run, as in the Tim Pawlenty example—cannot be conclusively measured. Do party leaders steer some potential candidates toward primaries while steering others away from them? Undoubtedly. This can potentially have the effect of changing the nature of competition; races with multiple viable candidates may contain a large number of insurgent or outsider candidates simply because these are candidates who have resisted the entreaties of party leaders to step down. Conversely, uncompetitive primaries may belie the real competition that went on—multiple strong candidates may have expressed an interest in running and explored their chances but ultimately have decided not to run, leaving the appearance that the competition for the nomination is less competitive than it actually has been. It is difficult to verify whether candidates have been encouraged to run or discouraged from running because neither type of candidate is likely to discuss this pressure, and party elites are not likely to admit such a role (Dominguez 2005, 20, 113).

This discussion of the role of parties in primaries leads us, then, to perhaps the largest question about primaries—and the question that has been most thoroughly explored over the past several decades. Do competitive primaries harm the nominees' general election prospects? Do they lower the chance that the party will win the seat? There are many stories of this happening at the presidential level—some argue, for instance, that the primary challenges to incumbent presidents Jimmy Carter in 1980 and George H.W. Bush in 1992 cost these presidents the election, while others merely say that the primary challenges were symptoms of problems Carter and Bush were having (Glad 1995). Some academic studies of presidential elections have found only limited evidence that this happens; Patricia Southwell (1986) studied survey data on presidential elections in the 1970s and 1980s, concluding that there was some defection of disgruntled primary voters in 1972, from the Democratic Party to President Nixon, and from Republicans unhappy with the nomination of Ronald Reagan in 1980 to third party candidate John Anderson. Southwell cautions, however, that what she calls "the politics of disgruntlement" is a relatively limited phenomenon in presidential elections. Other studies, however, have shown that divisive primaries can harm candidates (particularly Democratic candidates) in the states where primary competition was particularly heated (Lengle, Owen, and Sonner 1995).

Are the effects of divisiveness in congressional elections different? There are compelling reasons to expect that they are. Because congressional elections are lower visibility races, divisiveness in the primary may leave voters with impressions of the candidates that the candidates themselves have difficulty correcting; presidential candidates, on the other hand, get plenty of time to soothe hurt feelings. In addition, there is less at stake in congressional races—a voter may have greater reason to break with his or her party or abstain from voting if he or she thinks the nominee is a rotten person. Studies of the divisiveness of congressional primaries have had mixed results—Hacker (1965) argued that they have no effect on general election outcomes; in a study of Senate primaries, Bernstein (1977) argued that they hurt the stronger party but not the weaker party; Kenney and Rice (1987) found similar results in Senate and gubernatorial races. A 1975 study of House races by Pierson and Smith found that divisive primaries hurt in competitive districts but not in uncompetitive ones.[11] Alvarez, Canon, and Sellers (1995) find that general election challengers benefit from competitive primaries while incumbents' general election fortunes are harmed by competitive primaries; these effects are magnified when primary dates are close to the general election.

All of these studies have equated divisiveness with closeness, a problem that Alan Ware (1979) criticizes—why should we expect a close race to be more divisive than a lopsided one? After all, the dynamics of a race can change such that what at one time appeared to be a close race became less close following a series of harsh negative advertisements, or a long-shot challenger may, in desperation, engage in more divisive campaign tactics than a candidate who is close to winning. Ware analogizes campaigns to sporting events, pointing out that the final score often does not reflect how evenly matched the teams are, only that one team may have given up toward the end.

More recent studies of divisiveness have also criticized the methodology of these earlier studies. Jeffrey Lazarus (2005) summarizes the preponderant theme of the early literature—divisive primaries help challengers and hurt incumbents (or help "outsider candidates" and harm "insider candidates") in the general election—and then argues that this literature has matters backwards. Lazarus argues that more candidates will get into a race when their chance of winning the seat is higher, so the appropriate thing to look at is the number of candidates running, not necessarily the closeness of the race. The more candidates that there are in a primary, and the more money that is spent in the primary, the better the party does in the general election—not because multiple candidates have run or spent money, but because the emergence of multiple candidates and the high level of spending are a consequence of the likelihood that the primary nominee will win the general election. The effects here are stronger for the out party, or nonincumbent party, than for the incumbent party. Another recent study, by Johnson, Petersheim, and Wasson (2010) generally corroborates Lazarus's results but measures the effects of the primary date on general election outcomes; the authors contend that competitive late primaries yield better general election results for out parties. The excitement generated by nonincumbent primaries, in this accounting, dissipates quickly but can have an effect on general elections if the primary and general elections are close enough.

Perhaps the most mathematically sophisticated study of primary divisiveness was conducted by Hirano and Snyder (2011), who argue that competitive primaries can actually strengthen candidates' chances in the general election under certain conditions. Candidates seeking the nomination will need to concentrate their efforts in particular parts of the district or among certain types of voters. In comparing precinct-level primary and general election outcomes, Hirano and Snyder discover that in the general election candidates often outperform expectations in areas where they appear to have had strong primary support. Although the authors' method does not actually enable one to know why this is the case, it is easy to imagine that if a candidates has done door-to-door campaigning in a particular neighborhood during the primary, the people with whom he or she spoke may well remember that visit when they vote in the general election. Studies of candidate emergence among state legislators have also shown that candidates can develop a "personal vote" in particular geographic areas of the district during or before the primaries, which carries over into the general election (Carson et al. 2012).

Divisiveness, then, is easier to explain using particular anecdotes than it is to measure quantitatively. Political parties have clearly taken steps to assert control over primaries since their inception, and it would likely be futile to argue that they should never do this. Whatever the aggregate results on whether divisiveness is a problem show, party leaders would likely argue that sometimes it is and sometimes it isn't. This is one area of primary strategy where the judgments of political insiders, even if they are occasionally wrong, are likely based on subtle knowledge of individual races and individual candidates that may elude the attention of voters (or political scientists).

Interest Groups

Many organized interests function as part of the political parties' extended networks. That is, decision-making within the leadership of the Democratic Party must include leaders of civil rights groups, organized labor, environmental groups, and so forth, while decision-making within the Republican Party leadership includes participants from major business organizations, gun rights groups, evangelicals, and other social and fiscal conservatives. While many of these groups may take their cues about whom to support from the parties, it is important to note that the goals of even the most partisan of interest groups differ from those of the parties. A conventional distinction made among interest groups is among those that seek access to politicians and those that seek to influence policy and elections. Access-oriented groups tend to support legislators who are likely to be elected or reelected, and are unlikely to become involved in contested primaries. Groups that seek influence, on the other hand, may choose candidates to back in primaries, although again they are likely to focus their attention on candidates who have a good chance of winning. In the case of primaries, candidates expected to be competitive in the general election may curry support from organized interests, but groups may well wait until after the primary election to contribute. If a group has partisan goals, after all, it may be more concerned with which party wins than with which candidate wins.

This is not to say that there are not some groups that have sought to play an active role in primaries. Interest groups that have sought to recruit candidates, such as EMILY's List (which backs female Democrats), the Club for Growth (fiscal conservatives), or the Gay and Lesbian Victory Fund have sought to provide resources to a small number of primary candidates, providing contributions early in their campaigns in order to propel them to the front of the primary field. The Club for Growth, in particular, has spoken of the importance even of small contributions early in a primary candidate's campaign (Kraushaar 2011). Support from such groups is important in part because it serves as a signal to other organizations about the qualifications of these candidates. It is difficult to make generalizations about interest group strategy in primary campaigns in part because interest groups are not major players in very many primaries, and in part because there is so much variation in the nature of primaries and primary competition. As we shall see in subsequent chapters, however, the types of interest groups that take an active role in primary elections and the role that PAC money plays in primaries are very different from the patterns we observe in congressional general election campaigns.

Candidates

It is difficult to generalize about candidate strategy in primaries, in part because candidate strategies are so heavily dependent upon the competitiveness of the primary and the value of the nomination, and in part because candidates have little control over the context of the primary. As we saw above, political parties have maneuvered for much of the past century to adapt primary rules to their liking and to encourage or discourage particular types of candidates. Candidates must take the rules surrounding the primary as a given. Of course, different types of primaries will encourage or discourage particular types of candidates in their decisions to run for office, but it is difficult to study the decision-making calculus of people who thought about running in a primary but ultimately decided against it.

Although we will defer much of the discussion of how candidates campaign to the next three chapters, there are several different factors worthy of addressing that shape the types of candidates who run and the wisdom of running particular types of campaigns. These factors can be conveniently sorted into national factors, which shape all primaries in a given year; state or district factors, which affect the particular primary in which a candidate runs but can differ across the country; and characteristics of the particular set of candidates in the primary itself. The first and second sets of factors are largely beyond the control of candidates (although they can, again, choose whether to run or not based upon them) while the third set is somewhat within the control of the candidates.

The Context of the Primary: What Candidates Cannot Control

Although congressional primaries tend to attract scant attention from the public, the degree of attention paid to primaries depends in part on whether there is a presidential election taking place and, more broadly, on the general political mood of the nation. The Republican nomination is more worth having, for instance, if the year is expected to be a good year for Republicans. Just as the CSAE studies listed above raised the possibility that higher turnout for one party's candidates in the primaries bodes well for that party in the general election (even though this claim is not necessarily true), so media accounts of the 2010 primaries took note of the large number of Republican candidates who ran in the primaries and speculated that this was a sign of the Republican success that would follow in November. Studies of candidate emergence have also taken note of other year effects—in 1992, ballyhooed by many in the media as "the year of the woman" in congressional elections, it is entirely possible that some female candidates sought to run because there was so much discussion of the rise of female candidates. Paul Herrnson's (2012, 40–74) text on congressional elections notes that candidates' "strategic ambition" depends in part on national patterns and that the general anti-incumbent mood that has been so pronounced over the past four elections (and at other times over the past few decades as well) can encourage primary candidacies.

National trends will not, of course, be felt equally in all parts of the country. A congressional aspirant in a safely partisan district with an entrenched incumbent likely will need to worry more about when the incumbent will retire than about what the national mood is. Given the decision to run, however, there is a second set of factors that can influence candidates' prospects for victory. One of the most explored of these is the nature of the state's primary laws. As discussed in Chapter 2, it has long been believed that whether primaries are open or closed—or, to include the less common cases, whether there is a blanket primary or a runoff—can influence the number of candidates who run and the prospects for particular types of candidates. Research on the influence of primary type has not always supported the conventional wisdom and it is complicated by state-level variation in ballot access laws, filing fees, and endorsement procedures (Ansolabehere and Gerber 1996; Galderisi and Ezra 2001). Similarly, as we have seen above, preprimary conventions or other formal party endorsements can also reduce the number of candidates who run (McNitt 1980).

The next logical question, then, is what types of candidates are affected by variations in state-level primary rules. Kanthak and Morton (2001) use the adjusted Americans for Democratic Action scores for general election winners and conclude that semi-open and semi-closed primaries produce more moderate candidates than do pure closed or pure open primaries. Studies that have merely distinguished between open and closed primaries using this methodology have generally failed to find significant differences (Telford 1965). While there are compelling reasons to suspect that having primary competition at all advantages more ideologically extreme candidates (Burden 2001), and that open primaries produce more moderate candidates than closed ones (Gerber and Morton 1998), part of the reason these theoretical arguments have proven difficult to test is that the party's core voters may prize electability over ideological purity. Recent studies of legislative elections in California (Alvarez and Sinclair 2012; Hassell 2012) have shown that blanket primaries produce legislators who are at least less partisan in their legislative activity, and thus presumable more moderate. One important factor that interacts with primary type, however, is the date of the primary—if candidates adopt positions in order to win the primary, they may shift their positions once they have won the nomination, but their ability to do so will be affected by how much time they have between the primary and the general election (Galderisi and Ezra 2001).

Finally, each primary has its own dynamics, irrespective of national moods or state-level laws. While these factors may influence the number of candidates who enter a race or the composition of the electorate, ultimately a primary candidate must evaluate the strategies of his or her opponents in order to determine how best to campaign. To take a hypothetical example, even if some state laws and some elections might tend to advantage conservative candidates in a Republican primary, this does not guarantee that conservatives will necessarily win in any given Republican primary. Perhaps no strong conservative candidates enter a particular race, in which case a more moderate candidate might win by default. Or perhaps too many conservative candidates run, splitting the conservative vote and enabling a candidate with support from moderates to win the primary with a plurality of the vote. Perhaps the moderate candidate has a nonideological advantage over any potential conservative opponents—he or she comes from a well-known political family, or is able to outspend his or her opponents. In short, the nature of the field in a given primary may well be more important than the state or national context.

Position-Taking in Primaries: What Candidates Can Control

Let us now consider ideological competition in primaries. The classic spatial model of candidate competition holds that in a two-candidate race, both candidates will maximize their vote share and chance of winning by seeking the position at the ideological center of the electorate. If we assume that candidates know how liberal Democratic primary voters are and can arrange them from least liberal to most liberal, candidates in a two-candidate Democratic primary will seek to find the views of the candidate in the middle of that array and take positions at that point. It is perhaps unrealistic to assume that candidates have this sort of knowledge, but if they have a general sense of how liberal or conservative voters are they can at least try to do this. For instance, two candidates competing for the Democratic nomination in a district in rural Oklahoma will likely agree that the winning position will be a much more conservative one than the position two competing candidates might seek in a district in San Francisco. If two candidates are able to successfully converge on matters of policy, then voters either will be indifferent between them or will vote based on something other than ideology—whose personality they like better, who appears to have the strongest leadership credentials, or who is the most morally upstanding candidate.

The imperative to court the median voter only applies, however, to two-candidate elections. If there are three or more candidates running, candidates will need to differentiate themselves from each other. If two candidates have adopted identical views at the median of the voters' preference distribution, a third candidate may enter just to the right or left of the other two, commanding the votes of 49 percent of the voters and leaving the other two candidates to split the remaining 51 percent. There is no position one can take in a three- or more candidate race that ensures a victory or a split of the votes, so if candidates were able to change ideological positions at will we would simply expect that the candidate who had the good fortune to have taken the right position (relative to the other candidates) would win. If, in addition, we imagine that candidates can look at where the other candidates stand and change their own positions, chaos would ensue. Those who develop spatial theories of voting have noted the problems of such outcomes for democracy—there is no way to ensure that candidates who actually represent the views of a majority of voters are elected.[12]

This was one of the main concerns of some of the scholars who evaluated the consequences of early primaries (see, e.g., Meyer 1902, 277). Preprimary conventions had the effect of reducing the number of candidates running, if not to two then at least to a somewhat winnowed field. The Utah primary, as was noted in Chapter 2, ensures that no more than two candidates compete in the nomination.

Runoff elections in Southern states and the "top two" blanket primary in California also winnow the field in order to ensure that somewhat more representative candidates win. Evidence on whether plurality winners are actually a problem has always been mixed (Merriam and Overacker 1928, 211; Lamis 1984a), but spatial theories at least indicate that the potential always exists in primaries, and anecdotal accounts of presidential nomination campaigns abound in explanations of why the parties have at times nominated candidates who were not particularly representative of the party (e.g., Popkin 2012).

All of this presumes, of course, that candidates have the freedom to adopt whatever positions they want. This is a debatable assumption. Literature on presidential primaries has argued that by the time someone runs for president, the candidate is constrained by his or her past record. When John Kerry ran for the Democratic presidential nomination in 2004, he had a history of votes and positions taken as a senator from Massachusetts, so he would possibly not have been credible had he argued that he was actually very conservative. On the other hand, less well known candidates, or candidates without a lengthy history of position taking, may have more flexibility—such arguments have been made about Barack Obama's 2008 campaign (Popkin 2012), Mitt Romney's 2012 campaign, and about why senators and representatives, who must adopt positions on nearly everything during their time in office, are often at a disadvantage in races against governors, who often do not have established positions on many national issues (Pika, Maltese, and Thomas 2002, 39–41). There is evidence, however, that presidential candidates do have some flexibility in changing their campaigns after they win the nomination—Democrats can run to the left in the primaries and to the center in the general election, or vice versa for Republicans.[13] This has been said to be partially a function of moderating their positions and partly a function of talking about different things—talking about guns, abortion, or other issues that partisans may care about in the primary but then addressing the economy, foreign affairs, or so-called "valence issues" such as competence and leadership in the general election.[14]

In the case of congressional campaigns, candidate flexibility is likewise dependent in part on the individual candidate's record. A House member running for the Senate, or a state legislator running for the House, may have limited ideological flexibility while a successful businessperson may be able to adopt positions aimed at winning the election. The difference again, however, between congressional primaries and presidential primaries is in their visibility. The risk of being dubbed a "flip flopper" if one is a presidential candidate may be much higher than the risk for a congressional primary candidate. Congressional candidates, on the other hand, begin their campaigns with a base of supporters who know them, so the cost of alienating one's core supporters by changing positions may well be higher than the risk involved in sticking to one's positions and trying to boost turnout among those who agree with the candidate on policy or steering the conversation away from unpopular policy positions.[15]

Another consequence of the low visibility of congressional primaries, however, is the limited role that ideology may play. Research on municipal elections, for instance, has noted that voters have limited enough knowledge about many candidates that cues such as a candidate's ethnicity (even if only known through the candidate's last name on the ballot), race, or gender may be a better predictor of voting than ideology. Herrnson and Gimpel (1995) argue that population diversity is a stronger predictor of competitive primaries than any other factor—a diverse district might well ensure that, for instance, candidates of different races or with very different geographic bases of support appear on the same primary ballot. A congressional district whose population is split between two different medium-sized cities may see perennial competition between candidates from these cities, and in such instances geography will matter more than ideology. If one city is somewhat larger than the other, perhaps that city's candidates will always win. One can use the same sort of logic we used for ideology to make sense of this situation. To take one illustrative example, roughly half of the Massachusetts population resides in the Boston area, giving Boston candidates a healthy advantage in statewide races. In the 2006 governor and lieutenant governor primaries, however, three candidates ran for each office—two from Boston and one from west of Boston. In both races, the candidate from west of Boston won. These races were not determined solely by geography, but competition between different regions of the state arguably played a greater role than did ideology.

As Hirano and Snyder (2011) contend, these sorts of nonideological competitions may in part explain the persistence of candidates' support from the primary to the general election. If we can observe that a candidate did well in a particular precinct in the primary, then went on to do better in that precinct in the general election than one might expect based on partisanship or on his or her party's past performance, this may mean that the candidate campaigned extensively there and the voters remembered him or her when the general election arrived. Alternately, it may be that the candidate has an Italian surname and this is an Italian neighborhood. There is an advantage in a multi-candidate race of standing out, of representing an important bloc of voters in word or in appearance, if only to allow a candidate to add to the limited amount of information voters have when they go to the polls. This sort of "standing out" can take a variety of forms; as Branton (2009) has shown, it can advantage women or minority candidates, but as many accounts of Southern primaries have argued, such competition can also lead to demagoguery and efforts to establish one's self through incendiary rhetoric (Key 1949; Yates 1972; Kousser 1974; Lublin 2004).

Many of these general concepts about candidate strategy will reappear in subsequent chapters as we distinguish between open seat primaries, challenger primaries, and incumbent primaries. There is much more to candidate strategy than we have discussed here—I have said little, for instance, about the financing of election campaigns or the actual organizational decisions that go into campaigning. The general factors I have outlined above, however are all matters that primary candidates must take into account, even if the import of these factors varies according to the type of race in which the candidates are running.

What We Know about Congressional Primaries, and What We Only Infer

There are several rather well defined areas of research related to congressional primaries, but there is still much that we do not know. In Chapter 2, we explored twelve different questions that were raised at the time the direct primary was introduced. Since that time, there has been extensive research on the consequences of different primary types (in terms of the number of candidates and the types of candidates who win), on trends in voter turnout, on the dynamics of runoff elections, on the divisiveness of primaries, and on the effects of primary competition on incumbent legislators. Despite these findings, however, there have been few comprehensive treatments of congressional primaries and many of our ideas about primaries are in fact inferences drawn from other types of elections or from theoretical literature.

Comparing American Primaries with Other Nations' Candidate Selection Processes

American primaries have been a source of fascination for European political scientists because they represent a type of candidate selection in which, as Hazan and Rahat (2010, 53) put matters, the criteria for candidacy are highly inclusive (that is, there are few restrictions on who can run in a primary) and the selectorate (or the people who choose the nominee, in the U.S. case, the primary voters) is also highly inclusive. Although no other democracy has a system as inclusive as the American system on both grounds, the existence of less inclusive candidacy rules and selectorates enables us to see what might happen were changes made in either of these two areas. That is, it is well documented that when the selectorate is less inclusive, there is less probability of candidates without a strong commitment to the party being chosen; make primaries less open and the comparative literature tells us party loyalty ought to increase and ideological outliers should be less common. Increase the requirements for candidacy (in the U.S. case, increase the number of signatures required to get on the ballot or institute a preprimary convention) and the number of candidates will be reduced, ensuring that primary competition will be less likely to result in unrepresentative candidates. We can see patterns when we look at other countries, even if the contextual variables in U.S. primaries and the subtlety of the differences between primary types and rules across the states makes research in the U.S. difficult.

Comparing Congressional and Presidential Primaries

Many apparent truths, as well as many canards, about competition in primaries are drawn from observations of presidential primaries over the past four decades. Although the best scholars of presidential primaries have been careful to note that the small number of primary elections held thus far limits the lessons we can take from them, there are many principles established in the literature on presidential primaries that can easily be used to talk about primary elections for other offices. The potentially unrepresentative electorate of presidential primaries poses the same problems that are said to affect congressional primaries; the dynamics of multi-candidate competition in presidential primaries are the same as those I have described above for congressional primaries; the advantage incumbents tend to hold in clearing the primary field except in unusual cases holds for presidential primaries as well as for congressional ones; and the phenomenon of ideological movement by candidates has been much more thoroughly studied for presidential primary candidates than for congressional primary candidates.

The premier treatments of the presidential primary dynamics, such as Larry Bartels' *Presidential Primaries and the Dynamics of Public Choice* (1988), however, also emphasize the differences between presidential and congressional primaries and the caution one must use in applying the lessons of presidential primaries to other types of primary elections. Bartels' treatment of primaries emphasizes their sequential nature; candidates seek to generate momentum over a series of primary elections, held at different times, in front of different types of electorates, with different election rules, and (as the primary season goes on and less competitive candidates drop out) with different opponents. There are clearly some lessons that can be learned from, for instance, comparing open and closed primary results, but it is important to remember as well that in many instances the "winner" of a presidential primary is not even the candidate who received the most votes. In some instances, candidates strive to exceed expectations, trumpet a strong second-place showing, or skip some states' primaries altogether when their chances do not look good. The lessons about primary strategy one can take from these types of decisions have little to do with one-shot congressional primaries. Perhaps comparisons can be made with two-step primaries such as the runoff or the top two primary, but even here we cannot clearly make claims to have learned anything substantive. Much of the presidential primary literature also focuses on the financing of these elections—the allocation decisions candidates must make, or, in the days before the demise of the presidential primary matching fund system, the state-by-state spending limits. The winnowing that takes place in congressional primaries, when it does happen, is a function of financial problems or candidates' expectations about what will happen, not of voting results.

As a final note on presidential primaries, one must remember that credible presidential candidates are, in all likelihood, better candidates than the average

106 The Strategic Context of Congressional Primaries

congressional primary candidate. This means that presidential primary candidates will make better decisions, will be better known to the public, and will receive more scrutiny from the media and from voters. More voters pay attention to presidential primaries, although one must not overstate the differences. Figure 3.6 compares turnout in presidential and nonpresidential primaries since 1972 (the year the McGovern-Fraser reforms were implemented). While turnout in presidential primaries is not, with the exception of 2008, dramatically higher than in congressional primaries (and in some years is lower), this difference can be explained in part by the fact that in many years the nomination is effectively decided before most states get a chance to vote, and in years with an unopposed incumbent seeking renomination (1984, 1996, and 2004 in the graph) one party's supporters have no reason to vote in any of the presidential primaries other than to select delegates or, in some states, members of the state party committee. In states that matter in presidential primaries, turnout tends to exceed turnout in

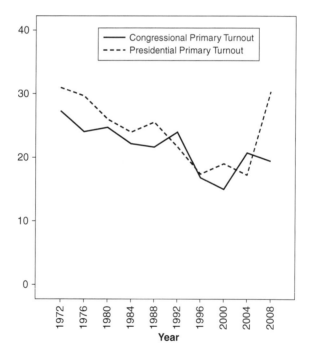

FIGURE 3.6 Presidential and Nonpresidential Primary Turnout Compared, 1972–2008

Source: Author's depiction of data provided by the American University Center for the Study of the American Electorate, www.american.edu/spa/cdem/csae.cfm

Note: Nonpresidential primary data are for gubernatorial and senatorial primaries (using the higher of the two where states have both), taken as a percentage of all eligible voters. Presidential data are for primaries only, not caucuses.

nonpresidential primaries substantially—for instance, turnout in New Hampshire presidential primaries has, according to the CSAE data, exceeded 40 percent of the electorate in years where both parties have contested primaries. Given these factors, it seems evident that American voters at least are more aware of presidential primary competition than they are of the nature of congressional primary competition in their own states or districts.

Findings in the literature on presidential primaries should, then, be taken with a grain of salt—the intuitions behind them are in many instances sensible and in cases where we cannot actually gather hard data on congressional primaries, they make an adequate substitute.

Comparing House and Senate Primaries

One might make similar arguments about Senate and House primaries. The reader may have noticed that much of the information provided in this chapter applies specifically to either House or Senate primaries, but not both. In particular, the turnout data used to generate the various graphs in this chapter and used in many studies of the effects of primary laws come from Senate races. It is difficult to assess whether the sorts of differences listed above regarding presidential and congressional primaries also pertain to comparisons between Senate and House primaries. Senate general election races tend, on average, to be more competitive and more expensive (per capita) than House races, and senators are more powerful and better known than House members. This could indicate that some of the same matters, in terms of candidate quality and candidate visibility, are relevant. On the other hand, presidential and congressional primaries are in many states held on different dates, so in order for voters to decide to vote in both primaries they need to make two separate trips to the polls. Senate and House primaries fall on the same day and are listed on the same ballot, so voters who have chosen to vote in a primary for the Senate or for governor have already made the decision to show up and merely have to take the extra step of moving further down the ballot to vote in the House primary. This is not to say that some voters will not "roll off," leaving the oval for House primary candidates blank, but the difference may well not be as large as differences between presidential and nonpresidential primary turnout can be. In the upcoming three chapters we will explore some other differences between House and Senate primaries, using the palette of strategic terms and ideas that we have presented in this chapter.

Open Seats, Challengers, and Incumbents

The most important distinction one can draw about primaries, however, is the distinction between open seat candidates, challengers, and incumbents. This is a conventional distinction in literature on congressional general elections. Because incumbency is such an important determinant of general election outcomes, and because congressional incumbents begin their campaigns from a very different place and with different resources than nonincumbents, it is important to separate these campaign types and avoid, where possible, generalities about congressional candidates. It is far easier to run for Congress than it is to seek nomination to office in many other democratic nations, and in some congressional districts it is not very difficult to get the nomination of a major party. It is, however, very difficult to win congressional elections or even to make campaigns competitive.

In the next three chapters we will consider three types of primaries separately—open seat primaries, challenger primaries (that is, primaries whose victor is expected to face the incumbent in the general election), and primaries in which an incumbent is running. These distinctions still leave a substantial amount of variation—some open seats will be competitive in the general election while others will almost certainly be won by one party; some victors in challenger primaries have a real chance to defeat the incumbent in the general election while others will almost certainly lose. We will explore these variations in the subsequent chapters as well. The distinction between open seat candidates, challengers, and incumbents is also, in my estimation, a distinction that can be used to explain competition in House primaries just as well as in Senate primaries. It is not the only way to distinguish between elections, and in a few cases (such as incumbent-versus-incumbent primaries brought on by redistricting, or in lopsidedly partisan districts) it is not at all illuminating. After we have explored these three primary types we will spend a chapter looking at unusual types of primaries where these distinctions are not very useful.

The data that we can bring to bear on these different types of primaries also differ. In the case of incumbent primaries, we have a variety of information on the incumbent that can explain primary competition—information such as the incumbent's performance in past elections, his or her voting record in Congress, how much money he or she has raised in the past, and so on. Because incumbent primaries are relatively uncommon it is also possible to gather and synthesize more qualitative information on them. Information on the incumbent remains somewhat useful in looking at open seat or challenger races—we can, for instance, use the incumbent's prior vote share or congressional voting record to assess the chance that nominees in challenger or open seat primaries will win the general election. It is more difficult, however, to come up with information on non-incumbent candidates themselves, apart from their fundraising or vote share, that we can use to make statements about them. It is harder to identify liberals and conservatives, for instance, among nonincumbents than it is among incumbents.

The core of this book, then, is an effort to describe the dynamics of three very different types of primaries—primaries in which the value of the nomination varies substantially and, in consequence, where the goals of voters, parties, and candidates also vary. Candidate selection has been referred to in other democratic nations as a "secret garden"—that is, it is hidden from view and almost entirely subject to the whims of often unaccountable and unknown party leaders.[16] In some instances American primaries may seem this way as well. Despite their low visibility and the obscurity of many primary candidates (and many primaries), Americans have the good fortune to have the ability to gather information and make more sense of our candidate selection process than one can in other nations. We shall begin to do so in the next chapter.

Notes

1. I use data from the CSAE through the 2010 elections. At the time this book went to press, CSAE had not released data for the 2012 election.
2. The CSAE website (www.american.edu/spa/cdem/csae.cfm) provides further documentation on method. States where there was neither a senatorial nor a gubernatorial primary are excluded from each year's calculations.
3. I do not provide explicit state-level comparisons of primary and general election turnout here; the various CSAE election year reports do provide some of this information and discuss the lack of correlation. One can, however, find rough support for the Jewell and Olson conclusions on the relationship between primary and general election turnout simply by comparing the figures using CSAE data with the general election results shown in Figure 3.5 (presented later in this chapter).
4. For a review of literature on this subject see Blais 2006.
5. This is a pattern that has been found in research on party activists and convention delegates; see Heaney et al. 2012.
6. Norrander's study was of Democratic and Republican presidential primary voters in 1980; she cautions that some of the findings may reflect the nature of support for the individual candidates running in that election, but she also argues that primary turnout will always be influenced in part by who the candidates are (Norrander 1986). Other studies that consider different elections (Keeter and Zukin 1983, Geer 1986, Norrander 1991) have found similar results.
7. Overreports of voting are common in all political surveys, a phenomenon generally attributed to respondents' desire to present their actions in socially acceptable ways; for discussion and a review of literature on the subject see Burden 2000.
8. See Achen and Bartels (2006) for a review of arguments for and against the use of ideological scales.
9. These figures are for the primary only. Because of California's top two primary, Sherman and Berman would face each other again in the general election. These numbers are from the candidates' preprimary reports. The discrepancy between money raised and money spent exists because both candidates had balances left over from prior elections.
10. Dominguez (2005, 9–10) also notes an alternative hypothesis—party elites may merely be seeking to curry favor with likely winners, and therefore may converge on the strongest candidates not in an effort to forestall competition but to ingratiate themselves with the likely winner. Although this hypothesis is difficult to disprove, Dominguez concludes that, because convergence often appears even in races where there is no candidate that is clearly the strongest, this alternative hypothesis is unlikely to be true.

11 For other studies of divisiveness, see Johnson and Gibson 1974; Born 1981; Kenney and Rice 1984; Kenney 1988; Miller, Jewell, and Sigelman 1988; Berry and Canon 1993.
12 A formal explanation of the dynamics of multi-candidate elections can be found in Enelow and Hinich 1984, 36–103; Hinich and Munger 1994, 76–79.
13 For explanations of this logic and an evaluation of whether it actually happens, see Page 1978 on presidential elections, Burden 2001 on congressional elections.
14 For an application of the distinction between ideological and valence issues to congressional elections see Stone and Simas 2010.
15 There are many formal models describing position change between a primary and a general election; see, for instance, Oak 2006, Adams and Merrill 2008, Agranov 2011.
16 This phrase purportedly was coined by British journalist Anthony Howard; see Hazan and Rahat 2010, 7; Cross and Blais 2012, 3.

4
OPEN SEAT PRIMARIES

The former Massachusetts congressman Barney Frank was first elected to the House of Representatives in 1980, winning a four-way Democratic primary to succeed the retiring Representative Robert Drinan. During thirty-two years in Congress, Frank was rarely seriously challenged; he ran seven times unopposed, and in all but his first and last reelection bids he won at least 65 percent of the vote. Given Frank's success in office, it was no surprise that when he announced his retirement from Congress in November of 2011 there was a long list of Democrats lining up to compete in the primary to replace him. Many Republicans, however, also expressed interest in running in the Republican primary for the nomination to contest for his seat as well. Frank's district had been redrawn for 2012 to make it slightly less Democratic; this change may have precipitated his retirement. In addition, Frank's opponent in 2010, Sean Bielat, had attracted the attention of Tea Party activists from around the country. Bielat had forced Frank to campaign more vigorously than he had in years, holding him to only 54 percent of the vote. While Bielat surely benefited from the anti-incumbent and anti-Obama mood of that year's election, he had shown that a Republican could run well in Frank's district. Bielat's lack of a political background likely inspired some more seasoned Republicans to look at running in the open seat primary for the Massachusetts Fourth District.

While the names of many prospective candidates were floated by the Boston media, the Fourth District primaries turned out not to be an exciting event. Bielat, who had moved away from the district following his 2010 loss, quickly reestablished residency there and restarted his campaign. Middlesex County Assistant District Attorney Joseph P. Kennedy III, grandson of former attorney general, senator, and presidential candidate Robert F. Kennedy and son of former

Congressman Joseph P. Kennedy II, announced his candidacy in February 2012. Although Kennedy's actual political experience would not have made him the obvious frontrunner in the race, his family history and his political connections ultimately persuaded other serious Democratic and Republican candidates that the race was not winnable. Kennedy won 90 percent of the Democratic primary vote against two minor candidates, and Bielat won the Republican nomination easily, with 70 percent of the vote. Kennedy went on to comfortably defeat Bielat in the general election.

The Massachusetts Fourth District primary races effectively ended long before voters had a chance to cast their votes. This is frequently the case—in fact, as we saw in Chapter 3, this may well be what parties want from primaries—but it is certainly not always the case. The nearby congressional district based in the Cape Cod area had seen contentious primaries on both the Democratic and Republican sides when the seat became open in 2010. Both the Democratic and Republican party primaries were duels between two strong candidates, both of whom had substantial political experience and a regional base of support within the district. Candidates in both of these races jousted over who would be the most electable candidate in the general election and whose record most foretold a successful congressional career. The Republican open seat primary in Western New Hampshire featured five candidates, all of whom enthusiastically sought support from Tea Party activists; the district's former representative, Charles Bass, ultimately prevailed, but at the cost, according to some observers, of presenting himself as a much more conservative candidate than his record in Congress warranted.[1] And two open seat primary races in 2010, in Republican primaries in Arizona and Indiana, yielded more than ten candidates. The winner in the Arizona race, Ben Quayle (son of the former vice president) received 21 percent of the vote.[2] In both of these races, the retiring incumbents had announced their retirements very abruptly and had done little to give order to their party's primary field.

The crucial questions in open seat primaries, then, have to do with the structure of competition. How many candidates (or at least, serious candidates) run, and how is the number of (serious) candidates influenced by the nature of the district, the nature of party competition, and the laws governing primaries? There is substantial variation among open seats—some districts are sufficiently partisan that it is clear which party will win the general election, while others are hotly contested. Open seats have traditionally been regarded by both major parties as worthy of their attention; the incumbency advantage in congressional elections is sufficiently high that open seats tend to be more competitive than incumbent-held seats. Whether this competitiveness yield wide-open races like the Arizona race, relatively structured ones like the Cape Cod race, or races that largely resolve themselves before the people actually vote, as in the race to succeed Barney Frank, has to do as much with the idiosyncrasies of individual candidates as it does with larger structural features. Much of the competition arguably takes place before potential candidates enter the race—some of these individuals might be dissuaded by party elites from running, while others try to gauge their chance against other potential candidates and make their decisions based on guesswork. Much of the competition in open seat races, then, is difficult to measure because it does not actually involve active campaigning. Yet, as I shall seek to demonstrate in this chapter, it is possible to make broader statements about what influences open seat primary competition and what has changed in open seat primary races over the past four decades. Open seat primaries are shaped by the expected competitiveness of the general election, but the approaches taken by the two major parties differ. The longer candidates have had to wait for a seat to open up, the more competitive the Democratic primary will be. Independent of this, however, Democratic primaries have become somewhat less competitive over the past four decades while Republican primaries have become more competitive.

The Significance of Open Congressional Seats

Open seat races tend to take place infrequently, but when they do happen they tend to attract a larger number of candidates than other types of primaries. This makes them convenient to study, given that there is more likely to be competition in open seat primaries than in the other types of primaries considered here. To a greater extent than in other types of primaries, we can observe the actual competition rather than making assumptions about why competition does or does not occur. It can, however, be difficult to describe the motivations of these candidates beyond the obvious fact that they are seeking to win. As we shall discuss later in this chapter, some political scientists have sought to measure the level of party support for primary candidates, but it is hard to categorize open seat candidates neatly.

When over 90 percent of incumbents routinely win reelection, with percentages that average well over 60 percent of the general election vote, it is natural that open seat races would receive substantial attention from political parties and from aspiring office seekers. Open seats are, as political scientists Ronald Keith Gaddie and Charles Bullock (2000) describe them, "where the action is"—over two-thirds of the members of Congress have gotten there by winning open seat races, the majority of switches in party control of congressional seats happen in open seat races, and open seat races tend to feature more evenly matched contests, in terms of vote share and in terms of the cost of campaigning, than do incumbent-challenger races. Open seat races also tend to more accurately reflect the partisan composition of their districts—there have been many examples over the past decades of Democratic incumbents who easily won reelection in districts that voted Republican for other offices, and vice versa. Open seat races provide a barometer of where voters actually stand on matters of policy.

Research on political ambition makes it clear why this is the case. Just as it is easier for parties to gain seats in open seat races than through defeating the other party's incumbents, so it is easier for aspiring members of Congress to wait for incumbents of their own party to retire or seek higher office than to run against him or her in a primary. All districts, then, have a queue of people who are interested in running for Congress but are waiting for the right opportunity. Anne Layzell and L. Marvin Overby wrote in 1994 about the queue of Democrats waiting to run for the congressional seat held by Representative Sidney Yates. Yates was first elected in 1948, and by the 1990s it was clear that he would retire sometime soon. Although this was a relatively safe Democratic district, encompassing left-leaning sections of Chicago and its northern suburbs, aspiring Republicans also tended to assume that they would fare better in an open seat race than in a matchup against the well-known Yates. Just having many potential candidates does not guarantee that there will be competition—after all, when Yates did finally retire in 1998, Democrat Jan Schakowsky decisively won the primary, with over 70 percent of the vote. It does, however, suggest that candidates who wait to run in open seat races will be strategic politicians—that for each open seat there will be at least a few potential candidates with prior political experience and with the connections within their party to mount a well-financed run for office.

What does all of this say about open seat primaries? The Massachusetts example suggests that we should not automatically assume that all open seat races will draw a crowd. It also suggests that we cannot rely too heavily on standard measures of candidate quality. Neither Kennedy nor Bielat had held prior political office, for instance, but both had demonstrated their political skills in other ways. It does, however, indicate that we should explore variations in the number and types of candidates who run across time and across types of districts. Ultimately, it is easier to discuss factors conducive to candidate emergence than it is to talk about characteristics of the candidates themselves. Many of the same characteristics that render open seat general elections competitive make open seat primaries competitive as well. Open seat nominations are, on average, more valuable than are nominations to take on an incumbent, and thus we should expect these primaries to look different from other types of primaries.

Why Open Seats Appear

In chapters on other types of primaries, we shall explore why primaries happen. This is not a particularly interesting question in regards to open seat primaries. The number of open seat primaries varies by year, for obvious reasons. In any given year some incumbents will retire or will seek to run for higher office. Patterns in incumbent retirements have been linked by political scientists to a small number of factors, which can be conveniently divided into factors specific to individual legislators and factors specific to the legislators' environment—that is, to the year in question.

Much of the calculus about retiring has to do with individual legislators' assessments of their own careers. Seats become open because legislators choose to move out or up. In a series of articles written in the early 1980s, John Hibbing (1982a, b, c) took note of the increase in open seats in the House of Representatives during the 1970s. This increase, according to his data analysis and his interviews with retired legislators, was driven by changes in the role of seniority in determining advancement in House committees, by members' frustrations over the difficulty of getting things done in Congress, and by changes in legislators' salaries and pensions. Hibbing discusses at length the role that ambition plays in decisions to retire; if a legislator has a realistic chance of becoming a committee or subcommittee chairman in the near future, he or she may well remain in Congress. If not, retirement becomes more attractive. Analyses of the abnormally high number of retirements in 1992 also noted changes in FEC laws governing whether members could keep unspent campaign funds as a reason for retirement (Groseclose and Krehbiel 1994; Hall and Van Houweling 1995). These reasons, as well as more obvious reasons for retirement such as age, are specific to individual legislators or to specific years. Apart from introducing dummy variables for individual elections, however, one cannot really use this information to make broader statements about changes in the number of open seats over time.

Furthermore, open seats do not arise solely because members of Congress choose to retire from politics. In the House, seats may open up because members have chosen to run for the Senate. These decisions are also influenced to a degree by idiosyncratic events—a senator retires and a representative who has been eying the seat for years decides it is his time, or a representative who has become frustrated with life in the House may leap at the opportunity to run for higher office even if victory appears unlikely (Brace 1984, 1985). The decision to seek higher office may be a natural occurrence among politicians, but such decisions are not necessarily rooted in realistic appraisals of legislators' chances of winning. During the 1990s, one piece of conventional wisdom among some House members was that after twelve or so years, a legislator ought to have a good understanding of his future prospects—if he or she was on a path to power in the House, this merited sticking around; if not, a legislator might opt either to retire or to seek higher office.[3] Such anecdotes, while not at all provable, might explain why some House members choose to run for the Senate even in races where their chances of victory are low.

Open seats may also occur, however, for reasons having to do with the broader political environment. Redistricting years, for instance, tend to feature a larger-than-average number of open seats; this is so in part simply because new seats are created, but also because incumbents may choose to retire rather than run in redrawn districts (see, e.g., Hall and Van Houweling 1995). Changes in party support may also matter; incumbents who expect they may lose may opt to retire rather than seek reelection, resulting in above-average numbers of open seats in years expected to be good years for one party (Highton 2011). Ambitious incumbents may also see favorable years for their party as good years to seek higher office; an ambitious House member may pursue a Senate seat if he or she senses favorable national trends. Anecdotal evidence also suggests that control of the House influences retirements—incumbents contemplating retirement may opt to stay for another term if they feel their party has a chance to win control of the House or lose control of the House. Democratic leaders, for instance, allegedly put pressure on members contemplating retirement in 2010 to stay and run again because they felt incumbents would be able to hold seats that might be possible Republican pickups if they were open. Conversely, it was reported that some Democratic incumbents chose to retire in 1996 and 1998 because they did not enjoy life in the minority and did not believe their party would regain the majority soon. While at least some open seats appear because of idiosyncratic decisions on the incumbent's part, more of them appear in some years than in others.

Most of what has been said so far concerns House primaries. Just as in other chapters, we shall explore differences between House and Senate open seat primary campaigns with the expectation that the greater competition in Senate races should encourage more serious candidates. One side effect of this is that we should expect the differences between open seat primary candidates and challenger party primary candidates to be less stark—if incumbents stand a greater chance of being unseated, the benefits that come from waiting until a Senate seat opens up are lower. Senate seats are also more competitive in terms of partisanship. In the following discussion we shall distinguish between open House seats that are safe for one party and those that are competitive; as election results over the past few decades have shown, there are very few states that have been reliably safe for one party in Senate races.

Why Open Seat Primaries Happen

Just as one can hypothesize about patterns in the occurrence of open seats, so perhaps one might predict competition for open seat primary nominations. Some nominations are more worth having than others, and thus one might expect variation in competition according to the reason a seat became open. In the case of the Barney Frank district, for instance, the threat of a 2012 general election challenge from Frank's 2010 opponent may have prompted his retirement—if so, one could argue, there should not be very much competition on the Republican side, and competition would occur on the Democratic side only if Democrats were not particularly frightened of Frank's opponent's strength in the general election. To systematize this a bit, the district's underlying partisanship, as reflected in its presidential voting patterns, might encourage or discourage competition.

Political parties and primary election laws can also determine whether competition occurs. States with a high threshold for appearing on the ballot may discourage competition, and strong political parties might also dissuade some primary candidates from running. The number of years the retiring incumbent has served might mean there were a larger number of ambitious politicians who had patiently waited their turn. Political trends, as well, might encourage or discourage candidates—Democrats might, for instance, have opted not to seek open seat nominations in 2010 out of concern that they would not be able to win the general election. In many instances these are difficult considerations to measure, and one could easily argue for plausible alternative scenarios. Yet these ideas suggest that one might be able to say something about the nature of primary competition—the number of candidates who emerge, the number of strong candidates who emerge, or the degree of fractionalization of the primary field—using these sorts of variables. We shall explore some of these in the next section.

Competition in Open Seat House Primaries, 1970–2012

Through the period from 1970 to 2012 there was an average of approximately forty-two open seats per election (excluding seats that became open because the incumbent was defeated in a primary and seats where the incumbent retired after winning the primary but before the general election). This percentage was slightly higher in the 1970s and 1990s than in the 1980s or 2000s, perhaps in part because of the institutional changes (in committee advancement and legislators' salaries) discussed above. It is also substantially higher in redistricting years than in other years—a function both of retirements and of the drawing of new districts in states gaining population. There is, however, no obvious correlation between seat swings and the number of open seats. In the high-turnover years of 1974 and 1994 there was an above-average number of open seats, but in 2006 there were only thirty-one open seats—the smallest number since 1990—and the number of open seats in 2008 and 2010 was also below average. The years with the fewest open seats were 1984 and 1988, years where there was relatively little turnover in the House.

Contested and Uncontested Primaries

Virtually all open seat races had a Democratic and Republican nominee, although in many instances there was no primary. There are generally three reasons why a primary might not be held—in some districts the nominee was chosen by convention, in some instances no candidate filed to run at all, and in many instances only one candidate ran and the party subsequently held no primary. State laws regarding one-candidate primaries differ; in some states even unopposed candidates must run in a primary, competing against write-ins or simply appearing on the ballot even without opposition, while other states do not list unopposed candidates on the ballot or list them but do not give the voter the option to vote for or against those candidates. It is difficult to draw conclusions about overall open

118 Open Seat Primaries

seat primary competition in convention states or when one considers districts that did not hold primaries, so the easiest thing to do is to assume that there is no salient difference between districts where one candidate ran and districts where there was no primary. This effectively creates a category for primaries where there was no competition.

Figure 4.1 shows the number of contested and uncontested open seat primaries by year. On average, about three-fourths of all primaries during this time period had some competition. If we first consider the number of primaries, the results are as we might expect given the discussion above of congressional retirements. The number of primaries is somewhat higher in the 1960s and 1990s than in the other two decades, and the number peaks in redistricting years. Beyond this the numbers are relatively consistent across the time period, apart from a possible increase in contestation over the past three election cycles. Party differences (not shown in the graph) are relatively minimal but they do correspond to other research on the parties. The Democratic Party, perhaps because of its majority status or its domination in the South, had far more contested primaries than did the Republican Party during the 1970s—84 percent of Democratic primaries were contested, as compared to only 63 percent of Republican primaries. This distance narrowed during

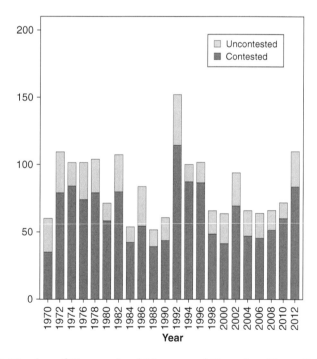

FIGURE 4.1 Number of Contested and Uncontested Open Seat House Primaries by Year and Party, 1970–2012

the 1990s and disappeared entirely by 1994; from that time on there tend to be more contested Republican primaries. In 1994, a high-water mark for the Republicans, every Republican open seat primary was contested, as compared to only 81 percent of Democratic primaries. One could seek to correlate this time trend with more short-term events, but there are no evident surges within the parties in the propensity of having a contested primary in surge years other than 2010. There is, in addition, no relationship between the party of the seat's retiring incumbent and contestation for the seat. There are no differences in the likelihood of having a contested primary related to whether a primary is open or closed although, unsurprisingly, states where the parties have a role, either formal or informal, in the nominating process have a lower percentage of contested primaries.

Simply looking at whether a primary was contested can tell us where to look at primary election results, but we are ultimately unable to draw conclusions about the nature of primary competition from comparing contested and uncontested primaries. On the one hand, an uncontested primary may be the result of the fact that few people believe the nomination is worth having; on the other, one strong candidate may effectively clear the field. We thus need to look more closely at other measures of competitiveness. There are several choices: first, we can look at the number of candidates who run, with an eye toward whether more candidates tend to run in particular types of open seat primaries; second, we might look at the level of competition, as reflected in the vote percentages of the first-place, second-place, or even third-place candidates; and finally, we can develop indices of the level of fractionalization in the primary field. The main idea in all of these measurements is that the number of candidates who run can tell us something about the nature of competition for the seat, but these numbers are often idiosyncratic—an open seat candidate who wins 90 percent of the primary vote against one or more opponents is, for all practical purposes, the same as an unopposed candidate. Let us consider each of these methods in turn.

The Number of Candidates

The number of candidates running in a primary may be first and foremost a function of a state's ballot access laws. States such as Maryland and Indiana, for instance, have low thresholds for qualifying to appear on the ballot and thus often have primaries in which some (or many) candidates are largely unknown to voters and finish with 1 or 2 percent of the vote, or less. It is difficult to determine when a candidate becomes worthy of study, but it seems unlikely that we could learn anything about primaries apart from ballot access differences by including all candidates who run. The analysis here sets a threshold of 5 percent of the primary vote for consideration—high enough to exclude candidates who are clearly simply running because they can, but low enough that we can see meaningful variation that can be attributed to factors other than ballot access.

There are many factors that may determine the number of candidates seeking a seat. First, there are political considerations. Is the nomination worth winning? That is, will the nominee stand a chance of winning the seat in the general election? There are several indicators that might ensure that candidates find the nomination worth having. These include the party of the retiring incumbent (that is, if the retiring incumbent is of one's own party, one would see evidence that his or her party could win the seat), the incumbent's previous vote share, and past presidential voting in the district. Second, there are structural and contextual factors. Does the party hold a nominating convention or endorse candidates? Has the party traditionally been organizationally strong in the state? For these variables I used an index constructed by Maisel, Gibson, and Ivry (1998) that measures the level of party involvement (on a 1–3 scale) and a 1–5 scale of party strength drawn from the work of David Mayhew (1986). In this category I also include dummy variables for whether the district is a majority minority district, whether the district has been redrawn, and whether the district is in the South. Third, and finally, following arguments such as the Layzell and Overby piece described above, I consider the number of terms the departing incumbent has served; this gives us some indication of whether there is a queue of potential candidates that have been waiting for the seat to open up.

Table 4.1 shows results of Poisson regressions for the number of candidates seeking the open seat nomination in each party.[4] In this equation I have categorized all uncontested primaries as having one candidate and I have counted each candidate who received over 5 percent of the vote. While acknowledging that there are many idiosyncrasies and much that is unpredictable about the number of candidates who run in any given primary, this table nonetheless shows some interesting patterns overall and within each party. Perhaps because incumbents frequently outperform the rest of their party ticket in their districts, neither the party of the retiring incumbent nor the retiring incumbent's most recent vote share are strong predictors of how many candidates will run to succeed him or her.[5] Presidential voting, however, has a strong influence on the number of candidates who run; here, I use the most recent presidential election for midterm years and the current election for presidential years, with the assumption that candidates can sense the prevailing political winds when they enter the race. The higher the Democratic presidential vote percentage, the more Democratic primary candidates emerge and the fewer Republican primary candidates emerge. In other words, the greater the prospects of the primary nominee winning the general election, the more candidates there are in the primary.

The other particularly important variable in structuring primary competition for both parties is the role of the party. The greater the party's role in the primary, the fewer candidates there are. This, again, is unsurprising, given that a formal party role in the primary is usually tantamount to limiting the number of candidates to one or two. What is noteworthy, however, is that few of the less

TABLE 4.1 Determinants of the Number of House Open Seat Primary Candidates, 1970–2012 (Poisson)

	Democratic Primaries	Republican Primaries
Political Context		
Party of Retiring Incumbent (0 = Dem, 1 = Rep)	−.11	−.08
Democratic Vote in Last Election	.01	−.01**
Democratic Presidential Vote in Last or Current Election	.02**	−.01**
Electoral Structure		
New Seat	.36	.59
Majority-Minority District	−.07	−.21
Redistricting Year	−.02	−.12
Party Role in Nomination (1–3)	−.21**	−.27**
Closed Primary	.05	.10*
Blanket Primary	−.41	−.09
Level of Party Organization (1–5)	−.02	−.02
South	−.03	−.06
Years Retiring Incumbent Served	.01**	.00
Decade	−.01**	.01**
Constant	22.4**	−17.0**
Log-Likelihood	−897.5	−938.8
N	932	933

* $p < .05$ ** $p < .01$

formal means by which primaries might be said to be structured have any effect at all. Closed primaries tend to produce fewer candidates than open primaries for Republicans, but not for Democrats.[6] The level of party strength has no effect on primary competition, although one might expect organizationally strong parties to have the ability to deliver the nomination for their preferred candidate—and presumably to deter others from entering the primary. New seats, redrawn seats, and majority-minority seats—seats which one might expect to attract a higher number of candidates—are no different from other open seats.

It is worth noting that if there is a queue of people waiting for seats to open up, the queue is more evident in Democratic primaries than in Republican primaries. This may be consistent with the fact that during this time period there were more Democratic incumbents and that Democratic incumbents over this time period served for longer—something consistent with the contention in the congressional retirement literature that legislators are more likely to retire when they expect to be in the minority for a long time or when they do not have satisfying prospects for advancement on committees. This is also consistent with the contention in popular literature on politics at this time that Democrats had a larger "farm team" for much of the 1970s and 1980s (Ehrenhalt 1992). The decade coefficient also points to a shift in the power of the parties—over the 1970 to 2012 period, the number of candidates in Democratic primaries declined, holding all else constant, and the number of Republican candidates increased.

Vote Percentages

Looking at the number of candidates who run in primaries is instructive, then, but it does not necessarily tell us anything about the nature of the competition between the candidates who do run. Nor does looking at the vote percentage of the winning candidates, given the large number of uncontested primaries and our lack of ability to clearly identify the reasons why individual primaries were not contested. We can, however, look at the vote percentages of the unsuccessful candidates. A high vote percentage for the second candidate (that is, approaching 50 percent) is indicative of a closely fought two-candidate race. Lower percentages indicate either that the primary vote was split among a larger number of candidates or that the winner received most of the votes; we cannot tell which of these two is the case simply by looking at the second-place candidate's votes. Third-place vote finishers are a little easier to interpret—because a third-place candidate cannot, by definition, receive more than 33 percent of the vote and because in order for the third-place candidate to approach doing this well the first-place and second-place candidates must both do poorly, a strong third-place candidate clearly indicates a more divided field.

The equations shown in Table 4.2 control for the winning candidate's vote percentage (shown in the top line of the table). Note here that the winning candidate's vote percentage is a weaker predictor of the second-place candidate's vote than of the third-place candidate's, given the competing explanations for second-place finishers' successes. The table shows significant predictors of second-place and third-place Democratic primary candidates (on the left) and second-place and third-place Republican primary candidates (on the right). Comparisons within the parties can tell us something about when primary votes are spread out among a number of candidates, when front-runners tend to win overwhelmingly, and when competition is balanced between two strong candidates.

First, let us consider the two types of Democratic candidate types. Third-place candidates tend to do best when they are running to replace a retiring Republican; this may indicate that these are districts where there is no party consensus about who the candidate should be. As we saw in Table 4.1, the number of Democratic candidates increases with Democratic presidential vote; this means that the vote is more spread out among candidates—that is, more competitive Democratic candidates run in better Democratic districts, yielding a higher vote share for the third-place candidate and a lower vote share for the second-place finisher. Although redistricting is not a strong predictor of a large number of candidates,

TABLE 4.2 Predictors of the Second-Place and Third-Place House Primary Candidates' Vote Percentages, 1970–2012 (OLS)

	Democratic Primaries		Republican Primaries	
	Second-Place Candidate	Third-Place Candidate	Second-Place Candidate	Third-Place Candidate
Winning Candidates Vote Pct.	−.22**	−.36**	−.12**	−.32**
Political Context				
Party of Retiring Incumbent (0 = Dem, 1 = Rep)	1.8	4.7*	−.02	2.5
Democratic Vote in Last Election	.05	.07	.04	.06
Democratic Presidential Vote in Last or Current Election	−.19**	.12*	−.07	.04
Electoral Structure				
New Seat	−4.8	−5.0	−8.8	6.9
Majority-Minority District	2.3	−5.7**	3.9	−11.0
Redistricting Year	−3.0*	2.6*	−1.9	−1.6
Party Role in Nomination (1–3)	2.6**	−1.2	1.1	−1.9
Closed Primary	−.07	−1.1	−.64	1.5
Blanket Primary	3.7	−1.7	.86	−4.3
Level of Party Organization (1−5)	−.64*	−.02	.09	−.18
South	−.99	2.1	−2.6*	.18
Years Retiring Incumbent Served	−.02	.04	.12*	.13
Decade	−.12**	.01	−.15*	.10*
Constant	293.3*	42.8*	330.2**	−181.3
N	645	343	588	198
F	5.9	9.7	2.5	2.3
R^2	.21	.44	.11	.33

* $p < .05$ ** $p < .01$

it does appear to produce more fractured fields, as third-place candidates perform better and second-place candidates correspondingly perform worse. Structural factors, such as the level of party organization or the party's role in nominations, tend to shape the fortunes of second-place candidates by winnowing the field or aiding the party's preferred candidate, but they have no effect on the fortunes of third-place candidates. Finally, the time trend variable indicates that second-place candidates have fared less well over time; the lack of a corresponding increase for third-place candidates suggests that the trend has been for primaries to become less competitive, for victorious candidates to do better.

It is also instructive to compare these results with the coefficients for Republican candidates. What is most important here is the overall lack of structure to Republican primary competition—neither the political nor the structural variables give us much insight into when the vote is split in Republican primaries. There is a time trend, as there is with Democrats, but this trend is also more difficult to interpret given that third-place Republican candidates perform slightly better over the same time frame.

One could undoubtedly perform analyses of the fortunes of fourth-place candidates, fifth-place candidates, and so on, but the analysis would become far more complicated. The important distinction between two-candidate and three-candidate primaries is that many of the formal devices of party control over primaries result in a winnowing of the field to no more than two competitive candidates. A race with two strong candidates also is still consistent with having a nominee preferred by most within the party, while stronger showings by third-place candidates and other less successful candidates indicate a lack of agreement within the party about the nominee. Given the extensive literature on the relationship between primary competition and general election competition and the numerous anecdotes about parties' efforts to reduce conflict in the primaries, competition between more than two candidates would seem indicative of weaker party roles in primaries.

Fractionalization

There are more precise social scientific tools for addressing the sorts of issues I have raised in the above discussion. Many studies of multi-candidate electoral competition, both in the United States and in other nations, make use of measures of fractionalization—that is, estimates of how divided the votes are among multiple candidates. The intuition behind these indices is that an election where one candidate gets most of the votes is not very fractionalized, even if there are multiple candidates; races with two candidates with similar vote share are split; and those with more than two equally competitive candidates are even more divided. One formula that has been used in several studies (Herrnson and Gimpel 1995, Hogan 2003, Brogan and Mendilow 2012) employs a fractionalization index that is operationalized as

$$F = 1 - \sum [(C_1)^2 + (C_2)^2 + (C_3)^2 + (C_4)^2 \ldots]$$

Where F is the fractionalization index, C_1 is the percentage of the total vote received by the first candidate, C_2 is the percentage of the total vote received by the second candidate, and so on.[7] This yields an index where a one-candidate race has a fractionalization index of zero and a race where two candidates split the vote would have a fractionalization index of 0.5 (or $1 - (0.5^2 + 0.5^2)$). The larger the number of similarly competitive candidates, the closer the index is to 1. For instance, a race with ten candidates who received 10 percent of the vote each would have an index of $1 - [(.1)^2 \times 10]$, or 0.9. A regression using the effects on the fractionalization index thus does not yield coefficients that are as intuitive as in some of the other equations here, but we are addressing the same subject as above in a much more precise manner.

Table 4.3 shows the relationship of the same variables we have discussed above to the fractionalization index. For ease of interpretation, I have multiplied the fractionalization index by 100, so a race without competition would have a score of zero and a highly competitive race such as the one in the above hypothetical example would have a score approaching 100. This table essentially returns us to the scenario presented in Table 4.1—the most important determinants of open seat competition are the potential for the nominee to win the general election (as predicted by the Democratic presidential vote percentage in the district, and the role of the party in informally or formally reducing competition. There are

TABLE 4.3 Determinants of Fractionalization in House Primaries, 1970–2012 (OLS)

	Democratic Primaries	Republican Primaries
Political Context		
Party of Retiring Incumbent (0 = Dem, 1 = Rep)	−7.7	−6.7
Democratic Vote in Last Election	−.10	−.35*
Democratic Presidential Vote in Last or Current Election	.55**	−.32*
Electoral Structure		
New Seat	17.6	37.0
Majority-Minority District	−3.8	−11.2*
Redistricting Year	−.87	−2.7
Party Role in Nomination (1–3)	−7.4**	−12.5**
Closed Primary	−.48	2.6
Blanket Primary	−14.2	10.8
Level of Party Organization (1–5)	−.36	−.17
South	2.2	−4.6
Years Retiring Incumbent Served	.09	.02
Decade	−.02	.49**
Constant	85.2	−872.1**
N	932	933

*p < .05 **p < .01
Democratic primaries: F = 4.67, p < .01, R^2 = .11
Republican primaries: F = 8.4, p < .01, R^2 = .20

slight differences between the parties, in that Republican primary competition is more influenced by the previous congressional vote in the district as well as the presidential vote, and there is as well a trend toward greater fractionalization over time in Republican primaries but not Democratic ones.

It thus appears that changes in the structure of competition in open seat primaries roughly parallel larger changes in American elections. Whatever measure one uses, it appears that open seat primaries have become somewhat more competitive, and that most of this change is due to the increasing strength of the Republican Party. The competition in open seat primaries is, however, largely driven by factors particular to the seat that has opened up—the greater the prospect of general election success, the greater the competition in the primary.

Evaluating Open Seat Primaries

At this point it may make sense to provide some examples of competition in open seat races. These accounts are nowhere near as plentiful as one might expect; few biographical or autobiographical works on members of Congress spend very much time discussing primary elections. Those that do, however, often show the unique nature of each open seat race. Linda Fowler and Robert McClure (1989) wrote an entire book on the 1984 open seat race to replace ten-term Representative Barber Conable in the congressional district based in Rochester, New York. For Fowler and McClure, what was most salient about this race was the uncertainty on the part of the candidates about how the race should be run. There were, the authors contend, at least ten potential candidates for every declared candidate, so as the primary field was taking shape none of the contestants could be sure how many opponents they would have, what issues would be most consequential in the race, or what their geographic or ideological base would be. This is, Fowler and McClure claim, in part a function of the fact that congressional district boundaries do not coincide with other types of boundaries—no one truly "knows" a congressional district save its incumbent representative. Some open seat candidates may represent parts of the district, but they are unlikely to know about the full district's "political personality." In races such as the New York race, long tenures for the incumbent also mean that there will be no one else who remembers what it is like to run in the district. House incumbents tend to win reelection comfortably even in districts that are not clearly safe for their party, so there may well be no clues about the true nature of the district. This could also explain why congressional staff members often appear as open seat candidates. For instance, former House Minority Leader Robert Michel represented a district based in Peoria, Illinois, for thirty-eight years; although this was a district with many Republican elected officials, and thus that one might expect to produce heated competition, Michel's Chief of Staff Ray LaHood defeated two veteran state legislators to win the three-candidate primary to replace Michel. Although there are, to my knowledge, no studies of the success rates of congressional staff members as candidates, the Fowler and McClure study shows why they can succeed—and why running in open seat primaries can be so difficult for so many other politicians.

Open seat strategy often, however, boils down to competition between different types of factions. Sometimes these factions are geographic—for instance, state legislators who represent part, but not all, of the district might vie for the nomination, pitting the interests of one geographic area against another. In other cases, competition can take place between liberals and conservatives, or between other types of ideological groupings. In many races both types of competition take place. In the open seat race in the Madison, Wisconsin, district in 1998, three local elected officials vied for the Democratic nomination. The winner, current Senator Tammy Baldwin, stood out, according to observers, as the only woman in the race; Baldwin was able to run not only as the representative of a geographic segment of the district but as a candidate who stood apart from the other two candidates by virtue of her gender and her attention to women's issues in the campaign (Canon 2001). Similarly, in the 1986 race to succeed Speaker of the House Tip O'Neill, the two strongest candidates in an eleven-candidate field represented strikingly different factions within the Democratic Party—the eventual winner, Joseph P. Kennedy II (father of the Kennedy discussed at the beginning of this chapter), won support from working class Democrats while his strongest opponent did well among university professors and better educated voters (Sullivan and Kenney 1987, 17–23).

The race to succeed O'Neill also shows how the incumbent can influence open seat competition. To some extent, O'Neill sought to play a role in this race—he announced his retirement early enough that all interested candidates had a chance to carefully test the waters before the race was underway, and he endorsed a candidate in the race (although he did not do so until shortly before the primary election date). The incumbent also can shape what voters expect from their representatives. Clearly O'Neill is an unusual example by virtue of his long tenure and his stature within Congress, and clearly races with a Kennedy running also take on a different complexion from the average House race. O'Neill had been in office for thirty-four years, so the candidates who aspired to succeed him had the same sort of uncertainty that those in the Rochester race trying to replace Conable had. Yet, as Sullivan and Kenney (1987, 11) point out, that district had been held for over half a century by prominent Democrats, so the voters expected that their representative would wield power in the House, would take an active interest in foreign affairs, and would play a large role in Massachusetts Democratic politics. Other districts may not expect quite so much of their representatives, but their interests in open seat races may well be shaped by their experience with the district's prior representative.

While incumbents may wield some power in primaries to replace them, however, there is little evidence that they can shape the general election. In many instances, incumbents are leaving office to run for higher office, so they may either be reluctant to endorse a successor or too busy to do so. Although there are common patterns across open seat primaries, what the above examples suggest most clearly is that open seat primaries at least have the potential to yield unpredictable consequences. Congressional elections that feature an incumbent, and the primaries on either side that lead up to incumbent-challenger races, are generally characterized in books on congressional elections as being, to some degree, referenda either on the incumbent's attentiveness to the district or on the incumbent's party. In either instance, there is a clear message. Open seat general elections may send a message about the parties, but it is not clear how one might interpret messages sent in open seat primaries.

This is so for three reasons. First, as discussed in Chapter 3, researchers have reached no conclusions about the relationship between primary election success and general election success. Some have contended that divisive primaries harm candidates' chances in the general election while others have argued that, particularly in open seat primaries, competitive primaries may actually help the victorious candidates in the general election by raising their visibility and testing their campaigning skills. There are certainly many anecdotes about the relationship between primary competition and general election outcomes. However, none of the various indices I use above—the number of candidates running, the vote shares of the losing candidates, or the fractionalization index—are correlated with general election vote share when one controls for district presidential voting. If open seat primaries are the scene of the greatest primary competition, then, this competition does not say anything about general election competition.

Second, open seat primary competition poses the possibility that many open seat nominees will be chosen by minorities of the primary electorate. That is, the more candidates there are, the greater the chance that the nominee will have received less than 50 percent of the vote, and may not have been the preferred choice of most voters. Literature on multicandidate elections in other nations has called attention to alternative voting schemes, such as cumulative voting, instant runoff voting, or the single transferable vote, which enable voters to rank order choices or designate a second choice candidate. The single round, plurality rule nature of most American primaries poses the possibility that candidates who would lose under any of these scenarios can win the election. In a crowded field, a candidate who either is not a strong general election candidate or is not representative of the district can win the nomination. In the data discussed here, 34.5 percent of open seat primaries yield nominees who win with less than a majority of the vote. The mean vote percentage for winners of contested primaries, in fact, is 52 percent over the full time period, and in six of the twenty-two election years covered here the mean is below 50 percent. If we couple this with the finding by Bullock and Johnson (1992) that approximately 70 percent of the winners of runoff elections—in House primaries in states where they do happen—were the frontrunners in the primary, we still have a group of perhaps 10 percent of primaries (30 percent of 34.5 percent) in which the winner would not have been chosen by the voters had there been a runoff. This may strike some readers as a large number—but, of course, it is not clear what this number means for representation or policymaking.

Third, open seat races sometimes, but not always, feature conflicts between well-defined factions. In 2010, for instance, many Republican open seat primaries pitted Tea Party-endorsed candidates against more conventional Republicans. In traditionally strong Democratic areas, conflicts between different wings of the party—as evidenced in the 1986 Massachusetts race discussed a few paragraphs ago—often play out. As noted in Chapter 3, recent work by, among others, Casey Dominguez (2005) and Hans Hassell (2012) has used network analyses to identify some of these factions. It is difficult, however, to identify enduring factions—the Tea Party, after all, has only been with us for two election cycles, and many issue-based factions can be specific to individual districts or specific election years. Certainly ideological conflict has been a mainstay of primary elections for some time, but thus far it has been difficult to use tools such as network analysis to place open seat candidates on any sort of ideological scale. Factional conflict also depends on who enters the race—the "liberal" candidate in a race may not have intended to run as a liberal when the race began, but if the other candidates who enter the race are to her right, then that is what she becomes.

Open seat primaries clearly confront us with a mixture of strategic and sincere choices on the part of candidates. That is, given the likelihood that a majority of open seat races feature candidates with realistic expectations of winning office, should they win the primary, many of those who run will adopt election-oriented strategies, and many of the supporters of open seat candidates will also adopt election-oriented strategies. This stands in contrast to other types of primary elections, in which the presence of incumbents—either in the primary or in the general election that will await the primary victor—often serves as a discouragement to election-seeking candidates and an encouragement to candidates with other reasons for running. Measuring these choices in open seat races is difficult. There is, however, one common coin to open seat races that we can draw upon—money. Although the large number of open seat candidates and the often serendipitous nature of open seat competition make it impossible to engage in the sorts of detailed considerations of who gives that I provide in the chapter on incumbent primaries, we can at a minimum explore the role of money overall in open seat races, as well as the role of party, interest group, and individual contributions in primary campaigns.

The Financing of Open Seat Primary Campaigns

Money clearly matters in primary elections of all sorts. It is, however, difficult to isolate the role of money in winning primaries, in part because fundraising during the primary depends so heavily on the candidates' expectations of winning the general election and the nature of competition in the primary. As in other chapters of this book, I consider here Federal Election Commission (FEC) data for contributions during the primary election only. For candidates defeated in the primary, this amount comprises their full FEC report for the year they ran for office; for successful candidates, I use the final preprimary report. I consider only candidates who had a contested primary, given that candidates who did not have primary opposition can be expected to raise money during the primary for the purpose of campaigning against their prospective general election opponent.

Figure 4.2 compares total primary cycle receipts for winning and losing open seat primary candidates in 2012. The average victorious candidate in 2012 raised just under $600,000. Roughly 75 percent of this money came in the form of individual contributions. The average successful open seat primary candidate received approximately $64,000 in PAC contributions and a negligible amount of party contributions. Party contributions, when they do arrive, tend to be received once the outcome of the race is evident. Many PACs, as well, prefer to support winners, although some PACs do contribute early in the primary period. Unsuccessful open seat primary candidates, in contrast, raised slightly less money from all sources; those who filed at all reported approximately $350,000, but of course

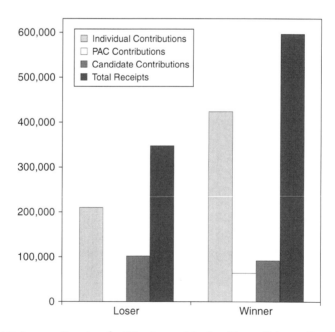

FIGURE 4.2 Average Receipts for Winning and Losing House Primary Candidates by Source, 2012

many primary candidates raise less than the $5,000 required to file with the FEC so the average for all primary losers is certainly far lower. Both winners and losers spent an average of $100,000 of their own money.

Other years show a similar distribution of funding sources to 2012; the lone exception of note is that the percentage of money spent by the candidates themselves was much higher in 2012 than it was in previous years. One striking feature of open seat primaries, however, is that apart from the fact that winners raise, on average, more than losers, it is hard to say that money plays a decisive role in open seat primaries. We can go about looking at this in two ways. First, we can try to measure the effect of money on vote share. This is complicated, of course, by the fact that not all primaries have the same number of candidates, and multi-candidate races will produce winners with lower vote shares than will two-candidate races. One could either control for the number of candidates or run separate regressions for two-candidate races, three-candidate races, and so forth. Whichever way one does it, though, the results are clear—when we insert a variable for the expected competitiveness of the general election, overall fundraising matters. When we break fundraising down further, however, the most important financial variable that matters is that for PAC contributions. If, as research on PACs has contended, most PACs are access-oriented—that is, they give to candidates who are likely to win—we are merely showing, then, that the candidates who are likely to win raise more money, not that having more money makes one likely to win. The competitiveness variable—scaled from 1 to 3 for a safe seat of the opposite party, a competitive seat, and a safe seat for the candidate's party—is intended to capture the fact that (as we shall see in Figure 4.3) there will be more overall fundraising for primaries that are more likely to determine the general election victor.[8] This variable also captures the possibility that candidates who expect to be competitive in their general election bids, should they win the primary, may be more likely to face strong opponents in the primary.

In Table 4.4 I have controlled for the number of candidates; the number is, as expected, highly significant. This is not an ideal way to measure the effect of finances in primaries with different numbers of candidates, but it is arguably the most straightforward way to provide evidence on the role of money for all primary candidates. I ran separate regressions for races with different numbers of candidates; while in all but the two-, three-, and four-candidate races the number of cases was rather small, the substantive effects of money were similar—in a regression using total receipts, money is significant, but if we break the receipts variable down into its component parts, only PAC contributions are significant. Were receipts particularly consequential in primary elections, we would expect individual contributions to be a significant determinant of vote share. Overall, they are weakly significant for Republicans, but not significant at all for Democrats.

132 Open Seat Primaries

TABLE 4.4 Determinants of Vote Share, Democratic and Republican House Open Seat Primary Candidates, 2000–2012 (OLS)

	Democrats	Republicans	All
Number of Candidates	−4.48★★	−3.06★★	−3.71★★
Year	.490	−.146	.169
Individual Contributions	.001	.005★	.003★
PAC Contributions	.100★★	.033★★	.062★★
Party Contributions	−.014	.100★★	.081
Candidate Contributions	.001	−.017	−.003
Competitiveness of Seat	−4.74★★	.811	−2.54★★
Constant	−925★	340	−285
N	401	406	807
F	34.1	25.1	49.7
R^2	.395	.292	.309

★ p < .05 ★★ p <.01

Note: Data drawn from FEC preprimary reports (for winners) and candidate summary file (for losers). All contribution variables are in thousands of dollars.

If money was a major predictor of success, we would expect that individual contributions would be significant in these regressions. Individual contributions, after all, comprise the majority of the money raised by primary candidates. We would not necessarily expect candidates' contributions to their own campaigns to be significant; while there are isolated cases of successful self-funded candidates, the conclusion of the literature on self-financing has been that candidates who spend large amounts of their own money do not tend to perform better than candidates who raise equivalent amounts from other sources (Steen 2006). We would expect PAC and party contributions to be significant, which indeed they are (though party contributions are only significant for Republicans). The likelihood of winning the seat in the general election decreases vote share for Democrats but not for Republicans.

Another sign that money is not particularly consequential in open seat primaries is the fact that, as Figure 4.3 shows, there is no clear evidence that successful open seat primary candidates raise more money today than they did a decade ago. For both parties, there are unusually prolific fundraisers who pull the party averages upwards in some of the years shown here. In 2008, for instance, Colorado Democrat Jared Polis raised $6.5 million for his successful open seat primary campaign, single-handedly increasing the Democratic average. In 2006, Republican Vern Buchanan raised $3.8 million in a successful open seat campaign in Florida. Only seven other open seat candidates raised over $2 million during the 2000 through 2010 period (although eight candidates did so in 2012). For the twelve years shown here, however, it appears evident that there has not been an increase in fundraising for open seat primaries. This is noteworthy because the overall cost of campaigns has increased during this time.

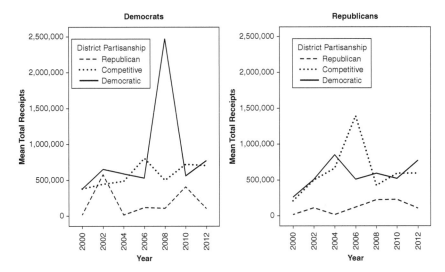

FIGURE 4.3 Receipts for Victorious Democratic and Republican House Open Seat Primary Candidates, 2000–2012

Figure 4.3 shows the average total receipts by party and by the expected competitiveness of the general election; the three lines show averages for seats that had been held comfortably by a Republican (that is, the Republican received over 60 percent of the vote in the last election), held comfortably by a Democrat, or had been competitive in the last election (that is, the incumbent received less than 60 percent of the vote). There is essentially no difference between candidates for safe open seats and candidates for competitive open seats. In the case of uncompetitive open seats—that is, seats where one's party received less than 40 percent of the vote in the last election and thus can expect difficulty in winning in the general election—fundraising has actually increased over the past decade for the disadvantaged party. This might indicate that past competitiveness is not a reliable barometer of current competitiveness, or it might indicate that parties are taking fewer seats for granted than in the past.

What can one conclude from this discussion of finances? It is clear that money is consequential for the outcomes of congressional general elections. It is also, however, easier to measure the results of fundraising because general elections are, with rare exceptions, two-candidate races. Even there, however, it is frequently necessary to look at the effects of fundraising for incumbent and nonincumbent candidates separately. None of the candidates we have considered in this chapter are incumbents, but there are, nonetheless, surely large differences in political experience or visibility that campaign fundraising itself does not reflect. Some candidates will be well-known within the district by dint of their previous tenure as a state representative, or they will have the campaign organization of the retiring incumbent working on their behalf. The fact that money appears not to be decisive in contested races may well show that other types of advantages, which do not translate into money during the primary election, are often important during primaries. Candidates who run for more valuable nominations—nominations that are more likely to lead to election to Congress—raise more money than other types of primary candidates, but in such races money tends not to be decisive in and of itself.

The claim here that PAC contributions frequently go to likely winners should not, however, be taken to mean that interest groups do not play a role in some open seat primaries. Groups that do choose to become involved in primaries have often reported that large independent expenditures can be far more important in the context of a multi-candidate primary than in a heated general election. The Club for Growth, a conservative organization that has supported many high profile challenges to incumbent legislators, has spent heavily on behalf of many open seat Republican primary candidates, including several current representatives. Liberal advocacy groups have adopted similar strategies. Of the eight open seat primary candidates who raised more than $400,000 from PACs, however, none were clearly reliant on ideological groups for support. Whatever support interest groups can provide to primary candidates, in other words, cannot clearly be boiled down to money.

Senate Open Seat Primaries

House open seat primaries are, as noted above, driven somewhat by the whims of incumbents. Because of the smaller number of Senate elections held every year, however, the occurrence of Senate open seat primaries is more idiosyncratic than is the case for House open seat primaries. That is, we can anticipate that House seats will open up in redistricting years, and we might expect that if one party anticipates a particularly poor showing one year, more incumbents of that party will retire. There are, of course, no redistricting years in the Senate; there is anecdotal evidence that partisan trends or anti-incumbent sentiment may influence the number of open Senate seats. Figure 4.4 shows some of this variation, depicting the number of Senate open seat primaries since 1970. The 2010 election, for instance featured the highest number of open seats in the past forty years. Other high turnover years, such as 1974, 1992, and 1994 show no marked increase in open seats. The 1980 election, which was one of the most volatile Senate general elections, had a relatively small number of open seats.

In Figure 4.4, as was the case for the equivalent House figure, I show the number of open seat primaries, not the number of open seats, and I show contested and uncontested primaries. With rare exceptions, each open seat yields two primaries. There were a total of 294 Senate open seat primaries between 1970 and 2012,

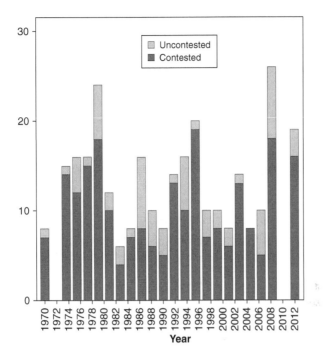

FIGURE 4.4 Number of Contested and Uncontested Open Seat Senate Primaries by Year, 1970–2012

an average of just under fourteen (or seven open seats) per year. Two hundred and twenty nine of these, or 77 percent, were contested. Nearly two thirds (63.9 percent, to be precise) of the contested primaries yielded a majority winner and 22 percent yielded a winner who received over three-fourths of the primary vote. These numbers are slightly higher than is the case in the House (though the difference falls just short of statistical significance). Although the average number of candidates tends actually to be higher than in House open seat primaries, Senate primaries are not, by this measure, more competitive than House primaries. The fractionalization measure in Senate open seats is actually slightly lower in Senate races than in House races (.40 in the Senate and .44 in the House), indicating that by this measure Senate primaries are less competitive than House primaries.

It is difficult to predict the number of candidates, the vote percentages for losing candidates, or the level of fractionalization in Senate open seat primaries using contextual variables. In the House, competition was determined in part by the district's past voting trends—the greater the prospects of victory, the more primary competition there is. Similarly, the number of years the departing incumbent had served was also hypothesized to increase competition, though it was only significant in the case of Democrats. In Senate open seat primaries, regressions using any of the measures of competition show only that the level of party control over the nomination process influences competition. This is somewhat tautological—as we saw in Chapter 1 for the Massachusetts 2012 Senate race, this is equivalent to saying that if parties have the tools to limit competition, there will be less competition.

How should one read the unpredictability of Senate competition? One could merely say that the smaller number of open Senate seats makes it difficult to predict the type of competition that will happen. There may, however, be more to the story. Senate nominations are clearly more valuable than House nominations because of the prestige of the chamber. It may be that every state has a few high-profile Senate aspirants of each party, while not all House districts have a strong candidate of each party waiting in the wings. There are also numerous examples of senators who represent states that would never support their party in presidential elections; in recent years, for instances, Democrats have won Senate elections in red states such as North and South Dakota, Montana, and Nebraska, while Republicans have won Senate seats in Democratic states such as Massachusetts and Maine. Gronke (2000, 112–20) has shown that voters know more about their senators than their representatives and are less likely to use partisanship as their sole cue in voting. Jacobson (2013, 233–45) has shown that although partisanship is becoming a stronger predictor of Senate general election voting than it was in previous years, fluctuations in party success in Senate elections appear to be somewhat independent of fluctuations in House elections. Parties, in other words, are less likely to write off Senate seats than they are to write off House seats, and as a consequence the state's voting history may not influence competition.

There is, however, one measure of competition that does seem shaped, to some degree, by the value of the Senate seat. Table 4.5 shows the average campaign receipts for the winning candidates in contested Senate primaries over the period from 2000 to 2012, according to the state's past or current Democratic presidential vote. Safe Democratic states are those where the Democratic presidential nominee received over 55 percent of the vote; competitive states are those where the Democrat received 45 to 55 percent of the vote, and safe Republican states are those where the Democrat received less than 45 percent of the presidential vote.[9] As the table makes clear, the role of money differs for the two parties. Among Democrats, the best funded candidates tend to be the winners of the safer Democratic seats—the candidates most likely to parlay their primary success into general election victory. The less Democratic the state is, the less well-funded is the Democratic nominee. The reverse is true for Republicans—the most expensive Republican campaigns tend to take place in the least hospitable states for Republicans. To be fair, the high number for Republicans in safe Democratic states is driven largely by one candidate—2010 and 2012 Connecticut Senate candidate Linda McMahon, who spent over $20 million in winning the 2010 primary and another $14 million to win in 2012. Absent McMahon, safe Democratic states

TABLE 4.5 Average Receipts for Victorious Senate Open Seat Primary Candidates, by Partisanship of State, 2000–2012

	Safe Democratic	Competitive	Safe Republican	All Races
Democrats				
Total Receipts	7,189,444	4,359,427	1,730,499	4,005,213
Individual Contributions	4,166,741	3,617,516	1,325,237	2,769,113
Party Contributions	11,634	16,255	7,358	11,063
PAC Contributions	399,090	515,687	209,04	348,740
Candidate Contributions	0	1,878	2,194	1,488
N	9	9	14	32
Republicans				
Total Receipts	5,761,190	4,408,436	4,087,211	4,625,061
Individual Contributions	2,564,974	3,575,536	2,561,024	2,876,074
Party Contributions	3,450	6,461	5,838	5,405
PAC Contributions	201,887	609,373	419,568	421,306
Candidate Contributions	1,661,178	20,429	67,708	731,640
N	11	13	18	42

Note: All data from FEC preprimary reports.

would feature approximately the same amount of Republican primary spending as competitive states. McMahon aside, however, the Republicans still look different from the Democrats. Republican races in safe Republican states do not attract the spending that characterizes Democratic primaries in Democratic states.[10]

The party differences are arguably a reflection of competition—although we cannot get at this using data on vote share, it appears from the campaign finance data that many safe Republican states are not competitive largely because candidates need less money during the primary. In several instances, Republican primary winners entered the race late but became frontrunners once they entered the race, and went on to raise ample money for the general election. For instance, 2010 Indiana Senate nominee Dan Coats entered the race only two months before the date of the primary election and raised only $445,000 during the primary. Coats was regarded as the likely nominee from the moment he entered the race, and he went on to raise nearly $5 million during the full election cycle. Coats is not that unusual among Republican nominees. It is somewhat of an irony, given the parties' reputations, that there is less money in Republican primaries than in Democratic ones.

There are a few other interesting features of Table 4.5. Republican winners rely far more on their own money than do Democrats. This is in part, again, a consequence of Ms. McMahon, but even apart from her campaign there is far more self-financing on the Republican side. Parties, as one might expect, play a minimal role in primaries. And PACs are active in a wide range of different types of Senate primaries. This is perhaps a reflection of my claims above that the small number of open Senate seats and the greater competition in Senate races makes for greater interest on the part of partisans; PACs contribute more to the winners of Senate races in competitive states, but they provide similar amounts among all types.

Senate primaries are, however, few enough in number that ultimately a small number of campaigns can have a great effect not only on aggregate data on Senate races, but on the way in which the media and the public think about Senate primaries. Consider, for instance, the claim presented in Chapter 1 that the Republican Party lost as many as five winnable Senate races in 2010 and 2012 by nominating unpopular or ideologically extreme candidates. Only one of these five, the Delaware primary in which political neophyte Christine O'Donnell narrowly defeated veteran Representative Mike Castle, was an open seat primary. Candidate spending clearly was not the decisive factor here—Castle raised and spent over $3.5 million while O'Donnell raised only $264,000. Yes, there was outside spending in this race as well, but even then, there is no way to extrapolate stories about how Senate primaries work. This primary received attention precisely because it was unusual. Less remarkable but more common, however, are races such as the 2012 Wisconsin open seat Republican primary; here, a veteran politician (former Governor Tommy Thompson) faced off against a wealthy businessman, the State Assembly Speaker, and a former member of the House of Representatives and Republican Senate nominee. There were clear ideological disagreements in this primary, and each of the four candidates had a base of support, but in the end Thompson, the candidate with the greatest statewide voter recognition, the greater appeal to PACs and out-of-state donors, and arguably the best chance of winning the general election, triumphed. Similarly, races such as the 2010 Ohio Democratic primary race between Lieutenant Governor Lee Fisher and Secretary of State Jennifer Brunner can be quite competitive, but whichever candidate won, the Democrats would have been represented by a candidate who had experience running, and winning, at the statewide level. Again, there is nothing surprising here.

One can draw upon media accounts of recent primaries to justify a wide range of theories about the characteristics of open seat primaries. Has ideology come to play a large role in open seat primaries? Accounts of the Texas Republican primary in 2012, where Lieutenant Governor David Dewhurst secured the support of Governor Rick Perry and many members of the Texas establishment, en route to winning a plurality of the primary vote but losing a subsequent runoff election to former Solicitor General Ted Cruz, suggest that many primaries do tend to feature well-defined ideological factions (Fernandez 2012). Do elite endorsements matter in primaries? Perhaps not, if the Nebraska Republican primary in 2012 is any indication; but it clearly depends which elites one is talking about. In that race, three candidates sought the Republican nomination—Attorney General Jon Bruning, State Treasurer Don Stenberg, and State Senator Deb Fischer. Bruning secured the support of many mainstream Nebraska Republicans, Stenberg received support (and money) from Senator Jim DeMint and the Club for Growth, and Fischer received a late endorsement and a round of prerecorded telephone calls from Sarah Palin. Although she was perhaps the least well-known candidate in the race and lacked the statewide platform of Bruning and Stenberg, Fischer prevailed by a narrow margin in the end (Weisman 2012, Zeleny 2012). Does money matter? The Nebraska race would suggest not, but then again Linda McMahon's 2010 and 2012 primary victories, in which she outspent her more politically experienced primary opponents several times over, mighty indicate that it does. Does electability matter to voters? McMahon's two victories might suggest not, given that pre-primary polls showed her primary opponents running even with their expected Democratic foes in the general election while McMahon was projected to run much further behind (Applebome 2012). Do Republican primaries follow a different logic than Democratic primaries? Well, 2010 and 2012 featured a much larger number of competitive primaries on the Republican side than the Democratic side, but the converse was true in 2002 and 2004. Given the small number of Senate open seat primaries per year, and the even smaller number that feature more than one strong candidate, party differences in Senate primaries seem more likely to be happenstance than to be the sign of some sort of difference in party culture or party factionalism.

There has also been much attention paid by the media to the role of Super PACs in congressional elections. Several of the open seat candidates running in 2012 were aided in their efforts by Super PACs. With almost no exceptions, however, Super PAC support came during the general election, not the primary. Super PACs may become consequential in primary elections—particularly, perhaps, in ideological conflicts such as those that took place in some of the 2012 Republican races—but there is little data out there at the moment to suggest that Super PAC spending was consequential in any of the 2012 primaries.

In the introduction to this section on Senate primaries, I noted that we simply lack the data to make the sorts of statements we can make about House races on the structure of competition. That does not mean that Senate primaries do not follow a similar logic to House races, only that we cannot prove that to be the case. The anecdotes above, however, suggest that journalists and political elites also frequently lack the tools to understand Senate primaries. Senate primaries often occur far from the glare of the national media, and pollsters not affiliated with Senate campaigns generally have little reason to survey voters. In the case of the three campaigns discussed above—the Connecticut, Texas, and Nebraska races—media coverage makes it clear that there was substantial volatility in these races, but that ultimately even veteran politicians had little clue about what was going to happen until just days before the election. In the Nebraska case, for instance, both party committees appeared to have counted out Fischer, the eventual nominee, for much of the campaign, and they had to scramble to find out exactly who she was and what she stood for once she had won the nomination (Weisman 2012). The apparent shifts in dynamics in the Texas and Nebraska races also meant that groups who had championed the candidacies of the eventual winners had a chance, after the race, to claim credit for what had gone on. The Club for Growth, for instance, issued a press release summarizing what it had done in Texas, while Independent Women's Voice, a little-known conservative organization, argued that its phone banking in Nebraska had been a pivotal part of Fischer's win (Heath and Higgins 2012, Keller 2012).

All of this does not suggest that the Senate is immune to the dynamics that affect House primaries. It is plausible that partisanship matters less because the differences in voter partisanship are less pronounced across states than across House districts, and that the parties are less likely to write off Senate seats. These anecdotes also do not suggest that money does not matter in Senate races, only that it is easy to find races where it is not decisive. What these anecdotes do suggest, however, is that unusual primary outcomes in the Senate will be scrutinized by politicians and the media for clues about what they mean; surprising Senate primary results will be held to mean something about the general election to come, while surprising House races will receive less attention.

Conclusions

In this chapter, I have tried to pull back the curtain to show the logic of open seat primaries. This effort has met with mixed results. In our exploration of patterns in House primaries in the number of candidates who run, the vote shares of winning and losing candidates, the level of fractionalization within the primary field, and the financing of winning and losing primary candidacies, a complicated picture has emerged. Political parties are able to limit the number of candidates and the level of competition in open seat primaries. That is, the formal and informal roles parties play in the nomination process can winnow the primary field. Yet other rules regarding who can vote in primaries do not have a measurable effect on open seat primaries. The two parties' open seat primaries have differed in consequential ways, however. The number of candidates and the competitiveness of the races is influenced by past voting in the district; the greater the likelihood of general election victory, the more likely it is that a large, competitive primary field will develop. This effect is stronger for Democrats than for Republicans. Democratic primaries are also more competitive the longer aspiring candidates have had to wait for the seat to open up. There are, in addition, year effects. These effects are largely out of candidates' control—more seats open up in some years than others, due to the idiosyncratic decisions of lawmakers. There is no clear relationship between the political climate in any particular year and the competitiveness of open seat primaries, but there is a trend toward greater competition in Republican primaries and less competition in Democratic primaries. This trend largely accords with changes in the parties' competitiveness across the country, the decline of the Democratic "solid South" and arguments that the Republican "farm team" has grown over the past few decades. We cannot assess whether these patterns hold for Senate primaries as well—there are reasons to expect that many of them do, but there is also a compelling case to be made that Senate races are treated differently by parties and by aspiring candidates because of the Senate's greater prestige and because of the larger and more diverse constituencies that senators represent.

Open seat elections have historically been treated as important opportunities for both parties. We thus have reason to suspect that they receive extra scrutiny from parties and potential candidates, even if the data we have do not allow us to conclusively prove this. In the introduction to this book, however, I discussed the role incumbency plays in congressional elections of all types. Literature on general elections has always treated the incumbency advantage as arguably the most important factor in understanding turnover in Congress. Although open seats, by definition, do not include the incumbent, incumbent members of Congress still loom large in shaping the contours of open seats in several ways. The structure of competition is determined in part by the tenure of the departing incumbent; as we discussed at the beginning of this chapter in regard to the race for Barney Frank's seat, some congressional seats open up only once in several decades, and the queue of aspirants for a seat within an incumbent's party may grow quite long the longer he or she stays in office. This can spill over into multi-candidate competition in the primary, but we have no means of saying when this will or will not be the case. The circumstances of an incumbent's departure also say much about primary competition for his or her seat. Did the incumbent have a preferred successor? Did he or she retire far enough ahead of the primary that anyone who wanted to run had time to develop a campaign? Did his or her departure happen because the district became inhospitable, either through redistricting or gradual change? One of the things that is so frustrating, and yet also so fascinating, about open seat primaries is the difficulty we have in gauging such intangibles.

Notes

1 Bass lost the seat to a Democrat two years later.
2 Quayle also lost his seat in 2012; the state's redistricting plan combined his district with a neighboring Republican's district, and Quayle lost the primary.

3 This was recounted to me by my own employer during my time as a House staffer; that employer chose to retire from Congress shortly after that, having served for six terms.
4 Poisson regression is the appropriate technique here because the dependent variable is a count variable. For those unfamiliar with Poisson regression, the approximate magnitude and significance of the coefficients can be read as if they were OLS variables without an appreciable loss of information in this case.
5 Note that vote shares are on a 0–100 scale here and in the subsequent tables, thus yielding rather large constants.
6 This variable is a dummy variable for pure closed primaries. I ran other regressions using dummy variables for semi-closed and semi-open primaries, but these variables were not significant and their presence does not change the equation noticeably. I omit them here and in other tables in this chapter in order to simplify the presentation of data, as is typical in most similar work on the effects of primary types.
7 The formula was developed by Canon (1978) in an article on primary competition in the South.
8 Here, as in Figure 4.3, I use the party's congressional vote in the previous election, employing a 40 percent threshold in determining competitiveness. Results are substantially the same when I use a scaled measure of vote in the previous election, presidential vote, or other standard measures of competitiveness.
9 Note that this is a different measure than I used above for House races. I use the previous House election vote there but I use presidential voting here. Other measures certainly could be used; the intent here is to break states into different types, so a categorical variable is superior to a continuous one for this purpose. I use presidential voting rather than Senate voting because less time has elapsed between the presidential election and the last senate election, so that is a better estimate of the state's current partisanship. I use a 55 percent cutoff for the purpose of making the three categories similar in size; using the 60 percent threshold I used for House races would place almost all states in the middle category.
10 Careful readers may note that the average total receipts numbers are in many columns somewhat larger than the averages of the different categories of receipts. This is because I have excluded transfers from this table. Many Senate candidates who are sitting House members transfer substantial sums from their House campaign accounts; these transfers are included in the FEC's total receipts categories.

5
CHALLENGER PRIMARIES

It was apparent long before November that the 2010 election would be a good one for Republicans. The natural tendency for the opposition party to pick up seats in Congress when the president is not on the ballot, coupled with the controversy surrounding the Affordable Care Act and the lingering effects of the recession ensured that the Republican Party would have good luck in recruiting strong candidates.

In South Dakota, Democrat Stephanie Herseth Sandlin had held the state's lone House seat since narrowly winning a special election in the summer of 2004. The Herseth family had a long history in South Dakota politics, and Herseth Sandlin had generally presented herself as a fiscally conservative Democrat. She had support from the National Rifle Association, she had voted against the Affordable Care Act, and she took positions similar to those of other North and South Dakota Democrats who had held on to House and Senate seats during the 2000s. Despite the state's Republican leanings at the presidential level, Herseth Sandlin had not faced serious opponents in either her 2006 or 2008 reelection bids. In 2010, however, three strong Republican candidates filed to run against her.[1] The Republican primary pitted two state representatives, Kristi Noem and Blake Curd, against the secretary of state, Chris Nelson. Curd had the advantage of representing Sioux Falls, the state's largest city, while Noem's district, to the west of Sioux Falls, lacked a major urban area. Nelson, however, appeared to be the early favorite, by virtue of the fact that he had won a statewide election. However, Nelson was not able to convert his statewide success into fundraising success, and he wound up raising only $156,000 while Noem and Curd both raised in excess of $400,000. Although there were few policy differences between the three candidates, by most accounts, the primary was devoid of personal attacks.

Each of the three touted his or her ability to defeat Herseth Sandlin. Noem, perhaps the least well-known of the three when the campaign began, touted her business experience and her quick rise in the state House of Representatives. She prevailed with 42 percent of the primary vote, to Nelson's 35 percent and Curd's 23 percent. Given that any of the three would have been a high quality opponent for Herseth Sandlin, the National Republican Campaign Committee had remained neutral during the primary but had made it clear that it was prepared to help the eventual winner. Noem went on to raise $2.3 million, and she narrowly bested Herseth Sandlin in the general election.

Another three-way primary took place in the Massachusetts Third District, for the right to challenge seven-term Democratic incumbent James McGovern. It was plausible that the right candidate could defeat McGovern, but it would be difficult. A Republican had held the district from 1992 to 1996, and Scott Brown had won a majority of votes in the district in his senate campaign. McGovern had, however, run unopposed in four of the past five elections, and he had amassed a sizeable war chest. He had been born and raised in Worcester, the district's major city, and he had devoted much attention to economic development in the city. Republicans at the national level had better prospects in other New England districts than they did in McGovern's district. Nonetheless, five candidates ran in the district's Republican primary.[2] One of these five, Brian Herr, had previously been elected as a selectman in the thirteen thousand person town of Hopkinton, on the district's eastern edge. Herr sought to position himself as a somewhat centrist Republican, and he sought to generate support in the eastern part of the district—where residents are more likely to see themselves as Boston suburbanites than as neighbors of Worcester. Herr raised $86,000 during the primary—far less than any of the South Dakota candidates, but more than three times as much as any of the other four candidates in his own race. None of the other four had prior political experience; they included an attorney, a physicist, a public defender, and a mortgage broker. Yet another candidate explored running in the primary but ultimately chose to run as an independent in the general election. The Republican primary was a spirited affair, with several debates and heated discussion of issues such as the flat tax, the presidential line item veto, whether President Obama is an atheist (and if so, whether that is a problem), and whether U.S.-born children of undocumented immigrants should be granted citizenship. There were substantial policy differences among the candidates; while the candidates did not have the resources to discuss these differences with the average voter, they all seemed to genuinely enjoy arguing with each other. In the end Marty Lamb, an attorney with ties to local Tea Party activists, scored an upset victory, winning 32 percent of the vote to Herr's 25 percent. Each of the other three had between 11 and 16 percent. The primary victory was, however, the high point of Lamb's campaign. After the race, Lamb spoke of how energizing the primary had been, and he expressed hope that the vigorous competition there would aid his general election bid. Although Lamb was the beneficiary of a small radio buy by a Nevada-based Super PAC, the NRCC did not help his campaign and McGovern cruised to a 57 to 39 percent win in November.

Democrat Marcy Kaptur has represented the congressional district based in Toledo, Ohio, since 1982. From 1986 through 2008 she consistently won over two-thirds of the general election vote. Kaptur is even more of a fixture in the House than McGovern, and although she has always had an opponent there have rarely been competitive primaries for the Republican nomination. There was one in 2010, however. Grocery executive Rich Iott faced retired Toledo police chief Jack Smith. Iott ran what one editorial referred to as a "glitzy" campaign, spending nearly $400,000.[3] All but $20,000 of this was his own money. Smith procured the endorsements of a few local newspapers, but was able to raise only $15,000. Neither Iott nor Smith had a long history within the Republican Party, and while party leaders did not discourage these candidates, neither candidate ran with the expectation that he would receive help in the general election. Iott won the primary easily, with 73 percent of the 17,400 votes cast in the primary. Iott was clearly saving his firepower for the general election, however. He went on to spend nearly $2 million—$1.7 million of which was his own money—but still won only 41 percent of the vote. This was the most anyone had received against Kaptur since 1984. Perhaps the most noteworthy aspect of Iott's general election campaign, however, was the release in October of photographs of Iott dressed in a Nazi uniform. The ensuing controversy ended any interest the NRCC might have had in the race.

These campaigns are all examples of the different forms that challenger primaries—that is, primaries whose winner will take on the district or state's incumbent member of Congress in the general election—can take. They are clearly not the only challenger primary types, but they do show the diversity of challenger primaries. The last chapter began with the presumption that open seat primaries will be particularly competitive, largely because open seat general elections are, on average, more competitive than general elections in which an incumbent is running. This chapter begins with the presumption that general elections featuring an incumbent are, on average, not very competitive. This does not necessarily mean that challenger primaries will not be competitive, but it does mean that in most cases the winner of a challenger primary will face an uphill climb in the general election. We can, therefore, expect to see different types of candidates, according to the winnability of the general election. In primaries for the nomination to face a vulnerable incumbent, as in the South Dakota race, we may well see competition between well-funded, experienced politicians who emphasize their political skills and deemphasize issue differences. Such competition may help the winner in the general election, it may draw political elites from outside of the district into the fray, and the candidates in such races may be good enough that there are no "bad" choices for the party.[4] Conversely, in primaries for the nomination to face an incumbent who is not particularly vulnerable, the primary is more likely to feature amateur politicians, such as those in Massachusetts, who are using their candidacies as vehicles to express strongly-held political views or to enhance their own name recognition in the pursuit of some other political office. We might expect competition to be more frequent in races where there is a vulnerable incumbent, but we should not assume out-party primary competition to be the sign of a vulnerable incumbent. Then again, we might expect primaries to be sleepy affairs, featuring perennial candidates or candidates who are unable to run district-wide campaigns due to a lack of resources. In some of these, the outcome may genuinely be in doubt, but in others, such as the Toledo race, the primary is a bump in the road for the better-funded candidate. In all of these races, however, it is the popularity of the incumbent that establishes the value of the nomination itself.

The Incumbency Advantage and Challenger Primaries

In every election since 1970, at least 85 percent of members of the House of Representatives have been reelected; in five of these elections, 98 percent of incumbents were reelected. Furthermore, a substantial majority of incumbents seeking reelection win with well over 60 percent of the vote. In only two election cycles (1974, for Republicans, and 2010, for Democrats) has the average vote share for incumbents of either party been less than 60 percent. In other words, the nomination to run in the general election against an incumbent is often not something worth fighting for. The popularity of the incumbent is the single most important factor in structuring competition in the opposing party's primaries.

Many incumbents therefore face no general election challenger at all. Over the past four decades, an average of fifty-nine incumbents has run unopposed each year. Figure 5.1 shows a breakdown of unopposed incumbents by party for each year. During the 1970s, large numbers of Democrats—more often than not in the South—ran unopposed. Since 1992, however, the numbers within each party have been even. In good years for Democrats, such as 2006, larger numbers of Democrats run unopposed, while in good years for Republicans, such as 2010, larger numbers of Republicans run unopposed. There are in addition many races in which token candidates run against incumbents. It is hard to come up with a solid definition of what a token candidate is, but some accounts of congressional races have discussed "token" candidates who are asked to run as a favor to the party, or file to run simply because they do not want the incumbent to be unopposed. There will also always be a percentage of voters in any congressional district who will vote for the out-party candidate no matter what. That is, there will certainly be some Republican voters who reside in overwhelmingly Democratic districts and who will vote for a Republican challenger even if they know absolutely nothing about him or her and even if that candidate has not actually

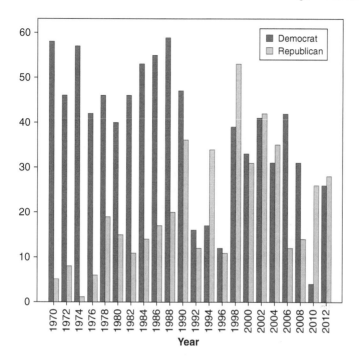

FIGURE 5.1 Number of Uncontested Incumbents by Year and Party, 1970–2012

campaigned. In the elections considered here, an average of fifty-four incumbents per year won reelection with over 75 percent of the vote, and four to five each year won with over 90 percent of the vote. If there are primary elections held to determine the out-party nominee for races such as these, they tend to be low turnout affairs where little money is spent by the candidates.

Most general election campaigns do, however, feature some competition. Although the incumbency advantage is driven in part by congressional districting practices and in part by the willingness of some voters to cross party lines to support a popular incumbent, the fact that even poorly financed general election challengers often get between 30 and 40 percent of the vote may well provide an incentive to some potential candidates and breed some level of primary competition. It all depends on the expectations of the candidates who enter a challenger primary.

Research on congressional campaigns has shown that candidates who seek to challenge a congressional incumbent generally know that the odds are against them. Robin Kolodny's (1998) study of the evolution of the Democratic and Republican congressional campaign committees shows that the party committees actively provide guidance to those who seek to challenge vulnerable incumbents. While the party campaign committees rarely endorse candidates before the primary, they do provide opposition research about the incumbent, recruit candidates to run in districts where they deem the incumbent to be vulnerable, and provide candidates with training on myriad campaign issues. In some races, the party committees also use primary results to determine whether candidates merit general election support (Herrnson 1988); this can provide an incentive to candidates to work hard for a convincing primary win. Party activists can also work to provide support for candidates even without an official endorsement (see Dominguez 2005). Several outside groups also provide training to prospective candidates and seek to encourage candidates to run; the Club for Growth (about which we will hear more in Chapter 6) has sought to recruit conservative candidates and back them in GOP primaries, and groups on the left such as Progressive Majority and Wellstone Action have also sought to train Democratic candidates. The absence of interest from such groups may well signify to a primary candidate that his general election prospects are dim, while attention from such organizations may serve as a sign that these groups will be helpful if and when the nomination is won.

Studies of general election challengers have taken note of the steep odds that face these candidates and have explored whether or not challengers are aware that they are likely to lose.[5] While some studies have focused on the role that self-deception plays in keeping a campaign going—it is hard to motivate yourself to campaign when you are certain you are going to lose—most research has concluded that challengers do not expect to win when they enter the race, and that they are not motivated solely by the prospect of victory. In my own work on this subject (Boatright 2004), I noted that candidates running against comfortable incumbents are actually less likely to adopt centrist views (relative to the district) than are competitive candidates. Primaries in such races, then, tend often to be forums for rallying the party faithful—in an overwhelmingly Democratic district, strongly conservative candidates can inspire their supporters by organizing a campaign around opposition to abortion, gun control, immigration, or other hot-button issues. This will not win them an election, but it can lead to an exciting campaign. If there are more competitive Republican candidates on the ballot—if the district is not competitive but the parties are competitive at the state level, for instance—such a campaign can help turn out voters and help the party. A better-than-expected showing in the primary can also position a candidate well for future campaigns. As we saw in the case of the 2012 open seat race to succeed Barney Frank, for instance, his 2010 opponent emerged as the presumptive 2012 nominee in large part because of his willingness to run aggressively against Frank in 2010.

These studies of general election dynamics show that many—perhaps most—congressional elections feature candidates who are not evenly matched and who plan their campaigns accordingly. This has implications for challenger primaries, yet it is hard to come up with ways to measure challenger primaries. We do have an important piece of information that we did not have in our discussion of open seat primaries—all of those who seek to run in a challenger primary are unhappy with the performance of the incumbent, and the incumbent's record thus influences how many candidates emerge and how successful these candidates are. We can separate out primaries to run against popular and threatened incumbents, but because the candidates who enter these primaries are often political neophytes, we cannot necessarily move beyond the tools we had in Chapter 4—the number of candidates, the fractionalization of the field, and the money raised by these candidates. We shall, therefore, rely on similar types of measurements here, while adding information on the incumbent—the incumbent's prior vote share, time in office, and ideological fit to the district.

Patterns of Competition in Challenger Primaries

The majority of nominations to face an incumbent, then, are not particularly heated affairs. An average of 63 percent of nominations are decided without any competition. As was discussed in Chapter 4, states vary in their laws regarding whether uncontested nominations are placed on the ballot; hence some primaries are not held at all, while in others one candidate appears on the ballot. Furthermore, in some states parties have the option to select a nominee if no one runs in the primary, so a lack of a primary does not necessarily indicate that there will be no candidate in the general election.

A one-candidate primary does not necessarily indicate that the party expects to lose the general election. As we saw in Chapter 1, Elizabeth Warren faced no primary opponent in her bid to challenge Scott Brown in the 2012 Massachusetts Senate race. A one-candidate primary may be an indication that one candidate has simply scared other candidates out of the race, or that party leaders have worked to clear the field for the candidate of their choice. In states that give parties a role in endorsing candidates or determining who will appear on the ballot, we can expect larger numbers of one-candidate primaries than in states without such restrictions.

Nonetheless, on average a primary with no candidate or one candidate generally is a sign that the incumbent will fare well in the general election. Figure 5.2 shows the average challenger party vote share in the general election according to the number of out-party primary candidates. In both parties, the presence of a larger number of primary candidates corresponds to a lower margin of victory for the incumbent in the general election. One might argue, of course, that having a competitive primary (in terms of the number of candidates, or simply in terms of whether there is more than one candidate) leads to an increased vote share for the general election challenger, but research on this has been inconclusive.[6] There is an almost identical relationship between the number of candidates and the challenger's party's vote in the *last* election, which suggests that the number of candidates that emerges is more of a consequence of the potential for victory than it is a determinant of it.

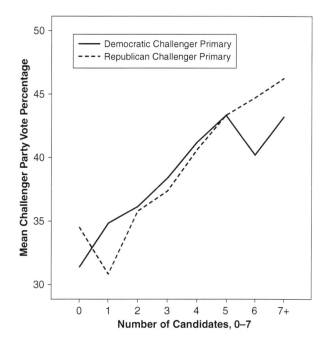

FIGURE 5.2 Challenger Party Primary Competition and General Election Results, 1970-2012

Merely having a primary with more than one candidate running, however, does not in itself mean that the primary is actually competitive. Just as a general election race where the incumbent receives over 60 percent of the vote is a sign that the incumbent was not truly threatened, so a primary where one candidate receives over 60 percent of the vote may not have been a race where the losing candidate ever had a chance. By this measure, slightly over half (56.9 percent) of the challenger primaries that take place are actually competitive, and only 39.7 percent of two-candidate challenger primaries are competitive. There is no relationship, however, between having a close primary election result and having a competitive general election.

Measures of Competition

As in Chapter 4, let us briefly consider patterns in the number of candidates that emerge in each party's primaries. Table 5.1 shows determinants of the number of candidates for each party. Table 5.2 shows the determinants of fractionalization in each party's primaries, using the same formula as in Chapter 4 and multiplying the index by 100 for ease of interpretation. In each of these tables, it is apparent that challenger primaries are far more sensitive to political and institutional variations

TABLE 5.1 Determinants of the Number of House Challenger Party Primary Candidates, 1970–2012 (Poisson)

	Democratic Primaries	Republican Primaries
Political Context		
Democratic Vote in Last Election	.010**	−.011**
Democratic Presidential Vote in Last or Current Election	.007**	−.006**
DW-NOMINATE Score of Incumbent	−.131	−.058
Electoral Structure		
Majority Minority District	.303**	.047
Party Role in Nomination (1–3)	−.238**	−.238**
Closed Primary	.280**	.242**
Semiclosed Primary	.106	.059
Semiopen Primary	.276**	.308**
Blanket Primary	.199*	.003
Level of Party Organization (1–5)	−.006	−.005
South	−.295**	−.318**
Years Incumbent Served	−.002	.000
Decade	−.007**	.010**
Intercept	13.7**	−17.9**
Log-Likelihood	−3964	−4847
N	3755	4840

*p < .05 **p < .01

than are open seat primaries. In other words, many of the variables we had reason to expect to be significant in explaining competition in open seat primaries were not, but most of these variables are significant in our explanations of competition in challenger primaries.

To wit, Table 5.1 shows that the number of candidates in both parties is strongly influenced by district partisanship, with more Democratic districts (according to both presidential and congressional voting) seeing more challenger party primary candidates. The converse is true for Republicans—there are more Republican primary candidates in districts that are more Republican by both measures. There is, as well, a time trend at work, with a growing number of Republican primary candidates and a declining number of Democratic candidates. As we saw in Chapter 4, these patterns exist for open seat primaries as well. Primary rules, however, also influence the number of candidates who emerge in challenger primaries; this was not true for open seat races. In both parties, closed primaries and semi-open primaries have more candidates, and states that allow parties a formal or informal role in primaries see fewer candidates of both parties. There is also less competition, in both parties, in challenger primaries in Southern states.

TABLE 5.2 Determinants of Fractionalization in House Challenger Primaries, 1970–2012 (OLS)

	Democratic Primaries	Republican Primaries
Political Context		
Democratic Vote in Last Election	.38**	−.38**
Democratic Presidential Vote in Last or Current Election	.06	−.24**
DW-NOMINATE Score of Incumbent	−3.1	−6.6*
Electoral Structure		
Majority Minority District	12.8**	2.6
Redistricting Year	2.9*	2.0
Party Role in Nomination (1–3)	−6.7**	−6.7**
Closed Primary	9.0**	6.3**
Semiclosed Primary	4.2*	2.5
Semiopen Primary	10.5**	10.0**
Blanket Primary	3.0	−2.1
Level of Party Organization (1–5)	−1.2**	−.70*
South	−12.3**	−12.5**
Years Incumbent Served	.08	.02
Decade	−1.8**	.08*
Constant	360.6**	−112.6

* $p < .05$ ** $p < .01$
Democratic primaries: $F = 14.1$, $p < .01$, $R^2 = .074$
Republican primaries: $F = 25.5$, $p < .01$, $R^2 = .104$

Similarly, the level of fractionalization in challenger primaries is determined in part by the partisanship of the district, but it also is higher in states with a role for the parties in endorsing candidates, in states with closed primaries and semi-open primaries—and, for Democrats, in states with semi-closed primaries as well. This is a pattern identified in other studies. McNitt (1980, 1982) noted in his two studies of state-level primaries that it defied expectations that open primaries in these races were less competitive. Westley, Calcagno, and Ault (2004) suggest that closed primaries might be more competitive because more ideological candidates will have a better chance to win. If this is the case, it might make sense that challenger primaries, which I suggested at the outset of the chapter might well be a forum for more ideologically extreme candidacies, would exhibit this pattern. The McNitt (1980) study also comments on the lack of competition in Southern primaries, noting that, insofar as Southern states often have run-offs, the lack of competition was all the more notable because the runoff might encourage competition.

In both of these tables characteristics of the incumbent are somewhat relevant. Unsurprisingly, the incumbent's vote percentage in the prior election affects competition in each of these measures. A more popular incumbent tends to attract fewer opponents.[7] The length of the incumbent's tenure, however, does not affect the number of challengers who emerge. For Republican challengers, however, the ideological extremity of the incumbent also affects competition. Table 5.2 shows that more conservative Democrats tend to attract fewer opponents (that is, to have fewer Republicans vying for the nomination to challenge them), controlling for district partisanship, than do more liberal Democrats.

While this is one factor among many that one might use to describe the nature of challenger primaries, it is important in that it shows the strategic nature of entry into out-party primaries. It also shows the effects of ideological diversity within the Democratic Party. Figure 5.3 shows challenger party primary competition according to the incumbent's ideological fit to the district. In the left-hand side graph, each dot represents a Democratic incumbent. The x-axis here is Democratic presidential vote while the y-axis is the Democratic incumbent's DW-Nominate score, a measure of ideological positioning where −1 is a particularly liberal incumbent and 1 is a particularly conservative incumbent. For Democratic incumbents, the more Democratic the district, the more liberal, on average, is the incumbent representative. The fit line in this graph shows the trend here.

This pattern is not interesting in and of itself, however; this pattern can help us to understand primary competition as well. In Chapter 6, we shall see how ideological fit influences the decision to wage a primary challenge against a sitting incumbent. For the purposes of looking at challenger primaries, however, let us consider a very rough measure of primary competition. The dots in Figure 5.3 are distinguished according to whether the victor in the challenger party primary was held to less than 60 percent of the vote—that is, whether there were at least two relatively competitive candidates. The darker dots are races that were competitive, while the lighter dots are races that were not. For Republicans (Figure 5.3, left), it is clear that there are few competitive primaries for the nomination to run against Democrats who are conservative *relative to their district*. This is in part because many of these Democrats are from the South—where, as we have seen, there are fewer competitive challenger primaries. Even when one excludes Southern races, though, the pattern remains. Fewer Republicans line up to challenge conservative Democrats.

There is no such pattern for Democrats seeking to challenge Republicans (Figure 5.3, right), however. This does not mean that Democrats do not behave strategically; rather, it is a consequence of the fact that Republican incumbents in the years studied are not as likely to adapt their policies to their districts as are Democrats. Candidates of both parties, as the tables indicate, respond to a variety of features of the district and the political context, but we cannot see whether they are responding to the incumbent's ideological fit to the district when incumbents do not provide us any obvious means of seeing whether they tailor their positions to their district.

154 Challenger Primaries

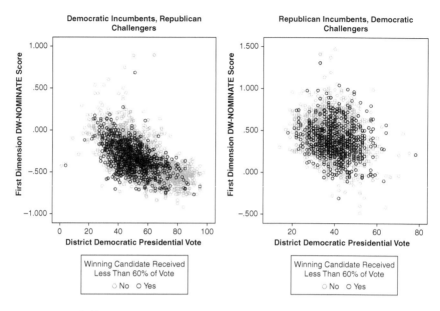

FIGURE 5.3 Challenger Party Primary Competition by the Incumbent's Ideological Fit to the District, 1970–2012

Challenger Primaries and General Election Competition

We saw in Chapter 4 that there is little relationship between open seat primaries and the broader political environment. In other words, whether a particular election year is expected to be a good one for the Democratic or Republican Party has little bearing on how many candidates emerge in open seat primaries. This is the case for several reasons. Open seats are sufficiently rare that there will not necessarily be enough of them that they reflect broader political trends. Aspiring local politicians may regard an open seat as a once-in-a-lifetime chance to run for Congress, so they likely will not be deterred by the popularity of the president or by other factors beyond their control. Political parties also tend to view open seats as being more competitive than incumbent-held seats, so they will not necessarily abandon these races simply because the overall prognosis for their party looks bad in that year.

Challenger primaries are, however, another story. Literature on the party campaign committees suggests that the most important goal of these committees tends to be protection of incumbents. In a good year for the party—for instance, in a year when the party is expected to win the presidency, or in a midterm election year when the other party holds the presidency—a party may choose to go on "offense," targeting a number of vulnerable incumbents in the other party for defeat. Conversely, in a bad year, a party may prioritize helping its own threatened

Challenger Primaries 155

incumbents and will not necessarily work with a large number of challengers. In 2010, for instance, the Democratic Congressional Campaign Committee made independent expenditures for only two general election challengers; unsurprisingly, only one Democratic challenger won a general election in that year.[8] In 2006, when no Republican challengers won seats in Congress, the National Republican Congressional Committee spent all of its money supporting incumbents and backing open seat candidates while the Democratic Party backed many challengers. Furthermore, DCCC leaders actively profiled the types of candidates who would run well in particular districts and recruited candidates who fit these profiles (Gottlieb 2009, 53).

Most elections, of course, fall somewhere in between these two extremes. It is to be expected that prospective candidates think about whether it is a good year to take on an incumbent when they file to run in a primary. Figure 5.4 shows this to be the case in recent election years. During the 1970s, there routinely was greater competition in Democratic primaries, whether one uses the number of candidates (on the left-hand side in the figure) or the fractionalization index (on the right-hand side) as a measure of competition. By the 1990s, however, this difference had disappeared. In elections from 1992 onward there is a rough correspondence between the party's fortunes in the general election and challenger primary competition. In 1992, a chaotic year for both parties' general election candidates, competition surges in both parties, but it surges more so for Republicans. Republican challenger primaries continue to be more competitive in 1994 and 1996. Competition in both parties' challenger primaries declines in 1998 and remains low through 2002; these were election years with particularly low turnover compared to those that preceded them. In 2006 competition within

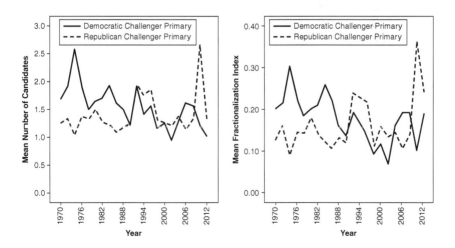

FIGURE 5.4 Challenger Primary Competition by Party, 1970–2012

Democratic challenger primaries surges, and in 2010 Republican challenger primaries are dramatically more competitive than they had been in any other year in this time series. Clearly, then, competition in challenger primaries is strongly shaped by the political environment even if many individual challengers' campaigns are not.

It is important, however, not to overstate the relationship between stronger partisan tides and candidate and party decisions. Robin Kolodny's (1998, 208) history of the parties' congressional campaign committees identified 1994 as a pivotal election for these committees because it was the first in which the NRCC broke with its norm of reflexively devoting most of its attention to protecting incumbents. In that year, the NRCC required incumbents to actually demonstrate that they needed the party's help. It devoted most of its attention to recruiting and training challengers and open seat candidates, and it sought to provide a recognizable platform that branded these nonincumbents—a platform that became the Contract with America. While the contract did not become a major feature in the election until the primaries were over, it was developed while primaries were still taking place, and primary candidates were encouraged to discuss it in their races. The Democratic Party followed suit in 1996, rolling out its "Families First" agenda well in advance of the general election. Although Kolodny's book was published not long after that election, it is evident that in subsequent elections, both parties have sought to present their nonincumbent candidates as a team and to present some set of principles that encompassed all of these candidates' campaigns. On the one hand, these efforts may be an attempt to brand the nonincumbents for donors, and these brands have at times provided few concrete policy details. On the other, these efforts have now taken place in good years and bad years, and as the parties have become further polarized during this time they have at least served both as a recruiting tool for the parties and as a set of ideas to which candidates can attach themselves.

Finally, much of the literature on primary competition suggests that competitive primaries help challengers in the general election. The problem in measuring this, however, is that, as we have seen, competitive challenger primaries are likely to occur when an incumbent is vulnerable to begin with (Alvarez, Canon, and Sellers 1995; Lazarus 2005). Earlier in this chapter, I noted that the number of challenger primary candidates appears to have no bearing on the general election result, but it is possible that there are other measures of primary competitiveness that do matter. If one seeks to predict incumbent vote share using two simple variables—the incumbent's prior vote share and the fractionalization of the challenger party primary—it is clear that primary competition does correspond to an increase in the challenger's party's general election vote. The problem with such an approach, however, is that we have no undisputable measurements of whether an incumbent is vulnerable before the election. Prior vote share may be some indication, but as we saw in the South Dakota case, prior vote share may well have more to do with the political circumstances of the prior election (whether, for instance, it was a midterm or a presidential year) than with the incumbent's popularity. The incumbent may, in addition, have done something unpopular—become embroiled in a scandal or cast an unpopular vote—in the intervening time. There are good theoretical reasons to suspect that incumbents and their prospective general election opponents look upon primaries differently, but it is hard to find proof that challenger primaries have an effect on general elections—too much depends on the tone of that primary, its visibility to the public, and perhaps its proximity to the general election (Johnson, Petersheim, and Wasson 2010).

The Role of Money in Challenger Primaries

In Chapter 4, we saw the difficulty of drawing connections between primary election fundraising and success. In some cases, candidates raise large amounts of money for the purpose of winning the primary; in others, candidates who expect to win the primary easily begin to stockpile funds for use in the general election. The same pattern holds for challenger primaries. We can, therefore, safely conclude that many unopposed primary candidates raise money during the primary but spend little of it on the primary electorate. This is not universally true—some primary candidates may well raise money because they simply do not know whether they will face a competitive primary or not, and others may use their fundraising prowess to scare away potential opponents. For instance, Lance Pressl, the general election challenger to Illinois Republican Representative Phil Crane in 2000, began raising money for his campaign early in the year, but did not know until the primary filing deadline that he would not have a primary opponent. Pressl nonetheless used some of his money in order to have a strong enough primary showing to demonstrate to party leaders that he did have support (Sidlow 2003).

Such cases may well be common, but it is difficult to study the role of money in one-candidate primaries. I thus restrict the focus of this section of the chapter to primaries with more than one candidate. Having two candidates does not ensure that we have two candidates who raised money—the threshold for FEC filings is $5,000, so it is certainly possible for a candidate to garner votes in the primary without filing. It does, however, ensure that a primary candidate cannot simply assume victory.

Earlier in this chapter, we saw that challenger primaries are rarely very competitive. Many challengers run unopposed, and in many instances where there are two or more candidates, one candidate still is able to coast to victory. The same pattern is evident when one considers the financing of challenger primaries. In challenger primaries, 1,393 candidates running with opposition filed FEC reports in the election years from 2000 through 2010. Of these 1,393, 246 faced opponents who raised too little to file with the FEC. This leaves us with only 1,147

158 Challenger Primaries

candidates running in 537 primaries during these seven election cycles where more than one candidate raised money—an average of 77 races a year, despite the fact that nearly 400 incumbents seek reelection in each of these years. There are only 73 primaries from 2000 through 2010 where more than two candidates filed FEC reports; of these 73, 45 took place in 2010.

There are isolated cases in the data of very high-spending primaries. There were twenty races over this period of time where three or more candidates raised in excess of $100,000; these races include the South Dakota race discussed at the beginning of this chapter. There were sixteen races where two candidates raised in excess of $1,000,000. It is tempting in both cases to posit reasons for such high spending—some of the districts in this latter category feature former incumbents seeking to regain their seats (such was the case for former Kansas Republican Jim Ryun in 2008); others feature candidates spending their own money (as, for instance, in the three-way 2002 race to take on vulnerable Maryland Republican Connie Morella) or take place in very wealthy districts; and still others feature candidates who would go on to win congressional seats in subsequent elections, as for Texas Republican Francisco "Quico" Canseco, who lost the 2008 Republican primary but won the primary, and the general election, in 2010. Whatever the causes of high spending on challenger primaries, however, there are too few of them to draw firm conclusions. On average there is not very much money raised in challenger primaries; as Figure 5.5 shows, the

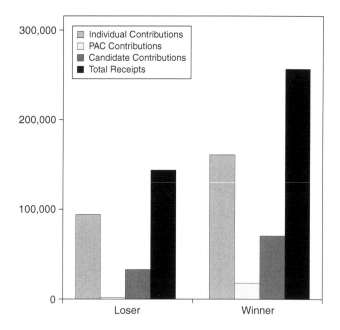

FIGURE 5.5 Sources of Funds for Challenger Primary Winners and Losers, 2012

average primary winner in 2012 raised slightly over $250,000 while the average loser who filed with the FEC raised just under $150,000. This is a similar ratio to that of open seat primaries (shown in the previous chapter, Figure 4.2), but the numbers here are less than half of those in open seat races. There, the average winner raised approximately $500,000 and the average loser raised about $300,000. Challenger primary winners have an edge over their opponents in PAC contributions—many of which are presumably given because the outcome of the race is clear to these PACs. Winners and losers both rely much more on their own funds than do open seat candidates, but losers rely more heavily on their own funds than do winners.

The cost of winning a primary also grew steadily over the decade; in 2000, the average primary winner raised barely over $100,000, while in 2010 the average winner raised over $300,000. Figure 5.6 shows this trend. This increase may be partially due to the doubling of individual contribution limits that was part of the Bipartisan Campaign Reform Act (BCRA), though there is no dramatic increase in 2004, the year BCRA took effect. It is more likely a consequence of the races that draw competition. Remember that we are only considering primaries where

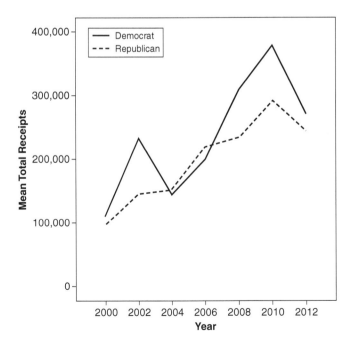

FIGURE 5.6 Average Total Receipts for Challenger Primary Winners, by Party, 2000–2012

there are multiple candidates here; in a good year for one party, there will be more such races. This has a paradoxical effect—many eager but poorly financed candidates may run if they feel the partisan winds will be at their back, leading to a lower average fundraising total. In 2010, then, Democratic primary winners substantially outraised Republican primary winners; the 34 Democratic challengers who ran in competitive primaries raised an average of $378,000 while the 146 Republicans who ran in competitive primaries raised an average of $292,000. Following this pattern, Republican primary winners outraised Democratic primary winners in 2006 and there was little difference between the parties in 2000 or 2004. Democratic winners outraised Republicans in 2002 and 2008, however, perhaps indicating that there is still some randomness to this pattern. Primary cycle receipts for challengers of both parties declined slightly in 2012.

One problem with making comparisons between open seat primaries and challenger primaries, however, is that there is much greater variation across races in the value of winning the nomination to run against an incumbent than there is across open seat races. We can speak of overall trends in the cost of winning the nomination to face an incumbent, but what is most of interest here is the expected competitiveness of the race. It is difficult, however, to come up with a priori measures of how competitive a race will be. As we saw in the South Dakota case, the same incumbent can face minimal opposition one year and then lose her seat in the next. We can get a general sense of competitiveness, however, if we group races based on the incumbent's party's presidential vote share in the current or previous election. While this is not perfect, it corresponds to discussion in the media about district competitiveness; media commentators often make reference to "mismatch" districts where one party won a house election and the other won the majority of votes for president. Similarly, distinctions can be made between districts where the presidential competitors each can count on at least 40 percent of the vote and those where they cannot.

Figure 5.7, then, shows changes in the primary fundraising for the victors in each party, according to the competitiveness of the district. The three lines show fundraising in "mismatch" districts, in districts where the incumbent's party's presidential candidate received between 50 and 60 percent of the vote, and in districts where the incumbent's party's presidential candidate received over 60 percent of the vote. The party differences here are interesting. In both parties, fundraising is flat for the victors in races to face relatively secure incumbents. Fundraising also changes little for Democrats in districts where their presidential candidate was competitive but did not win. Fundraising for both parties' candidates in mismatch districts soared in the latter half of the decade, however. In the Republican Party, fundraising by candidates in slightly competitive districts also increased substantially. The increases suggest, first of all, that the cost of the nomination increases with the likelihood of winning the general election. It also shows, however, that in recent years money has flowed to potential general election winners much

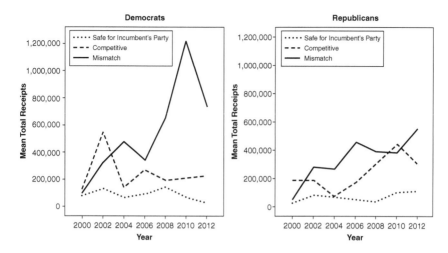

FIGURE 5.7 Average Total Receipts for Primary Winners, by Party and Competitiveness, 2000–2012

earlier than it did in the first few years of the decade. While we cannot prove that parties and their allies had a role in this, it does appear that there is some connection between this increase and the high general election turnover of these years.[9]

Finally, let us consider the relationship between fundraising and vote share for challenger primary candidates. We saw in Chapter 4 that contributions from political action committees are positively and significantly related to vote share, but that no other financial variables are significant when controlling for the number of candidates and the competitiveness of the seat. In the case of challenger primaries, Table 5.3 shows that candidate contributions are not related to vote percentage, but all other contribution types (individuals, parties, and PACs) are. In keeping with our other findings on the financing of challenger primaries, it seems that money flows much more directly toward winners than is the case in open seat races. It is to be expected, as well, that candidate contributions are not related to vote share; as discussed in the previous chapter, most research on self-financing has found that most self-financed candidates do not fare particularly well.

In sum, money matters far more in challenger primaries than in open seat races. This is so in part because challenger primaries tend to be less competitive than open seat races. Fewer candidates run, in part because the odds of beating an incumbent are so low. When strong candidates do emerge, they may well secure the backing of party leaders and use that backing to scare away opponents and to dominate fundraising. This is not the case in all challenger primaries, but the relationship between money and success is clearly there. There is in addition some evidence that political parties have made more of an effort in recent years to select and support strong challengers. This is particularly so in high turnover

TABLE 5.3 Determinants of Vote Share, Democratic and Republican House Challenger Primary Candidates, 2000–2012 (OLS)

	Democrats	*Republicans*	*All*
Number of Candidates	−7.61**	−4.37**	−5.15**
Year	−.315*	−.401**	−.319**
Individual Contributions	.008**	.008**	.008**
Party Contributions	1.00*	1.20*	1.10**
PAC Contributions	.032**	.052**	.038**
Candidate Contributions	−.005	.012	−.007
Competitiveness of Seat	−1.32	−2.28**	−1.86**
Constant	985.26*	865.43**	703.29**
N	635	800	1435
F	28.7	14.93	57.0
R^2	.24	.23	.22

* $p < .05$ ** $p < .01$

Note: Data drawn from FEC preprimary reports (for winners) and candidate summary file (for losers). All contribution variables in thousands of dollars.

years, as funds are concentrated among the small number of candidates seeking the nomination to run against incumbents in "mismatch" districts. This is all, perhaps, to be expected, but it bears repeating that challenger primaries have become more expensive over just the past three election cycles. Perhaps it was once the case that prospective general election challengers could defer their fundraising efforts until after they had won the primary; if this was once the case, it is clearly no longer so.

Senate Challenger Primaries

Challenger primaries in the Senate tend to be more competitive than those in the House. This is to be expected. The reelection rate of incumbent senators is lower than that of representatives—something that is both a consequence and a cause of primary competition. If senators are seen as being more vulnerable than House members, aspiring candidates may be less likely to wait for an open seat than will House aspirants. The appearance of strong candidates, in turn, can provide a greater threat to senators. The higher value of a Senate seat, compared to a House seat, also can lead to greater primary competition. States also tend to be less partisan than House districts, so there are very few Senate seats that are truly off-limits to either party.

Competition in Senate Challenger Primaries

Several statistics can be summoned to show the level of competition in Senate challenger primaries. Figure 5.8 shows the number of contested and uncontested

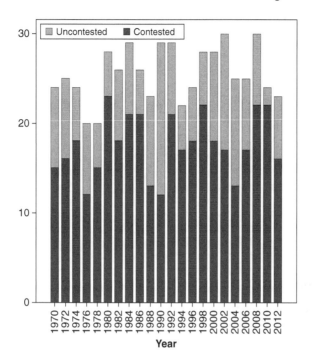

FIGURE 5.8 Number of Contested and Uncontested Senate Challenger Primaries by Year, 1970–2012

Senate primaries by year; in only one year (1990) were less than half of Senate challenger primaries contested; in some years, such as 2010, almost all of them were. The fractionalization index is also far higher in Senate challenger primaries than in House challenger primaries; for the full 1970 to 2012 series of elections, the average fractionalization index for the Senate is .37 while it is only .17 for House challenger primaries. Even in very competitive years such as 2010, the level of fractionalization is over twice as high in the Senate as it is in the House. And, to put matters in different terms, the average number of candidates in the House over the full 1970 to 2012 time series is 1.47, as compared to 2.86 in the Senate. In only one election year (2010) did the average number of House challenger primary candidates exceed two, while the average number of candidates in Senate challenger primaries is greater than two in every year except one (again, 1990). In 2010, there was an average of 3.96 candidates in challenger primaries.

In Chapter 1, we discussed recent debates within the Republican Party about the quality of its primary candidates. Many of the allegedly winnable Senate races that some analysts believe Republicans lost due to poor nominees were challenges to sitting Democrats. In 2010 in Nevada, for instance, State

Representative Sharron Angle won a three-way primary over a more experienced state senator and the 2006 Nevada secretary of state nominee, only to lose to Democrat Harry Reid in November. According to many, Angle was less competitive in the general election than the other candidates would have been. Similar stories were told about challenger primaries in Colorado in 2010 and in Missouri in 2012. In all of these races, however, national Republican Party leaders did not intervene. In other states, it is easy to see the wisdom of not intervening; there are several other elections over the past decade where less experienced candidates won competitive primaries and went on to defeat sitting incumbents. While one can certainly conclude from news coverage that Angle, Missouri Republican nominee Todd Akin, or Colorado nominee Ken Buck were not conventional Republican candidates, it is difficult to develop measurement tools to investigate whether they are part of a trend or anomalies. This is by no means a claim specific to Republicans; studies of Southern politics, for instance, have alleged that primary competition weakened Democratic challengers (Bain 1972; Craig and Austin 2008). Some older studies (Bernstein 1977) have alleged that Senate primary competition hurts the stronger party in a state, but the stronger party will, on average, be the party that already holds the Senate seat. Overall, when one takes into account the fact that winnable races will draw more primary candidates to begin with, the evidence seems to suggest that there is a slight advantage to having challenger primary competition (Alvarez, Canon, and Sellers 1995).

A competitive primary may, however, be a sign that there is no obvious party favorite in the race. Anecdotes abound, for instance, about efforts by party leaders to reduce primary competition and to gently (or not-so-gently) nudge other candidates out of the race. This was clearly what happened in the Elizabeth Warren race we discussed in Chapter 1. Many accounts of the 2002 Minnesota Senate election have also alleged that Karl Rove and other leaders in the Bush administration agreed that the mayor of St. Paul, Norm Coleman, would be the strongest nominee in a general election matchup with incumbent Democrat Paul Wellstone. Republican leaders reportedly steered Coleman's strongest potential primary opponent, Tim Pawlenty, toward the governor's race, promising support to Pawlenty in that race but not in a Senate campaign (Bai 2002). Pawlenty accepted the offer, and both candidates won their primaries and the subsequent general elections. Other such strategic decisions likely are common, but for understandable reasons it is not always possible to be certain about why some candidates choose not to run. What these cases show, however, is that it may at times be in the interest of parties to winnow the primary field; in other instances, party leaders themselves may be divided and may opt to avoid taking sides and let primary voters make the decision. This is one instance where challenger primaries serve the same purpose today that they were said to have served in the early years of the twentieth century.

The Financing of Senate Challenger Primaries

We have seen that Senate challenger primaries tend to be more competitive than are House challenger primaries. It is to be expected that Senate primary campaigns will cost more than House primary campaigns, if only because of the larger numbers of voters (in most states) and the greater prestige of the Senate. Even beyond this, however, the increased level of competition ensures that more money will be spent in Senate primaries. Table 5.4 presents average fundraising amounts for successful primary candidates over the past decade, broken out by party and by one measure of the potential competitiveness of the general election to follow, based on state presidential voting.[10] It should be noted, first of all, that there is a relationship between state size and campaign costs. The relationship is not necessarily linear—there have, for instance, been extremely expensive races in small states in recent years—but any variation according to state size is not captured here.

The data in this table show that Senate primaries tend to be quite competitive even when the odds of general election victory are slim. Democratic primary winners tend to raise nearly $800,000 even in states where Republicans are overwhelmingly favored, and Republican primary winners raise more than twice that in states where Democrats are strongly favored. Republicans in such states often spend a substantial amount of their own money; the average Republican

TABLE 5.4 Average Receipts for Victorious Senate Challenger Primary Candidates, by Partisanship of State, 2000–2012

	Safe Democratic	Competitive	Safe Republican	All Races
Democrats				
Total Receipts	2,657,447	2,216,392	786,763	1,560,722
Individual Contributions	2,120,636	1,617,291	567,608	1,149,173
Party Contributions	19,319	7,920	19,014	14,106
PAC Contributions	303,711	178,530	110,340	154,970
Candidate Contributions	0	301,372	10,467	138,983
N	4	24	26	54
Republicans				
Total Receipts	1,384,189	3,196,710	2,241,223	2,367,467
Individual Contributions	687,295	2,472,530	1,516,115	1,654,100
Party Contributions	708	9,347	6,600	5,592
PAC Contributions	25,844	194,047	356,598	144,498
Candidate Contributions	183,403	258,602	7,544	201,133
N	22	27	6	55

Note: All data from FEC preprimary reports.

primary victor in a Democratic state contributed over $200,000 to his or her own campaign.

There are a small number of challenger primaries in states where the challenger's party tends to perform well. Such states are not necessarily sure pickup opportunities for the challenger's party; 50 percent of the primary victors in these races went on to win the general election. These are, however, states where there should be a large number of strong candidates of the challenger's party. They include Democratic challenges in Maine, Rhode Island, and Oregon and Republican challenges in Arkansas, Georgia, Montana, and West Virginia. While there are few enough races here that the idiosyncrasies of individual candidates may matter, the party differences still are striking—Democrats spend heavily in their primaries while Republicans do not. These Democratic races are, in fact, more expensive on average than are Democratic primaries in more competitive states, while Republican races in Republican-leaning states are less expensive than Republican races elsewhere.

Variations in self-financing are also of interest. As noted above, Republicans running in heavily Democratic states tend to rely more on their own funds than do Republicans running elsewhere. Democratic primary candidates tend to self-finance more in races in competitive states. In keeping with others' findings on self-financing, however, very few of the candidates who spent their own money won (Steen 2006). Of the twenty candidates who spent more than $100,000 of their own money in the primary, only eight won their primaries and just two (current Democratic Senator Maria Cantwell of Washington and former Democratic Senator Mark Dayton of Minnesota) went on to win the general election. These two were among five candidates who spent over $3 million of their own money; four out of these five won their primaries. Perhaps, then, self-financing is not helpful unless one has the resources to spend several million dollars.

As was the case in open seat races, contributions from political action committees comprise a small percentage of primary candidates' funds, but PACs tend to give strategically. They are more strategic on the Republican side, however, than they are for Democrats. This difference is in part a consequence of labor union support for Democratic challengers. It has been noted that unions are more willing to support nonincumbent candidates than are other types of PACs (Sorauf 1992); here, the relatively generous PAC support for Democratic primary victors in Republican states is largely a sign that unions see virtue in backing long-shot Democrats.

Finally, lest we overemphasize the role of money in Senate challenger primaries, it is worth comparing the data here to those in Table 4.5 in the previous chapter. Primaries for the right to challenge a Senate incumbent do tend to feature a healthy amount of competition and of spending, but they are still far less expensive than are open seat primaries. No matter how competitive the general election is expected to be, open seat primary candidates still raise far more money than do Senate challengers.

Conclusions

Challengers rarely win congressional elections. The low chance of victory for most challengers leads to rather subdued competition in the primaries for the right to take on an incumbent. Although many challenger primaries are not contested at all, however, there still are many reasons that candidates seek major party nominations. Not all candidates who run for Congress are running exclusively to win, and there are many instances of fiercely competitive primaries where candidates air occasionally unorthodox views. Challenger primaries do, however, often take place outside of the public eye. While Senate challenger primaries tend to require a substantial amount of money, many House challenger primaries are fought out by underfinanced candidates. There are enough challenger primaries, and there is enough diversity among challenger primaries, that it can be easy to see the effects of electoral structure—when the opportunity is there, candidates behave strategically. What is most fascinating, however, about challenger primaries can be the unstrategic behavior—the fact that candidates emerge despite daunting odds, and that a party nomination can have value even when it is unlikely to lead to general election victory.

Notes

1 For a summary of the primary see Ellis 2010.
2 For discussion of this primary see Dayal 2010, Morton 2010.
3 For coverage see *Morning Journal* 2010, *Norwalk Reflector* 2010.
4 For a detailed study of one such race see Sanford Gottlieb's (2009, 24–27) account of the 2002 primary for the nomination to challenge Republican Constance Morella in Maryland.
5 For examples of this literature, see Kingdon 1966; Leuthold 1968; Huckshorn and Spencer 1971; Fishel 1973; Maisel 1986.
6 For discussion see Lazarus 2005; Johnson, Petersheim, and Wasson 2010; Stone, Fulton, Maestas, and Maisel 2010; Carson, Crespin, Eaves, and Wanless 2012.
7 It is worth noting that in measuring the incumbent's prior vote share I exclude uncontested general elections. Including these would show an even stronger effect for prior vote share, but it would arguably be misleading; were I to do this, I would need to set the incumbent's vote share to 100 percent, which would overestimate the incumbent's actual popularity. I follow most other studies, then, in excluding such races.
8 These two were Colleen Hanabusa, who defeated a Republican incumbent in Hawaii, and Thomas White, for whom the party spent only $9,000 in his unsuccessful campaign in Nebraska.

9 It should be noted that these categories are not apportioned evenly between the parties; by this measure there are more safe districts and mismatch districts held by Democratic incumbents than there are for Republicans. Redistricting cycles here (2002 and 2012) should also be treated with caution; changes in district composition can often render districts more competitive even when they do not significantly alter the partisanship of the district.

10 As in Chapter 4, safe seats are those where one party's nominee received more than 55 percent of the two-party vote while competitive seats are those where neither candidate received that much. While this is in some ways a flawed measure, it draws on more recent elections than the incumbent senator's last bid.

6
INCUMBENT PRIMARIES

> The faction that now dominates the Republican Party . . . they think government is always the enemy, they're always right, and compromise is weakness. Just in the last couple of elections, they defeated two distinguished Republican senators because they dared to cooperate with Democrats on issues important to the future of the country, even national security. They beat a Republican congressman with almost 100 percent voting record on every conservative score because he said he realized he did not have to hate the president to disagree with him. Boy, that was a non-starter, and they threw him out.
> —President Bill Clinton, speaking at the Democratic National Convention, September 5, 2012

In four of the past five election cycles, at least one incumbent member of the Senate has found himself or herself in a pitched political battle to win renomination. In 2004, moderate Pennsylvania Republican Arlen Specter, narrowly won renomination for a fifth term in the Senate, defeating Representative Pat Toomey by a 51 to 49 percent margin. In 2006, centrist Democrat and former vice presidential nominee Joseph Lieberman lost his primary in Connecticut to a wealthy liberal activist, but turned around and won the election running as an independent in an election seen by many as a referendum on Lieberman's hawkish views on the Iraq War. In that same year, Republican Senator Lincoln Chafee, son of Rhode Island's longtime Senator John Chafee, narrowly defeated a conservative challenger in his bid for renomination, only to be trounced by a Democrat in the general election. In 2010, five incumbent senators faced highly competitive primary foes. Specter switched parties in order to avoid a rematch with Toomey, only to be defeated in the Democratic primary; Arkansas's Blanche Lambert Lincoln barely squeaked by in her primary and then prevailed by a similarly small margin in a runoff election; Alaska's Lisa Murkowski followed in Lieberman's footsteps, losing her primary but winning the general election as an independent; and appointed Colorado Senator Michael Bennet beat back a strong challenge from the Speaker of the Colorado House of Representatives. Utah's Robert Bennett, who had sided with his Republican colleagues 90 percent of the time in his past term, did not even make it to the primary, coming in third in the voting at his state's Republican convention. Even John McCain, fresh off of his presidential bid, had to dip into his leftover presidential campaign funds to win the Arizona Republican primary. In each of these years at least one incumbent member of the House of Representatives also faced a primary challenger with a flair for raising money nationwide.

As we shall see below, these races were unusual. It is not uncommon for a few incumbents to face primary opponents, but the vast majority of incumbents who do have difficulty winning renomination have substantial personal baggage—they have been implicated in a scandal, they have grown old and failed to campaign vigorously, or they have the misfortune of representing districts where there have been longstanding factional conflicts within their parties. The common thread in the races discussed above, however, is that the incumbent had committed no moral or ethical transgressions; instead, these incumbents were accused of being too moderate or of consorting too often with the opposition party. What may be a winning general election strategy for Democrats in conservative states such as Arkansas, or for Republicans in liberal states like Rhode Island, may not be, or at least may no longer be, a winning strategy in primary elections.

Perhaps no election better exemplifies this dynamic than Richard Lugar's unsuccessful quest for renomination in 2012—one of the elections to which Bill Clinton is presumably referring in the above quote. As of 2012, Lugar was the longest-serving Republican senator. He was first elected in 1976; before that he served two terms as mayor of Indianapolis and was famously dubbed "America's Mayor" by President Nixon in 1972. During his time in the Senate, Lugar established a reputation as an expert on foreign affairs and nuclear weapons, and he ran unsuccessfully for president in 1996. During that time he did work closely with Democrats, but one would hardly call him a moderate; his party unity scores tended to top 90 percent during his final terms in office. Lugar was resoundingly defeated by a 61 to 39 percent margin in the 2012 primary, however, by Richard Mourdock, the Indiana state treasurer. Mourdock was endorsed by the Club for Growth and several Tea Party organizations, and ran ads attacking Lugar for his work with Democrats on nuclear nonproliferation. Lugar's defeat cannot entirely be attributed to allegations of centrism and bipartisanship; by 2012 he was eighty years old and, as Mourdock's campaign advertisements reminded voters, he had in fact given up his home in Indiana to reside in Washington fulltime. Yet statements after the election show that Lugar and Mourdock agreed on what the election was about. Lugar wrote that Mourdock's "embrace of an unrelenting partisan mindset is irreconcilable with my philosophy of governance and my experience of what brings results for Hoosiers in the Senate. In effect, what he has promised in this campaign is reflexive votes for a rejectionist orthodoxy and rigid opposition to the actions and proposals of the other party." Mourdock responded: "I have a mindset that says bipartisanship ought to consist of Democrats coming to the Republican point of view ... The fact is, you never compromise on principles. We are at that point where one side or the other has to win this argument. One side or the other will dominate" (Weinger 2012).

Conflicts such as these—instances of what the American media, party activists, and bloggers have dubbed "primarying"—are nothing new. Many prominent members of Congress have arrived there because of successful primary challenges or have run unsuccessful challenges before subsequently winning open seat races. Wisconsin's Joseph McCarthy and Texas's Lloyd Bentsen are two such examples; former Speaker of the House Newt Gingrich waged an unsuccessful primary challenge during the 1970s, and current Speaker John Boehner won his seat by taking on a Republican incumbent tarred by scandal. Primary challenges to incumbents are notable, however, because they are rare. They take on an outsized role in media coverage of primaries largely because they are more exciting than simply reporting on the inevitable victories of the vast majority of congressional incumbents. On the day after Richard Lugar's defeat, the web-based news magazine *Politico* featured an article entitled "GOP Senators Wonder: Am I Next?" (Raju 2012). Further down the page, in smaller font, *Politico* also had another story: "House Incumbents Cruise to Wins" (Isenstadt 2012). This second article led off thusly: "House incumbents had an easy night Tuesday as every member of Congress on the ballot in Indiana, North Carolina, and West Virginia won their primary elections." Clearly, the first article was much more exciting for political junkies, but the second may well have provided a more accurate summary of what really takes place in incumbent primaries.

The previous two chapters have shown that patterns of competition in open seat and out-party primaries are somewhat related to the popularity of the incumbent. In the case of open seat primaries, the endorsement of the seat's current representative can make a difference, although this certainly depends on his or her popularity and reasons for leaving. In the case of out-party primaries, the prospect of facing a popular incumbent in the general election may decrease the value of the nomination. This can result in lower-profile primaries, although they are not necessarily less competitive primaries. In both instances, the behind-the-scenes maneuverings of party leaders can shape the primary field, and the size of the field itself can provide clues about the nature of the general election race to follow.

The seat's current representative is part of the puzzle in these races, but he or she is by no means the only piece. Open seat primaries and out-party primaries can also be explained without spending time analyzing the incumbent. Why do open seat primaries happen? Because ambitious politicians want to win a congressional seat; in many instances, these candidates have waited several years for the incumbent to retire and for the seat to become available. Why do challenger primaries happen? At least some of the time, they also happen in part because ambitious politicians see a chance to win the seat, but they happen as well because these candidates sense that the incumbent may be vulnerable. This vulnerability may have something to do with the incumbent's conduct in office—that is, an incumbent may appear weak because of a scandal or other personal problems—but at least in some election years and in some districts out-party candidates may simply sense that voters would prefer to vote for them on partisan grounds. In both of these cases, candidates who demonstrate that they have a chance to win can depend on the help of interest groups, the party committees, and a network of large donors.

Primary challengers to incumbents, in contrast, can expect little help in their primary bids. Political parties virtually always support embattled incumbents, and most interest groups and individual donors will be reluctant to invest in a primary challenge. Although in recent years there have been a few instances of organized efforts to help primary challengers—something we shall discuss later in this chapter—primary challenges to incumbents occur far less frequently than do other types of congressional primaries, and when serious primary challenges to incumbents are mounted it is almost always because the incumbent has done something wrong.

In this chapter we shall therefore take a different approach to primaries than was the case in the previous two chapters. As we did in the previous chapters, we will begin with a look at changes in the number of candidates and the competitiveness of these candidates over time, and we will look as well at the financing of primary campaigns. Because it is not possible to separate incumbent fundraising for purposes of winning the primary from incumbent fundraising for purposes of winning the general election, however, we must confine our attention to fundraising by candidates challenging the incumbent. After looking at these data, we will then turn our attention to some of the reasons why incumbent primaries take place. These reasons are much less dependent upon national or district-level political trends than they are on the idiosyncrasies of the incumbent. We shall close the chapter with a look at the interests of political parties and interest groups in congressional primaries. However, in doing this we will look in particular at some recent high-profile primary challenges to incumbents and consider recent claims that so-called "primarying" is on the rise. This is a popular meme in contemporary politics, but as we shall see, the evidence behind this claim is mixed. To the extent that such campaigns have taken place over the past decade, they have taken place in instances where interest groups have sought to defeat certain incumbents, and they have often been presented as evidence of growing polarization between the political parties and their supporters.[1]

Patterns in Incumbent Primaries

From 1970 through 2012, 72 percent of House incumbents seeking renomination ran unopposed. Uncontested primaries are, then, the norm, but challenges are not uncommon. There is also substantial variation by year, as Figure 6.1 shows. From 1970 through 1986, more than one hundred incumbents faced primary opponents in each cycle, yet, since 1986 there have been only four elections (1992, 1994, 2010, and 2012) where over one hundred incumbents had opponents.

Merely noting that primaries have occurred is not, however, particularly illuminating. As we have discussed elsewhere in this book, the occurrence of primaries is often a function of the nature of state primary laws or of state political culture. The majority of primary challengers to incumbents fare rather poorly; the median vote percentage for incumbents who do face primary opponents is 80 percent. One might be tempted to look at Figure 6.1 and try to draw some conclusion about what the top years for challenges (for instance, to take the top four, 1984, 1992, 2010, and 2012) had in common. The answer, I suspect, is nothing. Figure 6.2 shows why. Here, three different levels of competitiveness are separated out—races where the incumbent received over 75 percent of the vote, races where the incumbent received between 60 and 75 percent, and races where the incumbent received 60 percent of the vote or less. This figure shows that while

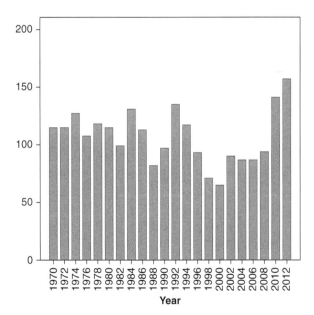

FIGURE 6.1 Number of Primary Challenges to Incumbent House Members, 1970–2012

174 Incumbent Primaries

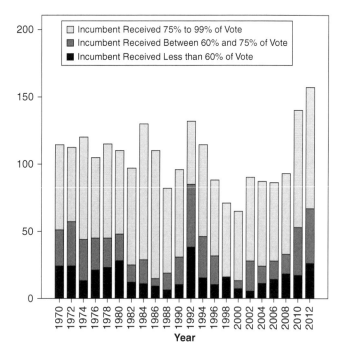

FIGURE 6.2 Number of Primary Challenges to Incumbent House Members, 1970–2012, by Level of Competitiveness

1984 had a large number of primary challengers, these were generally not serious ones. In 1992, many of the challengers did well—the proportion of challenges where the incumbent was held to less than 75 percent of the vote is the highest of any year in this time series. The years 2010 and 2012 featured large numbers in all categories—there were 141 incumbents who faced opponents in 2010 and 157 in 2012; these opponents were well-represented in all of our competitiveness categories.

There is, as it turns out, a substantial relationship (R = .662, p < .01) between general election volatility (as defined by the number of incumbents defeated in the general election) and the number of primaries where the incumbent received 75 percent of the vote or less. In high-turnover elections such as 1992, 1994, or 2010, in other words, there is a higher-than-average number of primary challenges. Conversely, the relatively sedate elections of 1988 and 1998 through 2004 (where fewer than seven incumbents were defeated, excluding incumbent vs. incumbent races), saw a smaller than average number of primary challenges. This relationship, furthermore, is driven mainly by Democratic challenges. Republican challenges follow no similar logic, although there have been far more Republican challenges over the past two decades than there were during the 1970s or 1980s. There is also no relationship between whether an election is held in a presidential year or midterm and the number of primaries, competitive or not. One should note that 2012 is unusual in this regard; relatively few incumbents were defeated—twenty incumbents lost, excluding primary losses and incumbent-incumbent matchups—although there was a high number of primary challenges.

We have, then, two obvious trends across the past four decades in the occurrence of primary challenges. First, there is an obvious decline in the number of primaries, whether one considers all primary challenges or merely those that are competitive, from the 1970s to the present day. Second, we have a growing homogenization of patterns of competition in incumbent primaries. By this, I mean to say that while there were variations in the occurrence of primaries by region or by electoral structure, these differences have disappeared. Primary challenges are related to volatility from 1980 on, but not at all during the 1970s. Why was there more competition in the 1970s? One potential explanation might be the dominance of the Democratic Party in the South during this era; as we saw in Chapter 2, a Democratic primary victory in the South was at one time tantamount to winning the election, and ideological or factional conflict in the South played out in primaries, not the general election. A quick look at Southern and non-Southern primaries, however, indicates that this is not the case. Figure 6.3 shows that primary competition in the South (whether one is concerned with all primary challenges or only competitive ones) follows the same pattern as competition in non-Southern states. Perhaps there was something else distinctive about

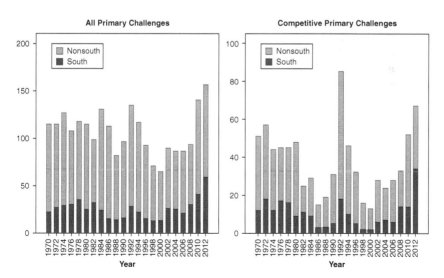

FIGURE 6.3 Primary Challenges to House Incumbents by Region of the Country, 1970–2012

the 1970s, or perhaps party organizations have become more effective at deterring primary opponents since that time.

Table 6.1 shows the limited role electoral structure plays in preventing or allowing challenges to incumbents. This table lists the percentage of competitive primaries (that is, those where the incumbent receives 75 percent of the vote or less) according to primary type and the party role in the nomination—that is, whether it can set a threshold for ballot access or provide a preprimary endorsement. This table shows that open primaries with an incumbent were far less competitive in the 1970s than they are today. Although the research on what role electoral rules play in encouraging primary opposition has reached no firm conclusions, the differences in this table suggest that electoral structure did play a role in the 1970s but not in subsequent decades. Parties, on the other hand, maintain the ability to limit competition in states where they do play a formal role in the primary. Parties with informal roles, however, have no effect on challenges to incumbents.

Senate primary challenges are far fewer in number than are House primary challenges. On average, eleven senators per year face some sort of primary challenge, but as in the House, these challenges tend not to be serious. The average number of competitive Senate primary challenges (that is, challenges where the incumbent was held to 75 percent or less of the vote) is slightly over three per year; it ranges from a high of eight (in 1980) to a low of zero (in 1984, 1988, and 2000). There is somewhat of a relationship between the percentage of Senate incumbents who face competitive challengers and the corresponding percentage of House incumbents. Figure 6.4 shows this relationship. The most consequential years for House challenges, 1992 and 2010, featured an above-average number

TABLE 6.1 The Relationship between State Primary Laws and Challenges to Incumbents

	1970s	1980s	1990s	2000s	2010s	Total
Primary Type						
Open	5.4%	5.5%	8.6%	4.8%	10.2%	6.5%
Closed	13.3	7.2	11.5	6.6	13.9	10.1
Blanket/Jungle	17.1	5.2	6.8	7.8	13.6	10.3
Party Role in Nomination						
Formal	7.7	5.9	5.6	6.5	8.1	6.6
Informal	13.9	7.9	14.4	6.4	14.0	11.0
None	13.3	6.6	10.5	6.6	14.6	9.9

Note: Percentages listed are the percentage of all primaries for each type in which the incumbent was held to less than 75 percent of the primary vote.

Source for Codings: Kanthak and Morton 2001; Maisel, Gibson, and Ivry 1998; adjusted by author for changes in subsequent years.

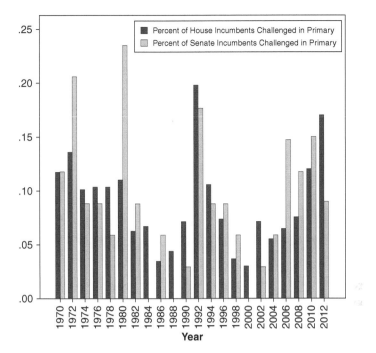

FIGURE 6.4 Competitive Primary Challenges to House and Senate Incumbents Compared

of Senate primary challenges, and the years with no competitive Senate primary challenges were all years with little competition in House incumbents' primaries. There are, however, some anomalous years; in 2012, for instance, sixty-six House incumbents were challenged (excluding incumbent-incumbent races), but only two Senate incumbents faced even minimally competitive primary opponents.

All of these trends (particularly those described for the House) provide more evidence of primary competition than does simply looking at the number of defeated incumbents. Between 1984 and 2008, no more than four incumbents lost their primaries, excluding incumbent vs. incumbent matches in redistricting years, which we shall discuss in the next chapter. Primary losses were more frequent in the years before that—eleven incumbents lost renomination in 1970, ten lost in 1974 and 1980, and eight lost in 1968 and 1978. Depending on how one counts, seven incumbents lost their primary bids in 2010—one (Robert Bennett) lost his bid to appear on the primary ballot, as discussed above, and Alaska's Lisa Murkowski lost in the primary but won the general election. Of the remaining five, two were mired in some sort of scandal and two others had recently switched parties. When one excludes races where two incumbents run against each other (a subject we shall take up in Chapter 7), six incumbents (one Senate, five House) were defeated in 2012.

Finally, it is evident that 2010 and 2012 are anomalous in terms of primary competition, if not in the number of incumbents who actually lost. Is this merely a function of the overall volatility of the 2010 election? It is here that gradations of competition become important. More primary challengers emerged in 2010—a function, perhaps, of Tea Party activism—but, as is the norm, most of these challengers were not particularly competitive. In the level of serious primary competition, 2010 and 1992 are the two anomalous years, but it is too early to tell whether 2010 is a harbinger of changes to come or whether it is simply like other high-turnover elections in regards to the number of competitive primary challengers.

Money and Primary Challenges

It is difficult to measure how much money incumbent members of Congress raise for the purpose of winning contested primaries, or how much of the money incumbents spend during primary season is spent for the purpose of winning the primary. Members of Congress raise and spend campaign money throughout their terms in office, in part to get a head start on their campaigns, in part because much of the money raised by incumbents is "access" money, money that is not necessarily solicited, and in part because incumbents seek to build campaign "war chests" that can deter challengers. Particularly in states with primaries as late as September, incumbents' primary campaigns and general election campaigns can be difficult to distinguish.

It is possible, however, to make some definitive statements about those who run against incumbents in primaries. First, and perhaps most obviously, the vast majority of candidates who file to run against incumbents raise very little money. In our discussion above, we distinguished between races in which the incumbent was held to less than 75 percent of the primary vote and those where he or she was not. For the purpose of looking at primary challenger fundraising, let us take a similar approach, focusing upon challengers who receive 25 percent or more of the primary vote. This is a slightly different set of races—in some instances, incumbents are held to less than 75 percent of the vote by multiple challengers, none of whom receive 25 percent of the vote. Yet this is a sensible cutoff—the Federal Election Commission only requires candidates to disclose information about their fundraising if they raise over $5,000, and a large majority of the primary challengers who receive less than 25 percent of the vote do not reach this threshold while the majority of those who exceed 25 percent do file with the FEC.

In the previous two chapters we explored the increase in fundraising for candidates in open seat and out-party challenger primaries. This increase corresponds to the increase in fundraising for general election candidates of all types. This increase is not particularly remarkable—inflation drives costs up, and the costs of campaigns have risen at a rate exceeding inflation for some time. What is noteworthy, however, is that challenger fundraising has not risen at a similar rate. Figure 6.5 shows the mean fundraising by year since 1980 for all competitive primary challengers broken out first by party, and then by two different levels of competitiveness.[2] In some years—particularly 1988 and 2002—the average is pulled upward by one or two anomalously expensive campaigns. Yet while there is clearly an increase in the amount of money it takes to run a competitive challenge from the 1980s to the 2000s, the increase is nowhere as dramatic as the increase for incumbents, general election candidates, or other types of primary candidates. The decline in 2008 and 2010, in particular, indicates that there is less of a correlation between fundraising and competitiveness for primary challenges to incumbents than there is for other candidate types. Or, to frame matters differently, these figures show that the vote share for primary challengers to incumbents has more to do with the incumbent's vulnerabilities than to the strengths of primary challengers. Simply being on the ballot at the right time and in the right place matters for primary challengers.

As we have seen in previous chapters, activity by interest groups and party committees is limited in primary elections. Incumbents, as presumptive nominees, can expect to raise money from political action committees throughout their tenure in office. Incumbents tend to raise slightly more than 40 percent of their money from political action committees. General election nonincumbents tend to fare somewhat worse; challengers raise somewhat less than 20 percent of their money from PACs and open seat candidates receive between 20 and 30 percent of their money from PACs. Self-funding, on the other hand, plays a greater role

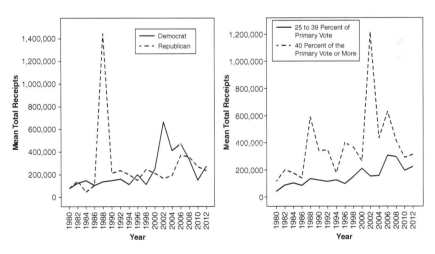

FIGURE 6.5 Average Receipts for Competitive Primary Challengers to Incumbents, by Party and by Level of Competitiveness

in the campaigns of nonincumbents than it does for incumbents, comprising as much as 20 percent of total funds raised by nonincumbents as opposed to less than 5 percent for incumbents. PACs play less of a role in Senate campaigns but the distinctions between incumbents and nonincumbents remain.

Figure 6.6 shows the sources of funds for competitive primary challengers to incumbents in the House. This figure shows that primary challengers are little different from general election challengers in the sources of their funds—PACs show no evidence of taking any greater of an interest in primary challengers than they have in the past, and self-funding plays a noticeable, but relatively consistent, role in the primary challengers' campaigns. The increase in fundraising by primary challengers during the 2000s is an increase in individual contributions. In addition, as Figure 6.7 shows, this is an increase in large individual contributions; there is no evidence of a surge in contributions from small donors across time.

As was the case above, there are too few cases of primary challenges in the Senate to present year-by-year patterns. Table 6.2, however, groups Senate challenges by decade. Even when we group challenges by decade we cannot be certain that the averages presented here are not unduly influenced by one or two races. The patterns presented here, however, do show a few trends that differ from House

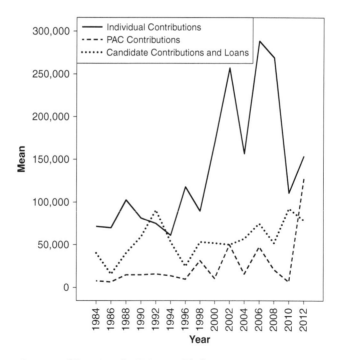

FIGURE 6.6 Sources of Receipts for Primary Challengers

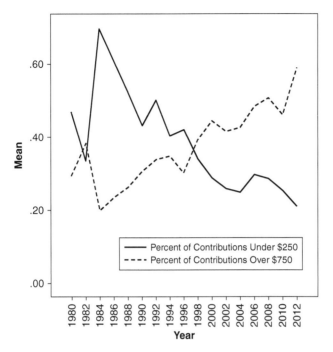

FIGURE 6.7 Average Percentage of Small and Large Contributions to Primary Challengers

TABLE 6.2 Campaign Finance for Senate Primary Challenges, 1980–2012

Decade	Average Receipts	Percent from Individuals	Percent from Candidate	Percent from PACs	Percent Small (< $750) Contributions	N
1980–1988	$241,365	76.3%	19.0%	4.6%	52.4%	10
1990–1998	732,537	55.2	36.3	5.5	46.3	14
2000–2008	1,870,959	50.9	29.7	3.6	38.7	10
2010–2012	2,536,135	71.8	16.3	2.0	64.3	7
Total	1,198,334	60.6	27.9	4.2	48.9	41

challenges. Most notably, the cost of a Senate challenge has clearly increased at a much more rapid rate than was the case in the House data. The increase in fundraising for Senate races has, however, come about primarily because of an increase in self-financing; Senate primary challengers are much more likely to contribute heavily to their own campaigns than are House challengers. This increase does not, however, account for nearly all of the increase in total money raised. Senate challengers have not become more dependent on large individual contributions than have House challengers; the rise in contributions in Senate challenges is driven in large part by a surge in small, often out-of-state contributions to several of the higher profile Senate challengers. Over the past two election cycles, Senate challengers have also relied much more on small contributors than they did in past years. Although they are few in number, Senate challenges have the potential to galvanize ideological donors nationwide.

The past two election cycles present somewhat of a puzzle. Both years featured a particularly large number of primary challenges. In the case of 2010, one might attribute the increase in the number of candidates to the influence of the Tea Party, or to the overall tumult of the 2010 general election. There was, however, a clear change in the rhetoric surrounding primary challenges to incumbents a few elections before that, and the surge during the earlier 2000s may have lent some credence to such language. The 2010 election was, however, somewhat orthogonal to that trend. More primary challengers emerged but less money, on average, flowed to their campaigns. The same was true in 2012 in the House, although the two Senate primary challengers looked more like the high-profile challengers of years past—they sought, with some success, to become national symbols of resistance to centrist Republican incumbents. If we look to what are perhaps the results political insiders care the most about—the numbers of incumbents defeated by primary challengers in these years—it is hard to argue that much has changed in incumbent primaries. As we shall see below, however, changes in the attention paid to selected primary challenges may have more subtle effects, effects that are difficult to accurately measure, on incumbent members of Congress.

Types of Primary Challenges to Incumbents

In any given congressional district, there is a large pool of potential congressional candidates. Numerous studies of congressional general elections have discussed the characteristics of congressional candidates, the strategic decision about whether or not to run, and the choice of what themes to raise in the campaign (see, e.g., Fowler and McClure 1989, Kazee 1994). The literature on political ambition is of limited applicability to most challenger vs. incumbent congressional primaries simply because savvy politicians will surely understand that their best chance at winning a congressional seat lies not in challenging an incumbent of their own party, but in waiting for that incumbent to retire or to seek higher office. This is the case even when the incumbent has obvious flaws (Layzell and Overby 1994). What this literature does suggest, however, is that while primaries are often a referendum on the incumbent, those who challenge the incumbent do not do so solely because of any one shortcoming of the incumbent. They run because they want the seat. The reasons reported for the challenge, then, may simply be the challenger's assessment of what is most likely to work, not the actual reason for the run.

The extent to which this is the case may vary according to the level of political experience of the challenger. Some analyses of primary challenges have sought to distinguish between those that feature a politically experienced challenger and those that do not (Pearson and Lawless 2008). Experienced challengers are more likely to be running to win than are inexperienced challengers. In general elections, for instance, single-issue candidates have at times noted that they have run to raise the visibility of their issue, without actually expecting to win (Boatright 2004). For primary challengers, the same logic would seem to apply. The problem, however, is that while it is hard enough to distinguish between reported reasons for a challenge, it is even harder to distinguish between the *actual* motivations of challengers.

A case study here may help to illustrate this dilemma. During the 1990s and 2000s, the city of Chicago was divided into seven congressional districts, most of which also stretched beyond city limits to include a small amount of suburban territory. Chicago is an overwhelmingly Democratic city; the city's members of Congress had little to worry about in the general election. One Chicago area representative, Dan Rostenkowski, lost his seat in 1994 to a Republican challenger following a criminal indictment against Rostenkowski, but this seat swung back to the Democrats in 1996. All of the city's other districts remained in Democratic hands throughout this time period.

Six of the city's seven districts have, however, had at least one competitive primary over the past twenty years, and the one that has not, the majority-minority Seventh District, was the scene of several competitive primaries in the 1970s and 1980s.[3] In these districts, victory in the primary is tantamount to winning the seat, so one could expect that many, if not most, of the primary challengers here are running to win.

The First District is a majority-minority district that encompasses much of the predominantly African-American south side of Chicago; the major white area of the district is the neighborhood of Hyde Park, an upper-middle class area that includes the University of Chicago. This was one of the first districts to elect an African-American representative; William Dawson represented the district from 1943 to 1970, and Harold Washington represented the district briefly before becoming the mayor of Chicago. From 1983 through the 1992 election, Charles Hayes, a trade union leader, held the district without any serious opposition. In 1992, however, Hayes was challenged by former Black Panther Bobby Rush. Rush criticized Hayes's lack of clout in Congress and insufficient attention to his district, and when the names from the House Banking scandal were released, Hayes's was at the top. Rush narrowly defeated Hayes in the primary, 42 percent to 39 percent. Rush has held the district comfortably ever since, with one exception. Following an unsuccessful 1999 run for Chicago mayor, Rush was challenged by State Senator Barack Obama. Rush turned back the challenge, winning 61 percent of the vote. Obama's challenge, according to his book *The*

Audacity of Hope, was fueled by ambition (Obama 2006, 105); he has little negative to say about Rush in his retelling of the race. There was little difference between the candidates on substantive policy issues. Obama, however, criticized Rush for his inattention to his congressional duties while running for mayor, and promised to be a more active member of Congress. Obama, a University of Chicago law professor, also sought to build a base among white voters in Hyde Park, an area where Rush had generally been considered weak. The two challenges in this district certainly have much to do with the ambitions of the challenger, but the two campaigns have revolved around criticisms of the incumbent's level of activity and ethics in office, not around the incumbent's voting record.

Illinois' Second District, which also is primarily comprised of African-American neighborhoods on the city's south side, was represented from 1980 to 1992 by Gus Savage, a civil rights activist. Savage's confrontational style limited his power in Congress, and he had become something of a pariah in Congress by the 1990s. Savage had difficulty in all of his primary bids, winning in the 1980s only because of the fractured primary field. In 1992, following allegations that he had sexually harassed a Peace Corps volunteer, Savage was handily defeated by community activist and Roosevelt University Professor Mel Reynolds. Reynolds, too, was dogged by scandal during his brief congressional career. He narrowly won renomination in 1994, and ultimately was forced to resign in 1995 as a result of sexual misconduct. Jesse Jackson, Jr. won the seat in a 1995 special election, and went unchallenged in the district's Democratic primaries until he, too, faced corruption charges in 2012. The challenges against Savage during the 1990s run the gamut of reasons, but the challenge that did him in in 1992, and the challenge Reynolds faced in 1994, clearly are all about scandal and ethics.

The Illinois Third District, which stretches through predominantly white areas of the city's southwest side into working class white suburbs beyond, was significantly altered in 1992. The 1992 Democratic primary featured two incumbents running against each other because Illinois lost a seat in that year's redistricting. The winner of this primary, William Lipinski, held the seat for fourteen more years before abruptly retiring shortly before the 2006 filing deadline. Lipinski's son, Daniel, won the 2006 primary without opposition. In 2008, the younger Lipinski held off two challengers. The stronger of the two, Mark Pera, criticized Lipinski for being too frequent a supporter of President Bush. Lipinski was likely seen as vulnerable in part because of his inexperience and his lack of political ties within the district—he had not resided in the district prior to winning the seat in 2006. The elder Lipinski and his son held virtually identical views on most policy matters, however, and the father was never challenged following his 1992 victory, suggesting that ideology was not all that mattered in this race.

The city's two white, north side incumbents during most of the 1980s and 1990s were Dan Rostenkowski and Sidney Yates. Both of these congressmen had accrued substantial power within Congress by this time. Rostenkowski was first elected in 1958, and by the 1980s had become chairman of the House Ways and Means Committee. Yates was first elected in 1948, and, with the exception of a two-year interlude following an unsuccessful run for the Senate in 1962, served until 1998. Yates was generally viewed as a champion for the National Endowment for the Arts, and was during the 1990s an Appropriations Subcommittee chairman. Rostenkowski was undoubtedly one of the most influential members of Congress, and was firmly allied with the city's Democratic establishment. His ethical scrapes, including allegations of mail fraud that eventually landed him in jail, prompted a challenge from political science professor and good-government advocate Dick Simpson in 1992. Simpson won 43 percent of the primary vote. Rostenkowski faced a field of four primary challengers in 1994, as his ethical troubles worsened, and he defeated Simpson and his other opponents with only 50 percent of the vote. He lost the 1994 general election. Yates also had the strong backing of the city's Democratic leaders, but in the late years of his career was dogged by criticisms regarding his ability to effectively represent the district. Yates's challengers never gained very much traction, but he was in his eighties by this time. Yates won 70 percent of the primary vote in 1990 and 65 percent in 1992 against relatively low-profile challengers. Yates's Republican opponents would pick up upon these criticisms in later elections (Layzell and Overby 1994; Boatright 2004, 132–36), but Yates left Congress on his own terms in 1998. The challenges in these two districts were prompted by obvious failings of the incumbents, but they were not supported by prominent party insiders, as the Obama and Reynolds challenges were.

Race has much to do with some primary challenges, in large part because majority-minority districts tend to be lopsidedly Democratic, forcing incumbents to focus their attentions more on the primary and less on the general election (see, e.g., Fenno 2003). The role of race is discussed in greater detail in the next chapter, but it merits some discussion here. Race is rarely a stated subtext of campaigns because when a primary challenge emerges in such districts both candidates are often of the same minority group. Many strong challenges of the 2000s—such as those to Earl Hilliard in Alabama and Cynthia McKinney in Georgia—have featured an African-American challenger who was able to draw the district's white vote. This is likely what Obama sought to do in 1992 as well. Conflict in such districts is also often generational, reflecting changes in the backgrounds of minority politicians. In a few instances, primary conflict can also be rooted in more subtle divisions. Chicago's Fourth District during the 1990s was a horseshoe-shaped district encompassing the city's Puerto Rican and Mexican neighborhoods. The district's representative, the Puerto Rican Luis Gutierrez, faced Mexican-American challengers in 1994, 1996, and 2002; each time, the challenger received between 30 and 40 percent of the primary vote. Appeals in these races tended to focus upon which communities were represented, or paid attention to, by the congressman. In the few instances where whites and blacks campaign against each other in primaries, race-based claims tend to be similar—whether a white representative can understand the issues of the black community, whether an African-American representative truly looks out for everyone in the district, and so forth.

No one (and certainly not President Obama's antagonists) would claim that Chicago politics bear much resemblance to politics in the rest of the United States. Yet this discussion of Chicago politics makes it clear that there is a lot going on in primaries—they are not all about the same thing, whether in Chicago or anywhere else. This complicates any effort to discern patterns within congressional primaries—how do we identify patterns, how do we relate them to trends in partisanship or anti-incumbent sentiment? Some may argue that a similar story could be told about general elections, but given that most voters identify the major parties with differing ideological views and that there are only two serious choices in congressional general elections, it is at least easier to do this in general election competition. The strategic concerns of a primary challenger have more to do with the incumbent than with the district's partisan leanings.[4] Analysts of congressional primaries may focus upon the consequences of a primary challenge for the party's candidate's general election fortunes, but it is not at all clear that challengers do this. As the Chicago cases show, we can make some rudimentary distinctions between types of challenges. However, there is no getting around the fact that this is a messy endeavor.

Complicating matters further, however, is the fact that all of the Chicago races discussed above took place in districts that have generally been reliably Democratic. Whoever wins the primary can expect to coast in the general election. There are some reasons to expect that primary challenges can be more frequent in these races—there is a large pool of ambitious Democrats who may not wish to wait their turn, and the Democratic Party does not have to worry that primary challenges will harm the party's general election prospects. Although the logic of these claims makes sense, the aggregate data discussed above, however, do not indicate that they are necessarily true. And even if they are more frequent, they merely indicate that there is a limited palette for those who challenge incumbents, and in most instances the race is more about the incumbent's failings than the challenger's qualifications for the job.

For an example of a different sort of challenge, one that took place in a less reliably partisan district, we have only to leave Chicago and head up the coast of Lake Michigan a few miles. Republican John Porter represented the district encompassing Evanston and other wealthy north Chicago suburbs from 1980 to 2000. Porter's district gave Bill Clinton 41 percent of its votes in 1992 (a plurality in this three-candidate race) and 50 percent of its votes in 1996. Porter was a fiscal conservative and a social moderate; most notably, he took a pro-choice stance on abortion during his time in Congress. Porter was renominated without challenge from 1982 through 1990, but he faced a string of challengers throughout the 1990s. His 1992 and 1994 challenger, anti-abortion activist

Kathleen Sullivan, garnered 40 percent of the primary vote in 1992 and 34 percent in 1994—enough, perhaps, to inspire other candidates to mount a broader critique of Porter. In 1996, conservative businessman Richard Rinaolo sought to run such a campaign, describing Porter as "a roadblock in the GOP revolution" (Fornek 1995) and as someone who was "out of touch with the Republican mainstream" (Black 1996). Rinaolo ultimately fared no better than Sullivan, winning 32 percent of the primary vote. While Rinaolo failed to unseat Porter, his campaign served to underscore the tension between the social moderates who have tended to represent this district and the rest of the GOP; Porter's successor, Mark Kirk, developed a similar profile in Congress, a profile that may well have helped him win the Republican nomination for Barack Obama's Senate seat in 2010. Kirk, like Porter, however, struggled to rein in the right wing of the party. In the 2010 Senate primary, Kirk faced several more conservative Republicans, and many Tea Party members expressed their discontent with his conservative credentials (McClelland 2010).

On its face, John Porter's primary challenges do not seem that different in their strategy than do some of the Chicago challengers, apart from the fact that they ran from the right in a Republican primary, as opposed to running from the left in a Democratic primary (as did Daniel Lipinski's opponents). Porter's district, however, may well not have been one that a conservative Republican could hold. In 2010, when Tea Party candidates dominated much of the public debate, the open seat race in this district featured a heated race between two candidates who aggressively sought to present themselves as moderates. Porter's opponents may not have been successful for this very reason, but their emergence bears similarities to many candidates who have sought, often with the help of organized interests, to "primary" opponents who are, in their eyes, insufficiently partisan. Porter's challengers are perhaps the exception to the rule I have established above—in these instances, it was not that John Porter had personal failings unrelated to politics (as the challengers to Mel Reynolds, Bobby Rush, or Sidney Yates argued); instead, these were challenges that were based on Porter's voting record. As we shall see below, there is some evidence that these types of challenges have become more frequent—or at least better publicized—over the past decade.

Categorizing Types of Primary Challenges

The discussion above of Chicago-area politics suggests that we need a typology of primary challenges in order to fully understand changes in incumbent primaries over time. The brief list of instances of "primarying" at the beginning of this chapter suggests that ideology may play a greater role in contemporary incumbent primaries than it once did. If we are to explore this claim, however, we need to reach back in time to measure the incidence of such challenges in the past and to seek to identify what other reasons for primary challenges exist. This is something that we were not able to do in our consideration of other types of primaries; ideology certainly matters in open seat primaries and challenger primaries, but it is easier to say whether incumbent primaries are "about" ideology than it is in other types of primaries because of the dominant role of incumbents. Any congressional primary where there is an incumbent winds up being about the incumbent, and the lines of attack in a challenge to an incumbent can be easily measured.

Doing this is consequential for a number of reasons. First, the limited number of primary challenges to incumbents enables us to measure variations in types of challenges across time. Does ideology play a greater role in primary challenges today than it once did? It seems that such an argument can be made, while variations in the number of incumbents challenged on the basis of scandal, of race, or of alleged incompetence would seem immune to any temporal variation—we have no reason to suspect, for instance, that members of Congress become more or less corrupt or more or less competent over time. Second, if we are able to categorize challenges we can look at how well candidates do—do ideological challengers outperform those who run against the incumbent on the basis of scandal? And third, we can consider primary divisiveness. In our earlier chapters, we reviewed the literature on whether contested primaries help or hurt nominees in the general election. While this literature has not arrived at definitive results, the divisiveness argument seems in many ways more relevant to incumbent primaries than to open seat or challenger primaries. Political parties may wish to clear the field for their preferred nominee in an open seat or challenger primary, but, as we have seen, there is little evidence that they are successful at doing this or that such efforts matter. If, however, incumbents are forced to spend money to fend off primary opponents, this is money that could otherwise be spent in the general election, so the claims for general election effects make a bit more sense. In addition, if one turns back to the presidential literature that has often been used to frame discussions of congressional primaries, anecdotes about the effects of, for instance, the primary challenges to Jimmy Carter in 1980 or George H.W. Bush in 1992 certainly suggest that a primary challenge is a sign of weakness for the incumbent. Looking at the reasons for primary challenges can help us develop expectations about when primary challengers are a sign of general election trouble for congressional incumbents.

Aggregate Data

From 1970 through 2012, there were 830 House primaries in which the incumbent was held to 75 percent or less of the vote. Of these, 577 were discussed at some length in each year's edition of the *Almanac of American Politics* or *Politics in America*, the two standard compendia of biographies of members of Congress. The descriptions of these primaries can easily be grouped into a relatively small number of categories; Table 6.3 lists these categories and the frequency of challenges

TABLE 6.3 Types of Primary Challenges to Incumbents, 1970–2012

Category	N	Percent of All Challenges	Percent of Categorizable Challenges
Scandal	106	12.8%	18.4%
Competence, Age	122	14.7	21.1
Single-Issue Challenges	55	6.7	9.7
Ideological Challenge from Center	32	3.9	5.5
Ideological Challenge from Left (Democrats) or Right (Republicans)	112	13.5	19.4
Other (Including Race, Party Factionalism, Redistricting)	149	18.9	25.7
No Reason Given	253	30.5	—
Total	830		

that fall into each of these categories.[5] It should be noted that most of these categories should be immune to trends over time. Some years (most notably, 1992) feature scandals that engulf an unusually large number of incumbents, but overall there is no reason to expect that the number of members of Congress accused of ethical misdeeds or incompetence should change in any systematic way over time. Likewise, the "other" category here includes challenges based on the incumbent's race (that is, for instance, that a white representative should not represent a district that is heavily African American or Latino), or on change in district composition brought about by redistricting.[6] These types of primaries are most common in the years following redistricting—in part because population changes brought about by that redistricting are most consequential in the election immediately following the redrawing of district lines, and in part because changes in the racial composition of districts also are sharpest immediately after redistricting. Single-issue challenges are also idiosyncratic in nature—the Vietnam War was a source of some challenges in the early 1970s, as was the Iraq War in the early 2000s, and busing and abortion also were the source of some challenges. Still other challenges have to do with the politics of individual districts; in one instance, traffic policies related to the Dallas airport spawned one challenge.

The lone area in which we might look for consistent changes across time is in ideological challenges—challenges such as those waged against Richard Lugar or Joseph Lieberman. Discussions of political polarization in Congress have focused upon the declining number of moderate Democrats and Republicans in Congress. The data on primary challenges suggest, however, that primary challenges in themselves are not a reason for this decline. Just as primary challenges to incumbents are rare, so ideological challenges are rare among the reasons for such challenges. Slightly more than 13 percent of the categorizable challenges to incumbents over the 1970 to 2012 time period are clearly instances of ideological challenges from the political extremes of the two parties—in other words, fewer than five challenges per year have to do with allegedly insufficient partisanship or fidelity to conservative or liberal principles on the part of the incumbent. In any given year, there are twice as many challenges based on personal failings of the incumbent than there are on ideology. Be this as it may, Figure 6.8 shows that the number of ideological challenges has been edging upward over the past three election cycles, while centrist challengers have disappeared entirely. Time frame, however, is important. There are more ideological challenges today than there were in the early 2000s or in the 1990s, but until 2008 the number of challenges remained lower than it had been in the 1970s. Ideological challengers did not, on average, do any better in terms of vote share than did ideological challengers in previous years—in fact, ideological challengers in 2010 and 2012 did less well, on average, than did similar challengers in 2006 and 2008.

Senate challenges show similar patterns, although again they are few enough in number to make graphical display unilluminating. On average, there are two to four cases of Senate primary challenges in each election cycle between 1970 and 2012, with a high of eight (1980) and a low of zero (1984, 1988, and 2000). In 1992, a year of unusually high primary competition in House races, there were six

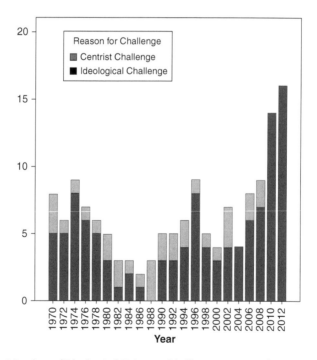

FIGURE 6.8 Number of Ideological Primary Challenges to Incumbents, 1970–2012

Senate incumbents who faced primary opposition, and in 2006 and 2010 there were five incumbents who faced primary challengers. Twenty senators faced challenges on the basis of ideology, and twelve of these twenty were challenged in the past five election cycles—Republican Arlen Specter in 2004 (from the right, as a Republican) and 2010 (from the left, as a Democrat), Republicans Lincoln Chafee and Mike DeWine and Democrat Joseph Lieberman in 2006, Democrat John Kerry in 2008, Democrats Blanche Lincoln and Michael Bennet and Republicans Lisa Murkowski and John McCain in 2010, and Republicans Richard Lugar and Orrin Hatch in 2012. Only two (Specter in 2010 and Lugar in 2012) failed to reach the general election, and given that Specter had recently switched parties, his was an unusual case. There is, as well, the case of Utah's Robert Bennett, who lost his bid to appear on the primary ballot in Utah in 2010.

One must take the patterns in the reasons for challenges with a grain of salt, however. The coding here relies on the reasons provided by nonpartisan, relatively objective sources, but the coding captures the reasons challengers have provided for their challenges, so they are not objectively "true" reasons. That is, if a challenger attacks an incumbent for scandalous behavior or incompetence, this does not mean that the incumbent has indeed engaged in questionable behavior or is in fact incompetent.[7] Likewise, a challenger who alleges that the incumbent is insufficiently conservative or insufficiently liberal may not be accurately portraying the incumbent's record. Furthermore, ideological extremism is somewhat related to the district; a moderate Republican who represents a district evenly split among the parties (or composed of relatively centrist Republican voters) may be out of step with his or her party, but not with his or her district. If this is the case, the challenger may not do well in the primary. And if an incumbent is not, in fact, as moderate as his or her challenger would have voters believe, the challenger may do poorly simply because the premise of the challenge does not ring true. One cannot, then, make claims about how well ideological challengers do without taking into account the composition of the district, the composition of the primary electorate, and the particulars of the incumbent's voting record. To an extent, then, we are measuring here avenues of attack for challengers, not necessarily faults on the part of the incumbent. True, a challenger who garners 25 or 30 percent of the vote by criticizing the incumbent's ideological leanings may arguably have something of a point, else he or she would not have done as well as he or she did. Yet the ceiling for a challenger's ideological attacks may vary by district.

Consequences of Primary Challenges

What does this suggest about the effects of primary challenges? A cynic might say that it suggests nothing, that even if one accepts the notion that there is more turbulence during primary season it affects a small number of incumbents, and even then it does not clearly affect their ability to retain their seats. One might look, as well, at the behavior of the incumbents who do face primary challenges, either during the term preceding the primary or the term immediately following the primary. There is no clear evidence of shifts in ideology among incumbents who face primary challenges, and, as noted earlier, we cannot easily separate out money raised and spent by incumbents for the purpose of winning the primary from money raised and spent for the purpose of winning the general election. This approach may be suspect, however, in that it selects out only the incumbents who have failed to scare away primary challengers—we are looking solely at incumbents who have not changed their behavior sufficiently to deter ideological challengers.

Anecdotes abound about incumbents who have prepared for the possibility of a primary challenge. Some moderates, such as Senator Olympia Snowe, may opt to retire (as Snowe did in 2012) rather than run against a determined primary challenger—although here we can only guess about Snowe's true reason for retiring. Others, such as senators John McCain, Charles Grassley, or Orrin Hatch, have been said to have raised money in anticipation of a primary challenge or to have abandoned moderate positions in order to immunize themselves against charges that they are too moderate (Calmes 2009). Similarly, anecdotes abound regarding the effects of primary challenges on the general election fortunes of incumbents who do face divisive challenges—Rhode Island's Lincoln Chafee, opposed by a conservative primary challenger in his 2006 campaign, ultimately lost his seat in the general election, and one can certainly speculate that this challenge damaged his moderate credentials in a state that has become increasingly skeptical of Republicans.[8]

There is no way to prove that incumbents think differently about primary challenges today than they ever did—perhaps cases such as McCain's, even if true, find an echo in challenges in the 1970s and 1980s. Yet if we are to consider anecdotes, it is possible to string together evidence that something has changed in the nature of ideological challenges. Consider the following narrative about challenges in the House over the past two decades:

Pennsylvania Republican Jim Greenwood's case is similar to that of John Porter, the Illinois Republican discussed above. Greenwood represented the Bucks County area of Pennsylvania, another quintessential suburban Republican district. Like Porter, Greenwood faced primary candidates in the mid-1990s who argued that he was too liberal, particularly on social issues. Greenwood faced a challenge from the right in every election year from 1996 through 2002; he received between 60 and 70 percent of the primary vote each time. A 1997 *Philadelphia Inquirer* article described Greenwood as "a man caught in the middle" (Mondics 1997). Although news accounts claimed that Greenwood generally ignored his opponents, his challengers during these election years frequently criticized his "liberal agenda," "extreme voting record," and lack of fidelity to "core Republican values" (Singer 1998). Greenwood's opponent in 1996, 2000, and 2002, conservative activist Tom Lingenfelter, dubbed himself the "real Republican candidate" in the race. Although Lingenfelter received 40 percent of the primary vote in 1996, he, and Greenwood's other primary opponent, a city council member, failed to reach this level in subsequent races. Greenwood abruptly retired shortly before the 2004 election, and the seat was won by another moderate Republican, who would go on to lose the seat to a Democrat in 2006. Lingenfelter continued to run for Congress as an independent in subsequent elections.

Republican Connie Morella represented the Maryland suburbs of Washington, D.C., from 1986 to 2002. Perhaps even more so than Porter, Morella needed to define herself as a moderate in order to win election in a district that voted heavily for Bill Clinton and Al Gore in the presidential elections of 1992, 1996, and 2000. Morella frequently broke with her party—most notably in her decision to vote against all four impeachment counts against President Clinton in 1998. Her 1996 primary challenger, Maryland Delegate Barrie Ciliberti, said of her votes on impeachment that "she has a reputation and a voting record, when she is in clutch positions, of supporting the Democrats and not her party" (Babington and Hsu 1998). Ciliberti held Morella to 65 percent of the primary vote in 1996—not a strong enough showing that Morella's renomination was ever threatened, but enough that Ciliberti was able to highlight conservatives' unhappiness with Morella. In 1994, Arnold Arnejaska, a political unknown, had held Morella to 70 percent. Arnejaska reportedly conferred with Ciliberti in 1996, and spoke to the *Washington Post* of his interest in finding a consensus conservative alternative to Morella to run in the primary (Abramowitz 1995). Although Morella did not face primary opponents in 1998 and 2000—and would ultimately lose her seat to a Democrat in 2002—news coverage throughout the 1990s portrayed her as someone who would be vulnerable were the right challenger to emerge.

The campaigns against Morella, Porter, and Greenwood never really caught fire. There were some, however, that did. Sherwood Boehlert, a Republican who represented the Oneida County area of New York, won only 65 percent of the primary vote in 1996; two relatively underfunded candidates, both of whom attacked Boehlert's stance on abortion, split the remainder of the vote. In 1998, Boehlert ran unopposed only after his potential primary opponent, a high school teacher named David Vickers, was disqualified from appearing on the ballot. In 2000 Vickers ran again; despite only spending $27,000, Vickers held Boehlert to only 57 percent of the vote. Vickers did not only criticize Boehlert's stance on abortion; he drew broader distinctions between the two on government spending and criticized Boehlert's stance on Cayuga Indian land claims in the district. Vickers also appeared as a minor party candidate on the general election ballot, winning 21 percent of the vote.

Inspired by Vickers's showing, Cayuga County Legislator David Walrath mounted an even stronger challenge in 2002. Walrath had enough money to hire a professional campaign team. Walrath took the same stances as had Vickers, and he also sought the endorsement of minor conservative parties (New York allows for cross-endorsements). Most importantly, Walrath received the endorsement of the Club for Growth, which pledged to "hold Boehlert's feet to the fire" (Dinan 2002). Boehlert barely edged out Walrath, 53 percent to 47 percent. As other, more politically experienced Republicans also toyed with the idea of entering the race (Kriss 2003), Walrath immediately began his 2004 campaign, courting the support of an array of conservative advocacy groups, including the American Conservative Union, the Club for Growth, Concerned Women for America, the National Rifle Association, and the National Right to Life Committee (*Roll Call* 2003). Boehlert waged a far more aggressive campaign in 2004, bringing in national Republican leaders to campaign with him and singling out Walrath for personal attacks (Lyman, Rapp, and Hurwitz 2004). Boehlert did somewhat better in 2004, winning 59 percent of the vote in his rematch with Walrath. Boehlert retired in 2006, a retirement that may have been hastened by his experience in the primaries.

Boehlert's experience shows the growing clout of conservative challengers in the primaries, and it is not unique. Several moderate senators, as well, had increasing trouble during the late 1990s and early 2000s. Pennsylvania Senator Arlen Specter, first elected in 1986, faced steadily increasing pressure from the right in his primaries. In 1992 and 1998 he was renominated with 65 and 67 percent, respectively, against underfunded conservative challengers, who often focused on abortion in their campaigns. In 2004, however, Specter faced sitting House member Pat Toomey. With the endorsement of the Club for Growth, the *National Review*, Paul Weyrich of the Heritage Foundation, and several other prominent conservatives, Toomey narrowly missed beating Specter, winning 49 percent of the primary vote. Toomey raised an estimated $1 million through contributions bundled by the Club for Growth (Barone and Cohen 2005, 1209) and benefitted from another $1 million in advocacy spending by the club. Toomey became president of the Club for Growth following his 2004 campaign, resigning to challenge Specter again in 2010. At this point, Specter switched parties rather than face another challenge from Toomey; he lost the Democratic primary for Senate in 2010 to a liberal challenger.

Were such primary challenges confined to the Republican Party, however, moderate Democrats would (obviously) have little to worry about. Although the accounts above show an increase in the seriousness of conservative primary challenges in the Republican Party, moderate Democrats in 2006 and 2008 were not immune to them either. The storyline for Democrats, however, is different—there are few instances of the sort of low-key primarying that Greenwood, Porter, and Morella faced. Instead, the major story of the 2006 primary season for Democrats was Ned Lamont's challenge to Joseph Lieberman in Connecticut. Lieberman, the Democratic vice presidential nominee in 2000, had never had primary opposition before, although throughout his career he had been more conservative than Connecticut's other Democratic senator—his ADA scores tended to be in the sixties while Connecticut Senator Chris Dodd consistently scored in the nineties. Lieberman won re-election easily in the general elections of 1994 and 2000 as well. Although in some instances incumbent senators can draw very experienced primary opponents (as was the case for Specter in 2004), Lamont did not appear to be a strong candidate on paper; his only prior political experience was an unsuccessful bid for the state Senate. Lamont's campaign began with a focus on Lieberman's support for the Iraq War, featuring an advertisement showing Lieberman embracing President Bush. As the campaign developed, however, Lamont broadened his critique to frame Lieberman as, in the words of a *New York Times* article, "a celebrity senator who has grown out of touch with constituents' concerns about jobs and affordable health care" (Healy 2006). Lamont drew upon the resources of liberal advocacy groups such as MoveOn.org to create an extensive email list of supporters and to generate support among liberal bloggers (see, e.g., Cohen 2008). Lamont narrowly defeated Lieberman in the Democratic primary. Connecticut does not, however, have laws preventing "sore losers" from running in the general election. With only a token Republican candidate in the general election, Lieberman was able to run as an independent candidate, garner some of the Democratic vote and most of the Republican vote, and defeat Lamont in the general election.[9]

These candidates all survived challenges from primary opponents who questioned their fidelity to their party. Other candidates have not been so lucky. Wayne Gilchrest, challenged several times during the 2000s and finally defeated in 2008, was a moderate Republican seeking to hold a middle-of-the-road district in Maryland; his opponent, Andy Harris, benefitted from bundled contributions gathered by the Club for Growth. Al Wynn, a suburban Maryland Democrat, was not even that conservative of a Democrat, but he was conservative enough that voters ultimately turned him out in his 2008 renomination bid; his challenger, Donna Edwards, was the beneficiary of large independent expenditures from MoveOn.org, the League of Conservation Voters, and several labor unions. And Chris Cannon was a relatively conservative Republican, but not conservative enough for Utah primary voters. In 2010, in an election that will be remembered for the Tea Party and for the success of so many conservative Republican candidates, a substantial number of moderates in both parties faced primary challengers, but only one House member, South Carolina Representative Bob Inglis, was defeated on account of his alleged moderation.[10]

If we put these races in context, however, it is evident that there is no clear narrative to be told about primary defeats. Figure 6.9 shows the number of defeats in House and Senate primaries dating all the way back to 1946. Apart from predictable spikes in redistricting years (the graph here includes races where one incumbent faces another), there is no clear trend over time, no relationship between the

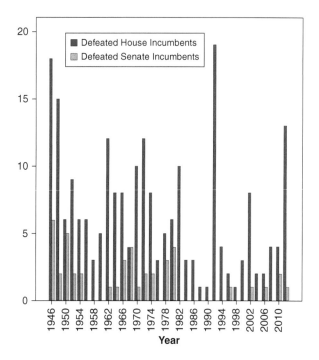

FIGURE 6.9 Incumbents Defeated in House and Senate Primaries, 1946–2012

Source: Hinckley 1981, 39, for 1946–1968 data; author's calculations for 1970–2012.

number of defeats and partisan swings, and no relationship between House and Senate defeats.

It is difficult to read very much into a small number of primary defeats, but it is also natural to do just this. Even if we have not been able to demonstrate that the nature of ideological primary challenges has changed, several features here stand out. First, a select number of primaries have clearly been nationalized to some degree, as the prevalence of outside money indicates. Second, the rhetorical impact of taking on one or two high-profile moderates may be of more value today than it was in previous years. Perhaps Morella would face stronger primary opposition today than she did in the 1990s; perhaps Sherwood Boehlert saw the writing on the wall and left Congress before those who opposed his moderate leanings could effectively unite around a candidate. While this narrative is hardly proof of any sort of change in primary challenges to incumbents, one could clearly argue that risk-averse congressional incumbents do not need proof that they are in trouble in order to change their ways. This narrative also suggests that the interests of political parties and interest groups in congressional primaries may be influenced by a small number of highly publicized primary challenges; groups and parties, as well, do not need proof that primaries today are any different in the past in order to invest resources in order to make them different.

Party and Group Interests in Incumbent Primaries

In the past two chapters, we established that political party organizations and outside interests are somewhat wary of taking sides in congressional primaries. While party operatives may encourage candidates to run for office and may even try to clear the field for their favored candidates, in many instances they maintain a stance of neutrality when there are multiple viable candidates vying for the party's nomination. Good candidates, after all, should be able to win primaries without the party's intervention. Access-oriented interest groups, likewise, prefer to aid candidates who they see as likely winners—and again, likely winners should be able to win primaries without outside assistance.

This is even more the case in primaries where there is already an incumbent present. It is almost unheard of for incumbents to be outspent in the primaries. Even incumbents accused of misdeeds have campaign organizations in place that can help them survive primary challenges, so involvement by the party committees on their behalf is not necessary, and involvement by party committees on behalf of their opponents can harm the party's general election prospects or result in difficult situations for the parties if the incumbent does, in the end, triumph. As we have seen above, organized interests play a minimal role in most primary challenges, and the groups that do get involved are those that care little about access to lawmakers.

There are some extreme cases where an incumbent is so unpopular that groups may rally around other candidates, but these are rare cases indeed. Current Speaker of the House John Boehner is one such candidate. Prior to serving in the House, Boehner served three terms as an Ohio state representative. He was one of two candidates running for the Republican nomination in 1990 against incumbent Buz Lukens, in a reliably Republican southern Ohio district. Lukens had been convicted in 1989 of soliciting sex from a minor, and he was widely seen as having virtually no chance of winning the nomination. As the stronger of Lukens's two opponents, Boehner raised $74,000 from PACs, including contributions from PACs affiliated with AT&T, Dow Chemical, National City Bank, and a variety of other groups that are infrequent players in other primary challenges. Boehner also received a $5,000 donation from the National Republican Campaign Committee. He easily won the primary and has gone on to win the general election in every year since with minimal Democratic opposition. Clearly, Boehner was a safe bet, but his case is unusual among primary challenges.

In races such as Boehner's, the incentive for parties and groups is simple—curry favor with the candidate most likely to win. This logic is certainly absent from races such as the challenges described above to veteran lawmakers such as

Joseph Lieberman or Alfred Wynn. Accordingly, most interest groups stay out, as do the party committees. Yet, as the descriptions above show, some groups become involved, and although the party committees do not enter these races, it is becoming more common for some party leaders to back primary challengers. What can we say about the incentives for these political actors?

Political Parties

It is natural for party campaign committees to stay out of primary challenges. The party campaign committees, after all, are run by members of Congress, and there has long been an unofficial rule that these committees will, wherever possible, seek to help any endangered incumbents.[11] Incumbents rarely receive direct contributions from the party committees early in their campaigns, simply because they do not need party money. Direct contributions, after all, are small enough that they have little impact on a campaign; in the case of a nonincumbent, party expenditures can serve as a signal that a party cares about a race, but party independent expenditures are far more consequential in dollar terms and tend be made during the general election, not the primary.

Incumbent members of Congress can, however, garner financial support or campaign assistance from popular members of their party. Here again, incumbents have a substantial edge over their primary opponents. Arkansas's Blanche Lambert Lincoln, for instance, received Leadership PAC contributions from several of her colleagues in the Senate, and one prominent fellow Arkansas Democrat, former President Bill Clinton, campaigned for her when she faced a primary challenger in 2010. One reason for political insiders, whether they be fellow members of Congress or other prominent individuals in the party, to side with threatened incumbents is that challenged incumbents will have personal ties with other lawmakers. Incumbents may well wish to call in favors from those whom they have helped in the past. Primary challengers do not have similar ties or political clout. Because incumbents usually ward off their primary opponents, more often than not the decision to help a challenged incumbent is also a safe bet for other politicians.

There are limits, however, to this sort of assistance, as senators Joe Lieberman and Lisa Murkowski found out. Both of these incumbent senators received some assistance from party leaders early in their campaigns, but as the date of the primary election approached, these party leaders equivocated. Lieberman received support from, among others, aspiring presidential candidate Hillary Clinton early in his campaign, and Senate Minority Leader Harry Reid sought to discourage Lieberman's primary foe, Ned Lamont, from running. After Lieberman lost the Democratic primary and opted to run as an independent, however, many Democrats rallied to Lamont's side (Medina 2006). Similarly, Lisa Murkowski lost the support of the National Republican Senatorial Committee and Senate Minority Leader Mitch McConnell after she lost her Republican primary in 2010, even though she, like Lieberman, opted to run as an independent and showed soon after the primary election that she had a good chance of winning the general election.

Party campaign committees, then, are highly risk-averse in their approach to primary challenges, and they also operate under a strict set of rules that discourage involvement in primaries. Party leaders, for the most part, are also risk averse, although slightly less so. There have been instances where party leaders have backed primary challengers, but these instances are unusual. Most notably, President Franklin Delano Roosevelt campaigned for a number of challengers to anti-New Deal Democrats in 1938 (Dunn 2012). Most historical accounts indicate that Roosevelt had a poor track record in helping these challengers get elected, and after the election he sought to mend fences with some of the Democrats he had campaigned against. With the exception of the support some members of George W. Bush's administration provided to Congressman John Sununu in his bid to unseat New Hampshire Senator Robert Smith in 2002, there are no other recent instances of presidents campaigning for primary challengers.[12]

One of the most notable features of primary challenges in 2010 and 2012, however, was the involvement of Senator Jim DeMint and his Leadership PAC, the Senate Conservatives Fund. DeMint presents an unusual case—as with many of the developments of 2010, his activities may be a harbinger of things to come or they may be a curiosity. DeMint took sides in several contested Republican primaries in both years. His Leadership PAC spent on behalf of Lisa Murkowski's opponent Joe Miller, but the expenditures were made during the general election, not the primary (Sarah Palin did campaign for Miller during the primary election). DeMint's activities sparked concern among some senators that DeMint would side with other primary opponents, sparking DeMint to announce in 2011 that he did not have plans to aid any Senate primary challengers in 2012 (although reports indicated that he did provide late support for Richard Mourdock in Indiana).[13] DeMint and Palin, however, are hardly typical Republicans—both have sought to ally themselves with a conservative movement that often is at odds with Republican Party orthodoxy.

Interest Groups

Just as the interests of DeMint and Palin are not always consonant with the interests of the Republican Party, so there are a select number of organized interests whose goals, while they are generally partisan, are not always in line with the goals of the parties they tend to support. Interest group scholars tend to make a distinction between groups that seek access, such as the banking PACs that supported John Boehner's primary bid, and those that seek influence, such as those that supported the campaigns of Donna Edwards and Pat Toomey.[14] There are very few PACs that see primary challenges as an appropriate venue for either access or influence. Table 6.4 shows the top PACs spending on behalf of primary

TABLE 6.4 Top Interest Groups Spending in Congressional Primary Challenges, 2000–2012

PAC	Number of Candidates Supported	Total
Service Employees International Union	6	$909,447
Club for Growth	11	439,084
MoveOn.org	3	407,296
League of Conservation Voters	6	216,361
EMILYs List	3	181,540
Total	21*	$2,153,728

* Some candidates received support from more than one group.

challengers since 2000 (this includes both direct contributions and independent expenditures). Overall, $6.2 million was spent by groups on behalf of primary challengers during this fourteen-year period.[15] These five PACs together spent over one-third of that total. And they spent this money on a total of twenty-one different candidates—a small fraction of the candidates waging primary bids against incumbents.

The relationship between campaign finance and primary success, as we have seen in this chapter and before, is complicated. Because primary turnout is so low and primary elections do not consistently garner public interest the way general election campaigns do, one or two large advertising campaigns, undertaken late in a campaign, can catch an incumbent napping. Some of the groups listed in the table above are well known for their attention to particular issues—for instance, EMILY's List has supported female candidates since its formation in 1985, the League of Conservation Voters was formed in 1969 and is one of the more politically active environmental groups in the country, and the National Rifle Association has existed for over a century and is the nation's largest gun rights organization. For such groups, activity during primaries might make sense if they are working against legislators hostile to their interests, and these groups are powerful enough that they need not worry about the repercussions that might come from losing. Other groups listed here, however, such as the Club for Growth and MoveOn.org, are newer organizations that have not historically had a singular issue focus. For such groups, the notoriety that comes from supporting a high-profile ideological challenger may increase their visibility and help these groups establish themselves. The Club for Growth, for instance, has singled out some incumbent Republicans for criticism long before challengers emerge; such efforts may inspire prospective challengers to approach the group for help in mounting a campaign. MoveOn and a number of smaller groups emulated the Club's tactics in identifying centrist Democrats to challenge in 2006 and 2008.

All of these groups, however, need to balance efforts to unseat moderate legislators against their own partisan preferences: do they want to unseat moderates so badly that they would risk handing the seat to the other party? The Club for Growth has been criticized by some Republican legislators for supporting conservative candidates who are unlikely to defeat Democrats in a general election, and liberal groups have faced similar criticisms. One intriguing development in 2012, however, was the formation of the Campaign for Primary Accountability, a Super PAC that made it its mission to support primary challengers of both parties, on the grounds that incumbents of both parties are responsible for the nation's problems. The group announced on its website that "ten percent of voters participate in the dominant primaries. This equates to an average of only 40,000–50,000 voters in each district. As pathetic as this seems, the low turnout in primaries represents a real opportunity. That's because just a small percentage of voters in any district can change the outcome of the primary and, therefore, change who will end up representing that district in Congress."[16] Although the Campaign for Primary Accountability spent money in opposition to several of the members of Congress defeated or seriously challenged in the 2012 primaries, it is not at all clear what role the Campaign's advertisements played in the election outcomes. Its advertisements may have made a difference in some races, or it may have strategically picked races where the incumbents were already in trouble so that it could claim credit when the incumbents lost.

There are, then, a very small number of established politicians who have an interest in encouraging primary competition, and a small coterie of organized interests that have focused their attention on congressional primaries. Given that a limited number of primary challenges are competitive in any given year, interest groups can have an impact if they focus on races where incumbents are vulnerable and where they can expect media coverage of their efforts. It is difficult to argue that the activities of groups or politicians determine the outcome in these races, but they clearly do play a part. To the extent that these efforts cause concern among other incumbents, they can be said to be a good investment of money.

Conclusions

Primary challenges to incumbents are noteworthy precisely because they are uncommon. One expects primaries for open seats, and in most congressional districts primaries for the nomination to face an incumbent in the general election are also not unusual. In fact, primary competition in these races is generally regarded as a positive thing. Primary challenges to incumbents, on the other hand, are more problematic. Challenges to incumbents who have ethical problems are, similarly, generally seen as a healthy thing. When Representative William Jefferson was found to have accepted illegal contributions or when Representative Gary Condit was investigated for his connection to the death of an intern in his office, few argued that primary opposition was in any way inappropriate. On the other hand, ideological challenges are often seen as a sign of the weakness of political parties or of heightened polarization in Congress and among party activists. As this chapter has shown, such fears may well be overblown—ideological challenges are neither novel nor demonstrably effective. There are, however, some signs that a select number of primary challenges have effectively been nationalized by organized interests or by politicians with something to gain by bucking their party. It is unclear whether this development will remain with us or not, but it does pose the possibility that the *threat* of a primary challenge can have an effect on the behavior of incumbents.

Notes

1 This chapter draws upon and updates my prior book (Boatright 2013) on primary challenges to incumbents.
2 We begin here with 1980 because it is the first year in which the Federal Election Commission made available computer files with candidate fundraising data. Chapters 4 and 5 drew upon only the past decade because of the need for a large number of computerized records of contributions; we can trace incumbents back further—using paper filings available at the Federal Election Commission office—because the number of challenged incumbents is so much smaller than was the number of candidates considered in Chapters 4 and 5.
3 All of the Chicago districts referred to by number in this section have had the same district numbers since 1992. While some suburban districts (such as that of John Porter, discussed below) have been changed substantially by redistricting, the districts in the city itself have been largely unchanged over the time period I discuss here.
4 Accounts of primary competition in other one-party areas of the country show similar patterns; in the case of the South, for instance, see the discussions of primary elections in Key 1949, Lamis 1984b, Rae 1994, Glaser 1996, and Berard 2001.
5 For further discussion of the coding method here see Boatright 2013.
6 I exclude from these calculations primaries in which two incumbents run against each other as a result of redistricting; for discussion of these types of primaries see Chapter 7.
7 I compared my coding of primary challenges where the incumbent is accused of scandal to the coding by Praino, Stockemer, and Moscardelli (2011) of formal investigations into scandals involving incumbents pursuing reelection. Praino and his coauthors find sixty-three such incumbents. Thirty-six of these sixty-three, or 57 percent, were held to less than 75 percent of the vote in the subsequent primary, and ten were defeated in the primary. However, sixty-one of the eighty-seven incumbents whose opponents alleged scandal (excluding multiple challenges to the same incumbents) were not, in fact, formally investigated for some sort of scandal.
8 For discussion of this race, see Laffey 2007.
9 Facing the likelihood of a Democratic opponent and a stronger Republican opponent in 2012, Lieberman chose to retire.

10 This is probably the congressman Clinton is referring to at the end of the quote that begins this chapter.
11 For discussion of congressional campaign committee decision-making, see Kolodny 1998, Currinder 2008.
12 For discussion of White House involvement in this race see Belluck 2002.
13 See Bravender 2012. DeMint stepped down from the Senate shortly after the 2012 election to become president of the Heritage Foundation. His Super PAC continues to exist, although DeMint has no formal role in running it.
14 For one among many interest group studies that explains the distinction between access and influence, see Wright 1996.
15 This figure includes direct contributions and independent expenditures. This is a pittance compared to overall spending by PACs; direct contributions from PACs to congressional candidates have increased from $250 million in 2000 to over $400 million in 2012, and independent expenditures on congressional races have grown to the point that they exceeded $300 million in 2010, according to Center for Responsive Politics data.
16 www.campaign4primaryaccountability.org/f_a_q, accessed February 8, 2014.

7

RACE, REDISTRICTING, AND PRIMARY ELECTIONS

The subject of race has been touched upon in various places in this book, enough to indicate that the politics of majority-minority districts at least have the potential to differ substantially from the politics of majority-white districts. This is the case in part because those racial minorities large enough to comprise a majority of voters in some House districts—African Americans, Latinos, and Asian Americans—have tended to vote overwhelmingly for the Democratic Party. Majority-minority districts, then, are with only rare exceptions Democratic districts, and they are more often than not so lopsidedly Democratic that the election that matters in these districts is not the general election but the Democratic primary.

Majority-minority districts are also unique among congressional districts in that their boundaries are subject to far more scrutiny than are those of other congressional districts. The Voting Rights Act Amendments of 1982 required states to create majority-minority districts where possible, and prohibited subsequent "retrogression," or reduction in the minority composition of such districts.[1] Majority-minority districts have thus tended to be a product of each decade's redistricting. We saw in earlier chapters that redistricting years tend to produce more tumultuous primary elections than do other years. The need to create or preserve majority-minority districts is one reason for this tumult; it can unsettle district lines and bring about competition in two ways. First, when majority-minority districts are created, these districts can attract a large field of competitors. Second, the need to establish or preserve majority-minority districts can mean that adjacent white districts have to be substantially redrawn, particularly in states that are losing seats.

The subject of race and of majority-minority districts raises a host of questions that will be considered in this chapter. The main question here is whether competition in primary elections in heavily African-American districts and heavily

Latino districts is different from competition in other congressional districts (we shall make some reference to heavily Asian-American districts as well, although there are far fewer of them). In order to ask this question, though, we cannot simply compare white districts to minority districts. Instead, we must ask whether primary competition in majority-minority districts is a function of race or merely of lopsidedness. That is, do primaries in districts that are, for instance, 70 percent African American and 75 percent Democratic resemble those in districts that are 75 percent Republican? Do they resemble primaries in districts that are 75 percent Democratic and mostly white? In other words, how do we know that primaries in majority-minority districts are about race?

We must, in addition, consider the disruptions caused by redistricting. Many studies of redistricting have focused upon the partisan consequences of majority-minority districts or on the partisanship inherent in gerrymandering. Fewer studies have looked at the way in which redistricting can shape primary elections. When districts lines are dramatically redrawn, how are primary elections affected? And how can one separate out competition brought about because of redistricting from other types of primary competition that just may happen to occur in redistricting years? In other words, how do we know when primaries that take place in years ending in a "2" are about redistricting?

Race and Redistricting in the 2012 Congressional Primaries

Let us begin our consideration of some recent congressional elections with the simple observation that majority-minority districts are also overwhelmingly Democratic districts. According to data gathered as part of the American National Election Studies (2012), in every election year since 1970, no more than 12 percent of African Americans have identified themselves as Republicans, and on average over 80 percent have identified themselves as Democrats. It is not uncommon for 90 percent or more of African Americans to vote for Democratic congressional candidates. While Latinos are not quite as overwhelmingly Democratic, they do tend to favor Democrats by healthy margins as well, giving Barack Obama 71 percent of their votes in 2012.[2] No Republican presidential candidate in the past forty years has received more than 40 percent of the Latino vote. There is less research on the voting habits of Asian Americans, but one survey following the 2012 election found that 77 percent of Asian Americans voted for Obama.[3]

The Voting Rights Act Amendments of 1982 mandate the creation of majority-minority districts where there is a sufficient concentration of nonwhite voters to do so. This is a rule that has received support from both parties, but for different reasons. For Democrats, the rule has cemented the party's alliance with African Americans and Latinos by ensuring the creation of a number of safe districts for minorities. For Republicans, the creation of such districts has in some states enabled the party to gain seats in surrounding areas. The creation of one district that is overwhelmingly Democratic can ensure the creation of several reliably, but not overwhelmingly, Republican districts in the areas surrounding it. Even in states controlled by Democrats, the creation of one or two majority-minority districts can make it difficult for legislators to protect white incumbents in surrounding areas. Once a majority-minority district has been created, the Democratic Party will have little need to work to protect the district's incumbent, and minority incumbents generally have more to fear from a primary challenger than from a general election challenger (a circumstance we shall explore more below). This also means, however, that in redistricting years minority incumbents are far less vulnerable than are white incumbents.

As an illustration of this point, consider the fortunes of Ohio's Democratic representatives in 2012. Ohio has historically had nearly equal numbers of Democrats and Republicans and has been a bellwether state in presidential elections. Republicans held twelve of the state's eighteen districts from 2002 through 2006; in 2006 Democrats gained one seat, and in 2008 Democrats gained four more, for a ten-to-six advantage. The party went on to lose five of these seats in 2010, as well as losing the governorship and control of the state House of Representatives. Republicans held a large enough majority in the legislature that they could do what they wished in redrawing the state's districts. The results are shown in Figure 7.1. One Democratic incumbent was clearly safe: Representative Marcia Fudge, who represented a district that was 56 percent African American. Fudge's district comprises predominantly African-American neighborhoods on the East Side of Cleveland, as well as the most liberal of the city's mostly white east side suburbs. This district had been majority-minority since the 1960s, and was from 1968 to 1998 represented by Louis Stokes, brother of Cleveland's first African-American mayor as well as a prominent Ohio civil rights figure in his own right. This district, then, was not only protected by law but had historical importance in the state as well. Fudge came into office in 2008, in an open seat race following the death of the district's prior incumbent. She faced no opposition in the 2012 primary, token opposition in the 2010 primary (two candidates who each received less than 10 percent of the vote), and no serious general election opponents. Fudge also has needed to raise very little money; she spent less than $100,000 the year she won the district, and she has raised and spent less than any other Ohio incumbent in the two elections since.

However, 2012 was very different for the Cleveland area's remaining white Democratic incumbent. Dennis Kucinich represented the city's white ethnic West side from 1996 until 2012. Kucinich's résumé included a controversial term as mayor of Cleveland and a pair of long-shot presidential bids. The legislature somehow managed to combine Kucinich's district with that of veteran Toledo Representative Marcy Kaptur, creating a solidly Democratic district that stretched over one hundred miles along a narrow strip of Lake Erie beach to combine two

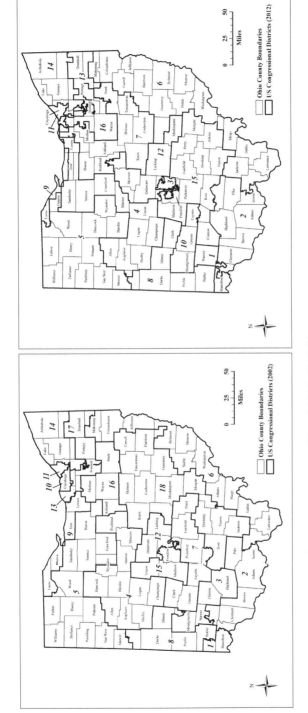

FIGURE 7.1 Ohio Congressional Districts 2002–2012 (a) and 2012–2022 (b)

Source: Ohio Secretary of State

large swaths of Democratic voters. *Roll Call* dubbed the new district one of the nation's five ugliest gerrymanders, pointing out that at high tide it was debatable whether the district really was contiguous (Toeplitz 2011).[4] Kucinich and Kaptur faced off in an incumbent-vs.-incumbent primary, which Kaptur won with 56 percent of the vote.[5]

A new district was also created in the Columbus area, (Franklin County), drawn such that it contained most of the city's minority voters—establishing what is commonly referred to as a "minority influence district"—along with solidly Democratic neighborhoods surrounding the Ohio State University. African Americans did not comprise a majority, but they do constitute an estimated 36 percent of the electorate—enough to give a black candidate a strong base from which to start (Myers and Bumgardner 2012). The creation of this district was a move that initially surprised some Democratic observers; Republicans had held both of the Columbus seats more often than not over the past two decades, but these seats always had been competitive. In creating the district, Republicans effectively conceded one seat to the Democrats while rendering the surrounding districts much safer for the party. In the four-way primary, former state House Minority Leader Joyce Beatty won 38 percent of the vote, narrowly defeating Mary Jo Kilroy, who had held a Columbus area House seat from 2008 to 2010. Beatty was one of two African-American candidates in the race; Kilroy is white. Although race likely played a role in the creation of the district and in aiding Beatty's reelection, media coverage of the primary tended to play down race as an issue. The African-American mayor of Columbus did endorse Beatty, but he also noted that he had supported Kilroy in the past and denied that his endorsement had anything to do with race (Eggert and Vardon 2011). The *Columbus Dispatch* described the race as a "friendly primary" where the candidates were "all liberals who strongly support President Barack Obama's agenda" (Eggert 2012).

Ohio's new district lines had much to do with race, for the minority candidates as well as the white candidates. This was the case even in primaries where the candidates did not make race an issue—the existence of these districts had to do with the Democratic leanings of African Americans. Ohio's experience is by no means typical—there is not necessarily an easy typology of types of majority-minority districts, or types of primaries in these districts—but it does point out the structural features established by race-conscious redistricting.

If we are to generalize from the two African-American representatives discussed here, though, we might begin by noting that many African-American legislators are freed from having to chase campaign cash as vigorously as do other representatives. This was the case for Ohio's Marcia Fudge, and if one compares African-American representatives in other states to their white colleagues, it is a common pattern. The lowest-spending Democrat in Pennsylvania in each of the races over the past decade has been the holder of the west Philadelphia majority-minority seat. Virginia's lone African-American representative, Bobby Scott, has spent less than half of what any other Virginia incumbent has spent in the past two elections. This is not, however, necessarily a comment about race. It is worth noting that there are several cases where electorally secure white representatives have been lucky enough to treat fundraising as an optional activity; this is the case, for instance, for safe Democratic representatives in Minneapolis. Some African-American representatives have argued that there is a racial element to this—their districts are poorer, and thus there is less money to be had.[6] But unless one expects a primary challenge or wishes to spend money to help the party or other candidates, less money is needed as well.

It is also noteworthy that Joyce Beatty's initial election campaign appears to have deemphasized race. Beatty's ties to the district's African-American community made her a strong primary candidate, but, as noted above, her strongest white opponent would certainly have had reason to be attentive to minorities' concerns had she won the race, and if one were to simply consider the candidates' issue positions, the two might not have been that different. Many studies of race and congressional elections note that in "minority influence" districts such as Beatty's, voters' considerations might take on more subtle concerns. Who is likely to establish constituent service offices in minority neighborhoods? Will the candidates instinctively recognize the obstacles minority constituents face? What will the racial makeup of the representative's staff be? Although some white representatives have successfully managed to present themselves as defenders of minority interests, primaries often can hinge on claims about descriptive representation. African-American candidates like Beatty who can win majority-white districts are still not common, but there have been examples of candidates over the past three decades in Missouri, Wisconsin, and Minnesota who have appealed both to minorities and white liberals.

The redrawing of congressional districts in 2012 fostered several other primary conflicts in which race played a role. Michigan, like Ohio, had a solid Republican legislative majority and slow population growth. The legislature chose to combine three Detroit-area districts (one predominantly white, two majority-minority) into two majority-minority districts. The boundaries of veteran African-American incumbent John Conyers' district changed somewhat, but the district remained heavily Democratic. Conyers did draw four primary opponents but still won easily. Hansen Clarke, Conyers' former chief of staff, had held the other majority-minority district leading up to the election. Clarke chose not to run against his former boss, running instead in a new district that included parts of his old district and parts of the Oakland County suburbs. Clarke is half African American and half South Asian; he appears to have won a slim majority of the district's African-American vote, but his white competitor, Representative Gary Peters, had significant support among minority voters as well. Peters ultimately combined support from black church leaders with overwhelming support in the suburbs to defeat Clarke (Gray 2012).

One might infer from the Ohio and Michigan cases that there is an "old guard" of civil rights era leaders in Congress who have emphasized race, but that there is a growing number of districts where race is not a decisive factor in elections. Such discussions often appear in the media—as in the *New York Times'* description of the primary contest between Charles Barron and Hakeem Jeffries for retiring Representative Edolphus Towns' Brooklyn-based seat:

> In some ways, the race offers a contrast between two different eras. Mr. Barron, 61, represents a throwback to the 1970s and 1980s, when black nationalists seemed to control the city's racial conversation, while Mr. Jeffries, 41, represents the more recent model of black leaders like President Obama; Newark's mayor, Cory A. Booker; and Gov. Deval Patrick of Massachusetts, who have earned establishment credentials and thrived by building coalitions with white liberals (Berger and Grynbaum 2012).

Such characterizations are also common in academic literature; in his study of African-American representatives, Richard Fenno quotes Philadelphia Representative Chakah Fattah remarking that African-American representatives elected in the 1960s and 1970s tended to be products of the civil rights movement, while contemporary (as of the 1990s) representatives tend to be career-oriented politicians (Fenno 2003, 116–17). This may be a matter that has particular salience among African Americans simply because there only have been a pair of generations worth of representatives. Then again, as we saw in Chapter 6, age is a common reason for primary challenges for all types of representatives.

Race can also structure primary conflict in the same fashion that parties have sought to winnow the field in some primaries. In the 2013 special election primary to replace Representative Jesse Jackson, Jr., seventeen African-American candidates filed to run in the Democratic primary, along with one white candidate. Jackson's former district, the Illinois second, is 62 percent African-American, covering parts of Chicago's south side and some south side suburbs. The lone white candidate, former Representative Debbie Halvorsen, had represented an adjoining district during the 2000s and was by no means hostile to black interests. African-American leaders, however, reportedly worked to encourage some candidates to drop out of the race so that the black vote would not be split to the extent that Halvorsen could win. Ultimately, the strongest African-American candidate, county administrator Robin Kelly, received the endorsements of many local clergy and other prominent figures. Her three most prominent opponents dropped out of the race well before the election.[7]

It is also important to note that racial conflict in primaries is not always a matter of whites and African Americans running against each other, or even of whites and minorities running against each other. The Latino-majority district in Chicago (which we discussed briefly in Chapter 6) has traditionally been referred to as the "earmuff district" because it encompasses two different Latino communities on different sides of the city, connected by a thin strip of land that makes the district's shape look like a pair of earmuffs. The Latino voters on the city's south side are predominantly of Mexican ancestry, while those on the north side are predominantly of Puerto Rican ancestry. There are slightly more Puerto Ricans in the district than Mexicans. The district's representative since its creation in 1992 has been Luis Gutierrez, who is Puerto Rican, but (as noted in Chapter 6) Gutierrez has occasionally drawn a primary challenge from a Mexican-American opponent. In cases such as these, there have been no explicit appeals to race, but the two competitors have drawn on different geographical bases of support. In the most recent California redistricting (discussed further in Chapter 8), a new district was drawn which is 51 percent Asian American; the Asian Americans in the district, however, are of different nationalities. Representative Michael Honda, who has been in Congress since 2000, currently represents the district. Honda is a Japanese American who spent time in an internment camp during World War II and has attracted support from many different ethnic constituencies. His new district, however, has a much larger Indian-American population than did his old district, and as a result some see him as being vulnerable to a challenge. As of this writing, Honda and former Assistant Commerce Secretary Ro Khanna (who is of Indian descent) are raising money in anticipation of a primary battle (Onishi 2013).

All of these stories indicate that race is an important consideration in understanding primary conflict. This is particularly the case when districts have been redrawn, and it can be an important consideration even when the district's electorate contains few minorities. In states such as Ohio, Illinois, Michigan, and others with one or more long-standing majority-minority districts, the legal need and the partisan need to preserve these districts is often one reason why white incumbents in neighboring areas face off against each other or are forced to run in substantially redrawn districts. These cases also, however, suggest that it is hard to make generalizations about primaries in majority-minority districts. There are many plausible assumptions one might make about these districts. Because there is little hope of Republican victory in such districts, perhaps they will feature more primary conflict; this is, after all, a more promising path to victory. They might feature more overt racial conflict—when white and minority candidates run against each other, does the campaign wind up being nastier, or explicitly about race? And finally, how much of a role does race play in primaries—how often do whites win primaries in majority-minority districts, and how often do minorities win them in majority-white districts?

Race, Redistricting, and Primaries: A Brief Historical Overview

There has always been a close connection between the race of the electorate and the race of the candidates who win elections. As we saw in Chapter 2, one of the reasons for the spread of primary elections in the United States was that they were an effective means for states to prevent the election of African-American candidates and to restrict the ability of African Americans to vote at all. While this was primarily a concern in the South, voting was sufficiently racialized in the North that there were never more than two African-American representatives in Congress from the end of Reconstruction until the 1954 election. The few African-American members who were elected hailed from inner city neighborhoods in New York and Chicago—cities where the concentration of black voters was sufficiently high that it was easier for white political bosses to create one exclusively black district than to spread African Americans among the districts of neighboring white representatives. Predominantly African-American districts were created in Detroit and Philadelphia in the 1950s and Los Angeles in the 1960s.

The representatives who held these seats—men such as Oscar De Priest and William Dawson in Chicago and Adam Clayton Powell in New York—gained reputations as civil rights pioneers, although they at times did face difficult challenges at home. The diverse political styles of some of these representatives are worth noting because they would become issues raised in future primaries in majority-minority districts in the future. Dawson (who served from 1943 to 1970) began his career as a Republican but later switched to the Democratic Party. During his tenure in Congress he benefitted from a friendly relationship with Mayor Richard Daley and Chicago's political machine; he was not a particularly high-profile legislator in Washington but by most accounts focused on securing benefits for his district. Powell, on the other hand, was a much more flamboyant politician; during his tenure in Congress he was an often confrontational advocate for civil rights. Powell lost the support of the New York political machine in the 1960s, repeatedly ran into legal trouble, and was narrowly ousted in the Democratic primary in 1970 by Charles Rangel. While Powell's outspoken stances in Congress were not the causes of these troubles, they may well have lost him support among his colleagues in Congress and among New York political leaders. Once the number of majority-minority districts grew, the tension between those who advocated "insider" strategies like Dawson and those who preferred more of an "outsider" approach would reappear.

During this time period there was only one African-American senator, the moderate Republican Edward Brooke of Massachusetts. Latinos were elected from congressional districts in New Mexico, Texas, and California; no more than three served at any one time until the 1970s. As is the case for African Americans, these districts were drawn not because states were ordered to create them but because the Latino populations of these areas made drawing the districts inevitable. New Mexico also sent a Latino senator to Washington beginning in the 1934 election. Upon its admission to the union in 1958, Hawaii (then, as now, a state with more people of Asian descent than whites) sent one Asian American to Congress, and both of the state's representatives were Asian Americans by 1965.

Two landmark changes reshaped congressional elections during the 1960s. First, beginning in 1962 the Supreme Court issued a series of decisions (*Baker v. Carr*, 369 U.S. 186 (1962); *Reynolds v. Sims*, 377 U.S. 533 (1964); and *Wesberry v. Sanders*, 376 U.S. 1 (1964)) that resulted in the requirement that states draw congressional districts of nearly equal populations. Prior to these decisions, many states had "malapportioned" their legislatures and congressional districts such that the votes of African Americans were often submerged in very large (in terms of population) districts. In northern states, urban districts often contained more voters than rural districts, and African Americans tended to live in urban areas. In the South, many districts were deliberately drawn to disenfranchise liberal voters regardless of race. By the 1970s, states did not have this option.

Second, the Voting Rights Act of 1965 outlawed poll taxes, literacy tests, and other practices that had been used in Southern states to prevent African Americans from voting. States could still seek to draw districts that made electing African Americans difficult, but African-American votes would have to go somewhere. Faced with these two requirements, more states drew districts with African-American majorities, and the number of African-American representatives increased to sixteen by 1974 and to twenty following the 1982 redistricting. This change (and the subsequent decades' developments, discussed below) is shown in Figures 7.2 and 7.3.

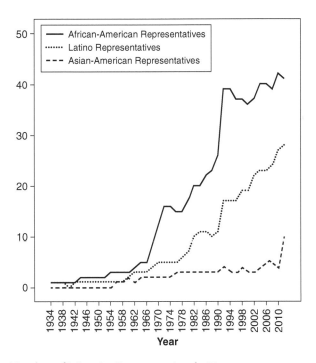

FIGURE 7.2 Number of Minority Representatives by Year

Source: Adapted from Ornstein, Mann, Malbin, and Rugg 2013, Tables 1–16, 1–17.

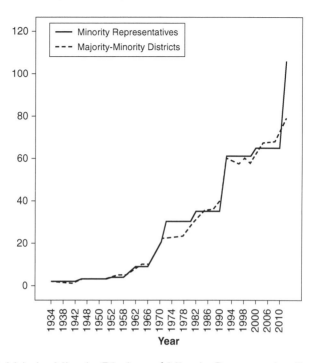

FIGURE 7.3 Majority-Minority Districts and Minority Representatives Compared

Source: For number of minority representatives: see Ornstein, Mann, Malbin, and Rugg 2013, Tables 1–16, 1–17. For number of majority minority districts: author's calculations.

By this time, African Americans had become one of the most reliable Democratic constituencies, but their political preferences also tended to be more liberal than those of white Democrats. In one-party Southern states such as Alabama and Mississippi—states with African-American populations of over 25 percent—the interests of whites and blacks were often so irreconcilable that districts where as many as one-third of the voters were African American could be counted on to comfortably reelect white representatives. As of 1990, for instance, five of Alabama's seven congressional districts had African-American populations between 28 and 37 percent; three of these districts were represented by white Democrats and the other two were represented by white Republicans (Bullock 2010, 75). Several political scientists have studied the relationship between the racial composition of a district and the likelihood that that district would elect an African American. On the one hand, even in the most racially polarized states some whites would vote for an African American, so a district with a black population of 40 to 45 percent might be expected to elect an African American; on the other, white voter turnout is often higher than that of African Americans and somewhat less than 100 percent of African Americans might be expected to vote for an

African-American candidate, so districts with African-American populations over 50 percent are not certain to elect an African American (Cameron, Epstein, and O'Halloran 1996).

In districts with a sizeable minority of African Americans (such as the Alabama districts described above), there was always the chance that an African-American candidate might prevail in a fractured Democratic field, but the mechanics of Southern primary laws provided a response to this. The runoff elections held in all Southern states but Virginia and South Carolina allowed white voters to coalesce behind one white candidate in the runoff. Faced with rapidly changing demographics, Democratic leaders in Virginia actually abandoned the state's direct primary (Sabato 1977). Jesse Jackson and other civil rights leaders argued that the runoff was discriminatory, but it was never actually proven that runoffs disadvantaged blacks in practice (Lamis 1984a; Bullock and Smith 1990). The fact remains, however, that African Americans were elected to Congress in Georgia and Texas in 1972, but Mississippi did not elect an African American until 1986 and Alabama did not elect one until after the 1992 redistricting. A 1986 Louisiana election held under the state's unusual "jungle primary" system resulted in a runoff that did include an African-American candidate; the white candidate (a Republican) prevailed, resulting in the only case of a congressional district that voted for Walter Mondale for president in 1984 being picked up by the Republicans in 1986 (Parent 2004).

In Northern districts, however, it was in the interest of white urban Democrats and of African Americans to draw one or two mostly African-American districts. As the number of African-American representatives grew, it became apparent that the new representatives would have more reason to fear primary challenges than to fear their Republican general election opponents (if they had any). Seven black representatives were defeated in primaries between 1970 and 1992; all but one were defeated by other black candidates, and the one who lost to a white candidate (Indiana Congresswoman Katie Hall) was a somewhat unusual case, as she represented a district that was not majority-black and had been elected under unusual circumstances.[8]

The original Voting Rights Act did not require evidence of nondiscrimination in the drawing of districts. Congress amended the Voting Rights Act in 1970, 1975, and 1982, gradually shifting its focus from proving that discrimination was intended to proving the discrimination was an effect of state actions regarding voting (Lublin 1997, 4–8; Bullock 2010, 57–59). The 1982 Voting Rights Act Amendments required the Department of Justice to consider discriminatory effects of congressional districting and broadened the act's scope to include minority groups beyond African Americans. States interpreted the amendments as an order to draw majority-minority districts anywhere it was feasible to do so. Seventeen new majority-minority districts were drawn in 1992, twelve of which were predominantly African-American and five of which were predominantly

Latino (Bullock 2010, 62). We have seen in each of the past three chapters that the 1992 election featured particularly tumultuous primaries; the establishment of these districts (and the consequent disruption of neighboring districts) was one reason for this.

We shall consider the dynamics surrounding the 1992 redistricting later in this chapter. For now, however, two points regarding this redistricting are pertinent. First, the 1992 redistricting featured several races in which veteran white incumbents were drawn into majority-minority districts. Nine-term representative Stephen Solarz, a leading voice of the Democratic Party on foreign policy issues, was drawn into a new district with a population which was 58 percent Latino. Solarz narrowly lost a five-way primary to a Latina candidate, Nydia Velasquez. Georgia congressman Charles Hatcher also tried unsuccessfully to retain a seat that was now 57 percent African American. Most white incumbents in such situations, however, either chose not to run for reelection or to run in neighboring white districts. Of the nineteen incumbents defeated in the 1992 primaries, nine were from states that had added a majority-minority district. Second, in 1994 the Republican Party gained fifty-two seats, winning its first House majority in forty years. Many of the seats Republicans gained were in Southern states whose districts had been "bleached" in order to create majority-minority districts. Scholars were divided on whether the creation of new majority-minority districts had caused the Republican gains (Hill 1995; Petrocik and Desposato 1998), but in subsequent elections the number of white Democrats in the South steadily diminished.

The 2002 redistricting was far less eventful than that of 1992, producing only four new majority-minority districts. The slower rate of increase was partially a consequence of the fact that there had not been sufficient growth in the minority population to draw more districts, but it also reflected Democrats' concerns about the consequences of drawing majority-minority districts. By 2012, however, the rapid growth of the nation's Latino population swelled the number of majority-minority districts to 106. Many of these districts were not drawn to advantage minorities; they simply became majority-minority over the course of the decade due to population changes. Some others contained many different ethnic groups but continued to elect white representatives. In some instances, districts that had been majority-black became districts that had a plurality of Latinos. The African-American California Representative Maxine Waters, for instance, had a district that was 50 percent African American and 37 percent Latino when she was first elected in 1990; her district is now 55 percent Latino and only 29 percent African American.

It is also possible that race has come to play less of a role in white Americans' voting habits than it once did. The vast majority of African American representatives come from districts that are either majority-black or at least majority-minority, but the number of African Americans who represent mostly white districts has grown substantially. Keith Ellison, for instance, represents a Minnesota district that is less than 20 percent black, and Indiana's André Carson represents a district that is slightly more than one-third black. There are two African-American senators: Cory Booker, elected in a New Jersey special election in 2013, and Tim Scott, a Republican from South Carolina appointed to the Senate in late 2012. Scott was elected to the House in the Republican wave election of 2010, and another African American, Allen West, was elected in a Florida district that was more than 90 percent white. Two Latino Republicans also won seats from districts in Washington and Idaho that are overwhelmingly white. In his study of race and redistricting, David Lublin (1997, 23–38) found that over 90 percent of the elections held between 1972 and 1994 in majority-black districts were won by African Americans, but African Americans won barely 1 percent of elections in majority-white districts. There were, then, a few unusual cases in the 1970s and 1980s, and there are a few unusual cases today. For the most part, however, the easiest way to increase the representation of minorities is to create majority-minority districts.

Most of the scholarship on race and redistricting has focused upon African Americans. In some ways, the politics surrounding the establishment of majority-minority districts are unique. African Americans were, until recently, the nation's largest minority group, and the original voting rights cases had to do with efforts to prevent African Americans from voting or winning elections. African Americans' places of residence have also been stable enough, and the size of the nation's African-American population has been stable enough, that there have been no new majority-black congressional districts drawn since the 1990s. In other words, there are limits to the number of majority-black districts that can be drawn, and the nation appears to have reached this limit.

The same cannot be said, however, about other minority groups. Between 1980 and 2010, the nation's Latino population more than tripled, going from 14 million to 52 million (Brown and Lopez 2013). New majority-Latino congressional districts were drawn in Arizona, Texas, California, and Florida in 2002 and 2012. In some districts, however, increases in the Latino population made some existing districts majority-minority even without changes in the district lines. In some cases, districts have become majority-minority but still retain a plurality of white voters. In others, growing Asian or Latino populations have established districts where three or more different races each have a large enough proportion of the population that cross-racial coalitions are necessary to win. As a point of comparison, there are twenty-nine congressional districts that are more than 45 percent African American; all but one of them are represented by African Americans, and that one district (based in Memphis, Tennessee) is represented by a Steve Cohen, a white civil rights lawyer who had a long track record of work in the city's African-American community before winning the seat. There are thirty-five districts with a majority-Latino population; seven of these seats are represented by Republicans, four are represented by white Democrats, one is represented by an African-American Democrat, and one is represented by an Asian-American Democrat. Neither race nor partisanship, then, are as decisive in Latino districts as in African-American districts. There are only two House districts where 45 percent or more of the population is Asian American, but there are ten where a plurality of the population is Asian American. Five of these ten districts are represented by Asian Americans.

There will certainly be much research over the coming decade on the politics of these new mixed-race districts. Existing research, however, suggests that majority-minority districts have several characteristics that are of relevance to primary elections. First, it has been argued that the existence of these districts can stimulate turnout (Barreto, Segura, and Woods 2004).[9] This is a finding that holds for African Americans and Latinos. The presumption here is that the presence of viable minority candidates encourages minorities to vote. This increase can advantage minority candidates in newly-drawn districts or in competitive primaries with white candidates. Second, Branton (2009) has found that the competitiveness of primaries increases with the minority composition of the district. This relationship is stronger in the North than in the South, and it is stronger in primaries with an incumbent running than it is in those with no incumbent running. These two findings suggest that there is indeed something different about majority-minority districts; the empowerment of minority voters can have unpredictable effects for the elections in which they vote and the candidates whom they elect.

This brief historical review has been intended to show that the politics of race in congressional primaries are inseparable from the politics of redistricting. Over the past four decades—but particularly since 1992—the districting requirements of the Voting Rights Act have created new majority-minority districts. In states gaining or losing seats, these requirements have also insulated the representatives of existing majority-minority districts from dramatic changes in their districts. White urban Democrats have thus been drawn into radically changed districts in metropolitan regions such as New York, Cleveland, Baltimore, Chicago, and Detroit. Race and ethnicity are not always overt themes in congressional primaries, but racial attitudes and the laws enacted to combat racism can play an important role in structuring competition.

Primary Elections in Majority-Minority Districts

It is easy to identify majority-minority districts in the data we have used over this book's past three chapters. The important question, however, is what we should compare them to. Over the period from 1970 through 2012, 96 percent of the victors in majority-minority districts were Democrats. The races won by Republicans were either aberrations (as was the case in Republican Joseph Cao's 2010 victory over scandal-plagued Democrat William Jefferson in New Orleans) or took place in districts that were not deliberately drawn as majority-minority districts, as was the case in several Texas and New Mexico districts. If majority-minority districts do feature unusual patterns of primary competition, those patterns should occur in the Democratic Party. Because of Democratic dominance in these districts, we also should be concerned mainly with the dynamics of incumbent primaries and open seat primaries, not challenger primaries.

Finally, majority-minority districts tend to be lopsidedly Democratic in their citizens' voting habits; the mean Democratic presidential vote in these districts is approximately 70 percent. In order to see whether competition in majority-minority districts is a function of something other than the partisanship of these districts, it makes sense to compare them to the small handful of majority-white districts with a Democratic presidential vote of 70 percent or more, and perhaps to districts with an average Republican presidential vote of 70 percent or over.

Incumbent Primaries

We start with a consideration of competition in incumbent primaries. Table 7.1 shows the percentage of incumbents who receive less than 75 percent of the primary vote across several different categories of districts. This table shows that no matter which comparison group one uses, incumbents in majority-minority districts are more likely to face primary opposition, and they are more likely to face competitive primary opponents.

This table strongly suggests that primary competition is more heated in majority-minority districts, although the overall level of competition is still not extremely high. If 16 percent of the incumbents in majority-minority districts

TABLE 7.1 Competition in Majority-Minority District Incumbent Primaries, 1970–2012

	Received Less than 75% of Primary Vote	Received Less than 60% of Primary Vote	N
Majority-Minority Democratic Incumbents	17.5%	8.2%	904
All Other Incumbents	9.1	3.8	7,651
All Other Democratic Incumbents	9.9	4.1	3,945
White Democratic Incumbents in Seats with > 70% Democratic Presidential Vote	5.4	1.5	129
Republican Incumbents in Seats with < 30% Democratic Presidential Vote	6.3	3.5	400

face opposition in any given year, this means that during the past decade, less than ten of the representatives in these districts faced a primary challenge. As Figure 7.4 shows, the percentage of majority-minority district incumbents who have faced primary challenges has consistently run higher than the percentage for other Democratic incumbents, but it has been below its four-decade average since the mid-1990s. In other words, majority-minority districts have become less competitive over the past few years. Perhaps this is a function of the increasing number of them.

Another important feature of this subset of primary challenges is the number of incumbents who have faced multiple challenges. As was discussed in Chapter 6, many challenges seem to have to do with the failings of particular incumbents or the idiosyncrasies of particular districts. Congressman William Clay, who represented a majority-minority district in St. Louis from 1970 through 2000, faced a primary challenge eight times, but always prevailed. Two Philadelphia-area representatives, Robert Nix and Thomas Foglietta, faced five primary challenges each during the 1970s, 1980s, and 1990s. Foglietta, who is white, often faced an African-American opponent. Nix served from 1958 to 1978, and during his last

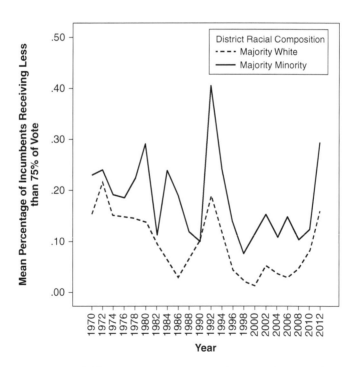

FIGURE 7.4 Primary Challenges to Majority-Minority Incumbents and Democratic Incumbents, 1970–2012

five bids he drew steadily stronger opponents in the Democratic primary, finally losing to William Gray in 1978. Most of the challenges to Nix had to do with his alleged lack of attentiveness to his district. The list of frequently-challenged majority-minority representatives also includes Chicago's Gus Savage (discussed in Chapter 6), challenged in every one of his six reelection bids, and California's Charles Wilson, challenged four times. Meanwhile, there are numerous majority-minority districts with long-tenured incumbents who never faced a primary opponent, as was the case in the Cleveland district we discussed earlier in the chapter. In sum, the number of majority-minority districts is still small enough that a few idiosyncratic districts or incumbents can give an impression that such districts encourage competition.

In Chapter 6, we also discussed the rationale for primary challenges. The coding method I have used here has its limitations. In the case of majority-minority districts, race may be a subtext of the challenge but not necessarily something that is discussed overtly. In addition, as was discussed in the Luis Gutierrez case, racial conflict in primaries may not be a matter of white candidates and African-American candidates contesting who should represent the district. It may, instead, be a matter of competing minority groups. Another example of such conflict took place during the 2012 primaries in Florida's majority-minority twenty-fourth district. While this district contains some of the city of Miami's largest African-American communities, the African-American community is split between African Americans who have been in the country for a long time and more recent Haitian immigrants. The district's representative, civil rights activist Frederica Wilson, faced a strong challenge from a Haitian-American opponent in 2012. The primary was not about overt hostility—Wilson has, by most accounts, a strong record of working for the Haitian-American community—but the competing candidates did draw upon different ethnic bases of support.

Table 7.2 shows some of the more prominent reasons for primary challenges to Democratic incumbents in majority-minority districts and in majority-white districts. As expected, race is a more frequent rationale for challenges in majority-minority districts than in others. Scandal and competence remain the two largest reasons for challenges, but they are slightly more frequent reasons in majority-minority districts. Ideology and issues play a much smaller role in majority-minority districts. It is perhaps not surprising that ideology matters less—these districts are predominantly liberal, as are their representatives, so there is little room for a challenge from the left and a centrist challenger would likely have little appeal to voters. It is harder to interpret the differences in the role of issues, but it is clear that there are fewer issue-based challenges in majority-minority districts.

These data provide some support for the claims made by, among others, Fenno (2003) and Swain (1993) about different representational styles. Fenno discusses Philadelphia Congressman Chaka Fattah's successful primary challenge

TABLE 7.2 Common Reasons for Primary Challenges in Majority-Minority Districts, 1970–2012

Reason for Challenge	Majority-White Democratic District Incumbents	Majority-Minority Democratic District Incumbents	N Majority-Minority Incumbents
Scandal	12.3%	17.8%	27
Competence/Age	15.1	17.1	29
Race	6.0	23.7	36
Issues	6.9	3.3	5
Ideology	13.9	5.9	9
Other/None Listed	45.8	32.2	46
Total N	382	152	152

to then-incumbent Lucien Blackwell, noting that Fattah and Blackwell differed in their willingness to court white voters, in their relationships with party leaders, and in their ambitions beyond Congress. Fenno notes that Fattah rarely felt he needed to explain his votes to his constituents, however—he, like Blackwell, voted reliably with the liberal wing of his party, and he rarely had any "tough votes."

To some extent, then, the differences between opponents like Fattah and Blackwell are a matter of style, and to some extent they may also be symptomatic of generational differences in beliefs about how minority members of Congress should behave. It is difficult to measure such characteristics, but successful challenges in majority-minority districts, such as Denise Majette's victory over Cynthia McKinney in Georgia in 2002 and Bobby Rush's defeat of Charlie Hayes in Chicago in 1992 appear to have had similar characteristics. Some recent research has also pointed to distinctive patterns of representation among Latino representatives (Wilson 2009). The number and heterogeneity of majority-minority districts has grown in recent years, as has the number of "minority influence" districts where minority voters can play a pivotal role in primaries. This increase may serve to heighten the role of conflicts over representational style, but it may also render majority-minority districts less unique. As Swain (1993) has noted, early minority representatives such as Charles Rangel, John Conyers, Louis Stokes, or Henry Gonzalez were seen by their constituents as more than simply members of Congress; they were civil rights trailblazers. Over four decades later, however, minority representatives may be less remarkable to their constituents, and they may be able to position themselves simply as members of Congress, rather than as part of a movement.

Open Seat and Challenger Primaries

There are good reasons to expect open seat primaries in majority-minority districts to be rare. These seats are, after all, safer than are most other seats, and when the Democratic Party regained its congressional majority in 2006, the party's use of seniority for choosing committee chairs resulted in the appointment of several new African-American chairs. This was not the case during the 1980s and 1990s—in part because of the creation of so many new majority-minority seats in 1992—but since 2006 representatives from majority-minority districts have, on average, been in Congress for two to three years more than their colleagues from mostly white districts.[10] With few exceptions, minority representatives also tend to stay in the House rather than pursue statewide office. Some racial minorities have won Senate seats, governorships, and, of course, the presidency, but the House may be the highest electoral goal if one does not wish to appeal to white voters. Apart from redistricting years, then, the appearance of open seats in these districts is a rare event. In at least two redistricting years, however—1992 and 2012—the growth in the number of majority-minority districts was largely responsible for those years' increases in open seat races. Figure 7.5 shows the frequency of these contests.

Primary competition among Democrats, then, is fierce when these seats do open up; the value of the seat and the lack of other options for progressively ambitious minorities draw more competitive challengers. Among Democrats, the average number of candidates in majority-minority open seat races is 4.4, while the average number in majority-white open seat races is 3.1. The level of fractionalization is also much higher in majority-minority districts; the index stands

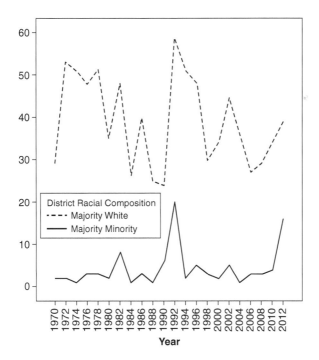

FIGURE 7.5 Number of Open Seat Races by District Racial Composition

at .57 in majority-minority districts, compared to .43 in majority-white districts. Unsurprisingly, the reverse is true for Republican candidates—the average number of candidates is only 2.1 in majority-minority districts as compared with 3.3 in other districts. The level of fractionalization is also lower among Republicans in majority-minority districts than it is for Republicans in other districts.

It is rare for there even to be primary competition for Republicans running to challenge incumbents in majority-minority districts; the average number of candidates in such primaries is barely over one, and the level of fractionalization, correspondingly, is very low. Over 75 percent of Republican challenger nominations are determined without primary competition.

Some minority representatives have contended that, because their constituencies tend to be poorer than mostly white districts, it is harder to raise money in majority-minority districts. Campaign finance data for open seat races bear this claim out. Since 2000, the average winner in Democratic primaries in majority-minority districts has raised just over $450,000, while winning primary candidates of both parties in majority-white districts have raised approximately $540,000. There were only eight majority minority districts where Republican open seat candidates even filed with the FEC; these eight candidates raised an average of slightly under $200,000. Republican challengers, however, fared even more poorly, raising on average only $82,300 to win their primaries.

Are primaries in majority-minority districts different, then? The evidence suggests that they are. This difference may have something to do with race—as long as discrimination limits the number of offices for which African Americans or other minorities can be competitive candidates, competition will be fiercer in districts where being a minority is an advantage. On the other hand, many of the characteristics of competition in majority-minority districts are really a function of their newness. The generational conflicts that have been suggested in many of these districts are largely a consequence of the newness of minority representatives; as the novelty wears off, so should these sorts of conflicts. Similarly, competition may also be caused by the combination of small numbers and idiosyncrasies of the representatives themselves. Surely there are many majority-white districts where the representative has faced frequent challenges, but when two or three minority representatives face these challenges, our perceptions of what majority-minority districts are like may be distorted. As a consequence of the growing number and growing diversity of majority-minority districts, as well as (one hopes) an increased willingness of whites to vote for minority candidates, all of these factors are likely to change over the coming decades.

Primaries in Redistricting Years

In each of the past three chapters, we have seen that primary competition changes in redistricting years. In Chapter 4, we saw that the number of open seats increases in redistricting years. In Chapter 5, we saw that in four of the five redistricting years considered here (all but 2002), competitiveness in challenger primaries increased for both parties. And most notably, in Chapter 6 we saw that primary challenges to incumbents increased noticeably in 1972, 1992, and 2002, even when we exclude incumbent-vs.-incumbent races; the number of challenges to incumbents was also relatively high in 2012, but 2012 was preceded by an unusually competitive year for incumbents. What is perhaps most noticeable in these time series is that the 1992 election, in which the Voting Right Act amendments mandating the establishment of majority-minority districts went into effect, stands out in all chapters as a particularly competitive year for all types of primaries.

It is difficult to prove that redistricting is related to all of these increases in competition. In some cases, it must be; in the case of open seats, for instance, we know that open seat primaries are on average more competitive than other primary types, and the act of reapportionment by definition creates new open seats. The loss of a congressional district in a state will also certainly force at least one incumbent either to retire or to compete with another incumbent in a primary or general election. In other cases, however, it can be difficult to disentangle the effects of redistricting from the effects of other factors. In the 1992 election, many incumbents who were challenged in their primaries were affected by the House Banking scandal. Some of the most prominent primary defeats of incumbents that year came in states such as Arkansas that were not very affected by redistricting. Similarly, some of the most competitive primaries in 2012 took place in states where redistricting did not dramatically change district lines but where Tea Party-supported Republican candidates took on more centrist Republicans. Yet redistricting clearly does play a role in many of these years' primaries.

One can draw four different scenarios from the literature on redistricting that are of relevance to primaries:

- First, states losing a congressional district will need to find a way to determine which incumbent will lose his or her seat. In some instances, incumbents have opted to retire or run for higher office before the redistricting process is complete; in 2012, for instance, Massachusetts was spared an incumbent-vs.-incumbent primary when the most senior member of the state's delegation announced his retirement, just days before the state's redistricting commission was to produce a new map. In instances where incumbents have not done this, however, considerations of seniority, of where in the state population loss is highest, or of partisanship may take precedence. Ohio lost two congressional districts in 1992; the legislature chose to develop a plan that would affect the parties equally. One district in the more Republican, southern part of the state was eliminated, forcing an incumbent-vs.-incumbent primary there, while another district in the more Democratic northern part of the state was also eliminated. The loss of this district would have forced

another incumbent-vs.-incumbent primary, but both of the affected Democrats retired rather than run in the new district.
- Second, in instances where one party controls the redistricting process, lines can be drawn to harm the opposition party. The state of Illinois lost one congressional seat in 2012. Democratic leaders in the state legislature, however, engineered a plan that resulted in the general election defeats of four congressional Republicans. They did this in part by placing Republicans Donald Manzullo and Adam Kinzinger, who both represented districts that had given Barack Obama 53 percent of their votes in 2008, into a much more conservative district, one that Obama (whose totals in Illinois likely exceed the state's normal Democratic vote, reflecting the fact that he is from there) lost by a 55–45 margin in 2012. The primary between Marcy Kaptur and Dennis Kucinich, discussed at the outset of this chapter, reflects similar partisan concerns on the part of the Republican Party.
- Third, in states with nonpartisan redistricting commissions, the commissions may be instructed, as part of their mandate, to disregard incumbency in constructing new districts. This has been the case in Iowa, where in 2002 and 2012 new district lines placed two incumbents in at least one district (Isenstadt 2011). In 2012, two Republicans were placed in the same district, two Democrats were placed in another, and two districts had no incumbent. Two of these incumbents responded, sensibly, by moving and running in the open districts. In California, however, the state's new nonpartisan citizen redistricting commission (discussed further in Chapter 8) produced a map of the state's fifty-three districts that resulted in two incumbent-vs.-incumbent primaries, one other instance where an incumbent was defeated by a challenger in a substantially redrawn district, and nine open seats.
- Fourth, the requirements for the establishment and preservation of majority-minority districts undoubtedly determine where primary competition will be. In predominantly Republican states, redistricting has often resulted in the "packing" of minority districts or in the placement of white Democrats into such districts. Georgia, for instance, added two heavily African-American districts in 1992; one white incumbent sought to hold onto one of these districts but lost in the primary. In the same year, however, the creation of new majority-minority districts in New York and Maryland resulted in primary losses for white Democrats—these states' delegations were Democratic enough that there was simply no way for legislators to draw majority-minority districts and preserve the Democratic districts that surrounded them. When states with majority-minority districts are losing seats, the state's legislators must produce plans that preserve these districts, so in cities such as Detroit or Cleveland, white Democrats whose districts border majority-minority districts are often vulnerable.

It is not possible to identify all of these patterns in the data we have at hand here. Some studies of the 2002 and 2012 elections have sought to measure changes in district composition from one election to the next (see, for instance, Crespin 2005). Such measurements are useful in predicting retirements or changes in partisan control. They can also, when coupled with data on the racial composition of old and new districts, help to determine the legality of redistricting plans. Incumbents can simply move from one district to another, however, and incumbency is a major determinant not only of primary competition but of the strategies of redistricting commissions. District change clearly does make some primaries more competitive, but there is no reason to expect that measuring the magnitude of change will be any more informative than simply noting that primaries tend to be more competitive in redistricting years.

There are, however, two things we can do with the data assembled here that give insight into the effects of redistricting on primaries. First, recall that the data on incumbent challenges in Chapter 6 were coded according to the reason for the challenge. In its biennial description of members of Congress and their districts, the *Almanac of American Politics* usually provides a brief account of the dominant issues in any major primary challenges. These descriptions do not prove that the primary was solely caused by redistricting, nor that redistricting was not a feature in challenges where other reasons were given. Yet the patterns in these descriptions do enable us to draw some conclusions about the effects of redistricting. To briefly summarize, there were thirty-seven challenges between 1970 and 2012 that the *Almanac* attributed to redistricting. All but two of these took place in the first year under the new districting plan, suggesting that when incumbents are harmed by redistricting, they are harmed immediately. Three redistricting-related challenges also took place in Texas in 2004, following the state's unusual mid-decade redistricting. Among the other thirty-two cases, there are clearly many that were precipitated by a state's gain or loss of a district, as well as several brought about in states with nonpartisan redistricting commissions. Many of these challenges were brought against incumbents who had faced, or would face, challenges based on other factors in other elections from around the same time, suggesting that they were weak incumbents to begin with.

One notable feature of challenges related to redistricting, however, is the exchange of general election competition for primary competition. In 2012, for instance, the state of Texas (which gained four seats that year) had several Republican representatives who had won traditionally Democratic districts in 2010. Representative Blake Farenthold had narrowly defeated veteran Democratic representative Solomon Ortiz, winning a district that was heavily Latino. When the state's districts were redrawn, Farenthold was given a much more Republican district; a consequence of getting this district was having to run against three other candidates in the primary. In the same year, Massachusetts sought to adjust its district lines after losing one seat. The state's entire delegation is Democratic, but, depending on how the lines are drawn, Republicans could possibly be competitive in one or more districts. Two Massachusetts Democrats faced serious primary opponents in 2012; in both cases, these opponents came from areas newly added to their districts. In western Massachusetts, State Senator Andrea Nuciforo had been patiently waiting for Representative John Olver to retire. When much of Olver's district was added to that of neighboring Representative Richard Neal, Nuciforo opted to run against Neal in the primary. Nuciforo won his home town and several other areas that had been added to Neal's district, but lost the primary by a 65 to 35 margin. Similarly, first-term Representative William Keating, who represented Cape Cod and parts of southeastern Massachusetts, had his home drawn out of his new district. Keating moved so he would reside in the newly drawn district (although there is no requirement that one has to live in one's district) and managed to hold off a competitive challenger in the primary. In all of these instances, incumbents were drawn into districts that were as safe, or safer, than their old districts, but they had to quickly introduce themselves to many new voters.

Farenthold, Neal, and Keating were fortunate to hold onto their seats; in other redistrictings, some incumbents have had the misfortune of adding territory represented by particularly popular or ambitious politicians. In 1992, California's veteran Republican Representative Robert Lagomarsino exchanged one safe Republican district for another, but his new district included multimillionaire Michael Huffington, who spent over $5 million to defeat Lagomarsino in the primary. Similar defeats took place in several states in other redistrictings.

Second, the clearest case where redistricting does influence primary election competition is in the instance of an incumbent-vs.-incumbent primary. Since 1992, there have been nineteen such races; these races are summarized in Table 7.3. In 1992 and 2002, there were eight incumbent-vs.-incumbent primaries. Seven of these (all but the 2002 Georgia race) took place in states losing a seat, and five of these (two races in Illinois and one race in Michigan, Ohio, and Pennsylvania) took place in states where the establishment (in 1992) or preservation (in 2002) of majority-minority districts likely guaranteed that the consolidated districts would be outside of the major cities. This is hardly definitive proof of anything—the rust belt states that have lost seats in recent elections all have substantial minority populations—but it does suggest that it is easy to predict where incumbents will be most inconvenienced by redistricting.

The 2012 redistricting is noteworthy for the number of incumbent-vs.-incumbent primaries it created. Seven of the eleven primaries were in states that were losing population. Among these were the Ohio and Pennsylvania races, where Republican legislators clearly sought to ensure the loss of a Democratic seat. In the Pennsylvania race, the Democratic primary winner ultimately lost the general election to a Republican. The Missouri and Michigan primaries both featured white incumbents seeking to win seats in majority-minority districts; the white candidate in Michigan was actually successful in doing so. And three of the primaries here were created by nonpartisan redistricting commissions. To

TABLE 7.3 Incumbent vs. Incumbent Primaries, 1992–2012

Year	Party	Winner	Loser	State	Percent of Winners Old District	Percent of Losers Old District	Winners Vote Percentage	Losers Vote Percentage
1992	Democrat	Lipinski	Russo	Illinois	39%	43%	58%	42%
1992	Democrat	Poshard	Bruce	Illinois	29	44	62	38
1992	**Republican**	**McEwen**	**Miller**	**Ohio**	**60**	**38**	**50**	**50**
1992	**Democrat**	**Mollohan**	**Staggers**	**West Virginia**	**72**	**28**	**60**	**40**
2002	**Republican**	**Linder**	**Barr**	**Georgia**	**34**	**19**	**65**	**35**
2002	Republican	Buyer	Kerns	Indiana	3	60	55	30
2002	**Democrat**	**Dingell**	**Rivers**	**Michigan**	**50**	**46**	**59**	**41**
2002	**Democrat**	**Murtha**	**Mascara**	**Pennsylvania**	**49**	**42**	**64**	**36**
2012	Republican	Schweikert	Quayle	Arizona	31	67	51	49
2012	Democrat	Sherman	Berman	California	29	71	60	40
2012	Democrat	Hahn	Richardson	California	16	47	60	40
2012	Republican	Mica	Adams	Florida	42	51	61	39
2012	Republican	Kinzinger	Manzullo	Illinois	31	44	54	46
2012	**Republican**	**Boustany**	**Landry**	**Louisiana**	**76**	**24**	**60**	**40**
2012	**Democrat**	**Peters**	**Clarke**	**Michigan**	**39**	**28**	**47**	**35**
2012	**Democrat**	**Clay**	**Carnahan**	**Missouri**	**70**	**30**	**63**	**34**
2012	**Democrat**	**Pascrell**	**Rothman**	**New Jersey**	**54**	**43**	**61**	**39**
2012	**Democrat**	**Kaptur**	**Kucinich**	**Ohio**	**47**	**39**	**56**	**40**
2012	Democrat	Critz	Altmire	Pennsylvania	29	64	52	48

Primary elections won by the candidate with the largest percentage of old constituents are in **bold**.

Source for district composition data: Missouri Census Data Center, University of Missouri. Online, http://mcdc.missouri.edu/.

some extent, these primaries show the consequences of heightened partisan conflict; although redistricting is always a partisan exercise, many news stories alleged that the new Republican majorities in several of these states engaged in a much more aggressive effort to gerrymander districts and preserve their party's congressional majority (e.g., Meyerson 2012). Several of the states with incumbent-vs.-incumbent primaries also had nearby open seat races, which meant that it was not necessary to force two incumbents to run against each other.

Table 7.3 also shows the unpredictability of incumbent-vs.-incumbent primaries. One might assume that when such races happen, the candidate who has brought the most constituents from his or her old district will be advantaged. I have put in bold the rows for races where the winner was the candidate who brought the most voters with him. The four right-hand columns show that there is no relationship here—half of the time the candidate who has the most prior constituents wins, half the time he or she loses. The table shows the percentage of each incumbent's old district that is included in the new district. These percentages do not precisely translate into potential primary votes; for instance, a Democrat may lose some of the Democratic areas of his district but retain Republican ones. Yet, given this caveat, there still are many cases where such inherited voters clearly do not determine the outcome. In three of the 2012 races, the winner had fewer than half as many prior constituents as did the loser; in one 1992 race, the eventual winner had a new constituency that included just 3 percent of the voters from his old district.

Redistricting years clearly have stimulated primary competition. Open seats are more competitive than races featuring an incumbent, and reapportionment and redistricting both create new open seats. There is also greater primary competition for incumbents in these years, however. The incumbents who are "losers" in these years are often those who had electoral problems to begin with. Apart from the disruptions caused by citizens' redistricting commissions such as the one in California, anecdotal accounts suggest that when incumbents are drawn into new, potentially hostile districts, it is because they have few friends in the legislature. It is no wonder, for instance, that Dennis Kucinich—a rather unconventional and polarizing politician—drew the short straw in Ohio in 2012. Often the incumbents harmed by redistricting retire or face stiffer competition in the general election. Yet the Kucinich example is not unusual. It is worth noting, in addition, that in the context of redistricting, primary competition is not always a problem—incumbents like Richard Neal and Blake Farenthold likely were happy to exchange the prospect of a strong general election opponent for a primary opponent who was a bit of an irritant. One of the reasons for the incumbency advantage is incumbents' familiarity with their districts; absent this, however, incumbents still have financial advantages and campaigning skills that can aid them even when redistricting prompts primary competition.

Conclusions

The pairing in this chapter of race and redistricting may strike some readers as a bit forced. Not all racial minorities reach office because of creative redistricting schemes, and not all redistricting plans are enacted for the purpose of enhancing minority representation. Yet for the past forty years, the alliance between the Democratic Party and African-American and Latino voters has meant that partisan goals in redistricting have needed to take into account the distribution of minority voters within each state. The result of this has been the establishment of types of primary competition that are not captured in the other chapters of this book.

Many arguments have been made for and against the establishment of majority-minority districts. Advocates of these districts have emphasized the importance of descriptive representation—of ensuring that minorities are present in Congress to speak on behalf of minority constituents. Critics have countered that these districts "ghettoize" minority politicians, effectively conceding some congressional seats to African-Americans and Latinos while denying minorities any real power within Congress. Our look at primary competition in these districts does not allow us to address somewhat normative questions such as these. The findings in this chapter do suggest, however, that primaries in majority-minority districts are not as simple as they are caricatured to be. Incumbents in these districts are not necessarily secure simply because of the districts they represent, but some successful minority incumbents have avoided serious primary challenges. The conventional distinction between majority-minority districts and the neighboring "bleached" districts is also overly simplified; as our consideration of redistricting here shows, one cannot fully understand the displacement of voters in redistricting years without considering the dynamics of primaries where incumbents seek to appeal to new voters. A look at primary competition in these districts, then, can add richness to debates about the appropriateness of race-conscious districting and about partisan goals in redistricting.

Notes

1 These amendments took effect in the next decade's redistricting, so they are responsible for the increase in majority-minority seats in 1992. See Bullock 2010, 52–62 for discussion.
2 These data are taken from Pew Foundation surveys (Lopez and Taylor 2012).
3 This is a survey conducted by the Asian-American Legal Defense and Education Fund; see http://aaldef.org/press-releases/press-release/new-findings-asian-american-vote-in-2012-varied-widely-by-ethnic-group-and-geographic-location.html, accessed November 26, 2013.
4 If so, this is an example of "duck contiguity," so named because a duck could walk from any one point in the district to another. Even if this were the case, this would not necessarily make the district unconstitutional; many coastal congressional districts include islands or cross waterways.

5 For discussion of this primary see Allen and Isenstadt 2012, Gomez 2012.
6 See, for instance, discussions of the Congressional Black Caucus's concerns about campaign finance reform, as in Clymer 2001.
7 This primary also received national attention because of extensive Super PAC spending in opposition to Halvorsen. For discussion of the race, see Yaccino 2013.
8 See Swain 1993, 20–44, for a history of this period.
9 Gay (2001), however, finds that majority-minority districts have no effect on turnout among African Americans but that they do decrease white turnout.
10 From the early 1970s through 2004, the average number of years in office for the holders of majority-white and majority-minority districts was between eight and ten years. As of 2006, however, majority-minority representatives had served eleven years in office while their colleagues had served slightly over eight years. This difference has persisted in the past three election cycles.

8
PRIMARY REFORM

It is easy to take the format of American elections for granted—we hold primary elections to determine our major party nominees, and we then hold a general election to choose between the two parties' nominees. As the previous chapters of this book have made clear, however, the way in which the party nominees are chosen has changed repeatedly over the past century. Some of these changes have been the results of sincere efforts to improve the election process, while others have been the results of efforts by the parties to increase their chances of winning elections.

In a sense, little has changed since the establishment of primary elections in the early twentieth century. In Chapter 2 we considered a lengthy list of concerns about primaries that were raised by politicians, academics, journalists, and political activists in the 1910s and 1920s. We still think about the same things in evaluating primaries. Some of these questions are probably unanswerable—we do not really know whether plurality winners are a problem for democracy, whether sore loser laws are a good idea, or whether there is any way to ensure that primaries are structured in order to produce the "best" candidates. Some of these questions have been thoroughly resolved. There are no longer serious debates, for instance, about whether primaries should be optional or whether they should be paid for by the parties or candidates. Yet many other questions from the time are still with us, and state governments, prompted in many cases by party leaders, researchers, or political activists, continue to tinker with the way in which primaries are held. Primaries are always being reformed, then; the purpose of this chapter is to look at recent changes in primary elections and to see if there is a pattern in these reforms—if our state-level systems of primary elections will look different in a decade or two than they do today.

Every so often one does encounter arguments that primaries should be abandoned entirely. In a 1992 back-and-forth on presidential primaries, for instance, prominent intellectuals fretted that political campaigning had become incompatible with governing, and some argued that primaries were part of the problem. *New York Times* columnist Tom Wicker (1992) argued that party conventions would likely choose more skilled candidates. Arthur Schlesinger, Jr. (1992) agreed with Wicker's fear that "our politicians are baffled by ... the long-term crises of our age," but went on to argue that "this fear will be stilled not by structural improvements in the political process but only by analytical improvements in the way we think about our problems."[1] Schlesinger is surely correct that we have no way of knowing whether changes in the structure of candidate selection will necessarily have the consequences that reformers wish them to have. Both of these authors were mainly concerned about presidential primaries, but their concerns can be applied equally well to congressional primaries. Throughout the twentieth century, we have seen that parties and candidates can adapt to changes in rules and ensure that these rules work to their advantage. There may be circumstances where well-respected incumbents are unexpectedly upended in their primaries, as has happened of late. There may be movements—such as the Nonpartisan League in the 1910s and perhaps the Tea Party today—that can use the primary process in an effort to directly challenge the two major parties. But these events and movements are intriguing precisely because they are not the norm. For the most part, primary elections are sleepy affairs that serve to effectively winnow candidates for the general election or to ensure that there is at least a mechanism for holding politicians accountable.

As both political parties discovered in the early twentieth century, the public strongly supports having primary elections. And as we shall see in our consideration of primary reform in California later in this chapter, majorities of the voters in both parties respond positively to arguments about making primaries more democratic or giving voters more of a choice in primaries—even when doing so might harm their party (Cain and Gerber 2002). There are thus limits to the sorts of changes in primary elections that the public will accept.

There are also legal limitations on how primary elections can be changed. While during the Progressive Era the Supreme Court was reluctant to allow governments to regulate primaries in any way—on the grounds that primaries were internal party affairs and the Constitution does not in any way recognize parties—today there is a small but coherent body of Supreme Court decisions on what sorts of primary reforms are legally permissible.

Although states have tinkered with their primary laws almost continually over the past century, we have not seen an intellectual or popular movement calling for change in our election system since the 1960s. There are, however, many smaller movements throughout the country. There have, as well, been some noteworthy changes in the administration of primaries. First and foremost among these is the decade-long effort to change California primaries, which resulted in 2012 in the establishment of a nonpartisan "top two" primary. Activists in several other states have sought to follow California's example, arguing that the top two primary will restore competition in single-party districts and will encourage candidates to appeal to voters who do not always support their party. Meanwhile, conservative activists in states such as Idaho and South Carolina have pushed their legislators to switch from open to closed primaries, arguing that their party's efforts to nominate candidates are being harmed by allowing voters not affiliated with the party to cast ballots. Despite a lack of evidence that change in either direction will necessarily have the results that activists have sought, it is clear that there is renewed attention being paid to primaries.

In this chapter we shall first consider the evolution of federal law regarding the structure of primary elections. We will then consider efforts in California to develop a nonpartisan primary system that is legally permissible. The California effort has generated much scholarly analysis of how primaries should be treated by the courts and of the effects that California's reforms have had on voters, candidates, and parties. We shall consider what the effects of the California reforms will be on other states' efforts to change primaries and we shall consider these effects in light of California's own turbulent electoral history. Following this discussion, we will briefly consider other states' reform efforts and some unconventional ideas about changing primary elections that have surfaced recently among political activists and academics.

The average citizen does not think about primary elections very much. One standard criticism of the Progressive Movement was that it expected citizens to care much more about its version of good government than it turns out they actually did. It is remarkable today that primaries received so much attention in the early twentieth century; it is perhaps just as remarkable that activists in California have managed to shepherd an ambitious plan to change primaries through the initiative process, over the objections of the two major parties. If citizens generally care little about primaries, however, it does not mean that the American citizen is unconcerned about broader matters of government dysfunction. Political scientists have been sounding the alarm for several years now that our two major parties are drifting further and further apart, and that this polarization has had and will continue to have implications for how well our government functions. It is not clear that primary elections are responsible for this or that reforming primaries will help, but primaries are often spoken of as part of the structural problem. In the closing section of this chapter we shall consider the relationship between primary reform and reform of campaign finance laws, voting laws, the redistricting process, and other structural features of our democratic election system.

The Supreme Court and Primary Elections

When primary elections were first introduced, it was generally assumed that the courts would have little to say about how they were regulated. In a 1905 article on the role of state governments in primaries, legal scholar Floyd Mecham contended that the state can neither restrict participation in primaries nor instruct parties on how to choose their nominees. The courts for some time held off on actually issuing rulings to this effect. During the 1900s and 1910s, as we have seen, states developed a wide variety of different types of primaries, and in some instances state courts weighed in to set limits on filing fees or to otherwise tweak legislators' actions. It was not until 1921, however, that the U.S. Supreme Court first took up a case concerning primaries. In 1910 Congress had passed the Federal Corrupt Practices Act (FCPA), which required disclosure of candidate spending, and in 1911 Congress amended the act to set limits on campaign spending by House and Senate candidates. In *Newberry v. United States* (256 U.S. 232 (1921)) the court struck down the spending limits as they applied to primaries, concluding that primary elections are internal party affairs and that Congress can do nothing to regulate primary elections.[2] Although the *Newberry* ruling only invalidated parts of the FCPA, its implication was clearly that Congress had no authority to intervene in other matters concerning primary elections. Not all state governments agreed with the Supreme Court, but the *Newberry* decision was the clearest statement of the court's views of primaries during this time.

The *Newberry* decision was greeted at the time much as the *Citizens United v. Federal Election Commission* decision was greeted in 2010—it was seen as a firm statement by the courts effectively putting an end to efforts to regulate primary elections and to regulate campaign finance. Congress responded much as it has to *Citizens United*, with quixotic efforts to amend the constitution or to increase the publicity of candidates' fundraising practices. The Senate even refused to seat two candidates (William S. Vare and Frank L. Smith) who—even absent any constitutional regulations on primary spending—it deemed to have spent too much in pursuit of the nomination.[3]

The court subsequently amended its thinking about regulating voting in primaries, if not its views on the role of money in primary elections. During the 1930s and 1940s the Supreme Court issued a series of rulings that have since come to be known as the "white primary" cases.[4] Southern states, as we discussed in Chapter 2, used primaries as a means of restricting the participation of African Americans in elections. At first, Southern states prohibited African Americans from voting at all in primaries—or at least in the Democratic primary. Since victory in the Democratic primary (or subsequent runoff) was tantamount to general election victory, African Americans were effectively disenfranchised. The state of Texas passed a law in 1923 prohibiting African Americans from voting; the court struck this law down in the *Nixon v. Herndon* (273 U.S. 536 (1927)) decision, concluding that this was a violation of African Americans' Fourteenth and Fifteenth Amendment rights to vote. Texas responded by directing the Democratic Party to prevent African Americans from voting in its primary; this practice was also found unconstitutional in the *Nixon v. Condon* (286 U.S. 73 (1932)) ruling. The court then concluded in its *Grovey v. Townsend* (295 U.S. 45 (1935)) decision, however, that it had no authority to require parties to allow African Americans to vote provided that the state had not been involved in preventing them from voting. That is, if a party took it upon itself to deny someone the right to participate in its primary, that person could not make a claim of discrimination.

The Supreme Court reversed itself a decade later in its *Smith v. Allwright* (321 U.S. 649 (1944)) decision. According to the court's logic in *Smith*, primaries do constitute state action because the state administers them; as a consequence, individual voters' civil rights cannot be denied by a party that holds a primary. Texas Democrats responded to this by creating an informal primary, known as the "jaybird primary," in which whites voted amongst themselves to choose a candidate who would then go on to run in the formal primary; that candidate's opponents in the jaybird primary would drop out at that point. In *Terry v. Adams* (345 U.S. 461 (1953)) the court struck this practice down as well, on the grounds that its sole purpose was to discriminate against African Americans and render their primary votes meaningless.

Cumulatively, the white primary cases carved out a large exception to the court's prohibition of federal involvement in primaries. The court now held that it could step in to require parties not to discriminate on the basis of race. This is an exception that legal scholars Samuel Issacharoff and Richard Pildes (1998) find problematic—not because of its laudable aims, but because when one takes these cases out of their Southern racial context, the court had in effect taken steps to reduce the autonomy of parties in choosing their own members.[5] The closed primary is, in effect, a primary in which parties restrict participation to members who have a certain standing in the party—as we saw in our discussion of early primaries, parties tended to require professions of loyalty from primary voters, to require advance registration, or to otherwise ensure that the voters would vote in the party's interest. The white primary cases were appropriate responses to Southern discrimination in part because the Democratic primary was the only meaningful primary, but the reasoning in these cases—particularly in *Terry v. Adams*—might have implications for other types of challenges. How can one make a legal distinction between a law excluding members of a certain race from a primary and a law excluding people with particular political views?

When such challenges were brought to the Supreme Court in the 1970s, however, the court proved to be uninterested in endorsing any particular type of primary. The court did strike down overly restrictive voting rules; in *Kusper v. Pontikes* (414 U.S. 51 (1973)) it struck down an Illinois registration law prohibiting voters from registering in one party's primary if they have voted in another party's primary in the previous twenty-three months. However, in the same year in *Rosario v. Rockefeller* (410 U.S. 752 (1973)) the court found New York's imposition of a thirty-day advance registration rule permissible. In *Morse v. Republican Party of Virginia* (517 U.S. 186 (1996)) the court held that Virginia could not impose a fee for participation in the state's nominating convention. In *Nader v. Schaeffer* (429 U.S.

989 (1976)) the court summarily affirmed a lower court decision rejecting voter claims that closed primaries violate their First and Fourteenth Amendment rights. The court, then, had stepped in to trim some primary laws that imposed a burden on individual voters, but it had done so in a way that avoided taking a position on the merits of different types of primary laws.

If federal and state governments were limited in their ability to dictate primary procedures to the states, however, national party organizations were held by the court to have the right to tell state parties how to conduct their primaries. In *Cousins v. Wigoda* (419 U.S. 477 (1975)), the Supreme Court resolved a challenge to the Illinois delegation at the 1972 Democratic Presidential Convention in favor of the party, concluding that national parties could set standards for states' delegate selection procedures (Wekkin 1984). While this did not speak to direct primary laws or subpresidential primaries, the Democratic Party invoked the decision in its subsequent push to require Wisconsin to close its primary. Wisconsin successfully resisted, and the party ultimately backed down from its threats not to recognize the state's delegates. The decade-long battle between Wisconsin and the DNC is somewhat of a sideline in the history of court decisions about primaries, but it does show both the extent of the court's deference to party organizations and Wisconsin's devotion to its primary rules. The episode provides a window into the standardization of primary rules following the McGovern-Fraser reforms; other states (such as Michigan) that were not as attached to the open primary were more compliant.

If there is a court doctrine on primary elections, however, it is embodied in two more consequential decisions. In *Tashjian v. Republican Party of Connecticut* (479 U.S. 208 (1986)), the court ruled on the Connecticut Republican Party's attempt to allow independents to vote in its primary. Connecticut state law required a closed primary. In a 5–4 decision, the court struck down Connecticut's law, holding that the state could not require a party to hold a closed primary. The decision split the court along ideological lines, with the court's liberals in the majority and its conservatives in the minority. Justice Thurgood Marshall, writing for the majority, took note of the possibility that citizens who are not registered members of the party may choose not to vote in the party's interests, but he held that the party, not the state, should be the judge of how best to ensure the integrity of the party's decision.

In *California Democratic Party v. Jones* (30 U.S. 567 (2000)), however, the court struck down California's recently enacted blanket primary law (more on this later in the chapter), concluding that while the state cannot force parties to hold closed primaries, it also cannot force parties to participate in a blanket primary. The 7–2 decision, authored by Justice Scalia (who had been among the dissenters in the *Tashjian* case), held that California's blanket primary compelled parties to allow registered members of the other party to vote in selected primary elections if they chose. Proponents of the blanket primary downplayed the idea that the blanket primary was really a means of selecting party nominees at all; instead, they argued, the blanket primary was merely a first-stage election. The court rejected this claim.

A common thread in these cases, according to legal scholars, has been the belief of the court in party autonomy. Despite the fact that the majorities in these two cases were quite different, one can link the two simply by saying that the court has concluded that parties should be free to establish their own nominating procedures except in instances where these procedures discriminate against prospective voters on nonpolitical grounds. As Persily (2002) summarizes matters, the court has been relatively unsympathetic to voters' arguments about rights except where civil rights are at stake. That is, it is okay for Democrats to exclude Republicans from their primaries, but it is not acceptable for Democrats to exclude African Americans or any other group that is not voluntary and political in nature. Given that party membership itself is easily changeable, this may be a reasonable distinction. Beyond this, however, parties receive substantial latitude from the courts in structuring their nominating processes. A frequently invoked decision in discussions of the *Jones* case, for instance, was the court's *Eu v. San Francisco County Democratic Central Committee* (489 U.S. 214 (1989)), where the court held that parties have a right to make preprimary endorsements. If parties can endorse primary candidates, then they have interests that precede the actual selection of their nominees.

The legal community split into three different factions, however, in its response to *Jones*. One faction, exemplified by political scientist Bruce Cain (2001), supported the *Jones* decision on the grounds that the establishment of the blanket primary was an effort by states to dictate the programmatic content of party nominations. Insofar as proponents of the blanket primary held that it would produce more moderate nominees, the establishment of the blanket primary was in effect telling Democrats and Republicans that they must allow members of the opposite party to participate in the selection of their nominees so as to choose nominees whose views might not be acceptable to those of the majority of registered party members. Cain concluded that the establishment of the blanket primary—by initiative, and over the objections of elected officials of both major parties—was about "using the state to predispose election outcomes to fall into a certain segment of the ideological spectrum and undermining the operation of the two-party system. This goes to the question of the neutrality of state action with respect to the content of political speech and representation." He felt that voter support for the initiative was easy to understand—the initiative was framed with reference to giving voters more choices in elections, a notion that seems unobjectionable but is, Cain argues, better suited to the market than to politics.[6] There was, he concluded, no compelling state interest in establishing the blanket primary and the court was correct to strike it down.

Another view on the *Jones* decision, however, was presented by law Professor Richard Hasen. Hasen agreed that *Jones* was consistent with *Tashjian*, but even before the *Jones* decision he had been critical of the court's deference to party autonomy (Hasen 1997). Parties should be able to control their internal affairs, argued Hasen (2001), but primaries are not internal party affairs—just as the Progressives had argued, once the state becomes involved in the administration of primaries they become public affairs. The blanket primary—and all contemporary primaries, Hasen argued—are merely means of winnowing the number of candidates so that voters have a manageable number of choices in the general election. Hasen disputed Cain's conclusions on the grounds that there is no evidence that blanket primaries would in fact change the ideological stances of the candidates; simply because some people hoped for this to be the case did not mean that it would be. Furthermore, Hasen argued, the state does not need a compelling interest to justify having a blanket primary. The blanket primary infringes upon no one's rights, and therefore a voter initiative to establish a blanket primary should not need a compelling interest. It was merely an expression of the electorate's preferences.

A third point of view, expressed by Samuel Issacharoff (2001), took issue with the court's emphasis on party autonomy. Issacharoff noted that he found many reasons why the blanket primary was problematic, but that these were matters of policy, not constitutionality (Hasen agreed with him on this point). The court's decision, he found, was so sweeping that it in effect made all primaries questionable. Issacharoff noted that there was no consensus that the blanket primary had had, or would have, any measurable effect on the ideological stances of party nominees; further, he surveyed literature on other states' blanket primaries and found no consensus on this. The court, then, had struck down a type of primary in part out of concern about what it might do. Any type of primary might be believed to have consequences for the type of nominee produced, so why should closed primaries, open primaries, or any other arrangement not be suspect? Furthermore, the court's belief in party autonomy seemed to suggest, for Issacharoff, that parties should in fact have the freedom not to hold primaries if they so choose. Issacharoff contended that the blanket primary likely would dilute the important organizing functions of parties and the importance of the party "brand" for voters, but these were not appropriate matters for the Supreme Court to consider. He worried about how the *Jones* decision would be used against other types of primary elections in the future.

Running through all of these responses is a debate that seems like a logical outgrowth of Progressive era concerns. The establishment of primaries was a response to the excessive and undemocratic power of party organizations in slating candidates, but primaries were established largely because the parties saw merit in democratizing and outsourcing their decision-making process. Legislators in the 1910s and 1920s worried about how to ensure that voters retained some loyalty to the party. Both Hasen and Issacharoff note that the court's reasoning in the *Tashjian* and *Jones* cases was indebted to V.O. Key's (1964) standard tripartite definition of parties as being comprised of the party organization, the party in government, and the party in the electorate. Key, as well as many other political scientists, used these distinctions to emphasize the benefits parties provide to the American political process.[7] But, Hasen argues, we long ago lost any meaningful way to define who the party in the electorate is. Today, he claims, party organizations have been replaced by a set of political experts who provide services to politicians, and the party in the electorate has disappeared. Instead, citizens vote, become active in politics, and so forth at election time but do not constitute a meaningful part of the party in any other way. Voters can choose to be members of parties merely by voting, as Justice Stevens noted in his *Jones* dissent; this should not privilege the position of the parties or allow parties to act in ways counter to the will of the voters. If voters wish to change the role of parties in elections, there is no reason why courts should prevent them from doing so. Hasen's accounting here largely draws upon standard political science views of party change such as John Aldrich's *Why Parties?* (1995), and he and Issacharoff draw our attention to the fact that the court's reference point in thinking about parties has been rather limited. On the one hand, the court's relatively paltry set of decisions on primaries can be seen as having some consistency, but neither its implications nor the court's future interpretation of primary laws are easy to predict.

One point that all of the various commentators on the *Jones* decision agree upon, however, is that the court's decisions on primary elections have favored major parties at the expense of minor parties. Both Hasen and Cain noted that the blanket primary did not make adequate provision for minor parties; Hasen argued that minor parties would be particularly susceptible to having nominees foisted upon them by nonmembers if they were to participate in the blanket primary, and Cain agreed that the historical role of minor parties entitles them to some rights in restricting their candidate selection processes. The Supreme Court has not, however, been sympathetic to minor parties' efforts to broaden their appeal in elections. In *Timmons v. Twin City Area New Party* (520 U.S. 351 (1997)) the New Party sought to practice fusion balloting, choosing as their own nominee the nominee of another party.[8] Although fusion balloting is currently practiced in New York and was once quite common, Minnesota had enacted a law prohibiting the practice.[9] The Supreme Court upheld the law, ruling in part that allowing minor parties to nominate major party candidates would confuse voters. Chief Justice William Rehnquist's majority opinion noted the stability that a two-party system provides, and concluded that this stability outweighed any First Amendment rights minor parties might have in selecting their candidates. In *Clingman v. Beaver* (544 U.S. 581 (2005)) the court denied the Libertarian Party of Oklahoma's attempt to open its primary to registered members of other parties (Oklahoma is a closed primary state). On its face, this case appears to be similar to *Tashjian*, but here the court did not grant a minor party the same level of autonomy it had granted to a major party years earlier (Chase 2007).

Amidst all of these rulings emphasizing the autonomy of major parties, however, Justice Scalia provided primary reform advocates with a way forward in his *Jones* opinion. The blanket primary was a means of selecting Democratic and Republican nominees. If a state wished to structure an election such that candidates ran as individuals, not as candidates for the nomination of any particular party, then such an election could truly serve as a means of winnowing candidates. Scalia outlined the parameters of what such an election would look like, noting that such an election would need to be structured so that it advanced candidates to the next round without reference to party. Nothing about the candidates other than their vote total would have any bearing on their eligibility to proceed to the next round. Although Scalia did not say this, some who interpreted the opinion speculated that candidates might choose to identify themselves in some manner on the ballot—to say that they would caucus with one party or the other, for instance. For all of the talk of party autonomy, some noted, Scalia's description in effect sanctioned nonpartisan primaries and dealt a longer-term blow to the parties (MacDonald 2002).

The *Jones* decision dealt an end to the California blanket primary, but it also invalidated blanket primary laws in Alaska and Washington. California and Washington responded to this by developing laws that conformed to Scalia's instructions. We shall consider California's experience in more detail in a moment. Washington, however, implemented by initiative a nonpartisan "top two" primary that received little attention from anyone outside of Washington and California. The Supreme Court did examine the Washington primary, however, and in *Washington State Grange v. Washington Republican Party* (127 S. Ct. 1373 (2007)) the court upheld the new primary law.[10] Scalia dissented, on the grounds that Washington allowed candidates to state on the ballot that they "prefer Democrats" or "prefer Republicans." For Scalia, this constituted a burden on the parties, who had no ability to prevent candidates from affiliating with them in this manner, but for Scalia's fellow conservative Clarence Thomas, who wrote the majority opinion, this was an acceptable bit of labeling.

The Supreme Court thus has preserved the variety of primary systems that have been in place for much of the century while providing reform advocates with a very narrow path forward. Although litigation regarding the California and Washington primaries continues, the legal options for primary reform are clear. In the next section we shall consider the politics behind recent primary reform efforts in the states.

The California Experience

Although this book has not consistently emphasized state differences, it is clear that one of the obstacles to drawing lessons from different types of primaries has been the variations in political culture across the different states. Southern primaries may not have been that different from Northern primaries in their mechanics, and variations in form (such as runoff elections) might have been worth evaluating as formal devices for selecting candidates. To evaluate Southern primaries without taking into account the role of race in Southern electoral politics and culture would, of course, be to miss the entire point of the Southern primary. Similarly, the lessons we can draw from the Wisconsin Progressives or the Nonpartisan League in North Dakota and Minnesota can tell us something about the effects of the direct primary, but again we cannot necessarily draw lessons from these without thinking about the geographical and cultural conditions that made politics in these states different from politics in the rest of the country. This is the case in California as well. California has historically had very different primary election laws and results than much of the rest of the nation, and its elections have been shaped in part by the state's experience with immigration, with economic development, and with the character of the state's Democratic and Republican leaders. California's highly publicized establishment of a nonpartisan "top two" primary for the 2012 election cycle is thus something that uniquely reflects California's political history. California's experience in 2012, in its blanket primary election of 1998, and in coming years are of some relevance in thinking about what other states might do, and there has been an abundance of research on the consequences of primary reform in California. We must, however, be cautious in interpreting this research.

The Backstory: Progressives and Primary Elections in California

California's experience with the direct primary has been among the most unusual in the country. Progressive era Governor Hiram Johnson was an early proponent of the direct primary—even before he became governor—and by most accounts Johnson used the state's primary laws to his advantage in his campaigns for governor and later for the Senate. California law from 1914 to 1958 allowed for cross-filing— candidates could run for the nomination of more than one party. This system allowed many candidates, predominantly Republicans and predominantly incumbents, to effectively win elections "at primary" by winning the nominations of both major parties. The law was amended twice, first in 1916 to require that candidates declare (although not publicly) a party affiliation; candidates could only proceed to the general election if they won the nomination of the party with which they affiliated. The law was amended again in 1952 to require candidates to list their party affiliation on the ballot. Throughout most of this period California politics were dominated by the Republican Party and by incumbents. The cross-filing system was abolished by Democrats once they had gained control of the state legislature in 1958.[11]

This history is of consequence in thinking about California's recent changes in its primary laws because it shows that California has had a history of relatively weak political parties and that Californians have reason to be skeptical of the political designs of those who have used primaries in the past. By most accounts, the

Progressive Movement in California was unable to separate itself from the legacy of Hiram Johnson, and as time went on the primary became a personality contest (see McWilliams 1949, 193; Lower 1993, 61). As one history of the state's politics recounted, the long-term effect of Progressivism was to create "an organized chaos of individual candidates, one-party dominance over the legislature and local government, and a lack of serious mainstream public debate about the ideological direction of the state and the country" (Bell 2012, 12). When political parties did seek to bring order to this process, it was generally done through informal means. By the 1950s Republican Party activists had created the California Republican Assembly (CRA) to hold their own informal nominating convention to try to limit primary competition and the Democrats had followed suit, establishing the California Democratic Council (CDC). These organizations were not always successful, but they did bring some order to the electoral process. Once the cross-filing system was abandoned, however, these organizations withered and parties were often vulnerable to efforts by activists on the left or right to get their candidates elected. In 1968, for instance, incumbent Republican Senator Thomas Kuchel lost his primary to a conservative challenger, and two years later veteran Democratic Congressman Jeffrey Cohelan was unseated in his primary by an anti-war candidate, Ronald Dellums (Delmatier, McIntosh, and Waters 1970, 429–42).

California, then, has long had a system of primary elections that has been quite different from any other state, its parties have experienced substantial difficulty in trying to use the primary system to their advantage, and California politics has over time resulted in a politics of personality and a politics in which extremist candidates are vulnerable to challenge. Finally, and this is of note for the implementation of the state's recent primary laws, California has been a state where direct democracy (another Progressive innovation) has allowed voters to bypass their elected officials in changing policy. Initiatives and referenda have become a regular feature of the California ballot, and according to some students of direct democracy, instead of being a tool of popular governance, they have become a means for special interests to create media campaigns to persuade voters to do what the legislature will not (see, e.g., Gerber 1999). California's two experiences with primary reform over the past two decades have been the result of referendum campaigns, and hence, while Californians certainly have had good reason to be cynical about the motives of politicians and to be unhappy with partisan conflict in California politics (see Masket 2009), the enactment of primary reform has also been a consequence of a broader and less focused disenchantment with politics (Bowler and Donovan 2002).

The Blanket Primary, 1998

In a low-turnout primary election in 1996, California voters approved Proposition 198, which established a blanket primary in which voters were provided with a list of all candidates for each office and could choose one candidate of any party.

The top vote-getter in each party would proceed to the general election. The initiative passed with 59.5 percent of the vote. There is little evidence that the average California voter knew very much about the consequences of the initiative. Spending on the initiative was low. Slightly under $1 million was spent on behalf of the initiative, most of which came from two moderate Republican politicians and one former Democratic legislator (Gaines and Tam Cho 2002). Opponents of the initiative spent slightly over $100,000; the bulk of this funding came from Rupert Murdoch and the California Republican Party (Gerber 2001). The main proponents of the initiative, including former representative and senate candidate Tom Campbell, were Republicans who had had difficulties with social conservatives in the party but had substantial support among Silicon Valley liberals. Opponents of the measure sought to fight it in other ways; according to some accounts the description of the measure in the voter handbook was biased against it, and the state legislature took steps to undermine the initiative (by, for instance, preventing it from applying to presidential primaries) soon after passage.

If the measure's proponents were hoping for dramatic changes in California politics, the 1998 election was not a particularly good year to look for them, especially at the congressional level. Nationally, 1998 was a virtual stalemate; over 98 percent of House incumbents were reelected and the major story dominating political news for much of the year was President Clinton's impending impeachment. With the economy in reasonably good shape, this was very much a status quo election.

There is, however, a surfeit of research analyzing the effects of the blanket primary. With the important caveat that the blanket primary was only in place for one election cycle, the findings of this research suggest that the blanket primary had a negligible effect on California politics. There was little crossover voting. Congressional primaries were actually less competitive than is the norm in California, voter turnout was down, and candidate spending remained similar to what it had been in 1996 (Tam Cho and Gaines 2002). There was little evidence that the blanket primary affected the fortunes of moderates, racial minorities, or women, although one study contended that it might have aided Latino Republicans (Gerber 2001, 2002; Caul and Tate 2002; Segura and Woods 2002). A study of the election conducted several years later argued that the blanket primary aided moderate candidates running in competitive districts, but the authors cautioned that this finding was more robust for state legislative races (because there were more of them) than for congressional races (Bullock and Clinton 2011). Perhaps most consequentially, most voters said when asked that they approved of the blanket primary, but the blanket primary appears not to have changed their feelings of political efficacy or approval of elected politicians (Gerber 2001).[12]

The consensus among researchers, then, was that the blanket primary did not live up to the predictions of either its supporters or its opponents. Perhaps this was a consequence of the dynamics of 1998, and perhaps politicians would have adjusted their behavior as they grew accustomed to campaigning in blanket primaries (Petrocik 2002). California's experience with cross-filing suggests that incumbents might have changed the way they campaign, using their position in office to reach out to voters of the other party. The Supreme Court's invalidation of the blanket primary, however, meant that there would be no way to know the answers to these questions.

The Top Two Primary, 2012

As noted above, the Supreme Court's decision striking down the blanket primary left California with a clear recourse—if primaries were strictly nonpartisan, then they would be constitutional, as a nonpartisan primary would not represent any sort of state interference in party activities. A 2004 proposition establishing a nonpartisan primary failed, garnering only 46 percent of the vote, in part because its proponents did not expend very much effort for it, in part because there were two conflicting and confusingly worded constitutional poison pill amendments to it on the ballot (Quinn and Alvarez 2010). In 2010, however, Californians narrowly (with 54 percent of the vote) passed Proposition 14, amending the state constitution to create a nonpartisan primary. In the same election year California voters also approved a constitutional amendment creating a nonpartisan redistricting commission. This ensured that the new primary and the new districting scheme both influenced the 2012 elections.

As was the case in 1996, the drive for the new primary law was led by a moderate Republican. State Senator Abel Maldonado led the fight to get the initiative on the ballot. Although both the Democratic and Republican parties opposed the initiative, it had sufficient support in the legislature that it was placed on the ballot not through petition but through an act of the legislature. In 2009 Maldonado allegedly secured support for the initiative from Republican Governor Arnold Schwarzenegger in exchange for supporting the governor's budget proposal. This support seems to have earned him enemies within the Republican Party, but Maldonado—who had spoken at the 2000 Republican convention and had been touted as one of the leading Latino politicians within the party—had been frustrated in Republican primaries for higher office in the past and likely saw the more open primary as a way forward (Chawkins and McGreevy 2009). Maldonado had actually won his seat in the blanket primary election of 1998 and was one of the Latino Republicans referred to as potential beneficiaries of that year's blanket primary (Segura and Woods 2002). Maldonado, who was appointed lieutenant governor by Schwarzenegger later the following year, did win the Republican nomination for lieutenant governor in 2010 but lost in the general election; he made it to the general election in 2012, losing narrowly to incumbent Democratic Representative Lois Capps. As other episodes in California political history have shown, it is difficult here to separate individual ambition and partisan conflict from more altruistic ideas about government reform.

It will take several election cycles to disentangle the effects of the new primary law from the consequences of the drastic changes wrought in 2012 by the redistricting commission. The composition of California's House delegation changed substantially; seven incumbents retired, in many instances because they were drawn into unfriendly districts. Seven other incumbents were defeated. Two of the defeated incumbents were Democrats forced into races with other Democratic incumbents; in both instances ideology appears to have been less relevant than other factors. Democrats Howard Berman and Brad Sherman, for instance, fought a bitter and expensive race that appears to have hinged primarily upon each other's competence. Likewise, the race between incumbent Democrats Janice Hahn and Laura Richardson revolved around ethical questions about Richardson's activities in Congress. Two other Democratic incumbents lost to nonincumbent Democratic opponents in races that featured allegations about the Democratic incumbents' character or tenure in office. In one district expected to be competitive, Republican Representative Gary Miller escaped unscathed because three Democratic candidates ran in the primary and the second-place candidate turned out to be another Republican (Blake 2012).

For all of this turmoil, it is not clear that the creation of the top two primary had an effect on the composition of the California delegation or on the engagement of voters in the election. Some media accounts professed to see signs that candidates were appealing across party lines. One article noted that many Republicans were more reluctant to sign their party's "no new taxes" pledge than would have been the case under the old system (Medina 2012); others noted that in the top two general election races featuring two candidates of the same party the candidates were very obviously trying to appeal to voters of the other party (Onishi 2012). The emergence of Super PACs on the political scene also ensured that in some races—particular the two-Democrat race featuring Representative Joe Baca—outside spending affected the issues under discussion.

Empirical researchers, however, have been more skeptical than have journalists. Kousser, Phillips, and Shor (2013) found that neither the new primary law nor the redistricting had a noticeable effect on the relationship between the ideological stances of the victorious candidates and the ideological views of their districts. Kousser, Lucas, Masket, and McGhee (2013) point out that both parties established endorsement mechanisms shortly after the passage of Proposition 14; these endorsements were not listed on the ballot but did appear in the voter guide, and candidates were free to mention the endorsements in their campaigning. The authors conclude that party endorsements were worth as much as 10 to 15 percentage points in the primary—enough to aid most incumbents and to blunt the effects of the nonpartisan primary. Masket (2012) also has noted that nearly 90 percent of party-endorsed legislative candidates proceeded to the general election, and that top two races featuring two members of the same party tended only to happen in congressional and legislative districts that were overwhelmingly partisan. In short, he concludes, the top two primary will have little effect on polarization because of the effect of party endorsements and because at least in the short run candidates tend to campaign to their party base in the primary.

Finally, a survey by Ahler, Citrin, and Lenz (2013; see also Ahler, Lenz, and Citrin 2013) of California voters also concluded that moderate candidates had no more support in the top two primary than they would have in a closed primary. They attribute this in part to the lack of familiarity voters and candidates have with running in a nonpartisan primary. Only 40 percent of the survey respondents said they even knew about the change, although most respondents said they preferred the new system to the old one. Fewer than half of respondents said that they could identify the moderate candidate in the race. These findings indicate that the nonpartisan primary may fail to encourage moderation simply because voters do not know enough about the candidates; perhaps it will be consequential in higher-profile races, but even then, whether it matters may be influenced by how candidates learn to use the primary rules to their advantage.

Unlike the blanket primary experiment, however, the top two primary will be a feature of California politics for long enough that it will be possible to study its effects. As we saw in our consideration of the Progressive Era, primary election reforms have a long history of failing to live up to their proponents' billing. Whether this is the case for the nonpartisan primary as well will depend in part on how candidates in California adapt to it and, perhaps, on how much attention the rest of the nation pays to California's experiment.

Primary Reform Everywhere Else: Legislation, Movements, and Ideas

Although California's reforms have drawn the most attention, several other states have explored establishing top two primaries; according to one study from 2012, legislation creating a top two primary has been introduced in six states—Alaska, Arizona, Idaho, Nevada, Utah, and Wyoming (Zhang 2012). Since that time Montana has also passed legislation to place a referendum creating a top two primary on the November 2014 ballot (Eaves 2013), and according to the "Stop Top Two" website, Mississippi and Florida are also considering top two legislation.[13] Most of these states are obviously in the same part of the country; they are also similar in that they have historically had weak party systems. Alaska used a blanket primary until the *Jones* decision and Idaho and Montana were both states where anti-party movements such as the Nonpartisan League found some traction early in the century. So all of these states have a political history that predisposes them to be skeptical of parties. As noted in Chapter 2, the Idaho Republican Party recently acted to close its primary (the Idaho Democratic Party still has an open primary), showing that movements toward more closed and more open primaries can flourish at the same time. Meanwhile, according to one recent study, as of 2011 legislation to close primaries had been introduced in thirteen states and legislation to open primaries had been introduced in eleven states (Hassell 2013).

Arizona's top two primary initiative, modeled on the California plan and buttressed with some diligent research into the plan's likely effects (see Berman 2012) failed miserably at the polls in November 2012, garnering just 33 percent of the vote. Unlike both the 1996 and 2010 California initiatives, which had support from Democratic and Republican voters as well as independents, the Arizona initiative received support only from independent voters (Wyloge 2013). Supporters of the initiative reportedly spent over $1 million on it, more than its opponents spent, but several prominent Democrats and Republicans campaigned against the top two proposition. Oregon voters also overwhelmingly rejected the top two primary in 2008 by the same margin that it lost by in Arizona; Quinn and Alvarez (2010) contend that the Oregon defeat took place because the language of the initiative was confusing and did not correspond to the language about open primaries used by the initiative's proponents during the campaign. Despite these setbacks, however, the top two primary has proven to be appealing to activists of many different sorts. While it is easy to see its appeal among those who advocate more broadly for institutional reform, it has also found support among Democratic and Republican politicians concerned about the effects of minor parties; in Montana, for instance, the lead sponsor of the legislation to hold a referendum on the top two primary is a Republican who worried that Libertarian candidates were siphoning off Republican votes (Eaves 2013).

There is currently somewhat of a disconnect between scholarly voices on primary reform and political activists. As we have seen, well-respected legal scholars such as Richard Hasen and Bruce Cain have taken strong stances on primary reform, and many of the leading California political scientists have taken their analysis of the effects of the rules change in California quite seriously. The coalitions for and against the top two primary, however, lack well-known political figures.

The most prominent organization with a national presence advocating for the top two primary and for opening up primaries more generally is a New York-based group called independentvoting.org, which has its roots in the New York Independence Party and former minor party presidential candidate Lenora Fulani's political organization. Chapters of the group have been established in many different states, including some where there is no legislative support for the idea. Independentvoting.org has a broader commitment to, as its name suggests, promoting the interests of independent voters, and it has advocated for open primaries on the grounds that a growing percentage of Americans do not affiliate with either party and that these individuals should be able to vote in primary elections without doing so; in essence, the group's position resembles the claims made in the *Nader v. Schaeffer* case. Harry Kresky, the group's chief lawyer, has lent his assistance to groups pushing to open up primaries in several states, including the successful effort to stop South Carolina from closing its primary.[14] Kresky also received a boost when journalist Linda Killian (2012, 255) discussed his views on primary reform in her recent book *The Swing Vote*. Other journalists have described the Independence Party as a "cult like" organization (Robbins 2009), and despite the group's national reach it remains deeply controversial in New York. Other organizations have championed the top two primary, including the California-based Foundation for Independent Voter Education (FIVE), but to date this movement lacks a well-known national spokesperson.

Like the top two advocates, the largest national group opposing the top two primary is also a product of anti-party politics. The national organization Stop Top Two counts among its supporters a few Democrats and Republicans who had sought to stop the top two primary in California, but its major source of funding is an organization named Free and Equal Elections, a 501(c) group that includes leaders of the Libertarian Party, the Constitution Party, and the Green Party. As Richard Hasen predicted, these parties have objected not only to the winnowing effect of the top two primary but to the fact that parties have no say in whether candidates can list their party on the ballot. The group counts among its supporters former presidential candidates Jill Stein, Gary Johnson, Ralph Nader, and John Anderson, as well as former Independent Governor of Minnesota Jesse Ventura. Civil liberties groups such as Fair Vote and the American Civil Liberties Union also support the group.

The debate about the top two primary, then, is being conducted largely by groups and individuals outside of the two party system, and there is little agreement between the two sides on the effects of changing primary laws or even on which approach offers the voters more choices. It is a debate that is certain to draw in more of the political mainstream if the top two primary spreads beyond California.

If the debate over primaries is not at the moment fully engaged, it has generated some fascinating proposals from within academia. We will just sample three of these here:

- Washington University law Professor David S. Law (2012) notes that the U.S. Constitution is anomalous in its failure to mention parties; he estimates that two-thirds of world constitutions do make explicit reference to the rights and responsibilities of parties. The lack of reference to parties has led the Supreme Court to avoid placing restrictions upon parties, and as a result we have no certainty that any primary system can be imposed upon parties. Law's solution is simple—amend the constitution to require parties to hold open primaries. This solution is similar to the proposed amendment overturning the court's *Citizens United v. Federal Election Commission* in that it would provide a straightforward means of addressing judicial intransigence. The problem with such an approach, of course, is that amending the constitution is a time-consuming process and would require not only increased public dissatisfaction with the primary process but a consensus that open primaries are in fact a solution to political polarization. As we have seen, the research on this question has not discerned clear differences in the outcomes of different primary systems.

- Emory University law Professor David Kang has established himself as the leading advocate for the repeal of sore loser laws. Sore loser laws, which we discussed briefly in Chapter 2, prohibit candidates who have lost a primary election from running in the general election as an independent or as the nominee of another party. Kang has chronicled the history of such laws, noting that in the early twentieth century, when such laws were uncommon, candidates could seek the nomination of a major party but then run as an independent or as the nominee of a minor party if they lost the primary. Kang (2011) notes that only about half of the states had sore loser laws in 2007, but that nearly all do today. He touts the repeal of sore loser laws as a means of encouraging moderation, insofar as primary winners would need to build support among the supporters of a losing primary candidate lest that candidate run against them in the general election. He has spoken of former Florida Governor Charlie Crist and Alaska Senator Lisa Murkowski as two candidates who would have benefitted from repeal of such laws (Kang 2010). In the absence of sore loser laws, a candidate with appeal among partisans of both parties can also run in a primary without being obligated to cater exclusively to party members. From a legal point of view, repealing sore loser laws is also more feasible than interfering with the actual conduct of primaries. The Supreme Court has already upheld sore loser laws (in the *Storer v. Brown*, 415 U.S. 724 (1974), decision). In the long run, removing sore loser laws would result in primary elections that are informal affairs that confer an advantage upon a party nominee (like, ironically, the "jaybird" primary) but are neither a certain means of winnowing the field nor, as they are in one-party districts, tantamount to a general election. In a subsequent empirical piece, Burden, Jones, and Kang (2013) estimate that sore loser laws explain approximately 10 percent of the ideological polarization between the two parties in Congress; no other primary rule has a significant influence on polarization.
- Another proposal, from Christopher Elmendorf and David Schleicher (2012) is to encourage the establishment of advisory primaries. Such primaries could be sponsored by any citizen group, and candidates could choose which advisory primary to enter as long as they only entered one. Under this proposal, the winners of the two advisory primaries with the highest turnout would then appear on the general election ballot. One benefit of such an approach would be that it might increase the information voters receive

about candidates; a candidate could be identified on the general election ballot by the name of the primary he or she won. This sort of approach is also reminiscent of the straw polls held in advance of some presidential primaries—candidates have the freedom to choose where to compete and can use these choices to seek to advance toward the general election. This proposal is offered by the authors as a suggestion that there are many other ways candidates could be selected, but it is not part of an active reform program.

There are, in short, many intriguing ideas about changing our primary elections that are under discussion. This is nothing new; the rules of primary elections have changed repeatedly over the past century, and even in their early years many unusual variations on primary laws appeared. There is little research that suggests a liberal or a conservative approach to primaries, let alone a way forward for those who would seek a middle way or a nonpartisan approach. There are certainly signs that primary reform occupies a more prominent place on the public agenda than it has for decades, but if this is so it is unclear what this prominence means.

A Piece of a Much Larger Puzzle

Are congressional primaries broken? In this book we have reviewed a wide variety of claims about the conduct and consequences of primary elections. One obvious conclusion one can draw from this book is that primary elections have always been a subject of contention, and states, politicians, and political activists have periodically sought to change the mechanics of primary elections. Yet it is also evident today that there has been renewed scholarly attention to the alleged problems caused by primary elections. Former Congressman Mickey Edwards (2013), writing in the *Atlantic Monthly*, recommends a six-step plan to "turn Republicans and Democrats into Americans." The plan includes several changes in congressional procedure, but his first two recommendations are requiring open primaries and establishing nonpartisan redistricting commissions. Veteran journalist Linda Killian (2012, 49) bemoans the steps to which parties have gone to sideline swing voters, and points to changes in the media, the growth of special interests and lobbyists, campaign finance laws, redistricting, and closed primaries as causes of "hyperpartisanship" in Congress. Killian recommends opening up primaries, although she is skeptical of California's reforms. She emphasizes that change to or preservation of open primaries must be accompanied by changes in ballot access, campaign financing, and voter registration laws if we are to see any effects. Brookings Institution scholar Thomas Mann (2006, 280) contends that primaries, campaign financing patterns, and redistricting are three of the major institutional sources of congressional partisan polarization.

One common thread in all of these claims is that it is not just primary elections that are held to be a cause of political polarization, congressional dysfunction, or public dissatisfaction with Congress. Many of those who have discussed changing primaries have spoken more generally about the way in which government institutions stand in the way of the public will. It is important to understand calls for primary reform as part of a broader movement for institutional reform, but it is also important to understand how primary reform differs from other types of reform efforts.

To illustrate this point, let us think back to the origins of primary elections. The establishment of the direct primary came at a moment when Progressive Reformers were pushing for many different sorts of changes in government. The direct primary thus fit in with the direct election of senators, recall elections, initiatives and referenda, and other institutional changes in that all of these proposals sought to democratize government and to reduce the power of political parties and unelected political bosses. It is easy to see the philosophical links between all of these proposals. Yet, as we saw in Chapter 2, the direct primary was the most widely adopted Progressive Era reform precisely because the targets of the Progressives' derision—political parties—understood that they could use primaries to their own advantage. The adoption of the direct primary thus had some intriguing consequences, but some consequences, such as the increase in spending and the increased security of incumbents, were clearly not what the Progressives wanted. Many of the predicted consequences of primaries failed to happen, as well, because political parties were able to gain some control of nominations through the establishment of preprimary conventions and through efforts at candidate recruitment. Primaries, then, were introduced at a time when many other reforms were also on the political agenda, but they were distinct in their popularity and their lack of effectiveness.

The same may be true today. Consider Thomas Mann's discussion above of primaries, redistricting, and campaign finance. These are all what are called "process issues," issues that have to do with how politics is conducted rather than with what sorts of policies politicians enact, but they are believed by many to have consequences for the policies made by government. It may make sense to think about reform plans that incorporate all three of these issues, if not more. After all, the California top two primary discussed above happened to be implemented at the same time as the state's new redistricting process, and it may be that the pairing of the two reforms will yet yield consequences far greater than would the establishment of only one of these reforms. The lack of effects stemming from California's 1998 blanket primary certainly indicates that this is a strong possibility.

Yet primaries are different from Mann's other two issues, perhaps in the same way that primaries differed from other Progressive reforms. Among academics, there may not be a clear sense of the consequences of different campaign finance reform proposals, but the battle lines have been clearly drawn for over a decade. Liberal reformers have sought to place greater restrictions on campaign spending, and perhaps to increase public financing of campaigns, while conservatives have sought to do away with restrictions. Similarly, those who have advocated redistricting reform have been in general agreement that redistricting commissions are preferable. There is no consensus on what the reformist approach to primaries is, nor what the liberal or conservative stance on primary reform should be. Perhaps the drive for the top two primary represents the dominant reformist sentiment of the moment, but this is hardly a monolithic movement. So if there is a problem, it is a problem without a clear solution.

One characteristic of public sentiment about matters of political process is that they are of relatively low salience to voters. To draw parallels again with campaign finance reform, anti-reform politicians such as Senate Minority Leader Mitch McConnell are wont to point out that when citizens are asked to name the most important problems facing the country, they do not name campaign finance.[15] Nor, one might add, do they mention any process issues—they name policy issues or larger challenges for the government such as taxes, defense, terrorism, or simply the economy and jobs. There is to my knowledge no public opinion data on the subject of primary elections, but it seems likely that citizens do not spontaneously name primaries as a problem. In fact, the Ahler, Citrin, and Lenz (2013) study indicated that in 2012 most California voters were unaware that their state had changed its primary laws. If that was the case in 2012 in California, it seems almost certain that most voters cannot explain what sort of primary system their state has or whether they would prefer a different system.

Despite this lack of knowledge, however, it is irrefutable that American voters feel a growing sense of detachment from their political institutions and are receptive to all manner of reform proposals. This is a phenomenon that has been referred to as the "democratic deficit" and that has been documented in many Western democracies over the past three decades (Dalton 2004). While voters in these nations may not have a thorough knowledge of how to change their political institutions, they respond positively to arguments about increasing democracy, about increasing transparency within government, and about increasing the accountability of politicians. In the case of campaign finance, this has manifested itself in high levels of public approval for reforms when they are described to survey respondents. Similarly, when changes in primary elections are framed for citizens as a matter of increasing choice, of increasing democracy, or of making politicians more accountable, voters respond enthusiastically. The problem here is that citizens' desires for reform are not sated by changes—precisely because citizens may not notice when changes have occurred. When the direct primary was introduced, it was very popular—citizens in virtually every state thought that primaries were a good idea, but this approval did not translate into higher levels of voting, higher levels of support for the political parties, or a sense that a better sort of politician was elected through the direct primary. The same logic seems likely to apply to changes in primary elections today.

We are left, then, with three paradoxes. First, our primary election laws are constantly in flux, yet most American citizens, when they think at all about primaries, think about them as a standard feature of political life, not something malleable. We take primaries for granted, even though they are a distinctly American phenomenon and are not by any means the best way of choosing candidates for office. Second, when voters are offered reform proposals, they tend to be enthusiastic, but they do not tend to notice when reforms are enacted. Voters are still enthusiastic about reforming the reforms. And third, we have never had strong evidence that changes in primary election laws yield the sorts of changes that reform advocates say that they will—yet this lack of effects may in itself be a reason for reform opponents not to fear reform. If primary reforms will not necessarily reduce political polarization, if they will not necessarily weaken parties or strengthen particular types of candidates, what is the rationale for them? How can one argue for reforms that do not yield substantial effects?

One possible response to this question is to simply note that there is a virtue in bringing order to our political process. In her book on presidential primaries, Barbara Norrander (2010, 94–118) discusses the logic of establishing regional primaries for presidential candidates. This, she argues, may simply be a matter of fairness. It makes sense to have presidential candidates campaign in a particular part of the country at a particular time, and it makes sense to rotate primaries so that Iowa and New Hampshire don't necessarily get to go first all of the time. This might not produce different kinds of politicians, but it seems, perhaps, like a fair way to do things. In the case of congressional primaries, it may also make sense to group congressional primary elections in this manner, or to separate them entirely. Is it fair to congressional primary candidates to place them on the same ballot as the presidential candidates? Perhaps it is, perhaps it is not, but a discussion of fairness avoids discussing the consequences of primaries and focuses instead on our views about how best to select candidates.

Similarly, consider the discussion earlier in this chapter about sore loser laws. When one starts discussing the effect of sore loser laws on the kinds of politicians who are elected—when one frames the repeal of sore loser laws as a way to aid centrist politicians and punish extremists—one is presenting a way to judge sore loser laws by their effects, not their fairness. Maybe it is not fair to give politicians a chance to run after they have lost a primary. Or perhaps it is, and perhaps primary elections are merely a means of allowing candidates to call themselves Democrats or Republicans on the ballot. One's position on this matter has little to do with results and more to do with beliefs about what elections are, what parties are, and what rights candidates and voters have.

This book does not seek to offer answers to questions such as these. In this concluding chapter, however, I have sought to provide a survey of the limits reformers face in changing primary elections, and of the options for change under discussion. Perhaps in a decade, when this book has started to fall out of date and (perhaps) a new one takes its place, some of the reforms discussed here will have become reality. And perhaps primary elections will have changed. The evidence suggests that reforms will not have predictable effects on primaries, and the data presented in this book suggest that when primaries do change, they change for reasons unrelated to the precise laws that govern how primaries are conducted. It is tempting to say that the outlook for primary reform is not promising. Many states will tinker with their laws, but there will not be a big reform movement, and even if there is it may not change our political system as much as one might think.

And yet, for all of this cynical talk about the political system, it is important to conclude by noting that Progressives realized this as well. Charles Merriam (1908, 176) concluded his book *Primary Elections* by saying that "the direct primary system is, therefore, to be regarded as an opportunity, not a result. It signifies the opening of a broad avenue of approach to democracy in party affairs, but not the attainment of the goal." Much of the time, perhaps most of the time, Merriam argued, people would not take advantage of these opportunities. But sometimes they would. For all of its flaws, and in all of its forms, the direct primary offers an opportunity. In many of the anecdotes presented in this book, this opportunity has yielded a level of political engagement for citizens that would not be possible were we to use another method of choosing candidates. Most of the time primaries may be sleepy affairs, but sometimes they are not, and these times may be why we have direct primaries. And to the extent that the cause of primary reform has gotten citizens involved in politics—as it seems to have during the Progressive era, and as it has in some of the state-level movements discussed here—the cause cannot but be seen as a positive thing for our democracy.

Notes

1 I am indebted to Reynolds (2006, 8) for calling this dialogue to my attention.
2 For discussion of the circumstances of the case see Baker 2012.
3 For discussion see Pollock 1926, 19; Overacker 1932b, 242–46, 282–83; Heard 1960, 352.
4 For discussion of these cases see Issacharoff and Pildes 1998; Persily 2002.
5 Rosenblum (2008, 432) finds this intervention less problematic. She notes that during this period the court had also upheld laws which restricted the activities of the Communist Party USA on the grounds that it was not a "real" political party. Such determinations rest on a federal interest in the internal proceedings of party decision-making, an interest that can also be said to exist in the white primary cases.
6 See also Persily and Cain 2000 on this point.
7 See also Maisel and Bibby 2002 for discussion of the relevance of Key's distinctions to primary elections.
8 The New Party was a left-leaning party active during the 1980s and 1990s that had ties with the Jesse Jackson presidential campaigns, ACORN, and labor union activists.
9 See Argersinger 1995 for a discussion of the rise and decline of fusion balloting, and Argersinger 1995, 171–75, on the relationship between the prohibition of fusion balloting and the introduction of the direct primary.

10 For discussion see Birkenstock 2007; Zhang 2012.
11 Gaines and Tam Cho (2002) provide a categorization of California's different primary regimes.
12 This is a common finding in research on other types of process reforms; voters, for instance, support a wide range of campaign finance reforms but when these reforms are enacted, the reforms appear to have no effect on citizens' views (see Dalton 2004).
13 See the "Top Two Threat Barometer" at www.stoptoptwo.org, accessed June 19, 2013.
14 The independentvoting.org website discusses Kresky's role in this; see http://openprimaries.org/news/south-carolina-victory/, accessed November 29, 2013. Whether the group made a difference in the case is hard to determine; the state's Republican Party dropped its plan to sue over the state's open primary law following the resignation of the state party's chairman. It is not certain whether the chairman's resignation had anything to do with the primary effort or whether he left for other reasons and the incoming chairman simply had different priorities (see Winger 2013).
15 For discussion of the two different perspectives on citizens' preferences for campaign finance reform, see Grant and Rudolph 2004.

REFERENCES

Abramowitz, Alan. 2010. *The Disappearing Center*. New Haven, CT: Yale University Press.
Abramowitz, Michael. 1995. "Morella Race Lures No Key Democrats; Filing Deadline Passes for Maryland's Primaries." *Washington Post*, December 27.
Achen, Christopher H., and Larry M. Bartels. 2006. "It Feels Like We're Thinking: The Rationalizing Voter and Electoral Democracy." Paper presented at the Annual Meeting of the American Political Science Association, Philadelphia, PA.
Adams, James, and Samuel M. Merrill. 2008. "Candidate and Party Strategies in Two-Stage Elections Beginning with a Primary." *American Journal of Political Science* 52 (2): 344–59.
Agranov, Marina. 2011. "Flip-Flopping, Intense Primaries, and the Selection of Candidates." Unpublished ms., California Institute of Technology.
Ahler, Doug, Jack Citrin, and Gabriel S. Lenz. 2013. "Can California's New Primary Reduce Polarization? Probably Not." *The Monkey Cage*, March 27. Online, http://themonkeycage.org/2013/03/27/can-californias-new-primary-reduce-polarization-maybe-not/.
Ahler, Doug, Gabriel S. Lenz, and Jack Citrin. 2013. "Do Open Primaries Help Moderate Candidates? An Experimental Test on the California 2012 Primary." Paper presented at the Annual Meeting of the American Political Science Association, Chicago, IL.
Aldrich, John H. 1995. *Why Parties?* Chicago: University of Chicago Press.
Allen, Jonathan, and Alex Isenstadt. 2012. "Kucinich Loss Is End of an Era." *Politico*, March 7. Online, www.politico.com/news/stories/0312/73757.html.
Alvarez, R. Michael, and Betsy Sinclair. 2012. "Electoral Institutions and Legislative Behavior: The Effects of Primary Processes." *Political Research Quarterly* 65 (3): 544–57.
Alvarez, R. Michael, David T. Canon, and Patrick Sellers. 1995. "The Impact of Primaries on General Election Outcomes in the U.S. House and Senate." Unpublished ms., California Institute of Technology.
Alvarez, R. Michael, and Jonathan Nagler. 1998. "Analysis of Crossover and Strategic Voting." Unpublished ms., California Institute of Technology.
Alvarez, R. Michael, and Jonathan Nagler. 2002. "Should I Stay or Should I Go? Sincere and Strategic Crossover Voting in California Assembly Races." In *Voting at the Political Fault Line: California's Experiment with the Blanket Primary*, ed. Bruce E. Cain and Elisabeth R. Gerber. Berkeley: University of California Press, pp. 107–23.

American National Election Studies. 2012. *The ANES Guide to Public Opinion and Electoral Behavior.* Ann Arbor: University of Michigan, Center for Political Studies [producer and distributor].

Anderson, Frank Maloy. 1902. "The Test of the Minnesota Primary Election System." *Annals of the American Academy of Political and Social Sciences* 20: 142–52.

Ansolabehere, Stephen. 2012. *Cooperative Congressional Election Study, 2010: Common Content* [Computer File] Release 1: February 26, 2012. Cambridge, MA: Harvard University [producer]. Online, http://cces.gov.harvard.edu.

Ansolabehere, Stephen, and Alan Gerber. 1996. "The Effects of Filing Fees and Petition Requirements on U.S. House Elections." *Legislative Studies Quarterly* 21 (2): 249–64.

Ansolabehere, Stephen, John Mark Hansen, Shigeo Hirano, and James M. Snyder, Jr. 2006. "The Decline of Competition in US Primary Elections, 1908–2004." In *The Marketplace of Democracy: Electoral Competition and American Politics*, ed. Michael P. McDonald and John Samples. Washington, DC: Brookings Institution and Cato Institute, pp. 74–101.

Ansolabehere, Stephen, John Mark Hansen, Shigeo Hirano, and James M. Snyder, Jr. 2007. "The Incumbency Advantage in U.S. Primary Elections." *Electoral Studies* 26 (3): 660–68.

Ansolabehere, Stephen, John Mark Hansen, Shigeo Hirano, and James M. Snyder, Jr. 2010. "More Democracy: The Direct Primary and Competition in U.S. House Elections." *Studies in American Political Development* 24 (2): 190–205.

Applebome, Peter. 2012. "Connecticut Faces Fight for Senate, Inside GOP." *New York Times*, May 16.

Arcenaux, Kevin, and David W. Nickerson. 2009. "Who is Mobilized to Vote? A Re-Analysis of Eleven Randomized Field Experiments." *American Journal of Political Science* 53 (1): 1–21.

Argersinger, Peter H. 1995. *The Limits of Agrarian Radicalism: Western Populism and American Politics.* Lawrence: University Press of Kansas.

Aylwsworth, L.E. 1910. "Primary Elections—Illinois." *American Political Science Review* 4 (4): 569–71.

Babington, Charles, and Spencer S. Hsu. 1998. "Little Fallout for Morella on Votes against Impeachment." *Washington Post*, December 24.

Bai, Matt. 2002. "Rove's Way." *New York Times*, October 20.

Bain, Chester W. 1972. "South Carolina: Partisan Prelude." In *The Changing Politics of the South*, ed. William C. Havard. Baton Rouge: University of Louisiana Press, pp. 588–636.

Baker, Paula. 2012. *Curbing Campaign Cash: Henry Ford, Truman Newberry, and the Politics of Progressive Reform.* Lawrence: University of Kansas Press.

Bakvis, Herman, ed. 1991. *Canadian Political Parties.* Research Studies: Royal Commission on Electoral Reform and Party Financing, Vol. 13. Toronto: Dundurn Press.

Barone, Michael, and Richard E. Cohen. 2005. *Almanac of American Politics 2006.* Washington, DC: National Journal Group.

Barreto, Matt A., Gary M. Segura, and Nathan D. Woods. 2004. "The Mobilizing Effect of Majority-Minority Districts on Latino Turnout." *American Political Science Review* 98 (1): 65–75.

Bartels, Larry M. 1988. *Presidential Primaries and the Dynamics of Public Choice.* Princeton, NJ: Princeton University Press.

Beard, Charles A. 1910. "The Direct Primary in New York." *Proceedings of the American Political Science Association* 7: 187–98.

Bell, Jonathan. 2012. *California Crucible: The Forging of Modern American Liberalism*. Philadelphia: University of Pennsylvania Press.
Belluck, Pam. 2002. "A GOP Primary Strains Party Ties and Bush Loyalties." *New York Times*, July 7.
Berard, Stanley P. 2001. *Southern Democrats in the U. S. House of Representatives*. Norman: University of Oklahoma Press.
Berdahl, Clarence A. 1923. "The Operation of the Richards Primary." *Annals of the American Academy of Political and Social Science* 106: 158–71.
Berger, Joseph, and Michael W. Grynbaum. 2012. "In Brooklyn, a Longtime Provocateur Surges in a Primary Race for Congress." *New York Times*, June 15.
Berman, David R. 2012. "Top-Two Proposition: What Nonpartisan Elections Could Mean for Arizona." Phoenix, AZ: Morrison Institute, Arizona State University.
Bernstein, Robert A. 1977. "Divisive Primaries Do Hurt: US Senate Races, 1956–1972." *American Political Science Review* 71 (2): 540–45.
Berry, William D., and Bradley C. Canon. 1993. "Explaining the Competitiveness of Gubernatorial Primaries." *Journal of Politics* 55 (2): 454–71.
Birkenstock, Joseph M. 2007. "U.S. Supreme Court Case Preview: Did I-872 Take Washington State's Voters on an Unconstitutional Detour? Partisanship in Primaries in *Washington v. Washington State Republican Party*." *Election Law Journal* 6 (4): 394–98.
Black, Bob. 1996. "Blagojevich Takes Fifth; Political Pull Yanks Win Back from Kaszak." *Chicago Sun-Times*, 20 March.
Blais, Andre. 2006. "What Affects Voter Turnout?" *Annual Review of Political Science* 9: 111–25.
Blake, Aaron. 2012. "California Primary Results: GOP Catches a 'Top-Two' Break." *Washington Post*, June 8.
Boatright, Robert G. 2004. *Expressive Politics: Issue Strategies of Congressional Challengers*. Columbus: Ohio State University Press.
Boatright, Robert G. 2013. *Getting Primaried: The Changing Politics of Congressional Primary Challenges*. Ann Arbor: University of Michigan Press.
Boots, Ralph S. 1922. "The Trend of the Direct Primary." *American Political Science Review* 16 (3): 412–31.
Born, Richard. 1981. "The Influence of House Primary Election Divisiveness on General Election Margins, 1962–1976." *Journal of Politics* 43 (3): 640–61.
Bowler, Shaun, and Todd Donovan. 2002. "Political Reform Via the Initiative Process: What Voters Think about When They Change the Rules." In *Voting at the Political Fault Line: California's Experiment with the Blanket Primary*, eds. Bruce E. Cain and Elisabeth R. Gerber. Berkeley: University of California Press, pp. 36–58.
Brace, Paul. 1984. "Progressive Ambition in the House: A Probabilistic Approach." *Journal of Politics* 46 (2): 556–71.
Brace, Paul. 1985. "A Probabilistic Approach to Retirement from the U.S. Congress." *Legislative Studies Quarterly* 10 (1): 107–23.
Branton, Regina. 2009. "The Importance of Race and Ethnicity in Congressional Primary Elections." *Political Research Quarterly* 62 (3): 459–73.
Bravender, Robin. 2012. "DeMint Fueled Lugar Fight." *Politico*, May 18. Online, www.politico.com/news/stories/0512/76493.html.
Brogan, Michael J., and Jonathan Mendilow. 2012. "Public Party Funding and Intraparty Competition: Clean Elections in Maine and Arizona." *International Journal of Humanities and Social Science* 2 (6): 120–32.

Brown, Anna, and Mark Hugo Lopez. 2013. "Mapping the Latino Population by State, City, and County." Washington, DC: Pew Foundation Hispanic Trends Project. Online, www.pewhispanic.org/files/2013/08/latino_populations_in_the_states_counties_and_cities_FINAL.pdf.

Bruhn, Kathleen. 2011. "Electing Extremists? Party Primaries and Legislative Candidates in Mexico." Unpublished ms., University of California, Santa Barbara.

Bullock, Charles S. 2010. *Redistricting: The Most Political Activity in America*. Lanham, MD: Rowman and Littlefield.

Bullock, Charles S., and Loch K. Johnson. 1992. *Runoff Elections in the United States*. Chapel Hill: University of North Carolina Press.

Bullock, Charles S., and A. Brock Smith. 1990. "Black Success in Local Runoff Elections." *Journal of Politics* 52 (4): 1205–20.

Bullock, Will, and Joshua D. Clinton. 2011. "More a Molehill than a Mountain: The Effects of the Blanket Primary on Elected Officials' Behavior from California." *Journal of Politics* 73 (3): 1–16.

Burden, Barry C. 2000. "Voter Turnout and the National Election Studies." *Political Analysis* 8 (4): 389–98.

Burden, Barry C. 2001. "The Polarizing Effects of Congressional Primaries." In *Congressional Primaries and the Politics of Representation*, eds. Peter F. Galderisi, Marni Ezra, and Michael Lyons. Lanham, MD: Rowman and Littlefield, pp. 95–115.

Burden, Barry C., Bradley Jones, and Michael S. Kang. 2013. "Nominations and the Supply of Candidates: The Connection between Sore Loser Laws and Congressional Polarization." Unpublished ms., University of Wisconsin.

Burnham, Walter Dean. 1965. "The Changing Shape of the American Political Universe." *American Political Science Review* 59: 7–28.

Cain, Bruce E. 2001. "Party Autonomy and Two-Party Electoral Competition." *University of Pennsylvania Law Review* 149 (3): 793–814.

Cain, Bruce E., and Elisabeth R. Gerber. 2002. "California's Experiment with the Blanket Primary." In *Voting at the Political Fault Line: California's Experiment with the Blanket Primary*, eds. Bruce E. Cain and Elisabeth R. Gerber. Berkeley: University of California Press, pp. 3–11.

Cain, Bruce E., and Megan Mullin. 2002. "Strategies and Rules: Lessons from the 2000 Presidential Primary." In *Voting at the Political Fault Line: California's Experiment with the Blanket Primary*, ed. Bruce E. Cain and Elisabeth R. Gerber. Berkeley: University of California Press, pp. 324–43.

Calmes, Jackie. 2009. "Congressional Memo: GOP Senator Draws Critics in Both Parties." *New York Times*, September 22.

Cameron, Charles, David Epstein, and Sharyn O'Halloran. 1996. "Do Majority-Minority Districts Maximize Substantive Black Representation in Congress?" *American Political Science Review* 90 (3): 794–812.

Canon, Bradley. 1978. "Factionalism in the South: A Test of Theory and a Revisitation of V.O. Key." *American Journal of Political Science* 22 (3): 833–48.

Canon, David T. 2001. "Wisconsin's Second District: History in the Making." In *The Battle for Congress*, ed. James A. Thurber. Washington, DC: Brookings Institution, pp. 199–238.

Carey, John M., and John Polga-Hecimovich. 2006. "Primary Elections and Candidate Strength in Latin America." *Journal of Politics* 68 (3): 530–43.

Carson, Jamie L., Michael H. Crespin, Carrie P. Eaves, and Emily Wanless. 2012. "Constituency Congruency and Candidate Competition in Primary Elections for the U.S. House." *State Politics and Policy Quarterly* 12 (2): 127–45.

Carson, Jamie L., and Jason M. Roberts. 2013. *Ambition, Competition, and Electoral Reform: The Politics of Congressional Elections across Time*. Ann Arbor: University of Michigan Press.

Caul, Miki, and Katherine Tate. 2002. "Thinner Ranks: Women as Candidates and California's Blanket Primary." In *Voting at the Political Fault Line: California's Experiment with the Blanket Primary*, eds. Bruce E. Cain and Elisabeth R. Gerber. Berkeley: University of California Press, pp. 234–47.

Chase, David A. 2007. "*Clingman v. Beaver*: Shifting Power from the Parties to the States." *University of California, Davis Law Review* 40: 1935–61.

Chawkins, Steve, and Patrick McGreevy. 2009. "Sen. Abel Maldonado Has Made a Name for Himself." *Los Angeles Times*, February 22.

Chrislock, Carl H. 1971. *The Progressive Era in Minnesota, 1899–1918*. St. Paul: Minnesota Historical Society.

Clymer, Adam. 2001. "Black Caucus Members Find Themselves Courted Heavily in Soft Money Fight." *New York Times*, July 12.

Cohen, Diana Tracy. 2008. "Netroots: Ned Lamont, Social Capital, and the Liberal Blogosphere." *Connecticut Public Interest Law Journal* 8 (1): 43–63.

Committee on Political Parties. American Political Science Association. 1950. "Toward a More Responsible Two Party System." *American Political Science Review* 44, supplement.

Converse, Philip. 1972. "Change in the American Electorate." In *The Human Meaning of Social Change*, eds. Angus Campbell and Philip Converse. New York: Russell Sage. pp. 268–301.

Craig, Stephen C., and Roger Austin. 2008. "Elections and Partisan Change in Florida." In *Government and Politics in Florida*, 3rd ed., ed. J. Edwin Benton. Gainesville: University Press of Florida, pp. 48–89.

Crespin, Michael H. 2004. "Direct Primaries and the Openness of the Two Party System, 1904–1920." Unpublished ms., Michigan State University.

Crespin, Michael H. 2005. "Using Geographic Information Systems to Measure District Change, 2000–2002." *Political Analysis* 13 (2): 253–60.

Cross, William P., and Andre Blais. 2012. *Politics at the Centre*. Oxford: Oxford University Press.

Currinder, Marian. 2008. *Money in the House: Campaign Funds and Congressional Party Politics*. Boulder, CO: Westview Press.

Dallinger, Frederick. 1897. *Nominations for Elective Office*. Cambridge, MA: Harvard University Press.

Dalton, Russell J. 2004. *Democratic Challenges, Democratic Choices*. New York: Oxford University Press.

Davidson, Chandler. 1990. *Race and Class in Texas Politics*. Princeton, NJ: Princeton University Press.

Davis, James W. 1980. *Presidential Primaries: Road to the White House*, 2nd ed. Westport, CT: Greenwood Press.

Dayal, Priyanka. 2010. "Lamb Takes GOP: Winner Faces McGovern in November." *Worcester Telegram and Gazette*, September 15.

Delmatier, Royce D., Clarence F. McIntosh, and Earl G. Waters. 1970. *The Rumble of California Politics, 1848–1970*. New York: John Wiley and Sons.

Dinan, Stephen. 2002. "Rival Advocacy Groups Contend over GOP Candidates." *Washington Times*, September 15.

Dodds, H.W. 1923. "Removable Obstacles to the Success of the Direct Primary." *Annals of the American Academy of Political and Social Sciences* 106: 18–21.

Dominguez, Casey B.K. 2005. *Before the Primary: Party Participation in Congressional Nominating Processes*. Ph. D. dissertation, University of California, Berkeley.

Dominguez, Casey B.K. 2011. "Does the Party Matter? Endorsements in Congressional Primaries." *Political Research Quarterly* 64 (3): 534–44.

Dominguez, Casey B.K. 2013. "Before the Primary: How Party Elites and Ambitious Candidates Respond to Anticipated General Election Competitiveness." Paper presented at the Annual Meeting of the Midwest Political Science Association, Chicago, IL.

Donnelly, Thomas C. 1940. *Rocky Mountain Politics*. Albuquerque: University of New Mexico Press.

Dorr, Harold M. 1937. "Tightening the Direct Primary in Michigan: First Applications of the Filing Fee." *American Political Science Review* 31 (1): 56–65.

Dunn, Susan. 2012. *Roosevelt's Purge*. Cambridge, MA: Harvard/ Belknap Press.

Eagles, Munroe, Harold Jansen, Anthony Sayers, and Lisa Young. 2005. "Financing Federal Nomination Contests in Canada—An Overview of the 2004 Experience." Paper presented at the annual meeting of the Canadian Political Science Association, London, Ontario.

Eaves, Lucas. 2013. "Montana to Vote on Adding Nonpartisan Top Two Primary to 2014 Ballot." Independent Voter Network. Online, http://ivn.us/2013/04/19/montanans-could-adopt-a-nonpartisan-top-two-primary-in-2014/ (accessed June 20, 2013).

Edwards, George C. 2007. *Governing by Campaigning: The Politics of the Bush Presidency*. New York: Pearson.

Edwards, Mickey. 2013. "How to Turn Republicans and Democrats into Americans." *Atlantic Monthly*, May 29.

Eggert, David. 2012. "Joyce Beatty Wins Friendly 3rd District Primary." *Columbus Dispatch*, March 7.

Eggert, David, and Joe Vardon. 2011. "Mayor Backs Beatty for Congress." *Columbus Dispatch*, December 30.

Ehrenhalt, Alan. 1992. *The United States of Ambition*. New York: Times Books.

Ellis, Jonathan. 2010. "U.S. House: State Rep. Kristi Noem to Face Herseth Sandlin in Historic Clash." *Sioux Falls Argus Leader*, March 10.

Elmendorf, Christopher S., and David Schleicher. 2012. "Informing Consent: Voter Ignorance, Political Parties, and Election Law." Unpublished ms., University of California, Davis School of Law.

Enelow, James M., and Melvin J. Hinich. 1984. *The Spatial Theory of Voting: An Introduction*. New York: Cambridge University Press.

Epstein, Leon D. 2002. "A Persistent Quest." In *Responsible Partisanship: The Evolution of American Political Parties Since 1950*, eds. John C. Green and Paul S. Herrnson. Lawrence: University Press of Kansas, pp. 201–16.

Erickson, Lynda, and R.J. Carty. 1991. "Parties and Candidate Selection in the 1988 Canadian General Election." *Canadian Journal of Political Science* 24 (2): 331–49.

Ethington, Philip J. 1999. "The Metropolis and Multicultural Ethics: Direct Democracy versus Deliberative Democracy in the Progressive Era." In *Progressivism and the New Democracy*, eds. Sidney M. Milkis and Jerome M. Mileur. Amherst: University of Massachusetts Press, pp. 192–225.

Ewing, Cortez. 1953. *Primary Elections in the South: A Study in Uniparty Politics*. Norman: University of Oklahoma Press.
Fanning, C.E. 1905. *Selected Articles on Direct Primaries*. Minneapolis, MN: H.W. Wilson.
Farrell, David M. 2011. *Electoral Systems: A Comparative Introduction*, 2nd ed. New York: Palgrave Macmillan.
Feldman, H. 1917. "The Direct Primary in New York State." *American Political Science Review* 11 (3): 494–518.
Fenno, Richard F. 1973. *Congressmen in Committees*. Boston, MA: Little, Brown.
Fenno, Richard F. 1978. *Home Style: House Members in Their Districts*. Boston, MA: Little, Brown.
Fenno, Richard F. 2003. *Going Home: Black Representatives and Their Constituents*. Chicago: University of Chicago Press.
Fernandez, Manny. 2012. "Texas Race for Senate Reveals Rift on the Right." *New York Times*, June 10.
Fiorina, Morris P. 1989. *Congress: Keystone of the Washington Establishment*. New Haven, CT: Yale University Press.
Fishel, Jeff. 1973. *Party and Opposition: Congressional Challengers in American Politics*. New York: David McKay Company.
Flanigan, William H., and Nancy Zingale. 2006. *Political Behavior and the American Electorate*, 11th ed. Washington, DC: Congressional Quarterly Press.
Fornek, Scott. 1995. "Frias Takes on Gutierrez in 4th." *Chicago Sun-Times*, December 19.
Fortenberry, Charles N., and F. Glenn Abney. 1972. "Mississippi: Unreconstructed and Unredeemed." In *The Changing Politics of the South*, ed. William C. Havard. Baton Rouge: University of Louisiana Press, pp. 472–524.
Fowler, Linda L., and Robert D. McClure. 1989. *Political Ambition: Who Decides to Run for Congress*. New Haven, CT: Yale University Press.
Fowler, Robert Booth. 2008. *Wisconsin Votes: An Electoral History*. Madison: University of Wisconsin Press.
Gaddie, Ronald Keith, and Charles S. Bullock III. 2000. *Elections to Open Seats in the U.S. House: Where the Action is*. Lanham, MD: Rowman and Littlefield.
Gaines, Brian J., and Wendy K. Tam Cho. 2002. "Crossover Voting Before the Blanket." In *Voting at the Political Fault Line: California's Experiment with the Blanket Primary*, eds. Bruce E. Cain and Elisabeth R. Gerber. Berkeley: University of California Press, pp. 12–35.
Galderisi, Peter F., and Marni Ezra. 2001. "Congressional Primaries in Historical and Theoretical Context." In *Congressional Primaries and the Politics of Representation*, eds. Peter F. Galderisi, Marni Ezra, and Michael Lyons. Lanham, MD: Rowman and Littlefield, pp. 11–28.
Galderisi, Peter F., Marni Ezra, and Michael Lyons, eds. 2001. *Congressional Primaries and the Politics of Representation*. Lanham, MD: Rowman and Littlefield.
Gaston, Herbert E. 1920. *The Nonpartisan League*. New York: Harcourt, Brace, and Howe.
Gay, Claudine. 2001. "The Effect of Black Congressional Representation on Political Participation." *American Political Science Review* 95 (3): 589–602.
Geer, John. 1986. "Rules Governing Presidential Primaries." *Journal of Politics* 48 (4): 1006–25.
Geer, John G., and Mark E. Shere. 1992. "Party Competition and the Prisoner's Dilemma: An Argument for the Direct Primary." *Journal of Politics* 54 (3): 741–61.
Geiser, Karl F. 1923. "Defects in the Direct Primary." *Annals of the American Academy of Political and Social Sciences* 106: 31–39.

Gerber, Elisabeth R. 1999. *The Populist Paradox: Interest Group Influence and the Promise of Direct Legislation*. Princeton, NJ: Princeton University Press.

Gerber, Elisabeth R. 2001. "California's Experience with the Blanket Primary." In *Congressional Primaries and the Politics of Representation*, eds. Peter F. Galderisi, Marni Ezra, and Michael Lyons. Lanham, MD: Rowman and Littlefield, pp. 143–60.

Gerber, Elisabeth R. 2002. "Strategic Voting and Candidate Policy Positions." In *Voting at the Political Fault Line: California's Experiment with the Blanket Primary*, eds. Bruce E. Cain and Elisabeth R. Gerber. Berkeley: University of California Press, pp. 192–213.

Gerber, Elizabeth R., and Rebecca B. Morton. 1998. "Primary Election Systems and Representation." *Journal of Law, Economics, and Organization* 14 (2): 304–24.

Gieske, Millard L. 1979. *Minnesota Farmer-Laborism: The Third-Party Alternative*. Minneapolis: University of Minnesota Press.

Glad, Betty. 1995. "How George Bush Lost the Presidential Election of 1992." In *The Clinton Presidency: Campaigning, Governing, and the Psychology of Leadership*, ed. Stanley A. Renshon. Boulder, CO: Westview Press, pp. 11–36.

Glaser, James M. 1996. *Race, Campaign Politics, and the Realignment in the South*. New Haven, CT: Yale University Press.

Gomez, Henry J. 2012. "Marcy Kaptur Scores Huge Victory against Dennis Kucinich in Battle of Democratic Heavyweights." *Cleveland Plain Dealer*, March 7.

Goodnough, Abby. 2011. "Massachusetts Democrats Meet in First Senate Debate." *New York Times*, October 4.

Goodnough, Abby. 2012. "In Massachusetts Senate Race, Top Democrat Has a Rival." *New York Times*, May 26.

Gottlieb, Sanford. 2009. *Red to Blue: Congressman Chris Van Hollen and Grassroots Politics*. Boulder, CO: Paradigm Publishers.

Grant, J. Tobin, and Thomas J. Rudolph. 2004. *Expression versus Equality: The Politics of Campaign Finance Reform*. Columbus: Ohio State University Press.

Gray, Katherine. 2012. "Congressmen John Conyers, Gary Peters Score Big Leads in Latest Poll." *Detroit Free Press*, August 3.

Green, John C., and Paul S. Herrnson. 2002. "Party Development in the Twentieth Century: Laying the Foundations for Responsible Party Government?" In *Responsible Partisanship: The Evolution of American Political Parties Since 1950*, eds. John C. Green and Paul S. Herrnson. Lawrence: University Press of Kansas, pp. 37–60.

Greene, Lee S., and Jack E. Holmes. 1972. "Tennessee: A Politics of Peaceful Change." In *The Changing Politics of the South*, ed. William C. Havard. Baton Rouge: University of Louisiana Press, pp. 165–200.

Gronke, Paul. 2000. *The Electorate, the Campaign and the Office*. Ann Arbor: University of Michigan Press.

Groseclose, Timothy, and Keith Krehbiel. 1994. "Golden Parachutes, Rubber Checks, and Strategic Retirements from the 102nd House." *American Journal of Political Science* 38 (1): 75–99.

Guild, Frederic H. 1923. "The Operations of the Direct Primary in Indiana." *Annals of the American Academy of Political and Social Sciences* 106: 172–80.

Hacker, Andrew. 1965. "Does a 'Divisive' Primary Harm a Candidate's Chances?" *American Political Science Review* 59 (1): 105–10.

Hajnal, Zoltan L. 2010. *America's Uneven Democracy*. New York: Cambridge University Press.

Hall, Arnold Bennett. 1923. "The Direct Primary and Party Responsibility in Wisconsin." *Annals of the American Academy of Political and Social Sciences* 106: 40–54.

Hall, Richard L., and Robert P. Van Houweling. 1995. "Avarice and Ambition in Congress: Representatives' Decisions to Run or Retire from the U.S. House." *American Political Science Review* 89 (1): 121–36.

Hamby, Alonzo L. 1999. "Progressivism: A Century of Change and Rebirth." In *Progressivism and the New Democracy*, eds. Sidney M. Milkis and Jerome M. Mileur. Amherst: University of Massachusetts Press, pp. 40–80.

Hannan, William E. 1923. "Opinions of Public Men on the Value of the Direct Primary." *Annals of the American Academy of Political and Social Sciences* 106: 55–62.

Hasen, Richard L. 1997. "Entrenching the Duopoly: Why the Supreme Court Should Not Allow the States to Protect the Democrats and Republicans from Political Competition." *Supreme Court Review* 1997: 331–71.

Hasen, Richard L. 2001. "Do the Parties or the People Own the Electoral Process?" *University of Pennsylvania Law Review* 149 (3): 815–41.

Hassell, Hans J.G. 2012. *The Party's Primary: The Influence of the Party Hill Committees in Primary Elections for the House and Senate*. Ph. D. dissertation, University of California, San Diego.

Hassell, Hans J.G. 2013. "The Non-Existent Primary-Ideology Link, or Do Open Primaries Actually Limit Party Influence in Primary Elections?" Paper presented at the Annual State Politics and Policy Conference, Iowa City, IA.

Hazan, Reuven Y., and Gideon Rahat. 2010. *Democracy within Parties: Candidate Selection Methods and Their Political Consequences*. London: Oxford University Press.

Healy, Patrick. 2006. "Race Profile: The Connecticut Senate Race." *New York Times*. Online, www.nytimes.com/ref/washington/raceprofile_CONNECTICUTSENATE.html.

Heaney, Michael T., Seth Masket, Joanne Miller, and Dara Z. Strolovitch. 2012. "Polarized Networks: The Organizational Affiliations of National Party Convention Delegates." *American Behavioral Scientist* 56 (12): 1654–76.

Heard, Alexander. 1960. *The Costs of Democracy*. Chapel Hill: University of North Carolina Press.

Heath, Hadley, and Heather R. Higgins. 2012. "Fischer: Anatomy of an Upset." *Politico*, May 18. Online, www.politico.com/news/stories/0512/76506.html.

Heberlig, Eric S., and Bruce A. Larson. 2012. *Congressional Parties, Institutional Ambition, and the Financing of Majority Control*. Ann Arbor: University of Michigan Press.

Helderman, Rosalind. 2008. "Strategists Weigh In on Edwards/Wynn." *Washington Post*, February 15.

Herrnson, Paul S. 1988. *Party Campaigning in the 1980s*. Cambridge, MA: Harvard University Press.

Herrnson, Paul S. 2012. *Congressional Elections: Campaigning at Home and in Washington*, 6th ed. Washington, DC: Congressional Quarterly Press.

Herrnson, Paul S., and James G. Gimpel. 1995. "District Conditions and Primary Divisiveness in Elections." *Political Research Quarterly* 48 (1): 101–16.

Hibbing, John R. 1982a. "Voluntary Retirements from the House in the Twentieth Century." *Journal of Politics* 44 (4): 1020–34.

Hibbing, John R. 1982b. "Voluntary Retirement from the U.S. House: The Costs of Congressional Service." *Legislative Studies Quarterly* 7 (1): 57–74.

Hibbing, John R. 1982c. "Voluntary Retirement from the U.S. House of Representatives: Who Quits?" *American Journal of Political Science* 26 (3): 467–84.

Highton, Benjamin. 2011. "The Influence of Strategic Retirement on the Incumbency." *Journal of Theoretical Politics* 23 (4): 431–47.

Hill, Kevin. 1995. "Does the Creation of Majority Black Districts Aid Republicans?" *Journal of Politics* 57 (2): 384–401.

Hinckley, Barbara. 1981. *Congressional Elections*. Washington, DC: Congressional Quarterly Press.
Hinich, Melvin J., and Michael C. Munger. 1994. *Ideology and the Theory of Political Choice*. Ann Arbor: University of Michigan Press.
Hirano, Shigeo, and James M. Snyder. 2011. "The Direct Primary and Candidate-Centered Voting in U.S. Elections." Unpublished ms., Columbia University.
Hirschman, Albert O. 1970. *Exit, Voice, and Loyalty*. Cambridge, MA: Harvard University Press.
Hofnung, Menachem. 2008. "Unaccounted Competition: The Finance of Intraparty Elections." *Party Politics* 14 (6): 726–44.
Hofstadter, Richard. 1955. *The Age of Reform*. New York: Vintage Books.
Hogan, Robert E. 2003. "Competition in State Legislative Primary Elections." *Legislative Studies Quarterly* 28 (1): 103–26.
Holcombe, A.N. 1911. "Direct Primaries and the Second Ballot." *American Political Science Review* 5 (4): 535–52.
Holmes, Jack E. 1967. *Politics in New Mexico*. Albuquerque: University of New Mexico Press.
Horack, Frank E. 1923. "The Workings of the Direct Primary in Iowa, 1908–1922." *Annals of the American Academy of Political and Social Sciences* 106: 148–57.
Hormell, Orren Chalmer. 1923. "The Direct Primary Law in Maine and How It Worked." *Annals of the American Academy of Political and Social Sciences* 106: 128–41.
Huckshorn, Robert J., and Robert C. Spencer. 1971. *The Politics of Defeat*. Boston: University of Massachusetts Press.
Ichino, Nahomi, and Noah L. Nathan. 2013. "Do Primaries Improve Electoral Performance? Clientelism and Intra-Party Conflict in Ghana." *American Journal of Political Science* 57 (2): 428–41.
Isenstadt, Alex. 2011. "Iowa OKs Redistricting Plan." *Politico*, April 14. Online, www.politico.com/news/stories/0411/53209.html.
Isenstadt, Alex. 2012. "House Incumbents Cruise to Wins." *Politico*, May 9. Online, www.politico.com/news/stories/0512/76086.html.
Issacharoff, Samuel. 2001. "Private Parties with Public Purposes: Political Parties, Associational Freedoms, and Partisan Competition." *Columbia Law Review* 101 (2): 274–313.
Issacharoff, Samuel, and Richard H. Pildes. 1998. "Politics as Markets: Partisan Lockups of the Democratic Process." *Stanford Law Review* 50 (3): 643–717.
Jacobson, Gary C. 1987. "The Marginals Never Vanished: Incumbency and Competition in Elections to the U.S. House of Representatives, 1952–82." *American Journal of Political Science* 31 (1): 126–41.
Jacobson, Gary C. 1989. "Strategic Politicians and the Dynamics of U.S. House Elections, 1946–86." *American Political Science Review* 83 (3): 773–93.
Jacobson, Gary C. 2012. "The Electoral Origins of Polarized Politics: Evidence from the 2010 Cooperative Congressional Election Study." *American Behavioral Scientist* 56 (12): 1612–30.
Jacobson, Gary C. 2013. *The Politics of Congressional Elections*, 8th ed. New York: Pearson.
Jacobson, Gary C., and Samuel Kernell. 1981. *Strategy and Choice in Congressional Elections*. New Haven, CT: Yale University Press.
Jewell, Malcolm E., and David M. Olson. 1988. *Political Parties and Elections in American States*, 3rd ed. Chicago: Dorsey Press.

Johnson, Donald Bruce, and James R. Gibson. 1974. "The Divisive Primary Revisited: Party Activists in Iowa." *American Political Science Review* 68 (1): 67–77.

Johnson, Gregg B., Meredith-Joy Petersheim, and Jesse T. Wasson. 2010. "Divisive Primaries and Incumbent General Election Performance: Prospects and Costs in U.S. House Races." *American Politics Research* 38 (5): 931–55.

Jones, Walter Clyde. 1910. "The Direct Primary in Illinois." *Proceedings of the American Political Science Association* 7: 138–62.

Kang, Michael S. 2010. "The Tea Party and a Supply-Side Approach to Political Polarization." *Election Law Blog*, November 11. Online, http://electionlawblog.org/archives/017928.html.

Kang, Michael S. 2011. "Sore Loser Laws and Democratic Contestation." *Georgetown Law Journal* 99: 1013–75.

Kanthak, Kristin, and Rebecca Morton. 2001. "The Effects of Electoral Rules on Congressional Primaries." In *Congressional Primaries and the Politics of Representation*, eds. Peter F. Galderisi, Marni Ezra, and Michael Lyons. Lanham, MD: Rowman and Littlefield, pp. 116–31.

Kaufmann, Karen M., James G. Gimpel, and Adam H. Hoffman. 2003. "A Promise Fulfilled? Open Primaries and Representation." *Journal of Politics* 65 (2): 457–76.

Kazee, Thomas A. 1994. *Who Runs for Congress? Ambition, Context, and Candidate Emergence.* Washington, DC: Congressional Quarterly Press.

Keeter, Scott, and Cliff Zukin. 1983. *Uninformed Choice: The Failure of the New Presidential Nominating System.* New York: Praeger.

Keller, Barney. 2012. "Facts on the Impact of the Club for Growth Political Arms in the Texas Senate Race." Washington, DC: Club for Growth.

Kemahlioglu, Ozhe, Rebecca Weitz-Shapiro, and Shigeo Hirano. 2009. "Why Primaries in Latin American Presidential Elections?" *Journal of Politics* 71 (1): 339–52.

Kenney, Patrick J. 1986. "Explaining Primary Turnout: The Senatorial Case." *Legislative Studies Quarterly* 11 (1): 65–73.

Kenney, Patrick J., 1988. "Sorting Out the Effects of Primary Divisiveness in Congressional and Senatorial Elections." *Western Political Quarterly* 41 (4): 765–77.

Kenney, Patrick J., and Tom W. Rice. 1984. "The Effect of Primary Divisiveness in Gubernatorial and Senatorial Elections." *Journal of Politics* 46 (3): 904–15.

Kenney, Patrick J., and Tom W. Rice. 1987. "The Relationship between Divisive Primaries and General Election Outcomes." *American Journal of Political Science* 31 (1): 31–44.

Kettleborough, Charles. 1923a. "Digest of Primary Election Laws." *Annals of the American Academy of Political and Social Sciences* 106: 181–273.

Kettleborough, Charles. 1923b. "Direct Primaries." *Annals of the American Academy of Political and Social Sciences* 106: 11–17.

Key, V.O., Jr. 1949 [1984]. *Southern Politics in State and Nation.* Knoxville, TN: University of Tennessee Press.

Key, V.O., Jr. 1956. *American State Politics: An Introduction.* New York: Knopf.

Key, V.O., Jr. 1964. *Politics, Parties, and Pressure Groups*, 5th ed. New York: Crowell.

Killian, Linda. 2012. *The Swing Vote: The Untapped Power of Independents.* New York: St. Martins.

Kingdon, John W. 1966. *Candidates for Office: Beliefs and Strategies.* New York: Random House.

Kolodny, Robin. 1998. *Pursuing Majorities: Congressional Campaign Committees in American Politics.* Norman: University of Oklahoma Press.

Kousser, J. Morgan. 1974. *The Shaping of Southern Politics.* New Haven, CT: Yale University Press.
Kousser, Thad. 2002. "Crossing Over When It Counts: How the Motives of Voters in Blanket Primaries Are Revealed by Their Actions in General Elections." In *Voting at the Political Fault Line: California's Experiment with the Blanket Primary*, eds. Bruce E. Cain and Elisabeth R. Gerber. Berkeley: University of California Press, pp. 143–70.
Kousser, Thad, Scott Lucas, Seth Masket, and Eric McGhee. 2013. "Kingmakers or Cheerleaders? Party Power and the Causal Effects of Endorsements." Paper presented at the annual meeting of the Midwest Political Science Association, Chicago, IL.
Kousser, Thad, Justin Phillips, and Boris Shor. 2013. "Reform and Representation: Assessing California's Top-Two Primary and Redistricting Commission." Paper presented at the annual meeting of the Midwest Political Science Association, Chicago, IL.
Kraushaar, Josh. 2011. "Growth Industry." *National Journal*, September 17.
Kriss, Erik. 2003. "Rep. Boehlert May Face Primary Foe in 2004." *Syracuse Post-Standard*, May 23.
Kuzenski, John C., Charles S. Bullock, and Ronald Keith Gaddie, eds. 2006. *David Duke and the Politics of Race in the South.* Nashville, TN: Vanderbilt University Press.
Laffey, Steve. 2007. *Primary Mistake: How the Washington Republican Establishment Lost Everything in 2006 (and Sabotaged My Senatorial Campaign).* New York: Penguin.
Lamis, Alexander P. 1984a. "The Runoff Primary Controversy: Implications for Southern Politics." *PS: Political Science and Politics* 17 (4): 782–87.
Lamis, Alexander P. 1984b. *The Two-Party South.* New York: Oxford University Press.
LaTourette, Steven. 2012. "The Senate's 'Manchurian Candidates.'" *Politico*, November 12. Online, www.politico.com/news/stories/1112/83703.html.
Law, David S. 2012. "Where's the Party? The Constitution Should Make Party Primaries Open to All Voters." *Slate*, June 21. Online, http://hive.slate.com/hive/how-can-we-fix-constitution/article/wheres-the-party.
Lawrence, Eric, Todd Donovan, and Shaun Bowler. 2013. "The Adoption of Direct Primaries in the United States." *Party Politics* 19 (1): 3–18.
Layzell, Anne C., and L. Marvin Overby. 1994. "Biding Their Time in the Illinois 9th." In *Who Runs for Congress? Ambition, Context, and Candidate Emergence*, ed. Thomas A. Kazee. Washington, DC: Congressional Quarterly Press, pp. 150–64.
Lazarus, Jeffrey. 2005. "Unintended Consequences: Anticipation of General Election Outcomes and Primary Election Divisiveness." *Legislative Studies Quarterly* 30 (3): 435–61.
Lengle, James I., Diana Owen, and Molly W. Sonner. 1995. "Divisive Nominating Mechanisms and Democratic Party Electoral Prospects." *Journal of Politics* 57 (2): 370–83.
Leuthold, David A. 1968. *Electioneering in a Democracy.* New York: John Wiley and Sons.
Levendusky, Mathew. 2009. *The Partisan Sort: How Liberals Became Democrats and Conservatives Became Republicans.* Chicago: University of Chicago Press.
Lockard, Duane. 1959a. *Connecticut's Challenge Primary: A Study in Legislative Politics.* New York: Henry Holt.
Lockard, Duane. 1959b. *New England Politics.* Princeton, NJ: Princeton University Press.
Loeb, Isidor. 1910. "Direct Primaries in Missouri." *Proceedings of the American Political Science Association* 7: 163–74.
Lopez, Mark Hugo, and Paul Taylor. 2012. "Latino Voters in the 2012 Election." *Pew Research Hispanic Trends Project*, November 7. Online, www.pewhispanic.org/2012/11/07/latino-voters-in-the-2012-election/.

Lovejoy, Allen Fraser. 1941. *La Follette and the Establishment of the Direct Primary in Wisconsin, 1890–1904.* New Haven, CT: Yale University Press.
Lower, Richard Coke. 1993. *A Bloc of One: The Political Career of Hiram W. Johnson.* Stanford, CA: Stanford University Press.
Lowrie, S. Gale. 1911. "Second Choice Nomination Laws." *American Political Science Review* 5 (4): 600–04.
Lublin, David. 1997. *The Paradox of Representation: Racial Gerrymandering and Minority Interests in Congress.* Princeton, NJ: Princeton University Press.
Lublin, David. 2004. *The Republican South.* Princeton, NJ: Princeton University Press.
Lush, Charles K. 1907. "Primary Elections and Majority Nominations." *American Political Science Review* 2 (1): 43–47.
Lyman, Peter, Scott Rapp, and Jenny Hurwitz. 2004. "Hoffman Beats Dadey; Boehlert Over Walrath." *Syracuse Post-Standard*, September 15.
MacDonald, Teresa. 2002. "*California Democratic Party v. Jones*: Invalidation of the Blanket Primary." *Pepperdine Law Review* 29 (2): 319–41.
Maisel, L. Sandy. 1986. *From Obscurity to Oblivion: Running in the Congressional Primary.* Knoxville: University of Tennessee Press.
Maisel, L. Sandy, and John F. Bibby. 2002. "Election Laws, Court Rulings, Party Rules and Practices: Steps Toward and Away from a Stronger Party Role." In *Responsible Partisanship: The Evolution of American Political Parties Since 1950*, eds. John C. Green and Paul S. Herrnson. Lawrence: University Press of Kansas, pp. 61–82.
Maisel, L. Sandy, Cary T. Gibson, and Elizabeth J. Ivry. 1998. "The Continuing Importance of the Rules of the Game: Subpresidential Nominations in 1994 and 1996." In *The Parties Respond*, 3rd ed., ed. L. Sandy Maisel. Boulder, CO: Westview Press.
Mann, Thomas E. 2006. "Polarizing the House of Representatives: How Much Does Gerrymandering Matter?" In *Red and Blue Nation?*, Vol. 1, eds. Pietro S. Nivola and David W. Brady. Washington, DC: Brookings Institution, pp. 263–83.
Mann, Thomas E., and Norman J. Ornstein. 2008. *The Broken Branch: How Congress Is Failing America and How to Get It Back on Track.* New York: Oxford University Press.
Margulies, Herbert M. 1968. *The Decline of the Progressive Movement in Wisconsin.* Madison: State Historical Society of Wisconsin.
Masket, Seth E. 2007. "It Takes an Outsider: Extralegislative Organization and Partisanship in the California Assembly, 1849–2006." *American Journal of Political Science* 51 (3): 482–97.
Masket, Seth E. 2009. *No Middle Ground: How Informal Party Organizations Control Nominations and Polarize Legislatures.* Ann Arbor: University of Michigan Press.
Masket, Seth. 2013. "Can Polarization be Mitigated? California's Experience with the Top Two Primary." In *Politics to the Extreme*, ed. Scott A. Frisch and Sean Q. Kelly. New York: Palgrave Macmillan, pp. 205–18.
Mayhew, David R. 1974. *Congress: The Electoral Connection.* New Haven, CT: Yale University Press.
Mayhew, David R. 1986. *Placing Parties in American Politics.* Princeton, NJ: Princeton University Press.
McCarty, Nolan Keith T. Poole, and Howard Rosenthal. 2006. *Polarized America: The Dance of Ideology and Unequal Riches.* Cambridge, MA: MIT Press.
McClelland, Edward. 2010. "Can This Man Derail Mark Kirk More Than Mark Kirk Has Derailed Himself?" *NBC Chicago Online*, June 15. Online, www.nbcchicago.com/blogs/ward-room/Look-Out-On-Your-Right-Mark-Kirk-96382454.html#ixzz0qw5zhJZS.

McClintock, Miller. 1922. "Party Affiliation Tests in Primary Election Laws." *American Political Science Review* 16 (3): 465–67.
McGerr, Michael E. 1986. *The Decline of Popular Politics: The American North 1865–1928.* New York: Oxford University Press.
McGhee, Eric, Seth Masket, Boris Shor, and Nolan McCarty. 2010. "A Primary Cause of Partisanship? Nomination Systems and Legislator Ideology." Paper presented at the Annual Meeting of the American Political Science Association, Washington, DC.
McNitt, Andrew D. 1980. "The Effect of Preprimary Endorsement on Competition for Nominations: An Examination of Different Nominating Systems." *Journal of Politics* 42 (1): 257–66.
McNitt, Andrew. 1982. "A Comparison of Explanations of Competition for Gubernatorial and Senatorial Nominations." *Western Political Quarterly* 35 (2): 245–57.
McWilliams, Carey. 1949. *California: The Great Exception.* New York: Current Books.
Medina, Jennifer. 2006. "Mrs. Clinton Offers to Raise Money for Lamont Campaign." *New York Times*, August 26.
Medina, Jennifer. 2012. "Nonpartisan Primaries Face Test in California." *New York Times*, June 3.
Merriam, Charles. 1908. *Primary Elections.* Chicago: University of Chicago Press.
Merriam, Charles, and Louise Overacker. 1928. *Primary Elections.* Chicago: University of Chicago Press.
Meyer, Ernst Christopher. 1902. *Nominating Systems.* Madison, WI: The author.
Meyerson, Harold. 2012. "GOP's Gerrymandered Advantages." *Washington Post*, November 13.
Mileur, Jerome M. 1999. "The Legacy of Reform: Progressive Government, Regressive Politics." In *Progressivism and the New Democracy*, eds. Sidney M. Milkis and Jerome M. Mileur. Amherst: University of Massachusetts Press, pp. 259–88.
Milkis, Sidney M. 1999. "Progressivism, Then and Now." In *Progressivism and the New Democracy*, eds. Sidney M. Milkis and Jerome M. Mileur. Amherst: University of Massachusetts Press, pp. 1–39.
Miller, Penny M., Malcolm E. Jewell, and Lee Sigelman. 1988. "Divisive Primaries and Party Activists: Kentucky, 1979 and 1983." *Journal of Politics* 50 (2): 459–70.
Millspaugh, Arthur C. 1916. "The Operation of the Direct Primary in Michigan." *American Political Science Review* 10 (4): 710–26.
Moakley, Maureen, and Elmer Cornwell. 2001. *Rhode Island Politics and Government.* Lincoln: University of Nebraska Press.
Moncrief, Gary. 2012. "BSU's Moncrief: Idaho GOP Closed Primary Failed to Stop Crossover Voting, If It Was Occurring at All." *Idaho Statesman Blogs.* Online, http://voices.idahostatesman.com/2012/05/18/idahopolitics/bsus_moncrief_idaho_gop_closed_primary_failed_stop_crossover_vot, accessed June 12, 2012.
Mondics, Chris. 1997. "A Man Caught in the Middle: Jim Greenwood, a GOP Moderate in Congress, Knows He's Vulnerable from the Right and the Left." *Philadelphia Inquirer*, April 6.
Morlan, Robert L. 1955. *Political Prairie Fire: The Nonpartisan League, 1915–1922.* Minneapolis: University of Minnesota Press.
Morning Journal (Lorain, OH). 2010. "Our View Endorsement: Straight Talking Smith Best GOP Choice to Face Kaptur in 9th District." April 22.
Morton, Michael. 2010. "Lamb Wins Republican Primary, to Face McGovern." *MetroWest Daily News*, September 15.

Myers, Andrew, and Kati Bumgardner. 2012. "Ohio's Come-From-Behind Shocker." *Campaigns and Elections*, June 15.
Norrander, Barbara. 1986. "Measuring Primary Turnout in Aggregate Analysis." *Political Behavior* 8 (4): 356–73.
Norrander, Barbara. 1989. "Ideological Representativeness of Presidential Primary Voters." *American Journal of Political Science* 33 (3): 570–87.
Norrander, Barbara. 1991. "Explaining Individual Participation in Presidential Primaries." *Western Political Quarterly* 44 (3): 640–55.
Norrander, Barbara. 2010. *The Imperfect Primary: Oddities, Biases, and Strengths of the U.S. Presidential Nomination Process*. New York: Routledge.
Norrander, Barbara, and Kerri Stephens. 2012. "Primary Type and Polarization of State Electorates." Paper presented at the Annual State Politics and Policy Conference, Houston, TX.
Norrander, Barbara, Kerri Stephens, and Jay L. Wendland. 2013. "Primary Type, Polarization of State Electorates, and the Ideological Composition of Primary Electorates." Paper presented at the Annual Meeting of the Midwest Political Science Association, Chicago, IL.
Norris, George. 1923. "Why I Believe in the Direct Primary." *Annals of the American Academy of Political and Social Sciences* 106: 22–30.
Norwalk (OH) Reflector. 2010. "Iott Wins GOP Nomination to Run Against Kaptur in Fall; Latta Defeats Challenger in 5th District." July 28.
Oak, Mandar P. 2006. "On the Role of the Primary System in Candidate Selection." *Economics and Politics* 18 (2): 169–90.
Obama, Barack H. 2006. *The Audacity of Hope*. New York: Crown Publishers.
Omdahl, Lloyd B. 1961. *Insurgents: the Switch of the NPL to the Democratic Column*. Brianerd, MN: Lakeland Color Press.
Onishi, Norimitsu. 2012. "New Rules Upend House Re-Election Races in California." *New York Times*, September 24.
Onishi, Norimitsu. 2013. "Rivalries Begin to Emerge in a New Seat of Power." *New York Times*, February 27.
Ornstein, Norman J., Thomas E. Mann, Michael J. Malbin, and Andrew Rugg. 2013. *Vital Statistics on Congress*. Washington, DC: Brookings Institution and American Enterprise Institute. Online, www.brookings.edu/research/reports/2013/07/vital-statistics-congress-mann-ornstein.
Overacker, Louise. 1928. "Direct Primary Legislation in 1926–27." *American Political Science Review* 22 (2): 353–61.
Overacker, Louise. 1930. "Direct Primary Legislation in 1928–29." *American Political Science Review* 24 (2): 370–80.
Overacker, Louise. 1932a. "Direct Primary Legislation in 1930–31." *American Political Science Review* 26 (2): 294–300.
Overacker, Louise. 1932b. *Money in Elections*. New York: Macmillan.
Page, Benjamin I. 1978. *Choices and Echoes in Presidential Elections*. Chicago, IL: University of Chicago Press.
Parent, Wayne. 2004. *Inside the Carnival: Unmasking Louisiana Politics*. Baton Rouge: Louisiana State University Press.
Pearson, Kathryn, and Jennifer L. Lawless. 2008. "Primary Competition and Polarization in the U.S. House of Representatives." Paper presented at the Annual Meeting of the Midwest Political Science Association, Chicago, IL.

Persily, Nathaniel. 2002. "The Blanket Primary in the Courts: The Precedent and Implications of *California Democratic Party v. Jones*." In *Voting at the Political Fault Line: California's Experiment with the Blanket Primary*, eds. Bruce E. Cain and Elisabeth R. Gerber. Berkeley: University of California Press, pp. 303–23.

Persily, Nathaniel, and Bruce E. Cain. 2000. "The Legal Status of Political Parties: A Reassessment of Competing Paradigms." *Columbia Law Review* 100 (3): 775–812.

Petrocik, John R. 2002. "Candidate Strategy, Voter Response, and Party Cohesion." In *Voting at the Political Fault Line: California's Experiment with the Blanket Primary*, eds. Bruce E. Cain and Elisabeth R. Gerber. Berkeley: University of California Press, pp. 270–99.

Petrocik, John R. and Scott W. Desposato. 1998. "The Partisan Effects of Majority Minority Districting, 1992–1994." *Journal of Politics* 66 (1): 613–33.

Pierce, Neal R. 1973. *The Great Plains States of America*. New York: Norton.

Piereson, James E., and Terry B. Smith. 1975. "Primary Divisiveness and General Election Success: A Re-Examination." *Journal of Politics* 37 (2): 555–62.

Pika, Joseph A., John Anthony Maltese, and Norman C. Thomas. 2002. *The Politics of the Presidency*, 5th ed. Washington, DC: Congressional Quarterly Press.

Pollock, James K. 1926. *Party Campaign Funds*. New York: Alfred A. Knopf.

Popkin, Samuel L. 2012. *The Candidate: What It Takes to Win—and Hold—the White House*. New York: Oxford University Press.

Praino, Rodrigo, Daniel Stockemer, and Vincent G. Moscardelli. 2011. "The Lingering Effect of Scandal in Congressional Elections: Incumbents, Challengers, and Voters." Paper presented at the Annual Meeting of the Northeastern Political Science Association, Philadelphia, PA.

Quinn, T. Anthony, and R. Michael Alvarez. 2010. *Primary Process Reform in California*. Sacramento: California Forward.

Rae, Nicol C. 1994. *Southern Democrats*. New York: Oxford University Press.

Raju, Manu. 2012. "GOP Senators Wonder: Am I Next?" *Politico*, May 9. Online, www.politico.com/news/stories/0512/76078.html.

Ranney, Austin. 1968. "The Representativeness of Primary Electorates." *Midwest Journal of Political Science* 12 (2): 224–38.

Ranney, Austin. 1972. "Turnout and Representation in Presidential Primary Elections." *American Political Science Review* 66 (1): 21–37.

Ranney, Austin. 1975. *Curing the Mischiefs of Faction: Party Reform in America*. Berkeley: University of California Press.

Ranney, Austin, and Leon D. Epstein. 1966. "The Two Electorates: Voters and Non-Voters in a Wisconsin Primary." *Journal of Politics* 28 (3): 598–616.

Ray, P. Orman. 1919. "Recent Primary and Election Laws." *American Political Science Review* 13 (2): 264–74.

Reid, Bill G. 1977. "John Miller Baer: Nonpartisan League Cartoonist and Congressman." *North Dakota History* 44 (1): 4–13.

Reynolds, John F. 2006. *The Demise of the American Convention System, 1880–1911*. New York: Cambridge University Press.

Ritter, Gretchen, 1997. *Goldbugs and Greenbacks: The Antimonopoly Tradition and the Politics of Finance in America*. New York: Cambridge University Press.

Robbins, Tom. 2009. "Bloomy Gives $250K to Independence Party." *Village Voice*, July 16. Online, http://blogs.villagevoice.com/runninscared/2009/07/bloomy_gives_25.php.

Rolfe, Meredith. 2012. *Voter Turnout*. New York: Cambridge University Press.

Roll Call. 2003. "New York: Reynolds not Worried about Boehlert Seat." May 26. Online, www.rollcall.com/issues/48_96/-1703-1.html.
Rosenblum, Nancy L. 2008. *On the Side of the Angels: An Appreciation of Parties and Partisanship.* Princeton, NJ: Princeton University Press.
Rosenstone, Steven J., and John Mark Hansen. 1993. *Mobilization, Participation, and Democracy in America.* New York: Macmillan.
Sabato, Larry. 1977. *The Democratic Party Primary in Virginia.* Charlottesville: University of Virginia Press.
Salvanto, Anthony M., and Martin P. Wattenberg. 2002. "Peeking Under the Blanket: A Direct Look at Crossover Voting in the 1998 Primary." In *Voting at the Political Fault Line: California's Experiment with the Blanket Primary,* eds. Bruce E. Cain and Elisabeth R. Gerber. Berkeley: University of California Press, pp. 124–40.
Sandri, Giulia, and Antonella Seddone. 2012. "Primaries and Political Parties in Europe: A Proposal for a Tailored Framework." Paper presented at the European Consortium for Political Research Joint Session of Workshops, University of Antwerp, Belgium.
Schlesinger, Arthur, Jr. 1992. "Faded Glory." *New York Times Magazine,* July 12.
Schlesinger, Joseph A. 1966. *Ambition and Politics: Political Careers in the United States.* Chicago: Rand McNally.
Schlesinger, Joseph A. 1994. *Political Parties and the Winning of Office.* Ann Arbor: University of Michigan Press.
Schwartz, Mildred. 2006. *Party Movements in the United States and Canada.* Lanham, MD: Rowman and Littlefield.
Seelye, Katharine Q. 2012. "Warren Fends off Party Challenger in Massachusetts Race." *New York Times,* June 2.
Segura, Gary M., and Nathan D. Woods. 2002. "Targets of Opportunity: California's Blanket Primary and the Political Representation of Latinos." In *Voting at the Political Fault Line: California's Experiment with the Blanket Primary,* eds. Bruce E. Cain and Elisabeth R. Gerber. Berkeley: University of California Press, pp. 248–69.
Sides, John, Jonathan Cohen, and Jack Citrin. 2002. "The Causes and Consequences of Crossover Voting in the 1998 California Elections." In *Voting at the Political Fault Line: California's Experiment with the Blanket Primary,* eds. Bruce E. Cain and Elisabeth R. Gerber. Berkeley: University of California Press, pp. 77–106.
Sides, John, and Lynn Vavreck. 2013. "On the Representativeness of Primary Electorates." Paper present at the "Political Representation: Fifty Years after Miller and Stokes" conference, Vanderbilt University, Nashville, TN.
Sidlow, Edward I. 2003. *Challenging the Incumbent: An Underdog's Undertaking.* Washington, DC: Congressional Quarterly Press.
Sinclair, Barbara. 2011. *Unorthodox Lawmaking: New Legislative Processes in the U.S. Congress,* 4th ed. Washington, DC: Congressional Quarterly.
Singer, Rena. 1998. "Greenwood Faces Challenge from Both Sides of the Aisle." *Philadelphia Inquirer,* February 10.
Sobieraj, Sarah. 2011. *Soundbitten: The Perils of Media-Centered Political Activism.* New York: New York University Press.
Sorauf, Frank. 1992. *Inside Campaign Finance: Myths and Realities.* New Haven, CT: Yale University Press.
South Dakota Legislative Research Council. 2005. "Direct Primaries and the Democratization of the Party Nominating Process." Pierre: South Dakota Legislative Research Council, Issue Memorandum 96–02.

Southwell, Patricia. 1986. "The Politics of Disgruntlement: Nonvoting and Defection among Supporters of Nomination Losers, 1968–1984." *Political Behavior* 8 (1): 81–95.
Steen, Jennifer A. 2006. *Self-Financed Candidates in Congressional Elections*. Ann Arbor: University of Michigan Press.
Stone, Walter J., Sarah A. Fulton, Cherie D. Maestas, and L. Sandy Maisel. 2010. "Incumbency Reconsidered: Prospects, Strategic Retirement, and Incumbent Quality in U.S. House Elections." *Journal of Politics* 72 (1): 178–90.
Stone, Walter J., and Elizabeth N. Simas. 2010. "Candidate Valence and Ideological Positions in U.S. House Elections." *American Journal of Political Science* 54 (2): 371–88.
Sullivan, Gerald, and Michael Kenney. 1987. *The Race for the Eighth*. New York: Harper & Row.
Sundquist, James L. 1983. *Dynamics of the Party System: Alignment and Realignment of Political Parties in the United States*. Washington, DC: Brookings Institution.
Swain, Carol M. 1993. *Black Faces, Black Interests: The Representation of African-Americans in Congress*. Cambridge, MA: Harvard University Press.
Tam Cho, Wendy K., and Brian J. Gaines. 2002. "Candidates, Donors, and Voters in California's Blanket Primary Elections." In *Voting at the Political Fault Line: California's Experiment with the Blanket Primary*, eds. Bruce E. Cain and Elisabeth R. Gerber. Berkeley: University of California Press, pp. 171–91.
Telford, Ira Ralph. 1965. "Types of Primary and Party Responsibility." *American Political Science Review* 59 (1): 117–18.
Theriault, Sean. 2008. *Party Polarization in Congress*. New York: Cambridge University Press.
Toeplitz, Shira. 2011. "Top 5 Ugliest Districts: Partisan Gerrymandering 101." *Roll Call*, November 10, www.rollcall.com/features/Election-Preview_2011/election/top-5-ugliest-districts-210224-1.html.
Unger, Nancy C. 2000. *Fighting Bob La Follette: The Righteous Reformer*. Chapel Hill: University of North Carolina Press.
Valencia, Milton J. 2012. "Low Voter Turnout Predicted for Rare Thursday Primary." *Boston Globe*, September 4.
Verplanck, J. Delancey. 1906. "A Problem of Primaries." *Annals of the American Academy of Political and Social Sciences* 28: 84–94.
Wallace, Schuyler C. 1923. "Pre-Primary Conventions." *Annals of the American Academy of Political and Social Sciences* 106: 97–104.
Ware, Alan. 1979. "'Divisive' Primaries: The Important Questions." *British Journal of Political Science* 9 (3): 381–84.
Ware, Alan. 2000. "Anti-Partism and Party Control of Political Reform in the United States: The Case of the Australian Ballot." *British Journal of Political Science* 30 (1): 1–29.
Ware, Alan. 2002. *The American Direct Primary: Party Institutionalization and Transformation in the North*. New York: Cambridge University Press.
Ware, Alan. 2006. *The Democratic Party Heads North, 1877–1962*. New York: Oxford University Press.
Wattenberg, Martin P. 2012. *Is Voting for Young People?* New York: Pearson.
Weeks, O. Douglas. 1948. "The White Primary: 1944–1948." *American Political Science Review* 42 (3): 500–10.
Weinger, Mackenzie. 2012. "Richard Mourdock Dismisses Dick Lugar Attack." *Politico*, May 12.
Weisman, Jonathan. 2012. "Nebraska State Senator Upsets Rivals for GOP Nomination." *New York Times*, May 15.

Wekkin, Gary D. 1984. *Democrat versus Democrat: The National Party's Campaign to Close the Wisconsin Primary*. Columbia: University of Missouri Press.

West, Victor J. 1923. "The California Direct Primary." *Annals of the American Academy of Political and Social Sciences* 106: 116–27.

Westley, Christopher, Peter T. Calcagno, and Richard Ault. 2004. "Primary Election Systems and Candidate Deviation." *Eastern Economic Journal* 30 (3): 365–76.

White, John Kenneth. 1983. *The Fractured Electorate: Political Parties and Social Change in Southern New England*. Hanover, NH: University Press of New England.

White, John Kenneth, and Jerome M. Mileur. 2002. "In the Spirit of their Times: 'Toward a More Responsible Two-Party System' and Party Politics." In *Responsible Partisanship: The Evolution of American Political Parties Since 1950*, eds. John C. Green and Paul S. Herrnson. Lawrence: University Press of Kansas, pp. 13–36.

Wicker, Tom. 1992. "Let Some Smoke In." *New York Times Magazine*, June 14.

Wiebe, Robert H. 1967. *The Search for Order, 1877–1920*. Westport, CT: Greenwood Press.

Williams, Benjamin H. 1923. "Prevention of Minority Nominations for State Offices in the Direct Primary." *Annals of the American Academy of Political and Social Sciences* 106: 111–15.

Wilson, Walter. 2009. "Latino Representation on Congressional Websites." *Legislative Studies Quarterly* 34 (3): 427–48.

Winger, Richard. 2013. "South Carolina Republican Party Withdraws from Its Own Lawsuit Against Open Primary." *Ballot Access News*, June 13. Online, www.ballot-access.org/2013/06/south-carolina-republican-party-withdraws-from-its-own-lawsuit-against-open-primary/.

Wolfinger, Raymond E., and Steven J. Rosenstone. 1980. *Who Votes?* New Haven, CT: Yale University Press.

Wright, John R. 1996. *Interest Groups and Congress*. Boston: Allyn and Bacon.

Wyloge, Evan. 2013. "Failed Top-Two Primary Measure Had Most Support among Independent Voters." *Arizona Capitol Times*. Online, www.azcir.org/2013/02/23/failed-top-two-primary-measure-had-most-support-among-independent-voters/.

Yaccino, Steven. 2013. "Candidate Who Backs Gun Control Wins Race." *New York Times*, February 26.

Yates, Richard E. 1972. "Arkansas: Independent and Unpredictable." In *The Changing Politics of the South*, ed. William C. Havard. Baton Rouge: University of Louisiana Press, pp. 233–93.

Zeleny, Jeff. 2012. "Insurgent Threatens Republican Plans in Nebraska Senate Primary." *New York Times*, May 14.

Zhang, Chenwei. 2012. "Towards a More Perfect Elections: Improving the Top-Two Primary for Congressional and State Races." *Ohio State Law Journal* 73 (3): 615–50.

Zimmerman, Joseph P. 2008. *The Government and Politics of New York State*, 2nd ed. Albany: State University of New York Press.

INDEX

Note: Page numbers followed by *t* indicate a table. Those followed by *f* indicate a figure.

advantages of primaries *see* strategic contexts of primaries
advisory primaries 251–2
Affordable Care Act 90, 143
African-Americans: civil rights legislation and 61, 204, 213, 215–16, 225, 231n1; Democratic Party leanings of 58–9, 205–11, 214; electoral victories of 211–18; exclusion from Southern primaries of 29, 57–9, 61, 212, 236–8, 256n5; as representatives of white districts 216–17; voter turnout of 218; *see also* majority-minority districts; race and ethnicity; redistricting
Ahler, Doug 248, 254
Akin, Todd 7, 164
Alabama: adoption of direct primary laws in 37*t*; African-American representatives from 215; Democratic Party in 214; factional differences in 57; 2012 primary dates in 63*t*; type of primary in 65*t*
Alaska: adoption of direct primary laws in 37*t*; blanket primary system in 68, 242; Independent candidates in 41, 72n16, 170, 177; sore loser candidates in 41, 72n16; top two primary initiative in 248; 2012 primary dates in 63*t*
Aldrich, John 19–20, 241

Almanac of American Politics 188, 226
Alvarez, R. Michael 96
American Conservative Union 193
The American Direct Primary (Ware), 6
American National Election Studies seven-point scale 86, 205
American Party 35
American Political Science Association (APSA), 59–60, 73n27
Americans for Democratic Action scores 100
American University Center for the Study of the American Electorate (CSAE), 78–82, 106*f*, 109nn1–3
Ames, A.A. "Doc", 33
Anderson, John 96
Angle, Sharron 164
Ansolabehere, Stephen 61
anti-party politics 250
Argersinger, Peter 47, 73n21
Arizona: adoption of direct primary laws in 37*t*; incumbent-vs.-incumbent primaries in 229*t*; top two primary initiative in 248–9; 2010 open seat primary in 112, 141n2; 2012 primary dates in 63*t*; type of primary in 65*t*
Arkansas: adoption of direct primary laws in 37*t*; redistricting in 225; 2012 primary dates in 63*t*; type of primary in 65*t*

Arnejaska, Arnold 193
Asian Americans 205, 211, 212, 217–18; *see also* race and ethnicity
The Audacity of Hope (Obama), 183–4
Ault, Richard 152
Australian ballot 31

Baer, John Miller 51–2
Baker v. Carr 212–13
Baldwin, Tammy 127
ballot access thresholds 72n11, 116–17, 119, 176, 252
barriers to voting 84, 85
Barron, Charles 210
Bartels, Larry 105
Bass, Charles 112, 141n1
Beatty, Jeff 2
Beatty, Joyce 208–9
Bennet, Michael 170, 191
Bennett, Robert 170, 177, 191
Bentsen, Lloyd 171
Berman, Howard 91, 109n9, 247
Bernstein, Robert A. 96
Bibby, John F. 73n30
Bielat, Sean 111
Bipartisan Campaign Reform Act (BCRA), 159–60
Blackwell, Lucien 222
Blais, Andre 16
blanket primaries 65t, 67–8, 74n31, 100, 102, 238–9, 242, 244–6
bleached districts 216, 231
Boehlert, Sherwod 193–4, 196
Boehner, John 171, 197, 199
Booker, Cory 217
Borah, William 50, 53–4
bosses; *see* party bosses and machines
Bowler, Shaun 47
Branton, Regina 42, 103, 218
Brooke, Edward 212
Brown, Scott 3–6, 144
Bruhn, Kathleen 15
Bruning, Jon 139
Brunner, Jennifer 138
Buchanan, Vern 132
Buck, Ken 164
Buckley v. Valeo 66
Bullock, Charles 113, 128–9
Burden, Barry C. 251
Burnham, Walter Dean 46
Bush, George H. W. 95–6, 188
Bush, George W. 199
Byrd, Harry 57

Cain, Bruce 239–41, 249
Calcagno, Peter T. 152
California 54, 242–8; adoption of direct primary laws in 34, 37t, 38, 46; blanket primaries in 68, 74n31, 100, 102, 238–9, 242, 244–6; cross-filing candidates in 72n17, 243, 245; history of primaries in 243–6; incumbent-vs.-incumbent primaries in 92, 109n9, 229t; majority-minority districts in 211; redistricting in 228; sore loser candidates in 72n17; top two primary system in 68, 102, 234–5, 242–8, 253–4; 2012 primary dates in 63t
California Democratic Party v. Jones 238–42
campaign finance; *see* financing of primaries
Campaign for Primary Accountability 201
Campbell, Tom 245
Canadian candidate selection process 13–14
candidates: impact of state law on 99–100; inclusive criteria for 104; political party endorsement of 40–1, 46, 49–50, 66, 91, 94–5, 109n10; political party funding of 10–11, 92, 94–5, 109n9; position-taking of 101–4; quality considerations of 17–18, 42–3, 105–6, 163–4; race and ethnicity of 211–18; selection methods for 11–17, 104; strategic contexts of primaries and 98–104; valence issues of 102
Cannon, Chris 195
Canon, David T. 96, 142n7
Canseco, Francisco "Quico", 158
Cantwell, Maria 166
Cao, Joseph 218
Capps, Lois 246
Capuano, Michael 2
Card, Andrew 1
Carey, John M. 14
Carson, André 217
Carson, Jamie L. 73n27
Carter, Jimmy 95–96, 188
Castle, Mike 91, 138
Chafee, Lincoln 169, 191, 192
challenger primaries 19–21, 22, 40, 107–9, 143–67, 171–2; determinants of vote share in 162t; district partisanship in 151t, 152; electoral structure and 151–2t; fractionalization index for 150–3, 163; funding

sources of 157–8; general election competitiveness and 145–6, 149–57, 160–1, 168n9; incumbency advantages in 146–9; incumbent characteristics in 151–2*t* 153, 167n7; incumbent vulnerability and 146–8, 156–7, 162; interest group involvement in 148; in majority-minority districts 224; number of candidates in 149–52, 157–8; political contexts of 151*t*, 154–7; political party support in 147–8, 154–5, 167n8; rates of 155–6, 162–3; role of money in 157–62, 168n9; for Senate races 162–7; in 2010, 143–6, 163–4; unopposed races in 149–50, 157; value of winning in 160–1
Chase, Ken 1
checks and balance system 12
Chicago's incumbent primaries 183–7, 202n3
Chrislock, Carl 55
Ciliberti, Barrie 193
Citizens United v. Federal Elections Commission 236, 251
Citrin, Jack 248, 254
civil rights legislation 61, 204–6, 213, 215–16, 225, 231n1; *see also* U.S. Supreme Court
Clarke, Hansen 209
Clay, William 220
Clingman v. Beaver 241
Clinton, Bill 198, 245
Clinton, Hillary 44, 80, 198
closed primaries 23, 32, 38–9, 60, 64, 65*t*, 237; crossover voters and 33, 34; independent voters and 87; moderation of candidates and 100; number of candidates and 121, 152; switching from open to 68, 235, 250; Tea Party victories in 67; women's suffrage and 73n19; *see also* state law
Club for Growth 95, 98, 134; funding of challenger primaries by 148; funding of incumbent primaries by 170–1, 193, 195, 200–1; funding of open seat primaries by 139
Coakley, Martha 2–3
Coats, Dan 137
Cohelan, Jeffrey 243
Cohen, Steve 217
Coleman, Norm 92–3, 164
Collins, Susan 3

Colorado: adoption of direct primary laws in 37*t*; age laws in 73n19; Tea Party primary victory of 2010 in 67, 91; 2010 challenger primary in 164; 2012 primary dates in 63*t*; type of primary in 65*t*
communications technology 61
Communist Party USA, 256n5
competence challenges 189, 221–2
competitiveness 61, 66–7; candidate strategy and 98–104; in challenger primaries 145–6, 149–57, 160–1; in close races 96–7; electoral structure and 120–2, 123*t*, 125*t*, 151–2*t*, 176; fractionalization index of 124–6, 135–6, 142n7, 150–3, 164, 224–5; of general elections 19–21, 145–9; ideological extremes and 90–1, 96; incumbency advantages and 19–21, 145–9; in incumbent primaries 172–6; in majority-minority districts 218; money and 11, 61; negative recruitment and 95; in open seat primaries 116–29, 134–7, 142nn4–9; party controls of 91–7, 101–2, 164; political contexts of 120, 121*t*, 123*t*, 125*t*, 151*t*; presidential vote share and 160–1, 168n9; redistricting and 224–30; requirements for candidacy and 104; of safe vs. competitive seats 131, 168n10; of Senate vs. House races 107, 134–7, 142n9, 162–4, 176–7; turnout and 83–4; types of factions in 127
Conable, Barber 126
Concerned Women for America 193
concurrent primaries 39
Condit, Gary 201–2
Congress: The Electoral Connection (Mayhew), 19–20
congressional campaign committees 47
Congressional Elections (Herrnson), 17–21
Congressional polarization 21, 67, 70–1
Congress: Keystone of the Washington Establishment (Fiorina), 19–20
Congressmen in Committees (Fenno), 19–20
Connecticut: adoption of direct primary laws in 35, 37*t*, 56; malapportionment in 60–1; McMahon's Senate races in 136–7, 139–41; sore loser candidates in 41, 56, 72n16, 169, 195; 2012 primary dates in 63*t*; type of primary in 65*t*

consequences of primary challenges 47, 191–7; fundraising as 192; incumbent defeats as 193–6; nationalization of primaries as 196–7; retirement as 192
conservative voter turnout 88–90
contagion effect 45–6
contemporary era (1968–), 28–9, 60–71; adoption of open primaries in 64–5, 73nn30–1; advertising by candidates in 69; campaign finance law and 66; communications technology in 61; congressional redistricting in 60–1; decline in competitiveness in 61, 66–7; delegate apportionment rules in 28; extremist candidates in 67–8, 69; gerrymandered districts in 69; inclusivity debates in 29; party polarization in 66–8, 70; potential reforms in 23, 233–56; presidential primary reforms of 60, 61–4
Contract with America 156
convention system 46, 69, 71, 234; *see also* preprimary conventions
Conyers, John 209, 222
Cooperative Congressional Election Survey (CCES), 86–90
costs of voting 84, 85
Cousins v. Wigoda 238
Crane, Phil 157
Crespin, Michael 47
Crist, Charlie 251
Cross, William P. 16
cross-filing candidates 72n17, 243, 245
crossover voters 33, 34, 65, 74n31
Cruz, Ted 138–9
CSAE; *see* American University Center for the Study of the American Electorate
Curd, Blake 143–4

Daley, Richard 62, 212
Dallinger, Frederick 25–7, 30, 69
Davis, James W. 28–9, 48, 71n3
Dawes, Charles 54–5
Dawson, William 183, 212
Dayton, Mark 166
DeFranco, Marisa 4
Delaware: adoption of direct primary laws in 37*t*; Tea Party primary victory of 2010 in 67, 91; 2012 primary dates in 63*t*; type of primary in 65*t*
Dellums, Ronald 243
DeMint, Jim 139, 199, 203n13

The Demise of the American Convention System 1880–1911 (Reynolds), 32
democratic deficit 254
Democratic Party: challenger primaries in 151*t*, 152–55, 167n8; Congressional seniority and 223; Convention of 1968 of 27–8, 61–2, 73n29; factional conflict in 129, 194–5; Families First agenda of 156; funding of Senate primaries by 136–8, 166; ideological diversity of 153–4; interest groups and PACs allied with 97–8, 134, 166, 195, 200–1; in majority-minority districts 205–6, 219; minority voters in 58–9, 204–11, 214; open seat primaries in 121–2; self-financing candidates in 166; in Southern states 29, 175–6; 2010 primary voters of 86–90
democratizing of elections 26–7, 44, 46
demography of voters 85–90
De Priest, Oscar 212
Dewhurst, David 138–9
DeWine, Mike 191
direct primaries (as term), 71n1; *see also* historical overview of primaries; strategic contexts of primaries; types of primaries
divisiveness; *see* competitiveness
Dominguez, Casey 94, 109n10, 129
Donovan, Todd 47
Drinan, Robert 111
Duke, David 91

Edwards, Donna 64, 195, 199
Edwards, Mickey 252
electoral structure; *see* state law
Ellison, Keith 217
Elmendorf, Christopher 251–2
EMILY's List 95, 98, 200–1
Engler, John 73n30
Ethington, Philip 42
ethnicity; *see* race and ethnicity
Eu v. San Francisco County Democratic Central Committee 239
Ewing, Cortez 57, 73n25
Ezra, Marni 6

factionalism; *see* ideological challenges
Families First agenda 156
Farenthold, Blake 227, 230
Farmer-Labor Party 53–4
Fattah, Chakah 210, 221–2

Federal Corrupt Practices Act 49, 236
Federal Elections and Campaigns Act (FECA), 66
Federal Elections Commission (FEC) data: on challenger primaries 157–9; on incumbent primaries 178, 202n2; on open seat primaries 130, 142n10
Fenno, Richard 19–20, 210, 221–2
filing fees 40
financing of primaries 10–11, 41–2, 49–50, 66, 70, 233; of challenger primaries 147–8, 157–62; competitiveness and 11, 61, 131–4; contribution limits in 66, 92; disclosure in 66; of election administration 12, 39, 45–6; Federal Elections Commission (FEC) data on 130, 142n10, 157–9, 178, 202n2; of incumbent primaries 172, 179–82, 203n15; inferences about candidates based on 11; interest group involvement in 98, 134, 148; in majority-minority districts 224; of open seat primaries 129–34; from out-of-state sources 182; by PACs 66, 130–1, 158*f*, 159, 179–80, 197–201, 203n15; by political parties 10–11, 92, 94–5, 109n9, 130, 136–7, 142n10, 147–8, 165*t*, 197–9; in presidential primaries 105; reforms in 252–4; self-funding candidates and 66, 138, 145, 165–6, 180, 181; in Senate races 136–7, 138, 165–7; spending limits in 49, 66, 115; by Super PACs 139; Supreme Court decisions on 49, 66, 236, 251; *see also* role of money in primaries
Fiorina, Morris 19–20
Fischer, Deb 139
Fisher, Lee 138
Flanigan, William H. 82
Florida: adoption of direct primary laws in 37*t*; factional interests in 57; incumbent-vs.-incumbent primaries in 229*t*; 2012 primary dates in 63*t*; type of primary in 65*t*
Foglietta, Thomas 220
Ford, Henry 49
Foundation for Independent Voter Education (FIVE), 250
Fowler, Linda 126–7
fractionalization index: of challenger primaries 150–3, 163; for open seat primaries 124–6, 135–36, 142n7, 224–5
Frank, Barney 111–12, 116, 141, 148
Fraser, Donald 62; *see also* McGovern-Fraser Commission reforms
Free and Equal Elections 250
Fudge, Marcia 206, 208
Fulani, Lenora 249–50
Fulbright, William 58
funding of primaries; *see* financing of primaries
fusion balloting 35, 72nn10–11, 241

Gaddie, Ronald Keith 113
Galderisi, Peter F. 6
Gaston, Herbert 24, 48–9
Gay, Claudine 232n9
Gay and Lesbian Victory Fund 98
gender 42
general elections 21, 41; demographics of voters in 22, 85, 87, 88*t*; incumbency advantages in 19–21, 145–9, 156–7; in majority-minority districts 22–3; prospects after challenger primaries in 149–57, 160–1; prospects after competitive primaries in 95–6; Super PAC support in 139; timing of primary elections and 39, 76, 79–81, 97; voter turnout in 82–4
George, Milton 24, 229*t*
Georgia: adoption of direct primary laws in 37*t*; African-American representatives from 215; incumbent-vs.-incumbent primaries in 229*t*; majority-minority districts in 226; 2012 primary dates in 63*t*; type of primary in 65*t*
getting primaried 7–8, 20–2; *see also* incumbent primaries
Getting Primaried (Boatright), 6
Ghana's candidate selection process 15–16
Gibson, Cary T. 120
Gilchrest, Wayne 195
Gimpel, James G. 64–5, 103
Gingrich, Newt 171
Goldwater, Barry 73n26
Gonzalez, Henry 222
Grassley, Charles 192
Gray, William 221
Great Depression 48
Greenwood, Jim 192–3
Gronke, Paul 136

Grovey v. Townsend 236–7
Gutierrez, Luis 185, 211, 221

Hacker, Andrew 96
Hahn, Janice 247
Hall, Arnold Bennett 75–6
Hall, Katie 215
Halvorsen, Debbie 210, 232n7
Hamby, Alonzo 42
Hammond, Winfield 45
Hanabusa, Colleen 167n8
Hannan, William 59–60
Hansen, John M. 61
Harris, Andy 195
Hasen, Richard 239–41, 249, 250
Hassell, Hans 94–95, 129
Hatch, Orrin 191, 192
Hatcher, Charles 216
Hawaii 37*t*, 63*t*, 65*t*
Hayes, Charles 183, 222
Hazan, Reuven Y. 12, 17, 104
Hearst, William Randolph 73n18
Helgeson, Henry 51
Heritage Foundation 203n13
Herr, Brian 144
Herrnson, Paul S. 17–21, 99, 103
Hibbing, John 115
Hilliard, Earl 185
Hirano, Shigeo 14, 16, 61, 97, 103
Hirschman, Alfred O. 16
historical overview of primaries 22, 24–71; on adoption of direct primaries 33–8, 46, 56; on contemporary era reforms 28–9, 60–71, 243–6; on direct election of senators 27, 31; on early optional primaries 26, 27, 31–3, 71n2; on limitations on suffrage 32; on mandatory primaries 31–2; on maturation phase of primaries 28–9, 48–60; on party bosses and machines 11, 20, 24, 26–7, 32, 70, 240–1; on Progressive Era reforms 11, 20, 24–47, 70, 235, 253; on regional differences 27; on secret ballots 31; in Southern states 56–60; on state administration of primaries 31–2; on Supreme Court rulings 235–42
Hoffman, Adam H. 64–5
Hofstadter, Richard 24–5
Holmes, Jack 56
Home Style (Fenno), 19–20
Honda, Michael 211
Hormell, Orren C. 35

House Banking scandal 225
Huffington, Michael 228
Hughes, Charles Evans 35
Humphrey, Hubert 62
hustling candidates 32

Ichino, Nahomi 15–16
Idaho: adoption of direct primary laws in 37*t*; closed primaries in 68, 249; Nonpartisan League in 53; top two primary initiative in 248–9; 2012 primary dates in 63*t*; type of primary in 65*t*
ideological challenges: candidate position-taking in 101–4; in challenger primaries 153, 154*f*; competitiveness and 90–7; in the contemporary era 66–8, 70; courting the center in 101; in incumbent primaries 170–1, 187–91, 202, 221–2; low visibility of 103; measures of ideological strength of 86–90; network analysis of 129; in open seat primaries 127, 129, 138–9; position changes in 102; in the retrenchment and maturation phase (1917–68), 29, 49–54, 57–8; in Senate races 190–1; sore loser laws and 251
ideological fit 153, 154*f*
Illinois: adoption of direct primary laws in 35–6, 37*t*; candidate quality in 42; Chicago's incumbent primaries in 183–7, 202n3; endorsed candidates in 40; incumbent-vs.-incumbent primaries in 229*t*; majority-minority districts in 210–11; 2012 primary dates in 63*t*; type of primary in 65*t*
inclusiveness 12
incumbency advantage 60, 73n27, 105; average vote-share and 146; challenger primaries and 146–9, 156–7; uncontested primaries and 146, 147*f*
incumbent primaries 7–8, 20–2, 107–9, 169–202; Campaign for Primary Accountability on 201; consequences of 191–7; diversity of challenges in 182–7; electoral structure and 176; financing of 172, 179–82, 203n15; ideological challenges in 7–8, 23, 67–9, 170–1, 187–91, 202, 221–2; incumbent-vs.-incumbent races 91, 109n9, 202n6, 206–8, 225; incumbent vulnerability in 172;

individual contributions in 180, 181*t*; interest group involvement in 170–1, 197, 199–201, 203n15; levels of competitiveness in 172–6; in majority-minority districts 206–11, 219–22; nationalization of 196–7; out-of-state financing in 182; party switching and 169–70; political party involvement in 172, 197–9; race and 185–6, 189; rates of 173, 175–8; reasons for 172, 201–2, 202n7, 221–2; redistricting and 189, 195, 225; role of money in 178–82; self-financing candidates in 180, 181; in Senate races 169–71, 176–8; state law and 176; of 2010 and 2012, 175, 178, 182; types of challenges in 188–9; uncontested races in 173; *see also* challenger primaries

incumbents 6, 9, 56, 107–9; campaign war chests of 178, 192; competitiveness in general elections of 17–21, 145–9; general election challengers of 19–22, 108; ideological fit and 153, 154*f*; open seat race endorsements by 9, 127–8; PAC support of 66; political party protection of 154–5; reelection rates of 11; voter knowledge about 84; voting records of 149; vulnerability of 146–8, 156–7, 162; *see also* challenger primaries; incumbent primaries

incumbent-vs.-incumbent races 91, 109n9, 202n6; redistricting and 206–8, 225, 226, 228–30; unpredictability of 229*t*, 230

Independence Party 249–50
independent voters 87, 90
independentvoting.org 245, 249–50, 257n14

Indiana 137; adoption of direct primary laws in 37*t*; ballot access laws in 119; incumbent-vs.-incumbent primaries in 229*t*; 2010 open seat primary in 112; 2012 primary dates in 63*t*; 2012 Republican primary in 170–1; type of primary in 65*t*

individual contribution limits 66, 92
influenza epidemic 48–9
Inglis, Bob 195, 203n10
interest groups 97–8; funding of challenger primaries by 148; funding of incumbent primaries by 193, 195; funding of open seat primaries by 134, 138, 139; fundraising by 98; interests in incumbent primaries of 197, 199–201; primary election endorsements by 95, 98, 170–1; recruiting of candidates by 148; types of 199

intra-party factionalism 29, 49–54; *see also* ideological challenges

Iott, Rich 145

Iowa 255; adoption of direct primary laws in 37*t*; redistricting in 226; 2012 primary dates in 63*t*; type of primary in 65*t*

Issacharoff, Samuel 237, 240–1
Ivry, Elizabeth J. 120

Jackson, Jesse 215
Jackson, Jesse, Jr. 184, 210
Jacobson, Gary C. 6, 17–21, 90, 136
jaybird primaries 237, 251
Jefferson, William 201–2, 218
Jeffries, Hakeem 210
Jewell, Malcolm E. 77–8, 85, 86
Johnson, Gregg B. 97
Johnson, Hiram 34, 38, 48, 243–4
Johnson, Loch K. 128–9
Johnson, Lyndon B. 62
Jones, Bradley 251
Jones, Walter Clyde 42
jungle primaries 67–8, 215

Kang, David 251
Kansas: adoption of direct primary laws in 37*t*; Nonpartisan League in 53; 2012 primary dates in 63*t*; type of primary in 65*t*

Kanthak, Kristin 100
Kaptur, Marcy 145, 206–8, 226
Kaufmann, Karen M. 64–5
Keating, William 228
Kefauver, Estes 62
Kelly, Robin 210, 232n7
Kemahlioglu, Ozhe 14, 16
Kennedy, Edward 1, 2, 6
Kennedy, John F. 62
Kennedy, Joseph P. II, 127
Kennedy, Joseph P. III, 111–12, 114
Kennedy, Robert F. 73n29
Kenney, Michael 9
Kenney, Patrick J. 96
Kentucky 37*t*, 63*t*, 65*t*
Kerry, John 1–2, 4–6, 23n3, 102, 191

Kettleborough, Charles 30, 39
Key, V.O. 38, 42, 46, 73n27; definition of parties of 240–1; on Southern politics 56–8, 61, 69
Khanna, Ro 211
Khazei, Alan 2
Killiam, Linda 250, 252
Kilroy, Mary Jo 208
Kinzinger, Adam 226
Kirk, Mark 187
Kirk, Paul 2
Kolodny, Robin 147–8, 156
Kousser, J. Morgan 58, 69
Kousser, Thad 247
Kresky, Harry 245, 250, 257n14
Kuchel, Thomas 243
Kucinich, Dennis 206–8, 226
Kusper v. Pontikes 64

La Follette, Robert 34, 38, 45
La Follette, Robert, Jr. 50
Lagomarsino, Robert 228
LaHood, Ray 126
Lamb, Marty 144–5
Lamont, Ned 194–5, 198
Latin American candidate selection process 14–15
Latinos 204–6, 210–12, 216–18; *see also* race and ethnicity
Law, David S. 250–1
Lawrence, Eric 47
Layzell, Anne 114, 120
Lazarus, Jeffrey 96–7
League of Conservation Voters 195, 200–1
Lenz, Gabriel S. 248, 254
Lieberman, Joseph 2; party support of 198; retirement of 202n9; 2006 general election of 72n16, 169; 2006 primary challenge of 7–8, 41, 189, 191, 194–5
Lincoln, Blanche Lambert 7–8, 170, 191, 198
Lingenfelter, Tom 193
Lipinski, Daniel 184
Lipinski, William 184
Louisiana 91; adoption of direct primary laws in 37t; African-American representatives from 215; incumbent-vs.-incumbent primaries in 229t; jungle primary system of 67–8, 215; 2012 primary dates in 63t; type of primary in 65t
Lower, Richard Coke 48
Lublin, David 58, 217

Lucas, Scott 247
Lugar, Richard 7, 170–1, 189, 191
Lukens, Buz 197
Lyons, Michael 6

machines; *see* party bosses and machines
Maine: adoption of direct primary laws in 35, 37t; candidate quality in 42; regional rivalries in 43; 2012 primary dates in 63t; type of primary in 65t
Maisel, L. Sandy 73n30, 120
Majette, Denise 222
majority-minority districts 22–3, 204–11, 226, 231; challenger primaries in 224; competitiveness of races in 218; Democratic dominance in 219; elected representatives of 214–17; financing of campaigns in 224; open seat primaries in 222–4, 232n10; primary elections in 218–24; redistricting and 216–18; safe seats in 206, 208–9; Southern bleached districts and 216, 231; turnout in 218; voter concerns in 209; *see also* race and ethnicity
malapportionment 60–1, 213
Maldonado, Abel 246
malicious voting 65
mandatory primaries 31–2, 38
Mann, Thomas 70, 252–3
Manzullo, Donald 226
Marshall, Thurgood 238
Maryland 64, 167n4, 193, 195, 199; adoption of direct primary laws in 37t; ballot access laws in 119; majority-minority districts in 226; 2012 primary dates in 63t; type of primary in 65t
Masket, Seth 247–8
Massachusetts: adoption of direct primary laws in 34, 37t; challenger primary in 144–5, 146; open seat races in 111–12, 114, 116, 127, 129, 148, 225; opposition to the direct primary in 54; preliminary elections in 34; preprimary conventions in 3–4, 41; redistricting in 111, 227–8; 2006–12 congressional primaries in 1–6, 41; 2006 state office primaries in 103; 2012 primary dates in 63t; type of primary in 65t; voter turnout 4; Warren's 2012 Senate race in 3–4, 93, 149, 164

maturation phase (1917–68); *see* retrenchment and maturation phase
Mayhew, David 19–20, 120
McCain, John 65, 170, 191, 192
McCarthy, Eugene 62
McCarthy, Joseph 50, 171
McClure, Robert 126–7
McConnell, Mitch 198–9, 254
McGhee, Eric 247
McGovern, George 62
McGovern, James 144–5
McGovern-Fraser Commission reforms 62, 64, 70, 106, 238
McKinney, Cynthia 185, 222
McMahon, Linda 136–9
McNitt, Andrew 94, 152
measurement tools 6
Mecham, Floyd 235–6
media coverage 43, 99–100; impact on turnout of 82–3; party polarization and 67; on Progressive Era primaries 30–1, 33, 43; on Senate primaries 139–40
Merriam, Charles 27, 30, 256; evaluation of direct primaries by 38, 40, 44, 71; on open primaries 64; on popularity of direct primaries 45–7; on public interest in primary reform 48
Meyer, Ernst Christopher 25–6, 30, 31, 38
Michel, Robert 126
Michigan: adoption of direct primary laws in 36; filing fees in 40; incumbent-vs.-incumbent primaries in 229*t*; majority-minority districts in 226; redistricting in 228–30; 2012 primary dates in 63*t*; 2012 redistricting in 209–10; type of primary in 65*t* 73n30
midterm elections 78–9, 81–3, 86–90
Mileur, Jerome M. 47
Miller, Gary 247
Miller, Joe 199
Minnesota: adoption of direct primary laws in 33–4, 37*t* 46; candidate quality in 42; opposition to the direct primary in 54; popularity of direct primaries in 45; preprimary conventions in 55–6; third party movements in 53–5; 2002 Senate primary in 92–3, 164; 2012 primary dates in 63*t*; type of primary in 65*t*
minority candidates 42
minority-influence districts 222

minority parties: fusion balloting and 35, 72nn10–11, 241; party endorsements in 50
mismatch districts 160–1, 168n9
Mississippi: adoption of direct primary laws in 37*t*; African-American representatives from 215; Democratic Party in 214; factional differences in 57; 2012 primary dates in 63*t*; type of primary in 65*t*
Missouri: adoption of direct primary laws in 36, 37*t*; incumbent-vs.-incumbent primaries in 229*t*; redistricting in 228–30; 2012 challenger primary in 164; 2012 primary dates in 63*t*; type of primary in 65*t*
modern primary system (1968–); *see* contemporary era
Montana: adoption of direct primary laws in 37*t*; Nonpartisan League in 53–54; top two primaries in 248; 2012 primary dates in 63*t*; type of primary in 65*t*
Morella, Connie 158, 193, 196
Morlan, Robert L. 50–3, 73n23
Morton, Rebecca 100
Moscardelli, Vincent G. 202n7
Mourdock, Richard 170, 199
MoveOn.org 195, 200–1
Murdoch, Rupert 245
Murkowski, Lisa: party support of 198–9; 2006 general election of 72n16, 170, 251; 2006 primary challenge of 41, 177, 191

Nader v. Schaeffer 250
Nathan, Noah L. 15–16
nationalization of congressional elections 18, 196–7
National Rifle Association 193, 200–1
National Right to Life Committee 193
Neal, Richard 5, 228, 230
Nebraska: adoption of direct primary laws in 36, 37*t*; Nonpartisan League in 53; 2012 primary dates in 63*t*; 2012 Senate primary in 139–41; type of primary in 65*t*
negative recruitment 95
Nelson, Chris 143–4
Nevada: adoption of direct primary laws in 37*t*; Tea Party primary victory of 2010 in 67, 91; top two primary initiative in 248; 2010 challenger

288 Index

primary in 163–4; 2012 primary dates in 63*t*; type of primary in 65*t*
Newberry, Truman 49
Newberry v. United States 49, 236
New Hampshire 255; adoption of direct primary laws in 37*t*; 2010 open seat primary in 112, 141n1; 2012 primary dates in 63*t*; type of primary in 65*t*; voter turnout in 107
New Jersey: adoption of direct primary laws in 37*t*; incumbent-vs.-incumbent primaries in 229*t*; 2012 primary dates in 63*t*; type of primary in 65*t*
New Mexico: adoption of direct primary laws in 37*t* 56; 2012 primary dates in 63*t*; type of primary in 65*t*
New York: adoption of direct primary laws in 35, 37*t*; age laws in 73n19; fusion balloting in 35, 72nn10–11, 241; majority-minority districts in 226; opposition to the direct primary in 54; 2012 primary dates in 63*t*; 2012 redistricting in 210; type of primary in 65*t*
Nineteenth Amendment 48
Nix, Robert 220–1
Nixon, Richard 96, 170
Nixon v. Condon 236
Nixon v. Herndon 236
Noem, Kristie 143–4
Nominations for Elective Office (Dallinger), 25–7
Nonpartisan League (NPL), 13–14, 50–5, 68, 73n23, 234
nonpartisan primaries 65*t*
nonpartisan redistricting commissions 226, 252
non-Southern states 49–56; African-American representatives from 215–17; patterns of primary competition in 175–6
Norrander, Barbara 77–81, 86, 109n6, 255
North Carolina: adoption of direct primary laws in 37*t*; Republican Party in 57; 2012 primary dates in 63*t*; type of primary in 65*t*
North Dakota: adoption of direct primary laws in 37*t*; third party factionalism in 50–5, 73n21, 73n23; 2012 primary dates in 63*t*; type of primary in 65*t*
Nuciforo, Andrea 228

Obama, Barack 44, 64, 67; 2008 primary races of 80, 91, 102; minority voters for 205; 2000 congressional race of 183–4
O'Donnell, Christine 91, 138
Ohio: 1992 redistricting in 225–6; adoption of direct primary laws in 37*t*; challenger primary in 145; incumbent-vs.-incumbent primaries in 206–8, 229*t* 230; majority-minority districts in 226; redistricting in 206–10, 228–30, 231n4; 2012 primary dates in 63*t*; 2012 Senate primary in 138; type of primary in 65*t*
Oklahoma: adoption of direct primary laws in 36, 37*t*; 2012 primary dates in 63*t*; type of primary in 65*t*
Olson, David M. 77–8, 85, 86
Olver, John 228
one-candidate primaries 117–19, 149–50, 157
O'Neill, Tip 127
open primaries 38–39, 60, 64–5, 73nn30–1, 252; candidate appeal in 65; centrist views in 65, 100; crossover voters in 33, 34, 65; independent voters in 87; switching to closed from 68, 235, 250; *see also* state law
open seat primaries 6, 19–20, 22, 107–9, 111–41, 171–2; ballot access laws and 119; competitiveness in 116–29, 134–7, 142nn4–9; electoral structure in 120–2, 123*t* 125*t*; factional conflicts in 127, 129; financing of 129–31, 138; fractionalization index for 124–6, 135–6, 142n7, 224–5; general election success and 128; ideological competition and 138–9; incumbent endorsements in 9, 127–8; interest group support in 134, 138; in majority-minority districts 222–4, 232n10; in the Massachusetts Fourth District (2012), 111–12, 114, 116; number of candidates and 117–19, 121, 152; plurality winners in 128–9; political contexts of 120, 121*t*, 123*t*, 125*t*, 154; rates of 117, 134–5; reasons for 114–16, 142n3, 225–6; redistricting and 115–17, 122–3; role of money in 131–4, 136–9; self-funding candidates in 138; for

Senate seats 134–40; significance of 113–14; Super PAC support in 139; vote percentages in 122–26; *see also* incumbents
optional primaries 26, 27, 31–3, 38
Oregon: adoption of direct primary laws in 37*t*; candidate statement requirements in 36; 2012 primary dates in 63*t*; type of primary in 65*t*
O'Reilly, Ed 2
Ornstein, Norman 70
Ortiz, Solomon 227
Outlook magazine 30–1
out-party primaries; *see* challenger primaries
Overacker, Louise 27, 30, 256; evaluation of direct primaries by 40, 71; on open primaries 64; on public interest in primary reform 48
Overby, L. Marvin 114, 120

Pagliuca, Steve 2
Palin, Sarah 94, 139, 199
participation; *see* turnout
parties; *see* political parties
partisanship 10, 86, 136; *see also* ideological challenges
partisan swings 10, 252
party bosses and machines 11, 20, 24, 26–7, 32, 42, 70, 240–1
Party Campaigning in the 1980s (Herrnson), 18
party-in-service 47
party switching 16, 169–70
Patrick, Deval 93
Paul, Ron 44
Pawlenty, Tim 93, 95, 164
Pennsylvania: adoption of direct primary laws in 37*t*; early primaries in 26, 71n2; incumbent-vs.-incumbent primaries in 229*t*; redistricting in 228–30; 2012 primary dates in 63*t*; type of primary in 65*t*
Pera, Mark 184
Persily, Nathaniel 239
Peters, Gary 209
Petersheim, Meredith-Joy 97
Phillips, Justin 247
Piereson, James E. 96
Pildes, Richard 237
plurality winners 12–13, 40–1, 76, 128–9
Poisson regression 120, 121*t* 142n4

polarization; *see* ideological challenges
Polga-Hecimovich, John 14
Polis, Jared 132
political action committees (PACs), 66; access-orientation of 131, 199; financing of challenger primaries by 158*f*, 159; financing of incumbent primaries by 179–80, 197–201, 203n15; financing of open seat primaries by 130–1; funding of Senate races by 138, 165*t* 166, 180–2; as Super PACs 139, 201, 232n7
political parties 20, 90–8; bosses and machines in 11, 20, 24, 26–27, 32, 42, 70, 240–1; campaign platforms of 36–7, 55, 72n13; candidate endorsements by 40–1, 46, 49–50, 66, 91, 94–5, 109n10; congressional campaign committees of 47; Congressional loyalty to 21; control of competition by 91–7, 101–2, 154–5, 164, 172; convention system of 46, 69, 71; funding of candidates by 10–11, 92, 94–5, 109n9, 147–8, 165*t*, 197–9; funding of election administration by 12, 45–6; fundraising by 94–5; incumbent primaries and 197–9; Key's definition of 240–1; leadership elections in 12; local caucuses of 25–6; nominating role of 7, 8–9, 11, 24–7, 75–6; partisan swings between 10, 252; polarization of 66–8, 70; preprimary conventions of 3–4, 8, 40–1, 49–50, 55–6, 60, 69, 101–2, 253; recruitment of candidates by 253; state law on 10; U.S. Supreme court on autonomy of 238–42, 250–1, 256n8; *see also* partisanship
Political Prairie Fire (Morlan), 50–3
The Politics of Congressional Elections (Jacobson), 17–21
Populist Movement 24–5, 47
Porter, John 186–7
post-Progressive Era; *see* retrenchment and maturation era
Powell, Adam Clayton 212
"Practical Reform of Primary Elections" conference of 1898, 32–3
Praino, Rodrigo 202n7
preprimary conventions 3–4, 8, 40–1, 253; benefits of 55–6, 60, 69; primary competition and 49–50, 101–2

presidential primaries 10, 22, 28–9, 38, 54, 72n14; candidate position-taking in 102; comparison with congressional primaries of 105–7; contemporary reforms of 60, 61–4; dates in 2012 of 63t; financing of 105; ideological challenges in 188; ideological movement of candidates in 105; ideological strength of voters in 86; incumbency advantage in 105; multicandidate competitiveness in 105; quality of candidates in 105–7; scholarship on 76; turnout and 63–4, 79–84, 106–7
Presidential Primaries and the Dynamics of Public Choice (Bartels), 105
Presidential Primaries: Road to the White House (Davis), 28–9, 48
Pressl, Lance 157
Primary Elections (Merriam and Overacker), 27, 64, 71, 256
primarying; *see* incumbent primaries
primary reform 23, 233–56; advisory primaries and 251–2; California's top two system and 23, 67–8, 102, 234–5, 242–8, 253–4; federal law and 235–42; financing of primaries and 252–4; open primaries and 252; organizations advocating for 249–50; public opinion on 245, 257n12; regional primaries and 255; sore loser laws and 251; switching from open to closed primaries as 68, 235, 250; through constitutional amendment 250–1; top two primary initiatives in 248–50; voter disinterest in 253–4
process issues 252–4
Progressive Era (1905–16), 11, 20, 24–49, 70, 71n3, 235, 253; adoption of direct primaries in 30–8, 46; citizen engagement ideals of 43–4, 48; democratization goals of 26–7, 44; evaluation of reforms of 38–44, 71; media interest in primaries of 30–1, 33, 43; party bosses and machines in 11, 20, 24, 26–7, 32, 42, 70, 240–1; political and social goals of 29–31; popularity of primaries in 44–7; Republican Party of 49–50; state government roles in 30; third parties of 47; thresholds for primaries in 72n11
Progressive Majority 148

proportional representation systems 12–13
public funding of election administration 12, 45–6
public role in primaries 20–1

quality of candidates 42–3; of challengers of incumbents 17–18, 163–4; in presidential primaries 105–6
Quayle, Ben 8, 112, 141n2

race and ethnicity 204–24; challenger primaries and 224; civil rights era leaders on 210; civil rights legislation on 61, 204–6, 213, 215–16, 225, 231n1; incumbent primaries and 185–6, 189, 219–22; majority-minority districts and 22–3, 204–11, 214–18; malapportionment practices and 60–1, 213; minority candidates and 42; in New Mexican primaries 56; open seat primaries and 222–4; political rhetoric on 58; of senators and representatives 211–18; in Southern primaries 29, 57–9, 236–8, 256n5; voter turnout and 218; *see also* African-Americans; Asian Americans; Latinos; redistricting
Rahat, Gideon 12, 17, 104
Rangel, Charles 212, 222
Rankin, Jeanette 53–4
Ranney, Austin 64
Reagan, Ronald 96
recruitment of candidates 95, 148, 253
redistricting 70, 111, 204–31; challenger primaries and 224; civil rights legislation on 61, 204–6, 213, 231n1; competitiveness and 224–30; disruptions caused by 205; evidence of nondiscrimination in 215–16; general election competition and 227–8; history of 211–18; incumbent primaries and 189, 195, 219–22, 225; incumbent-vs.-incumbent primaries and 225–6, 228–30; majority-minority districts and 22–3, 204–11, 226; malapportionment practices and 60–1, 213; minority influence districts and 222; 1992 primaries and 216, 225; by nonpartisan commissions 226, 252; open seat primaries and 115–17, 222–4; partisan gerrymandering in 69, 205;

population loss and 228–30; reforms in 252–4; under single-party control 226; Supreme Court decisions on 212–13; 2002 primaries and 216–17, 225; 2012 primaries and 205–11, 225; vote percentages and 122–23; *see also* race and ethnicity
reform; *see* primary reform
regional factors 27, 43, 56, 67–8; *see also* Southern states
regional primaries 255
registration drives 84
Rehnquist, William 241
Reid, Harry 164, 198
Republican Party: African Americans in 205; bleached districts of 216, 231; challenger primaries in 143–46, 151*t*, 152–5, 163–4, 167n8; competitive Senate primaries of 139; Contract with America of 156; funding of Senate primaries by 136–8, 166; ideological challenges in 129, 192–4; interest groups and PACs allied with 98, 134, 139, 166, 193, 200–1; majority-minority districts and 205–6; open seat primaries in 121–6; of the Progressive Era 49–50; self-funding candidates in 138, 145, 165–6; in Southern states 57, 118–19; support of incumbents by 155, 156; 2010 primary voters of 86–90; 2012 primaries of 7–8, 94, 138; white conservatives of 61
retrenchment and maturation phase (1917–68), 28–9, 48–60; adoption of direct primaries in 56; factional interests in 29, 49–54, 57–8; financing of candidates in 49–50, 66; in non-Southern states 49–56; opposition to the direct primary in 53–5; party endorsements in 49–50, 66; power of individuals in 59–60; preprimary conventions in 55–6, 60; primary administration focus in 29; scholarship on primaries in 48, 73n20; in Southern states 56–60, 66; "Toward a More Responsible Two Party System" report in 59–60, 73n27; voter turnout in 43
Reyes, Silvestre 8
Reynolds, John 32, 46
Reynolds, Mel 184
Reynolds v. Sims 60–1, 213

Rhode Island: adoption of direct primary laws in 35, 37*t*; 2012 primary dates in 63*t*; type of primary in 65*t*
Rice, Tom W. 96
Richards, R. O. 37
Richards primary (South Dakota), 36–7
Richardson, Laura 247
Rinaolo, Richard 187
Roberts, Jason M. 73n27
Robinson, Jack 3
role of money in primaries: in challenger primaries 157–62, 168n9; in incumbent primaries 178–82; in one-candidate primaries 157; in open seat primaries 131–4, 136–9; in primaries with more than one candidate 157; *see also* financing of primaries
Rolfe, Meredith 85–6
Romney, Mitt 102
Roosevelt, Franklin D. 199
Roosevelt, Theodore 35
Rosenblum, Nancy L. 256n5
Rostenkowski, Dan 183, 184–5
Rove, Karl 92–3, 164
rules; *see* state law
runoff elections 101–2; in Southern states 40–1, 215; winners of 128–9
Rush, Bobby 183–4, 222
Ryun, Jim 158

safe seats 131, 168n10, 208–9
Sandlin, Stephanie Herseth 143–4
Savage, Gus 184, 221
Scalia, Antonin 238, 242
scandal 189, 201–2, 221–2, 225
Schakowsky, Jan 114
Schattschneider, E.E. 46, 73n27
Schleicher, David 251–2
Schlesinger, Joseph 19–20, 234
Schwarzenegger, Arnold 246
Scott, Bobby 208–9
Scott, Kevin 1
Scott, Tim 217
secret ballots 31
self-financing candidates 66, 138, 145, 165–6, 180, 181
Sellers, Patrick 96
semi-closed primaries 65*t*, 100, 152
semi-open primaries 65*t*, 100
Senate Conservatives Fund 199, 203n13
Senate races: candidate quality in 164–5; challenger primaries in 162–7; competitiveness of 107, 134–7,

142n9, 162–4, 176–7; direct election in 31, 70; House members in 115–16; ideological challenges in 190–1; incumbent challenges in 169–71, 176–8; interest group and PAC involvement in 138, 139, 165*t*, 166, 180–2; Massachusetts's 2006–12 primaries for 1–6; media coverage of 139–40; open seat primaries in 134–40; out-of-state financing in 182; political party funding of 136–7, 142n10, 165*t*; role of money in 136–9, 165–7; self-funded candidates in 138; state appointment of 27
sequential primaries 39, 76, 79–81
Service Employees International Union 200–1
Sherman, Brad 91, 109n9, 247
Shor, Boris 247
Sides, John 90
Simpson, Dick 185
single-issue candidates 183, 189
Smith, Frank L. 236
Smith, Jack 145
Smith, Robert 199
Smith, Terry B. 96
Smith v. Allwright 58, 237
Snowe, Olympia 3, 8
Snyder, James M. Jr. 61, 97, 103
Socialist Party 35, 51
Solarz, Stephen 216
sore loser laws 41, 72nn16–17, 195, 251
South Carolina 250, 257n14; adoption of direct primary laws in 37*t*; factional differences in 57; 2012 primary dates in 63*t*; type of primary in 65*t*
South Dakota: adoption of direct primary laws in 34, 46; challenger primary in 143–4, 156, 158; preprimary conventions in 55, 69, 72n13; representative conventions in 36; Richards Primary Law of 36–37; 2012 primary dates in 63*t*; type of primary in 65*t*
Southern states 56–60; adoption of direct primaries in 37*t*, 38, 46; African-American candidates in 211–12, 214–15; African-American voters in 57–9, 61, 212; bleached districts of 216, 231; candidate rhetoric in 58, 69, 103; competitiveness of primaries in 66, 152, 164; Democratic Party in 29, 56–7, 56–60, 67, 118, 175–6, 214; factional interests in 57–8, 73n26; issueless primaries in 57–8, 61; malapportionment in 61, 213; politics of racial exclusion in 29, 57–9, 61, 236–8, 256n5; Republican Party in 57–9, 118–19; retrenchment and maturation phase in 56–60; runoff elections in 40–1, 215; uncontested primaries in 57, 73n25; voter turnout in 57
Southwell, Patricia 95–6
Sparkman, John 57
spatial theories of voting 101–2
Specter, Arlen 169–70, 191, 193
spot candidates 36
state administration of primaries 31–2, 39, 45–6
state law (electoral structure), 5, 10, 28, 30, 32; on ballot access 72n11, 116–17, 119, 176; on challenger primaries 151–2; disunity in 59–60; impact on candidates of 99–100; on incumbent primaries 176; on open seat primaries 120–2, 123*t*, 125*t*; on political party involvement 10; on uncontested primaries 117–18; on voter access 10, 32
Stenberg, Don 139
Stephens, Kerri 86
Stevens, John Paul 241
Stockemer, Daniel 202n7
Storer v. Brown 251
Stokes, Louis 206, 222
Stop Top Two 250
strategic contexts of primaries 22, 75–109; for candidates 98–104; compared to presidential primaries 105–7; competitiveness in 91–7, 101–2, 104, 107; courting the center in 101; fundraising in 94–5; ideological competition in 101–4; interest groups in 97–8; multiple candidates in 76; nature of the opponent in 100–1; negative recruitment in 95; nonideological competition in 103; plurality winners in 76; for political parties 90–8; standing out in 103; state law in 99–100; voter turnout in 77–90
strategic voting 65
structure of competition 5, 8, 9, 22
Sullivan, Gerald 9
Sullivan, Kathleen 187

Index

Sununu, John 199
Super PACs 139, 201, 232n7
Swain, Carol M. 221–2
The Swing Vote (Killian), 250, 252

Taft, William Howard 54–5
Talmadge, Herman 58
Tashjian v. Republican Party of Connecticut 238–41
Tea Party 3, 19, 23, 129, 234; populism of 25; primary election organizing by 84; 2010 races of 67, 91, 144, 178, 182, 187; 2012 victories of 138–9, 170–1, 225
Tennessee: adoption of direct primary laws in 37t; Republican Party in 57; 2012 primary dates in 63t; type of primary in 65t
Terry v. Adams 237
Texas: adoption of direct primary laws in 37t; African-American representatives from 215; factional interests in 57; redistricting in 227; 2012 primary dates in 63t; 2012 Senate primary in 138–41; type of primary in 65t; voter turnout in 57
third-party movements 24–5, 35, 47; of the Nonpartisan League (NPL), 50–5; in presidential campaigns 96
Thomas, Clarence 242
Thompson, Tommy 138
thresholds for ballot access 72n11, 116–17, 119, 176, 252
Thurmond, Strom 58
ticket balancing 43, 93
Tillman, "Pitchfork" Ben 58
timing of primary elections: early primaries and 101–2; late primaries and 97; voter turnout and 39, 76, 79–81, 107
Timmons v. Twin City Area New Party 241, 256n8
Toomey, Pat 169–70, 193, 199
top two primaries: advocacy groups against 250; advocacy groups for 249–50; in California 23, 67–8, 102, 234–5, 242–8, 253–4; state initiatives on 248–9
"Toward a More Responsible Two Party System" report (APSA), 59–60, 73n27
Townley, A.C. 50–1, 52
town meeting formats 25–6, 69

Towns, Edolphus 210
turnout in primaries 4–6, 8, 43–4, 48, 81–90; barriers to voting and 84, 85; competitiveness and 83–4; demographics of 85–7, 88t; frequency of elections and 84; high-profile state races and 78–9, 84; in House vs. Senate primaries 107; in majority-minority districts 218; measures of 77–81, 84–6; in midterm election years 78–9, 81–3, 106–7; overreporting of 87, 109n7; in presidential election years 63–4, 79–82, 84, 106–7; in Southern primaries 57; timing factors in 39, 76, 79–81, 107; U.S. rates of 17, 43, 48; women's suffrage and 48, 73n19; *see also* voters in primaries
2010 voter survey 86–90
types of primaries 22, 65t; blanket primaries 67–8, 100, 102, 238–9, 242, 244–6; closed primaries 23, 32, 38–9, 60, 64; extremist victories and 67–8; fusion balloting 35, 72nn10–11, 241; impact on candidates of 99–100; jaybird primaries 237, 251; jungle primaries 67–8, 215; open primaries 38–9, 60, 64–5; top two primaries 23, 67–8, 102, 234–5, 242–50, 253–4

U.S. Constitution 250–51
U.S. Supreme Court 235–42; on California's blanket primaries 68, 238–9, 242, 246; on campaign finance 49, 66, 236, 251; *Citizens United* decision of 236, 251; on Communist Party USA, 256n5; on fusion balloting 241; on independent voters 238; on political party autonomy 238–42, 250–1, 256n8; on redistricting 212–13; on sore loser laws 251; on voter rights 58, 64, 237; on Washington's top-two primaries 242; on white primaries 58, 236–8, 256n5
Utah: adoption of direct primary laws in 37t; runoffs and preprimary conventions in 40–1, 72n15, 101–2; top two primary initiative in 248; 2012 primary dates in 63t; type of primary in 65t

valence issues 102
Vare, William S. 236
Vavreck, Lynn 90
Velasquez, Nydia 216
Vermont: adoption of direct primary laws in 37*t*; 2012 primary dates in 63*t*; type of primary in 65*t*
Vickers, David 193
Virginia: abandonment of direct primaries in 215; adoption of direct primary laws in 37*t*; political factions in 57; 2012 primary dates in 63*t*; type of primary in 65*t*; voter turnout in 57
voice vs. exit 16
voters in primaries 77–90; African-American blocs of 58–9; beliefs on competitiveness of 83; beliefs on consequences of elections of 83–4; benefits of primaries for 77; crossover voting of 33, 34; demographics of 85–7, 88*t*; difference from nonvoters of 85; difference from voters in general elections of 22, 85; embeddedness in social networks of 85–6; ideological engagement of 86–90; party activism and 86, 109n5; party registration of 77; public engagement of 43–4, 48; state law on 10, 32, 77; time and effort required of 84; *see also* turnout
Voting Rights Act of 1964, 61, 213; amendments to 204, 205–6, 215–16, 225, 231n1; on discriminatory effects of redistricting 215–16

Walrath, David 193
Ware, Alan 6, 20; on close races 96; on consequences of direct primaries 47; on Crawford County (PA) primaries 71n2; on immigration and urbanization 32; on Minnesota's primary law 33; on party endorsements 49–50, 91; on popularity of direct primaries 45–7; on ticket balancing 43
Warren, Elizabeth 3–4, 93, 149, 164
Washington: adoption of direct primary laws in 37*t*; blanket primary system in 242; top two primary system in 68, 242; 2012 primary dates in 63*t*
Washington, Harold 183
Washington State Grange v. Washington Republican Party 242
Wasson, Jesse T. 97
Waters, Maxine 216
Weicker, Lowell 56
Weitz-Shapiro, Rebecca 14, 16
Wellstone, Paul 164
Wellstone Action 148
Wendland, Jay L. 86
Wesberry v. Sanders 213
West, Allen 217
West, Victor 43, 73n18
Westley, Christopher 152
Westminster Model 13
West Virginia: adoption of direct primary laws in 37*t*; incumbent-vs.-incumbent primaries in 229*t*; 2012 primary dates in 63*t*; type of primary in 65*t*
Weyrich, Paul 193
White, Thomas 167n8
white primaries 29, 57–9, 61, 236–8, 256n5
Why Parties? (Aldrich), 19–20, 241
Wicker, Tom 234
Wiebe, Robert H. 24–5
Wilson, Charles 221
Wilson, Frederica 221–2
Wilson, Woodrow 34
Wisconsin: adoption of direct primary laws in 34, 37*t*, 38, 46; battle with DNC of 238; Nonpartisan League in 53; popularity of direct primaries in 45; 2012 primary dates in 63*t*; 2012 recall election in 75; 2012 Senate primary in 138; type of primary in 65*t*
women's suffrage 31, 48, 73n19
World War I, 48, 51, 54
World War II, 48
Wynn, Albert 8, 64
Wyoming: adoption of direct primary laws in 37*t*; top two primary initiative in 248; 2012 primary dates in 63*t*; type of primary in 65*t*

Yates, Sidney 114, 184–5

Zingale, Nancy 82

Printed by PGSTL